KEEP THIS QUIET! IV
Ancient Secrets Revealed

Praise for the *Keep This Quiet!* Series

"A fascinating and very well written personal story, *Keep This Quiet!* III: *Initiations* is very highly recommended for both community and academic library collections. Also exceptionally commended are the first two volumes in this outstanding series, *Keep This Quiet! My Relationship with Hunter S. Thompson, Milton Klonsky, and Jan Mensaert*, and *Keep THIS Quiet Too!*"

—MIDWEST BOOK REVIEW

"In *Keep This Quiet!* III, Margaret expands greatly on some of the things she only briefly discussed in the first two books. The connections between physics and the mind are fascinating and oddly reassuring. Pick up all three books for the full scope of Margaret's story, but if you have a more scientific or (for the lack of a better term) spiritual bent, start with *Keep This Quiet!* III: *Initiations*. And if you have the chance to see Margaret speak, you owe it to yourself to go."

—BRADLEY JAMES WEBER, First Prize
Louisville Gonzo Fest literary contest 2014

"The first time I met Margaret, she sat down beside me (or, was it the other way around?) in a meeting, and immediately I knew I wanted to get to know her. She had a certain presence . . . a 'shining' . . . that was magnetic. The Universe must have been in agreement with my intuition, because over the years I was blessed to become her student and benefited greatly from her wise and loving teachings, but still, there was a certain mystery about her that was never revealed, for she very rarely talks about herself or her life. Now I know she was saving it all for this brilliant series of autobiographical revelations that comprise the *Keep This Quiet!* series. My advice . . . read them all, beginning with the first, and when you are done, await with bated breath the fourth (and, honestly, I hope not last!) installation of her mind and heart expanding sharings."

—JOY HAYNIE AYSCUE, Founder of Wake for Consciousness:
Sacred Realms

"I thought the whole series was remarkable, original, and transcendent!"
—RUSSELL D. PARK, board-certified transpersonal psychologist,
coauthor of *The Power of Humility*

Praise for *Keep This Quiet!* III: *Initiations*

"Margaret has done an amazing job witnessing for us all the deep path of walking with the Self. She has presented this information, while weaving the amazing discovery of the multi-layers of psychology and the depth the journey revealed."

—JYOTI, Spiritual Director, Center for Sacred Studies

"Jung & Pauli . . . Courageously, competently Harrell guided this reader through mazes of scientific exploration, all the while keeping her engaging 'anima' voice as lure to read on."

—PUANANI HARVEY, Advanced Studies Coordinator,
New Mexico Society of Jungian Analysts

"I could feel a welling form in my chest . . . An emotional surge was building, I was sure of it. I had no intention of heading it off. I was into this book for the duration."

—MARTIN FLYNN, owner of www.hstbooks.org

"As a practicing Reiki master, I received a great deal of insight from Harrell's spiritual study, as well as her ability to connect patterns and puns (Watergate/Flood Gate) with both humor and reverence."

—ALICE OSBORN, author of *Heroes without Capes*

"I've got my highlighter and am really appreciating the depth of Margaret's initiation and how much she did for her spiritual emergence!"
—**JONETTE CROWLEY**, author of *Soul Body Fusion*

"The information on the universal nature of each soul offers a good potential to remove some of the barriers or veils between otherwise divergent ways of thinking and believing. I'm glad Margaret is 'putting this out there.'"
—**AL MINER**, channel, author (with Lama Sing) of *Seed Thoughts*

"Margaret A. Harrell's *Keep This Quiet!* III is the real-life alchemical journey of her poet (co-creator with the creative forces of the universe) soul in which she intentionally determinedly makes the journey of initiation, juxtaposing apparently irreconcilable differences into a synthesis, a union of being. And she takes Hunter S. Thompson, Milton Klonsky, Jan Mensaert, Wolfgang Pauli, Carl Jung, and many others with her as she discovers and shares, with us, her own tao her way her I ching her Book of Changes. Thank you, Margaret, for sharing your transformative journey. When one of us is lifted up we are all lifted up. Thank You for the lift!!!!"
—**RON WHITEHEAD**, poet, author of *I Refuse,*
I Will Not Bow Down, I Will Not Give Up

"*Noteworthy:* One initiation exercise is 'Dream Interpretation.' Harrell relates the dream, provides the dream question raised, reveals her related real life event, and links all for interpretation."
—**MINDQUEST REVIEW OF BOOKS**

"I am quite impressed by *Keep This Quiet!* III . . . Most of all, parts 1 & 3 drew my special attention. The given information revealed, often clarified, so many aspects of my own quest in life . . . Now, if God, nature, or whatever, already put purpose in us, how stupid would it be if there weren't signs indicating to us if one was walking in the desired direction . . . Signals, signs and indications come to us through several layers of consciousness."
—**JEF CRAB**, founder of E.A.S.T.
(Energetic Awareness, Sensitivity & Transformation) Institute

Praise for *Keep This Quiet!* IV: *Ancient Secrets Revealed*

"A book of wonder—spirit, ghosts, hope, mysticism, mystery. If you ever had instincts, premonitions, or felt you are out of place or feel you know things—that there is a whole world beyond, there's more magic in this world than there's supposed to be—I feel this book is for you. Especially if you're in the last one third of your life and think, 'I want to unlock the mysteries, I want some answers, I'm not done.'"

—ALICE OSBORN, author of *Heroes without Capes*

About a scene with Hunter Thompson: "I read it as written by a sensitive woman, with perception both as strong and delicate as the strand on a spider's web, describing her experience."

—VIRGINIA PARROTT WILLIAMS, coauthor of *In Control: No More Snapping at Your Family, Skulking at Work, Steaming in the Grocery Line, Seething in Meetings, Stuffing Your Frustration*

"I finally got a chance to read through all of the sections . . . about Guruji [Dhyanyogi-ji] and Anandi Ma and I am blown away! Thanks to Margaret for writing all of these wonderful stories! She is such a gifted writer."

—JAN HANDEL, Dhyanyoga Centers Antioch administrator and meditation instructor

"Margaret Harrell is a skilled professional writer with excellent ability to communicate and weave esoteric ideas about science, psychology, philosophy, and spirituality. Richard Unger's channeled hand analysis description of her as a 'grand synthesizer' was apt and accurate."

—RON RATTNER, author of the forthcoming *From Litigation to Meditation: An ex-lawyer's spiritual metamorphosis from secular Hebrew to born again Hindu to uncertain Undo*

Keep This Quiet! IV
Ancient Secrets Revealed

Margaret A. Harrell

Saeculum University Press
USA and Romania

Visit us at http://www.margaretharrell.com/ and at

http://margaretharrell.com/news

Cover design by Gaelyn Larrick of www.wakingworld.com
Interior design series format by Bram Larrick

Publisher's Cataloging-In-Publication Data

(Prepared by The Donohue Group, Inc.)

Names: Harrell, Margaret A. (Margaret Ann), author, illustrator.

Title: Keep this quiet! IV, Ancient secrets revealed / Margaret A. Harrell.

Other titles: Ancient secrets revealed

Description: Newly revised, expanded, retitled. | Raleigh, NC ; Sibiu, Romania : Saeculum
University Press, [2018] | Previously published in 2016. | Includes bibliographical references
and index.

Identifiers: ISBN 9780692688663 (paperback)

Subjects: LCSH: Harrell, Margaret A. (Margaret Ann) | Spirituality. | Parapsychology. | Mind
and body. | Women authors, American--21st century--Biography. | LCGFT: Autobiographies.
| BISAC: BODY, MIND & SPIRIT / Inspiration & Personal Growth. | BIOGRAPHY &
AUTOBIOGRAPHY / Personal Memoirs. | PSYCHOLOGY / Movements / Transpersonal. |
BODY, MIND & SPIRIT / Mysticism.

Classification: LCC PS3558.A62498 Z46 2018 | DDC 818.5409--dc23

Library of Congress Control Number: 2017911641

Saeculum University Press
5048 Amber Clay Lane, Raleigh, NC 27612

A division of Saeculum University Press (SUP)
Didi-Ionel Cenuşer, publisher
B-dul Victoriei 5–7
550024 Sibiu, Romania

Didi-Ionel Cenuşer, publisher

Contents

PART THREE

PART FOUR

PART FIVE

Author's Note to the New Edition

I am peering into the past, trying to decipher—from newly retrieved materials in my garage—who I was in the 1990s (long before my 2018 self existed); who this person writing back then in my name was, this person I confidently spoke for in the first edition of *Keep This Quiet!* IV. But—findings in my garage now tell me—I didn't exactly remember "me." I "remembered" *who I am now*, how I got *to here*, I thought. Ah. It's not the case.

Often, when my 1990s self spoke for herself in "real time" *in the '90s*—resurrected in the garage papers—it's a surprising voice. To reopen these newly discovered documents, these confessions and accounts—steering me back there as into an old mine but with a real miner's light—transforms my internal records of me.

Many of the boxes I'd packed up in in August 2001 when I left Belgium and prophetically came to North Carolina to live, some earlier. But one day in late 2016 as they sat in the garage, guarding their secrets, someone warned me that cardboard could attract termites. That did it. Slowly I began to repackage the papers.

In writing the first volume of this series, I had the foolproof chronology of Hunter Thompson's letters to refer to. But *Keep This Quiet!* IV had no reference documents at all. Yet today, in the revised edition, I have them. Letters from me to me, especially missives I drafted to other people—often unmailed. I hadn't realized they would dispute my memory. Would contradict a lot of my assertions. So what did I leave, as in a bottle, for my "future self," me, right now? It fills in a lot of details. For in an Awakening, a lot that we're not ready for we discard, interpret wrongly. Now my mature self is ready—for what I recorded fresh off the inner waves: an unexplored, documented history I wasn't earlier able to reconstruct exactly this way. These writings, some of them twenty-five years old, shed new light on spots I dimly recalled; also, *time has finally caught up to what was ahead of the times* (such as when I, with spirit guides, predicted—in the future—"out of control events," in particular, grave dangers from misunderstood, highly energized, on-the-move archetypes, such as "Home").

Inserting them into the revised edition, I listen as with a conch shell to those waves of information my greater self brought, planted, sometimes prophesizing. This includes what appears to be almost fairy tale narrations, of multidimensional meanings. And so, I synched my life's advance notices with now, listening to this very bold, out-of-the-box thinking "past self," who, indeed, was quite different than what I thought. As she made her records before nontime became Time and unity consciousness and my multidimensional self expressed itself further (as we all do) in real-time variations of some of these and other insights all over the globe. NOW.

Author's Note to the 2016 Edition

I had intended to write this book as a simple storytelling record. The kind you find in a spiritual autobiography. But Western-type anchors kept creeping in. Perhaps the model was rather Carl Jung; he considered his autobiography—*Memories, Dreams, Reflections*—his "personal myth," a myth the collective unconscious asked for. He added that he had lived "the self-realization of the unconscious."

Jung dedicated his life to establishing his theory of the unconscious. ("The unconscious," to Jung, always meant both collective and personal.) He also believed in parapsychology, corresponding with J. B. Rhine, a pioneer in laboratory research into telepathy, precognition, clairvoyance, and psychokinesis, and privately discussed the topic with physicist Wolfgang Pauli. In the 1930s, philosopher Gerda Walther asked why he did not discuss parapsychology openly, "since he was after all convinced of the phenomenon's authenticity." Someone else chimed in, wondering whether Jung feared open support for it would cause him to lose face among scientists.

No, Jung answered. He was "more afraid of propagating a subject matter that can very easily have dangerous effects in the hands of unprepared people." He explained: "People will first have to take in and digest the other things I have to offer in psychology, and only then will they be ready for parapsychology. Now, it is still too early."[1]

Look what happened in the Manhattan Project, when the U.S. government brought together the "hundreds of physicists, mathematicians, and engineers . . . needed to design, build, and test the world's first atomic weapon"; the physics that made the bomb possible fell into the hands of those who wanted to build it—and then drop it on Hiroshima and Nagasaki. (Jung: "There is no H-bomb in Nature"; also, "By focusing almost singularly on developments in the outer physical world, what we have neglected is ourselves, our own inner nature.")[2]

Nature held the secret of splitting the atom, unleashing untold force. Similarly, in the yogic East there were hidden secrets. Nature held, in this other direction considered unscientific by many, unseen mysteries mastered by wisdom teachers throughout centuries but not taken seriously by—unprovable by—Western science.

These two vital types of secret required a readiness for release into the world. The discovery of atomic nuclear fission in the twentieth century led to atomic bomb detonations of "Little Boy" and "Fat Man" on Hiroshima and Nagasaki in August 1945, followed by a century of attempts to control the resulting arms race.

The other side of the globe had guarded its mystical secrets on palm leaves in India, in caves in the Himalayas, inside confounding insights in the *Tao Te Ching*. There's a significant difference in how the two big discoveries came about: through "yogic science" and "heart awakening" in the East and the scientific method in the West.

In the case of the East, paranormal feats (to use Western terminology), called *siddhis* in Sanskrit, were reached via consciousness. Only an expanded consciousness, an altered state, could get you there. Nature was revered. On the other hand, in the West, scientific breakthroughs into our whole modern technological world, which hit a major landmark with Newton's *Principia: Mathematical Principles of Natural Philosophy*, were more and more reached by overthrowing our relationship to nature, folk wisdom, and indigenous medicines, and by studying nature mathematically—quantifying matter—with rigorous reductionist logic.

Two vastly different approaches. One planet. What would happen when it began to draw closer in space-time, to where in a nanosecond a message in one part of the globe could reach another, miles and miles away? Of course, the yogis said that distance, like time, was a construct of our minds. What could the Earth make of these two vastly different treasures? As the Earth resets its priorities in turmoil today, we are finding out.

The "sides" were so far apart that in 1938 a retired U.S. Army lieutenant colonel wrote confidentially to J. B. Rhine at his parapsychology lab—which had been set up to investigate ESP and psychokinesis (PK) scientifically—about his telepathy experiences in the military; he had had to keep them a secret.

He explained that at the Army Signal Corps school (presumably the Training Center) he roomed with an "exceptionally bright" officer, later colonel, who had a telepathic gift. Under his tutorship the two men practiced together, and at their electricity exam one question stumped everybody. Both men wondered what the other was thinking. You can guess what happened. They were on opposite sides of the room, but—this lieutenant colonel reported—invented the same original equation and solved it identically! It was apparent there was no way they could have communicated "except by thought waves," he added, but when they graduated, neither was recommended for the Corps.[3]

In Volume IV of my *KTQ!* series, I, a Westerner, born into a small Southern U.S. town, discover many of these wisdom traditions and feel at home in them. Readers of earlier *Keep This Quiet!* volumes may want to wait some years to go into these new areas, and new readers already exploring these areas, I hope will jump in. So reader, beware. A lot here is new to the series as West meets East and logic meets mysticism.

In a broad sense, the two approaches tend to occupy different parts of the brain. For instance, at a certain point in meditation, in order to make room for the meditative right-cerebral-hemisphere brainwaves to step in, moving us into an altered state—thereby canceling out logical thought—the linear left cerebral hemisphere (the rational, thinking part of the brain) will need to at least temporarily retire from its gatekeeping, censoring role, and it may at first balk. The consensus, logical, sequential, rational reality is the specialty of the left cerebral hemisphere, while the nonlinear, nonverbal, image-making reality tends to be the specialty of the right. This is roughly speaking. Yet both belong to nature, to the hidden secrets of our planet. And together they comprise the youngest, most sophisticated part of the brain. In between the two hemispheres, nerve fibers (the corpus callosum) help them communicate.

Importantly, the East/West split just mentioned and the verbal/

visual brain hemisphere specialization operate in all of us every single day. But this sophisticated cerebrum, which is two thirds of the brain's mass, is not in control of our emotions. They don't listen to it. Ah ha. The problem is immediately clear.

And that's significant in understanding what happens in spiritual evolution. I have often seen people go easily into high energy states, have a wonderful experience in meditations, and I think: *Fantastic. Now their emotions won't get stuck, they'll have mastered emotional flow.* Not so. It usually doesn't work that way. In fact, it rarely does.

To find out why, take a look at *the limbic brain*: older, more instinctive, more governed by archetypes rather than thought. It's the realm of a lot of our personal and collective inheritance: of the archaic mind, the instincts. Often it surreptitiously, unconsciously, wages war with the thinking function, or mental body. These two mighty warriors inside a single person might not be on the same side. The head and the heart may see things not eye to eye but oppositely.

Many people in the West now meditate with ease. They may have visions, hear sounds. As the old teachers will tell you, this doesn't necessarily mean anything. It can be a distraction to the real spiritual path, *in which the person truly transforms, becomes One with God.* The goal isn't to do great psychic feats but to transform into a more evolved level of consciousness, of Knowing, they will tell you; the goal is to reach the state of feeling constantly unified with all life.

But putting that aside—the fact that many people have these experiences is a wonderful sign of being "on the path." And it's practical and useful; it's an individual journey.

So, many people today believe in spirit guides and past lives or just like to meditate for stress relief.

However, this is not necessarily being "awake." It doesn't necessarily equate with "thinking for yourself" or incarnating the energies you go into in meditation, which is further along the path.

When you go into altered energy states, you are in touch with the energy potential that you can bring into your own life in patterns. Why is it, though, that leaving these pure energies and their patterns in meditation, a person so often comes back into everyday reality and re-enters the old familiar patterns—the consensus reality ones, the problem ones, the habits that were banished temporarily during the frequencies in the meditation? What happens to all those warm and fuzzy feelings? That bliss? That Light? Those frequencies stay out there. They are for "Sunday" visits.

These other energies try, however, to find their way into our experiences, get the upper hand. But once out of the meditative realm, they often get transformed beyond recognition.

In the Exercises section in *Keep This Quiet!* III, I had readers hold energy between their palms, with the palms facing each other; they were to imagine that this was the energy they had for a project that day—compressed right between their hands. This is not just imaginary. On the energy level if you can mold energy of potential, connecting it abstractly with your mind and emotions, then when it gets down into everyday reality—crossing the boundary line between energy and matter—it literally turns into the matter of experience; the potential and frequency it had as pure energy stays with it as it translates and transforms in everyday life. The East distinguished between Shiva (pure consciousness) and Shakti (sacred energy of action). When the two unite (the divine masculine and divine feminine), then the energy of *pure consciousness, pure awareness without action,* enters *action,* and your life is transformed.

This is why people say thoughts are energy, intention is a force, or *thinking becomes biology* and can prevent and heal disease. (Thinking influences our cells, our unconscious, and in that way it can determine whether we are healthy or ill; our cells are listening to our expectations, and they try to comply with them, align with them; *after all, we are their environment; we shouldn't give them negative expectations to align with!*)

All these things are the next step, once you begin to develop energy skills, once you further develop consciousness. In the East this system was all laid out. Becoming One with God was the goal. Entering unity consciousness was. And—the key—it was a level of consciousness. As such, it expressed itself in meditation, heightening the electrical field around the brain, *and* expressed itself in daily life.

Until a human being could express the energy in life, the ego governed. Therefore, the guru system was set up, whereby the guru (as agreed upon knowingly by disciple and the guru) received a projection. The guru, being One with God, received the projection of the *inner guru of the disciple*. (This would be comparable, in the West, to *the inner Christ*.) This inner guru was likewise One with God but blocked. Being One with God meant having God consciousness, which translated into "You are God." Why? Because you are part of the All, you are "wired in."

It would take years, maybe reincarnations, but one day the inner guru (inner Christ) would overcome the ego. And that person would be "enlightened," seeing the unity of all things. A neuroscientist friend of mine told me a story. He was angry with a man, and suddenly he saw Meher Baba's face on that person's face. In that instant he was being taught by this famous guru; he knew that Meher Baba was demonstrating unity consciousness for him.

This Eastern system was breaking up by the time it began to cross to the U.S. to introduce itself. By that time, in the 1900s, the most esoteric gurus had already realized that a new system was coming in. For that reason they broke their centuries-old silence and began to spread teachings that had always been top secret, handed down one on one.

A friend once put the emerging paradigm into words for me. She said, it's "becoming your own authority." So the leading male gurus began passing their mantle to women, the feminine. The West didn't notice; they thought the old system was going on as usual and that they, in the West, were overturning it, when in fact it was intentionally overturning itself. No matter that you will still see some of the guru systems alive today. They are, most often, led by women.

To back up, it may seem like there's a big chasm between a delightful hour of meditation or an energy workshop and going to work every day, sitting at a computer (in that instant depending on the left hemisphere of your brain, a beta brain state, far from the meditative alpha or theta brain state).

Many people think energy work is just something they do outside their everyday life. It's relaxing, but it doesn't keep them from getting sick or help them save a marriage or finish a project or live in a state of peace or decide whom to vote for. This is wrong. Energy, as I learned in the process of the years covered in this book, IS our everyday experience. It's the "easy way," the fast track. If you can do something in a vision, or even unconsciously during a meditation, what is really happening? That version of events is now available to you. You might still overlook it. But with practice, you can master how to bring the atmosphere and results right into the health of your physical body and into your everyday decisions.

It takes a shift of consciousness, for this work you did in energy then has a long trip into matter. It's in a formless state. It's very possible potential. But to move into 3-D reality, it has to not be blocked by our thoughts or stopped in a screeching halt by an emotion (*that's ridiculous, I can't do it*). It has to shift from frequency to frequency, without losing its essence. And it has to fill our bodies. If we practice, this process will go faster, unhindered by unwanted emotions like guilt. Energy, I learned to be a fan of. Working in energy is now lifeblood to me. And I want to pass that lesson on to you or whoever will pick up some hints that will be useful in their own life.

If you have already been exposed to these ideas but didn't quite "get it," maybe this time it will click. Maybe this time it will appeal to that deep self trying to find a way in. Or it may be a refreshing reminder, illustrating what you already believe, helping anchor it even more, give you one more frame of reference assisting you to put it into practice automatically, as consciousness.

Let's go further into *Keep This Quiet!* with more things to keep quiet, this time in what the mind, the psyche, can do. The spirit. But wait. Let's don't keep quiet.

Prologue

In 1991, as this book opens, I was dealing with issues that a spirituality path had turned up. My old consciousness wouldn't do. It had no answers—not even peg holes to put some of the questions into.

Keep This Quiet! III ended as I was planning a trip to Owl Farm in Woody Creek, Colorado, to for the first time visit Hunter Thompson, whom I'd not seen for twenty-one years, not since 1969, when I moved out of New York City, where I'd copy edited his first book, *Hell's Angels* (Random House, 1967). At the time we first met in 1966 (over his manuscript), I'd been a Random House copy editor for a year. Eventually I became assistant editor—a title I was given unofficially by Editor-in-Chief Jim Silberman; my level of work, he said, required it. When working with heavyweight authors, such as NBC nightly news anchor Chet Huntley or U.S. Supreme Court First Amendment lawyer for Grove Press, Charles Rembar, I needed the clout. Rembar had successfully used the "redeeming social value" test to get now-classics like D. H. Lawrence's *Lady Chatterley's Lover*, which had been banned for obscenity, published in the U.S.

In the late 1960s there were not many women editors. But I didn't want to be a full editor anyway (Jim had offered me a chance to work my way up); it would take even more time away from my writing. Jobs at Random House were sought after and could be all-consuming, as in my case. In my scanty free time on weekends I holed up in my Greenwich Village brownstone apartment, a rent-controlled one-room walk-up, to write.

The *Hell's Angels* copy editing was done by expensive long-distance telephone (San Francisco or Colorado–New York City) and by letter—an exception to the rule. Normally, all writers came in, sat down in my tiny cubicle office, and we went page by page over the questions and suggestions. But Hunter stayed out West—living near the hippy Haight-Ashbury district in San Francisco, then Colorado.

We never met in person until his book-promotion tour in February 1967. But sight unseen, glued to the phone in late-night calls, we spent hours and hours together, nonetheless.

By hunches and electricity and hard focus on his book, we gradually discovered that we were falling for each other, though this didn't interfere with the work. Letters I kept—published in earlier *Keep This Quiet!* volumes—attested to the fact we were drawing close. And also that even in 1966 Hunter—having gotten stomped by the Angels the weekend after his very first letter to me—had an action-packed, a danger-fraught life spiked with hilarious comedy. And add in his absolute objection to authority. Who could resist?

Also, he listened closely to his instincts, was on good terms with them. Being on less good terms with mine, I was attracted to this. He would later write: "Fear is a healthy instinct, not a sign of weakness. It is a natural self-defense mechanism that is common to felines, wolves, hyenas, and most humans. Even fruit bats know fear, and I salute them for it. If you think the world is weird now, imagine how weird it would be if wild beasts had no fear."[4]

During the editing process we became secretly enamored, and at our first moment of flesh and blood meeting felt the shock of recognition of a lifelong connection. At least, speaking for myself. In one romantic tryst we spent a weekend in Los Angeles.

Then I left Random House in 1968, seeking more time to write. In 1970, I married a Belgian poet, Jan Mensaert, whom I'd met in Marrakesh, Morocco. I'd gone alone to Europe and wandered down into Morocco before joining Random House, in a last sally into freedom preceding the tied-down, one-week-vacation-a-year restrictions of a job. So, for four years while in New York City, I corresponded with Jan, and in late 1969, not long after I left Random House, we reunited in Germany for a month. Obviously, with much to discover about each other.

What I did know was he was a gifted artist and poet—in fact, he had two new published books of poetry by then—but foiled himself by self-destructive leanings. These included suicide attempts and alcoholism. Everything said: STAY AWAY. I did not listen. In modern parlance, he was a "bad boy," but a highly cultivated international bohemian. I swore I'd turn his life around and get his artist drive working for him. This meant returning to North Africa.

Later, when I lived in Moroccan villages with Jan, having married him in Belgium, and still later, after our separation, that bond with Hunter, though we were far apart in space, endured—occasionally sweetened by phone conversations but mostly under the radar of other events, other relationships.

For fourteen years I stayed married to Jan: a marriage that though technically still on the books afterwards, effectively ended in 1983. I left him—or fled from him—in Larache, Morocco. I say fled because I had not only discovered (he finally told me) he'd been gay when we married (a long story), but I also realized I was no match for his deep self-destructive tendencies. I had to lose myself, as the phrase goes, to live with him.

Finally waking up to the reality that I could not change things and did not want to continue in his lifestyle, not thinking he'd let me go, I left without warning. I lived the next few months with my mother in Greenville, North Carolina, then moved to Charlottesville, Virginia. In Charlottesville I worked at a dream lab for a year. During that time I plunged into my first spiritual workshops, at a new center called Openway. Which brings us up to October 1984. At that point I took a huge step—moving to Switzerland to study at the C. G. Jung Institute in Küsnacht/Zürich (1984–'87).

Meanwhile, Jan had been evicted from Morocco by corrupt officials so they could keep part of the $10,000 of his personal furniture sales (wired to him from the U.S. via a local bank); he relocated to Tienen, Belgium, with our mini-dachshund Snoep (another adventurous story covered in volume 2 of this series) and we corresponded now and then. He intent on getting me back, me equally intent on a new life.

I saw him again in 1984, when I flew to Tienen to retrieve Snoep after he fell victim to the dachshund disk disease—leading to a paralysis of the back legs.

So in October 1984, Snoep and I moved to Küsnacht. *Keep THIS Quiet!* III: *Initiations* covered my time in Switzerland, ending in 1991 in Belgium. Between 1984 and '87, I was enrolled in the C. G. Jung Institute Küsnacht, located on Lake Zurich in a suburb of Zurich; at this particular Institute, at the time, many people who taught or attended underwent transformation.

Not to be left out, in 1985, I had a significant initiation that altered my view of reality. Starting in September, I experienced—in Jungian terms—a "confrontation with the unconscious," or "with the Self."* As I saw it, it culminated nineteen years of learning *how to be strong as a female*—primarily through relationships with three ultra-strong male outlaw writers, who would never bow to authority of any sort but thought for themselves, rightly or wrongly.

And now I must introduce the third male who held a center focus in the first two volumes of *Keep This Quiet!* My initiation in Zurich was precipitated by his death—that is, the sudden (to me) death of New York City poet, essayist, and Blake scholar Milton Klonsky. In the days when I was at Random House and afterwards in Morocco, he had been my mentor and very close friend. Also, we'd dated. This included the period I was working on Hunter's book and other books at Random House.

I lived on Bleecker Street between Charles and Perry in Greenwich Village, not so far from where Hunter had lived in 1959 on Perry Street. Around the corner was Milton's walk-up apartment—or "aerie," as he once called it, which means an eagle's nest or hawk's nest perched on a cliff or mountaintop. And indeed, he had a high-up window overlooking the Village life below. But in more astute ways his perception had that aerie aspect. During his short illness and his death, November 29, 1981, I was in Morocco and no one said a word to me about it till a year later, in December 1982—which made the loss all the more traumatic. In hindsight I felt clearly that my 1981 dreams were littered

---

* For Jung the term "Self" represents "the totality of man"—conscious and unconscious—in accordance with the philosophy of the universal self in the ancient Hindu Upanishads.

with precognitive hints. In fact, my unconscious, it seemed, clearly tried to warn me. Jung said such anticipatory warnings are common, calling them the "shadow of the approach of a death."

But the dream hints were not the end of it. To say the least. It appeared to me when I arrived in Zurich in 1984, as it had the year before in Charlottesville, that the inimitable Klonsky had survived death and from the spirit world was guiding me.

This was a startling thought to me, as it fit into nothing in my past, nothing my psyche was equipped to handle, but I held onto it as a life raft, feeling abandoned. He had been my psychopomp into the world of rarefied ideas, though Hunter and Jan traveled there too, but Milton was a straight-up genius IQ without the sidetracks of a quirky lifestyle. He was the original Greenwich Village hipster or, as he put it, a "gangster-poet." In fact, he told me he'd been the first to use the word "hipster," in the 1940s. Today others, looking back, have applied the term "guru" or "cult" figure to him.

Nineteen years my senior, in frequent nights out with me he spoke quotable aphorisms of wisdom, digested into mouthfuls that I gave the protagonist of my novel—Robert—modeled on him. I had the habit of jotting down Milton's statements secretly, pouring over them; though plainly successful with women, he did not attract me with the romantic allure of the other two. In my novel Robert was in a similar position vis-à-vis the semiautobiographical Paula; that novel would, by the time it was published after a thirty-year incubation, be part novel, part revelatory consciousness exploration titled *Love in Transition: Voyage of Ulysses: Letters to Penelope*. That's ahead.

In Charlottesville, it had been in the confusion of thinking Milton still alive, experiencing him vividly in dreams and synchronicities— once a young woman even stopped to tell me she saw a very high being over my head, in conversation with me (was that possible?)—I'd opted, in late 1983, a year before Zurich, to consult my first psychic: the highly regarded Al Miner, channel of Lama Sing. His answer dumbfounded me. According to Lama Sing, not only was Milton still alive, guiding me, but I was in an off-Earth spirit group that was attempting to spread *its* consciousness—that is, "illuminating the *universal* nature of each human soul." He stipulated that this grouping I belonged to, that Milton belonged to, which was several realms in consciousness beyond the Earth—measured in "ability to accept"—was coordinating its transition with the Earth's transition. This breathtaking revelation really knocked my breath out, initially turning me to jelly inside, but I held on, trying to weigh and absorb everything that seemed now on my plate. So I supposed this was my own consciousness that appeared so foreign to me when met in this format.

Al Miner had started his psychic career reluctantly while being an early computer engineer: by an unlikely happenstance he spontaneously fell into trance channeling in his first hypnosis session. This session came about accidentally, though in synchronicity terms seemed destined. Subsequently, in repeated tests of psychics by Edgar Cayce's Association for Research and Enlightenment (A.R.E.), Al scored the highest in accuracy. Many believe he is the Sleeping Prophet Edgar Cayce's successor.

In a second reading, still in Charlottesville, Al Miner associated "illuminating *the universal nature of each soul*" with Christ consciousness. This phrase, he applied to my soul grouping project when I asked if one was currently under way. Yes—it was the "return home."

Though Milton knew Jewish mysticism well in his eclectic inner library, the Zurich Initiation (that he was instrumental in precipitating, beginning in September 1985) was into a level of consciousness even beyond the one where the physical Milton had lived (a level I'd not lived in). For example, the Initiation denied the validity of form recognition when it came to energy identity. A distinction easy enough to apply abstractly. But of course all of us recognize people literally by outer form. That's a given.

Following up on this idea, the former Milton, who was now part of a much larger spirit (an expression of "the universal nature of each soul," as Lama Sing put it) asked me—in regard to him—to let go of form recognition and look for his energy in a transpersonal way.

To give me a semblance of grounding, this "Initiator," a name I created for him in *Keep This Quiet!* III, told me to call him "Milton

Christ"—as the familiarity helped me anchor. He had no single form, he explained. Not only was he a spirit, he also perceived his energy to be in many people and followed it to those locations, applauding it there. But the Initiator also said that most people couldn't handle his light; it darkened them. He was electric, passionate.

It probably goes without saying that being identified with the burst and complexity of energy—it being prana, chi—his energy would translate in different directions in human terms. So that he could be found on many sides of issues we had. Sometimes, surely, the term "his" would not apply to locations of his energy, but at other times he was complex and multidimensional enough that he was a conscious vehicle of it.

With no Eastern training and minimal teaching in the metaphysics of Oneness, I had little if any experience in this level. How did one tread in these waters?

He expounded on the idea of "returning home" in terms of consciousness—that is, of Earth adopting a more expansive consciousness suited to the twenty-first century.

By November 1987, the Zurich Initiation had died down but its effects remained and would forever. By then I had a new boyfriend I thought compatible with my path, despite external appearances, and that month moved into his Tienen, Belgium, apartment. This was the handsome, humorous, sports-loving Flemish truck driver Willy Vanluyten. But a little over three years later, on January 6, 1991 (preceded by uncanny warnings), he died in a car crash. Having spoken to Hunter by phone in the U.S. a year earlier, I phoned him (among others) after the death.

Thrown off balance—but excited—by the energy beginning to permeate the apartment Willy and I had shared, I felt the need to reach out to an old friend, though I had close female friends in a weekly "Inner Landscaping" course in self-development in Brussels and in a mystical Tai Chi course in Leuven. But I wanted someone with a longer view of me, who wouldn't laugh outright at the fact that since Willy's death I had a nonphysical bell sounding in my apartment in response to thoughts. Who could I call? Someone who took "weirdness" in stride? Hunter.

Not that I told him right away about the bell or even about Willy, but I broached the topic of psychic experiences and he listened. At least, he didn't dismiss them outright, but said he preferred the word "intuition."

After numerous long calls January–April 1991, we found a window of opportunity to meet. It latched onto feelings never lost. We both felt the old tie that had never broken stirred up.

However, think about the unknown territory we had to cross now. Hunter did not know me as a mystic. He had only a clue or two about what was going on in my apartment—about which the reader will get more input coming right up. I did not know the extent of his increased drug use. It didn't matter. We knew something more basic, which held on despite these important things that should have driven us apart. Would it, when we met?

To prepare me, he mailed three photos of himself, along with correspondence with Don Henley. Henley, singer/drummer/songwriter of the Eagles ("Hotel California"), owned property close by in Woody Creek; he'd just invited Hunter to contribute an essay to a fund-raising book in support of the developer-threatened woods in which Henry David Thoreau's Walden Pond was located.

Hunter enclosed the back-and-forth. A fax cover sheet said his proposed contribution was "A Death in the Family"—about "the hideous death in life of a red fox." Though dated 1986 in the anthology *Generation of Swine*, the real date was April 26, 1991.

Knowing Hunter's disdain for developers, wouldn't you think he'd help Walden Pond out? But his sense of humor kicked in. Would I see the fun or be horrified? Sending me the correspondence was a test.

According to his essay, he'd discovered a nest of foxes "about 200 yards across the field from my front porch, and I am now in the process of killing them." He went on: in fifteen years "not even a rabid coyote has ever come up on my front porch and killed one of the family animals, or even chewed up one of the peacocks." Not so the fox.

Purportedly, Hunter erected a Have-a-Hart box with Salisbury steak inside, trapping the unlucky perpetrator; then he shoveled in feathers and peacock dung, driving the fox hysterical—after which he followed up with a spray of liquid glue and maced him in the eyes, at long last then freeing him. At least, that's the story.

Let loose, the suffering creature made another pass at a peacock. His fate? He was "shot . . . with a load of double-0 buckshot." As he was sent on his way there were "two huge red-tailed hawks . . . circling overhead preparing to take him into the food chain."

In an enclosed photo he thanked Don "for yr help last year when the Nazis made a run at me. Yr. neighbor HST"; the printed return address on the stationery read: "Congress of the United States."

A fax from *Rolling Stone* editor Bob Love was next in the packet. Love's reaction: "Don't let him change a word."

Don Henley fired back the same day: "Hunter, Hunter, Hunter."

Henley objected: the idea was to point out "how man and nature should live in *harmony*." If Hunter wanted "to write a scathing, sardonic, hit-piece, aim it at *man's folly*." Advocate, he suggested, "chop[ping] up the fucking developers and corporate swine at Dow Chemical"; or he could lash out at "the malignant world banking community; the beef barons who are hacking down the rain forests and overgrazing public range lands."

Henley closed with a tit-for-tat; he too had battled with nature— as a child. A peacock terrorized him till he clubbed it dead "with a Louisville Slugger (Hank Aaron model). So there. Touché. There's some fucking harmony for you."

From peacock killer to owner, not a good turn. What next? Instead of a concluding volley, the remaining enclosed text was a newspaper review, April 27, of William McKeen's biography of Hunter—a review authored by James S. Pope Jr. Hunter handwrote beside the byline: *"Remember him? Great Guy."*

Remember Pope? No. Had he been in New York with us?

The ironical correspondence made me laugh. To reacquaint us, he also enclosed—besides the text—three large photos of himself:

a bald, unattractive, aging Hunter piloting a boat off Key West; a glamorous, romantic-looking face; and a wild, bare-legged-in-the-snow Hunter aiming a gun at unknown quarry. That ought to cover what you might expect, he seemed to say. I sent him a photo taken in Portugal. He told me, "I've psyched myself up."

Left out of his bio was a recent stint in San Francisco, writing political columns for the *Examiner*, which were collected in *The Generation of Swine: Tales of Shame and Degradation in the '80s*. While in San Francisco, he took on a *Playboy* assignment to investigate "couples pornography," a variation on how *New York Times* journalist Gay Talese had daringly investigated changing sex trends

The author in Portugal 1990

in the U.S. In Hunter's case, not surprisingly, he threw himself into the research by spending a lot of time at the O'Farrell Theater, a famous night spot of striptease, porn and live sex. He called himself "the night manager," made himself business cards, and sold Random House the rights to a fictional version of the story. Though I don't remember hearing about this episode or about his 1980s girlfriend, Maria, I knew about an in-progress manuscript, *Polo Is My Life*, involving a similar protagonist.

May 1991, I got into the plane.

I was leaving behind—since Willy's death—a spooked apartment. A bell sound with no visible source that rang at key moments, in part to help me with the writing. I was still finishing *Love in Transition*, a novel I'd begun in 1965 in Paris, twenty-five years before. It wouldn't end.

In retrospect, I thought the end had pointedly eluded my discovery till the revelations after Milton's death in 1981 moved the writing in a different direction. But it was now ten years later. I was going to Woody Creek on the heels of Willy's death. His fatal accident in January had brought with it a new layer of parapsychological (if you are Western) and *siddhi* (if you are Eastern) incidents.

One interest of the Zurich Initiator had been in establishing an "archetype of the couple" (and along with it, the Sacred Marriage). In furthering this as it related to me, he'd used mentally, as a model, the pattern of my relationship with Hunter—which he seemed able to electrify a setting with. That was scandalous to me. But it was only one of his concerns. Another being important world challenges; for example, the threat of the growth of extremist groups, one of which might get some sort of a bomb. These warnings in 1985–'86 have seemed prescient to me with the more recent development of Al-Qaeda, ISIL, and other terrorists.

The Zurich Initiator predicted in 1985–'86 that the drive behind such groups would, unfortunately, merge with the ego's misunderstanding of the Archetype of Home—an archetype constellated in the psyche as the planet went to a higher level of consciousness. In Jungian terms, this meant it was activated in the collective unconscious. But there was danger, said the Initiator, if this archetype was taken literally. Another name for this drive, he said, was the "Archetype of the End of the World," meaning a *nonliteral* end of "the old Earth consciousness."

And now for Woody Creek. Hunter, prominent on the physical-world stage, had never insofar as he made public, focused on spiritual topics. He was an astute observer of the American scene and did a lot of saber-rattling, crushing hypocrisy. He spoke of himself as "a roadman for the Lords of karma" and a writer. My first energy teacher, Chris Van de Velde, had done "energy readings" in the late 1980s and early 1990s (he has since stopped). I'd had one and he told me, when looking into my soul line, that I had "a close relationship with Jesus. But not the Jesus of the Bible. The one who took his whip against the hypocrites."

Hmmm. So I was perhaps closely associated, on a soul level, with an anti-hypocrisy consciousness demonstrated by Jesus in the temple, using his whip to expel the money changers.

In 1991, I hesitantly, cautiously mentioned some concerns about my evolving psychic issues on the phone to Hunter, as stated above; in response, he told me he invented his alter ego Raoul Duke to deal with statements he didn't want to make as Hunter Thompson.

I recently found a (January 1992) note in which I said, "I had taken Hunter as confidante [in 1991], sensing I had to communicate with someone . . . and he was there, familiar with terror and such—with edges and motorcycle speed. And secrecy."

I didn't know what would happen on my trip—for instance, whether I'd arrive at Owl Farm with an audible nonphysical "bell" or other indications of Willy and company. Or indications—sometimes shenanigans—of the high-consciousness soul grouping I perceived to be around me. But Hunter and I went way back to 1966. We'd figured things out before.

What would happen when my new propensity toward spirituality met the man who would say, regarding his legacy, that he'd like to be known as the "voice of my generation"? And that "I heard the music, and I wrote to it. Some people beat drums. Some people strum guitars. It's all in the music you hear"?

PART ONE

Hunter, Kundalini, "A Road above a Road," In the Center of a Rampaging Archetype

Dream no small dreams, for they have no power to move the hearts of men.

—Goethe

James Joyce was a synthesizer, trying to bring in as much as he could. I am an analyzer, trying to leave out as much as I can.

—Samuel Beckett

— 1 —

A Peek into My Apartment

In "Synchronicity, Science and the *I Ching*," quantum physicist/*I Ching* expert Shantena Augusto Sabbadini states: "The assumption of orthodox Western science that there is no meaning to be gleaned from random events was certainly not shared by the ancient Chinese. These divinatory practices [exemplified in the *I Ching*] and their whole cosmology were based on a qualitative notion of time, in which all things happening at a given moment in time share some common features, are part of an organic pattern. Nothing therefore is entirely meaningless, and the entry point to understanding the overall pattern can be any detail of the moment, provided we are able to read it."[5]

Carl Jung wrote in his foreword to the *I Ching*:

The Chinese mind, as I see it at work in the *I Ching*, seems to be exclusively preoccupied with the chance aspect of events. What we call coincidence seems to be the chief concern of this peculiar mind, and what we worship as causality passes almost unnoticed. . . .

The manner in which the *I Ching* tends to look upon reality seems to disfavor our causalistic procedures. . . . The matter of interest seems to be the configuration formed by chance events in the moment of observation, and not at all the hypothetical reasons that seemingly account for the coincidence. While the Western mind carefully sifts, weighs, selects, classifies, isolates, the Chinese picture of the moment encompasses everything down to the minutest nonsensical detail, because all of the ingredients make up the observed moment. . . .

In other words, whoever invented the *I Ching* was convinced
that the hexagram worked out in a certain moment coincided with
the latter in quality no less than in time.[6]

I quote this to help set up the rest of the book. In the events that
follow—and the whole of *Keep This Quiet!* IV—it may sometimes
appear that I report random events, coincidences, and ungrounded
(to the West) anecdotes without explaining rationally how they could
be possible. But such "acausal" (to a purely materialistic view) events
immediately gain new clarity if seen inside frameworks such as the
above, which recognizes two types of time: clockwork (chronos) and
content-oriented (kairos). In the later, events can be "set up" energetically outside 3-D time and manifest in it at "the right," perhaps
synchronistic time.

For one thing, events that happen in the psyche—the mind—are
real, according to Carl Jung. They might come out of—and do feed
into—the collective unconscious: a pool all of us draw from not limited
by time and space. If something happens to me physically and I interpret it a certain way—even esoterically—then regardless of how someone else may explain it (or explain it away) or value it, it has a place in
the collective unconscious. It may be part of an activated archetype, an
archetype appearing far and wide, trying to become conscious.

Intuitively, we all experience our life as concrete and material.
But the psyche, in its roamings, is not limited to material reality.

Jung had mused back in 1929: "So far as I can grasp the nature of
the collective unconscious, it seems to me like an omnipresent continuum, an unextended Everywhere. That is to say, when something
happens here at point A which touches upon or affects the collective
unconscious, it happens everywhere."[7]

Having posited that "every atom in your body, astrophysicists
say, originated billions of years ago in a star or in the explosive aftermath of the Big Bang"[8]—that most of the elements *inside us and
elsewhere* are dust of exploded stars, maybe from a long-extinct "star
factory"— some scientists go further, telling us that space and time

are constructs of our 3-D minds. Hard (a.k.a, rigorous) science is joined by Carl Jung's psychology, which points out that mind (in each of us) is as ancient as life, and *remembers its past, its instincts*, and is as universal as the cosmos. Jung: "Just as the human body represents a whole museum of organs, each with a long evolutionary history behind it, so we should expect to find that the mind is organized in a similar way. It can no more be a product without history than is the body in which it exists."[9]

The collective unconscious and the particle world we are intertwined with (those "sparks of informative energy"[10]) will have a totally different sense of time and different preconditions than materialism. How do we reconcile this? Much further ahead a physicist, E. H. Walker, will give his definitions of what consciousness is.

Neuroscientist Norman S. Don, who will enter *Keep This Quiet!* IV also, did numerous experiments with psychic/engineer Olof Jonsson, who (along with three others), in a secret telepathic experiment set up by astronaut Captain Edgar Mitchell during his 1971 moon voyage, received Mitchell's transmission of symbols from a deck of Zener cards.* Zener cards, which have five symbols, had been routinely used by J. B Rhine in ESP experiments at Duke University. Mitchell said of his experiment, "Professionals in the fields thought it was very significant. In telepathy, space doesn't matter."[11]

In *Keep This Quiet!* III, I reported how, unknown to his scientific colleagues, Nobel Prize physicist Wolfgang Pauli's dreams were analyzed by Carl Jung. With Jung, Pauli came to believe that psyche and physics emerged from a unified psychophysical reality: a nonlocal—not bound by time and space—*unus mundus*. Jung and Pauli worked to establish this as fact.

In the seventeenth century this World Soul was basic to the world view. Nature was thought to be alive, a living being. Everywhere "correspondences" were found between nature and humans. Then, with seventeenth-century mathematician/astronomer Johannes Kepler

---

* The symbols are a star, a circle, three wavy lines, a square, and a cross.

and others, science began to demolish this belief—emphasizing reason and mathematical proof. And math could not, to Kepler's dismay, work on living matter. It could only calculate with "dead matter."

Statistical data depended on Large Numbers. The small numbers—the isolated, the individual, the personal—were lost in the Large Number calculations.

And so it stood when the two twentieth-century giants Jung and Pauli tried to find the way back to the lost moment in the seventeenth century when modern science, in its birth, cast aside the amniotic fluid of hermetic alchemy: the feminine, nonrational (not able to be understood by reason)—even "magic"—roots.

In the twentieth century, to many in consensus reality it was barely imaginable to believe without rational proof. But had the West become lopsided—the resulting world view off balance? Scientists, taking the conquest of nature further and further, arrived at, to Jung and Pauli's mutual horror, the atom bomb. Jung and Pauli said nature would retaliate. The archetypes would. The collective unconscious would. Nature wanted *wholeness*, they said. Symmetry.

The twentieth and twenty-first centuries saw the stirrings of a call to "reclaim the feminine" in the West—that is, yin (beside yang): intuition, the mystical, things reached by "inner Knowing," not proving (which to the Eastern yogis and other wisdom traditions was where Truth was). Could this lost half partner with the scientific, rational view to arrive at a healthy wholeness: a "tension of opposites"?

As he viewed Earth from space, Mitchell thought, *the rational man in me had to recognize the validity of the nonrational cognitive process.*

Jung wrote: "At times I feel as if I am spread out over the landscape and inside things, and am myself living in every tree, in the splashing of the waves, in the clouds and the animals that come and go, in the procession of the seasons. There is nothing . . . with which I am not linked."[12]

Against that backdrop, I hope the questions raised in the experiences recounted here are interesting and probe-worthy.

Enough of this Author Interruption. Now back to the story.

Before leaving Belgium for the U.S., let's take a last peek into my apartment at 46 Lunevillelaan ("Moonville Lane") in the small Flemish town of Tienen.

The housing complex was low rent, subsidized. Being on disability from accident injuries, Willy qualified. Not that any broken bones showed. As an international trucker, he'd had several wrecks before we met—ruled not his fault—such as when the brakes of a large transporter gave out. He wound up with half his bones broken, though they mended, leaving only some back pain, which he hid. The roomy walk-up overlooked a field, where he sometimes rode his dirt bike when the wheat fields weren't blooming.

He'd grown up desperately poor, leaving school at fourteen to help support his mother, and he identified fresh bread with rising out of poverty; so it was very important to him to have fresh bread on the table.

Willy's death in a car accident, at just under thirty-four, was preceded by warnings. On several nights, returning home late from a pub a half hour from Tienen, he "saw" with his inner eye a head-on collision into his windshield. Terrifying. He wasn't one to have visions. Obviously, this scared him. Further, even Russell Park picked a warning up—in a dream of a car accident when visiting us, sleeping on Willy's side of the bed. It was so convincing he almost telephoned a cab to take him to the airport rather than have Willy drive. To me, Russell's dream clearly harked back to ten years earlier, when I myself had a car-accident dream—in the "wave of announcements" preceding Milton Klonsky's death, the "shadow of the approach of death," as Carl Jung called it. See the Appendix on event balls for a sketch of the details. Also, see *Love in Transition* IV: *The Bedtime Tales of Jesus* (pages 122ff).

Sometimes near the end he would walk into my small writing room, hold a fresh-baked bread loaf up to my nose to smell, and say, inexplicably, "Hello, Mrs. Bell."

Oddly, after he died in a coincidence-riddled accident, the bell came. Let me explain.

In *Keep This Quiet!* III: *Initiations*, I described its first appearance. Helen Titchen Beeth, a translator in the European Commission, stayed with me immediately after Willy's death, helping with the grief. I wrote:

> "The bell" arrived in the first week after his death, while Helen was still there.
>
> When we were talking together about him, suddenly we both heard an electronic beep. "The sense was that we were saying something and he was confirming it," she recently recalled. "We went looking around the house for anything that might have made the noise and there was nothing." Reviving Willy's enigmatic comment "Hello, Mrs. Bell," it was to be yet one more "impossible"—this time day-to-day—occurrence the death left in its wake.
>
> Multiple times every day the bell was audible in the apartment—sounding something like the then-new watches that beeped on the hour. Only, there was no such watch in the apartment and not many in Belgium. Often it punctuated a thought or statement by me or something on TV. In those cases I felt it was "rung"—who knew how?—by Willy. Helen, who had a highly developed sense of "knowing," never doubted it.[13]

I was convinced of the obvious explanation—the bell was at times "rung," somehow, by Willy—but I also felt sure that at other times it was "rung" by a spirit group.

However, there are many explanations as to what acausal source might explain the bell. Jung had broached the subject in terms of synchronicity: "I well understand that you prefer to emphasize the archetypal implication in synchronicity . . . but I must say that I am equally interested, at times even more so, in the metaphysical aspects of the phenomena, and in the question: how does it come that even inanimate objects are capable of behaving as if they were acquainted with my thoughts? This is . . . a thoroughly paranoid speculation which one had better not ventilate in public, but I cannot deny my fervent interest in this aspect of the problem."[14]

I will go into the bell more later, as well as a phenomenon that soon accompanied it, "computer PK," but for the moment want to change the venue to Owl Farm.

The bell preceded, by a hair, my renewed contact with Hunter— about the only person I knew still alive who might not close his ears if I broached some topics, tentatively albeit, that newly consumed my life. Just an anecdote here and there, a question, a pause to hear how he digested it.

Not that we'd had a lot of contact recently. But always at big moments he came in. For instance, in 1984, en route to studies at the Jung Institute Zurich, I phoned him from New York and mentioned that I was experimenting with not drinking alcohol; he fired back with light repartee and witty depth. I thought his agility, fast mind, and insights might perfectly cast him as replacement for the confidante status Milton had had. It would also renew the amorous status Hunter occupied earlier, when I lived in New York, though he was married at the time and therefore in a situation that couldn't be taken further.

Now he was free. Though just barely. His most recent relationship ended around January 1991; his girlfriend chanced to be walking out the door against his protests at the very moment I phoned. A mere coincidence. But it set up the plan to meet in his Woody Creek hermitage, mid-May.

2

Woody Creek

Woody Creek is located in the Roaring Fork River valley in the Rockies. Both of us knew this meeting had been held in reserve, although some reserves are not called on. But we had clutched the possibility to our breasts privately. Such a meeting might not be the best idea, considering all the water gone under the dam. But we didn't care. Common sense might proclaim this was an impossible dream. But Hunter and I thought big.

He cleared his schedule of speaking gigs (they brought in $15,000 to $20,000 a pop, which he didn't say). Canceled everything, he said—in particular, a possible chance to interview Gorbachev. He added, it was "probably a ruse of an old girlfriend to get me to Russia."

Specifics aside, I took it that he'd given up something he cared about for this meeting—he had prioritized it.

I didn't know that Terry Sabonis-Chaffee, the girlfriend who'd just moved out, was in Moscow—or going to be (I don't know her arrival date). By all reports, she would *not* have invited him. I sent the photo earlier pictured, of me leaning against a car in Portugal in a colorful tie-top blouse and knee-length form-fitting tan skirt. I still had dancer's legs (because of Tai Chi).

To my surprise, *before* the photos revealing my current appearance arrived, Hunter committed to the rendezvous; he knew less than nothing of how time might have physically eroded me. At fifty-one,

I might be a white-haired, prune-wrinkled two-hundred pounds! He deleted that consideration, though he suddenly asked on the phone, "Do you still have those long"—he paused as if picturing the former me—"tresses"?

In 1966—likewise blind to appearance, when I was a Random House copy editor assigned to him in New York City—he hadn't known for months I was three years his junior, with Veronica Lake-style red hair. Long hair (or, as he was now saying, "tresses") had been my trademark since leaving my hometown, Greenville, North Carolina, where my mother had kept my hair cut short. She did that in reaction to how her mother kept hers, as a child, in long, dark ringlets.

I felt very excited about the 1991 trip. Didn't a part of him fit well with my initiations? Hadn't I already, in 1984, once mentioned "my new self," such as it was—little knowing how great the coming change would be? Hadn't he shown me his insightful-about-females side? Sometimes things just fell into place.

On the other hand, perhaps I should have prepared him for my transformation in the Zurich Initiation and its aftermath. But it hadn't interfered with my relationship with the rugged former truck driver Willy Vanluyten, the very virile, masculine, thirty-four-year-old, who—when I first met him in the Tienen hospital, where I was visiting my ex, Jan Mensaert—had been determined to kick a coke habit. He'd sunk into it (shooting up once a day for a year) in the depths of depression after his wife left, then filed a restraining order against his seeing their seven-year-old daughter.

Having doted on her, he'd been demoralized. Besides, many truck drivers used coke to stay awake on long trips across different European countries. But Willy wound up in the Tienen hospital after having bargained with the police that he'd reform if they expunged his record. They did. We met, fell in love, and I moved in.

A little over three years later, on January 6, 1991, came the fatal auto crash. It was wrapped in uncanny coincidences and increasingly urgent warnings I have only begun to allude to in this volume. For instance, Russell Park's dream of a terrifying car accident, in our apartment, appeared to act out literally my symbolic warning dream of Milton Klonsky's approaching death ten years before. And was part of a synchronicity involving yet another death—in January 1988, just after I moved in with Willy—of the painter René Pascal in Zurich. I had dreamed, before moving in with Willy, *that to go into his apartment was to go into René's apartment,* which underscored to me the energetic presence of the Initiator. Also, both René and Willy had reported feeling "stalked" by death in the month before they died. But that's a long story. I touch on in the Appendix on "event balls" and multidimensional gravity, which such multiplying synchronicities led me to speculate existed.

When Hunter and I later that same January renewed contact via phone, it was not that I wasn't mourning but with all that was going on in the apartment, he seemed to me to be singularly prepared for my odd circumstances—ultra-open-minded, one of very few I could share some of the events with, short of Willy's friends.

Yes, I knew, it was pushing things.

In May I sent questions to reputable psychic Mariah Martin, in Delaware, whom I'd occasionally contacted since she was first recommended to me by leading Charlottesville figures: Graciela Damewood (founder of Openway) and Bob Van de Castle (psychologist and director of the University of Virginia dream lab). I asked that Mariah mail the answers to Owl Farm. Then I went to North Carolina. Hunter phoned at my sister's home. It created a stir.

I landed at the tiny Aspen–Pitkin County Airport (it had one runway) in seat 5A at 3:52 p.m. May 13, on a flight from Raleigh-Durham via Chicago and Denver. How do I know the details? I recently found the ticket! Collecting my bags at the small carousel, I looked around. No Hunter. I didn't realize that as an extreme night owl, normally he'd still be asleep. His friend and historian Doug Brinkley wrote, "He took a fiendish pride in waking up . . . pals in the middle of the night. Sleep, as Hunter saw it, was for the weak and feeble."[15] Waiting nervously, bags at my side, I felt the kind of fading out of reality where logically you know he's coming but illogically you see he is not there and wonder if he really will walk through the door, or perhaps it's all a sham, a dream. Perhaps the whole airport will collapse before he enters, *though* you know it is entirely real and meant to be.

He walked in, so tall—was he six three?—I was taken aback, having forgotten. I had not watched a gradual change. This was full blast, meeting this physical giant who to me had been playful, direct, a huge force.

I'd seen a photo of him bald on the top, but hadn't realized he'd become a bit hefty. Minor details I was adjusting to, as he doubtless adjusted to me. He hoisted my bags up into his big hands and—not to be spotted by reporters—hurried us out of the baggage area. What were the first words? Maybe we summed up the moment in a telling, piercing glance. I was overwhelmed by the raw physical tangibility. In intangible ways it was as if I'd seen him yesterday, the familiar guy at my side. But many physical details were different. The loose, lanky, volatile, open, humorous early-thirties young man had given way to many unknowns—old and new at once.

In the Red Shark (his famous fire apple red 1971 Chevy Impala convertible that made appearances in his work, most notoriously in *Fear and Loathing in Las Vegas*), he immediately snorted cocaine. I'd never seen him do this. He told me he'd expected to stay awake the night before—and instead fell asleep and had been woken abruptly at the last minute, rushing out to pick me up before I disappeared into the past again.

As he sat so close beside me in the front seat, I said—not stopping to think—after he snorted the coke, "Do you have to do that, Hunter?" He looked at me and broke through any objection with that smile: "Margaret, it's not what you have to do. It's what you *want* to do." He wanted to be here, sniffing the coke. Of all his possibilities in the world, these were the two he wanted, chose.

What I remember clearly is the projection of his smile—it filled a bandwidth between our faces—poured energy right into me, straight to my heart, to the unpredictable. Time being drawn into the present in intensity inside that smile.

Earlier I hadn't seen him hooked on drugs. Obviously, I'd seen him, as was common in the '60s, when he felt like it smoke pot. Who didn't in those days? And—it's a vague memory—I can see a circle, a joint passed. My hand passing the joint. But that was long ago. Everyone back then in Greenwich Village was used to such scenes. My eventual husband, Jan Mensaert, when in Morocco, had smoked grass (or kif) to write.

Now at the wheel, a convulsive shiver; then he was like before, as if he'd accommodated every shift of substance that entered his body, allowed some in, thrown off the rest—he seemed perfectly sober and lucid. There were no bats on the horizon. Just he himself phenomenally *right there*. No gibbering maniac, no wild terrifying driver. Answering *why*, he turned his head to look right in my eyes with a sparkle in his, mischief, that totally relaxed, winning, charming smile that spread wide into the creases of his face. It was as if the smile was capturing all the focus, so that nothing else could be felt—just the feeling that emotes presence and frankness, that says: *This is me, take it or leave it.*

Answered, dimpling, "It's not what YOU HAVE to do, Margaret. It's what you WANT to do."

There is a phrase like that in *Fear and Loathing*. It was conveyed here with such impact, force, certainty, naturalness—resonating.

There was the sheer audacity that we'd accomplished Mission Impossible, sitting—after all these centuries between then and now—alone in the car. What would happen next?

All I could feel were his words, which dissipated the question as if there were no place for it to go. He had opened a door. The answer simply sat there, sinking in. There was no reply to it, hurled at me transparently like a ball of hot iron, an admission, a philosophy: he was doing what he wanted to do.

Looking at him smiling, I felt no distance between the fifty-three-year-old and spry twenty-seven-year-old.

But there were lifetimes of times where we grew in different choices. Could we get past them? Would they bar the way? Well, I was still game. And so was he. We were leaving ourselves wide open. There was a zest, a tinge of edginess. Riding together through this Unknown.

Prima facie, I couldn't disagree. Inside I felt: Yes, who can argue with that? If a person makes a conscious choice, how can you tell that person to make another choice? He went to great inconvenience—up at this hour, being a night owl—picking me up himself. What can I say? I am happy to be here. Let's keep going.

Let me quickly add that this is the only situation in which I can imagine reacting that way. I had been told that cocaine was an ego power trip, habit-forming. Supposedly it made *"holes in the aura"* through which negative energy entered. In every way counter-prescriptive to my spiritual initiations.

Yet he did not have a normal reaction. He did not cave in or have outbursts. He was the same, with 150 percent *charming, vulnerable* presence.

I'd seen a rush. But his intentional shaking seemed to settle the substance into place. He was not driving dangerously fast. At least, if he was, I didn't notice. Or remember. He didn't test me.

For those who find it hard to imagine Hunter being vulnerable, let me add that anyone deeply sensitive, in touch with his or her feelings, who lives in the moment volatilely—who is present, listening— is taking a risk in a relationship. No one has signed on for keeps. There is no insurance in love except its authentic nature. As long as it *is*, one can access it. If it dies, then one knows. Being particularly passionate and uninhibited, Hunter could fall deeply in love.

I had heard that (in Eastern esotericism) a great teacher could transmute poisons. If Hunter's body was doing that with these chemicals, somehow he'd learned to take in only what he wanted to, be it from a cigarette or a drug. Jim Silberman, his editor at Random House, once told me that Hunter's body was "a natural chemical factory." Still, it was rather surprising that now, in his fifties, he regularly took cocaine, sometimes with pot, acid or mushrooms, or with nothing. AND—TO JUDGE BY THIS MOMENT—REMAINED HIMSELF. Perhaps more so.

He suggested we stop off to catch the Lakers' game—drink margaritas, eat guacamole, my favorites!—at the Jerome. This is an Aspen luxury hotel opened in the 1880s in the silver mining boom, in walking distance, skis in tow, from Aspen Mountain. Rife with charm. No heads turned toward our small table as we sat down. "I told *no one* you were coming," he said. "Paparazzi *would have been at the airport*." It went to my heart, that he secluded us off in a room of scattered people.

We were reacquainting ourselves. I remember that Willy had stretched me to the limit when he shoplifted a few ultratiny clay figurines in Portugal and when I reacted said, "This is *me*"—conveying with sparse words that whatever *he* did was *him*—as if its "being *him*," not an abstraction, removed the persona non grata from around the tiny theft.

Hunter was delightful. Most people, with a few exceptions such as Sigmund Freud, do not react this way to coke. Freud—no one knowing the dangers at the time—without addiction or adverse reaction experimented with it, reporting "exhilaration and lasting euphoria," self-control, vigor, more ability to work, and no aftereffects of depression. Certainly, the friends of Willy I had seen addicted to coke were, by their own admission, a sorry sight. When Freud recommended it to a friend, he was horrified at the result. Intending to review a new edition of Freud's *Cocaine Papers* (1884) for *Rolling Stone* in 1973, Hunter, by his own account, first tried the stuff, and—we know the result.*

I was heart and soul plunged into hopes. He at least as convinced as I, I think, but also more reckless. To not see each other for twenty-one years while barreling at high speed in opposite directions might send chills down the noblest, gamest, most *up for it* adventurer or romantic. What habits might cramp us, cause us to buck?

---

* This date has been contradicted by one source, who reports he began taking cocaine earlier.

So far, we were melding, grooving, happy, ignoring consequences.

I'd last seen him in 1969 at his hotel room on Fifth Avenue, where I stayed the night and watched football the next day. Did the red "Chou de [pronounced 'Ciao D'] Hunter" I repainted on my palm in a dream every time it washed away *signify this moment*—recalling the "red ink" intensity of his letters to me in the '60s, not to mention the Red Shark; picking up a delicate, strong thread across two decades? Was this what I had vowed to myself in that dream never to let go of without one more chance—rewriting the red on my hand as it vanished?

But at our Hotel Jerome table a monster appeared—to splinter this idyll—a polite waiter, phone in hand. Deborah, Hunter's assistant, quite reasonably wanted to go over a few things before leaving.

I do not remember careening around curves—no one could drive more wildly (yet safely) than Willy—though speed was in the mind-boggling readjustments, the turn of the time dial backwards, then forwards, then in modulations; the in-the-moment excitement of having dropped our worlds to meet across continents and oceans and years. Zooming, my hair flying, along Highway 82, through the mountain landscape, we approached his ranch in the valley: his unpretentious one-story cabin.

Yellow dandelions dotted green grass. A peacock strutted and opened its tail. A sixteen-foot Birdview satellite dish stood a hundred yards from the cabin. Hunter called it a "full-bore, all-channels, 19 satellite Earth Station . . . including Spanish Reuters and the morning news from Bermuda."[16] Snow-banked slopes of mountains glided picturesquely down toward us.

As I stepped over the cabin threshold, I had a momentary jolt at seeing a sign from Dante's *Inferno* that read: ABANDON ALL HOPE, YE WHO ENTER HERE. Purposefully, Hunter led the way, carrying my bags. He headed past the kitchen counter (where his electric typewriter sat) into the bedroom. I followed. Without a word, he deposited the suitcases. *Hot damn! So we don't have to wade through that awkward bit.*

Not asking where I wanted to sleep, after twenty-one years and without overstepping, he thought the answer self-evident. I was relieved he was so natural, choosing the only suitable place. That over, we conferred with Deborah Fuller, who was going to leave her job to me for a day or so. Hot damn again! Now Hunter, the writer I had worked with so many months so long ago, sat down at at his writing perch in the kitchen and told me my assignment: *to keep him focused*—not let him wander *off subject*, which, he said, he had a tendency to do.

So we sat nose to nose, with a rustle underneath of the electricity. He had yet to switch from IBM Selectric to computer, which he never would. Looking around, I let my eyes sweep over the silent anchor faces on TV, coming in by satellite.

With Deborah gone, telephone messages from unanswered calls were broadcast out into the room over a speaker. He picked up only once, when a Fourth Amendment lawyer friend, using expletives, called his bluff.

I loved everything. We were a team. I loved that this person was so romantic, imaginative, so HIMSELF. I loved that being so private, he included me, that he had not been disappointed. And neither had I.

From here on, it's hard to say *what* happened *when*—of the minor details. They are merged, fused, moved around. In *Keep This Quiet!* IV, the first edition, I deduced I'd stayed only four days. Deduced it because my memory brought back to me point blank only the initial forty-eight hours and the last twenty-four. So the stay must have been ultrashort, I calculated. Contradicting that, I had the impression I'd stayed a week. But how to account for the time?

I still don't know. But that impression belatedly proved correct. Ticket dates don't lie. Holding the ticket in my hand in the garage, there's no denying I arrived the thirteenth. Sunning in the backyard in my blue flowered two-piece bathing suit—that happened when? Eating cheeseburgers at the Woody Creek Tavern, when? (A number of times, actually.) Hunter presenting me with two PART OF THE LEGEND Tavern T-shirts, for me and Jyoti—when? Seated by Hunter as he worked at the typewriter, when? (Well, every day.) So I'll just continue, placing the puzzle pieces as best I can. They need to make up a whole week.

The *New York Times* ("HUNTER S. THOMPSON, OUTLAW JOURNAL-
IST, IS DEAD AT 67," by Michael Slackman) reported that sometimes
Hunter implied he was "not really about guns and drugs, and tear-
ing up the pavement and planting grass, but about grabbing public
attention to focus on the failures of leadership, *the hypocrisy in society*."[17] (emphasis added)

At the typewriter—his fingers curled into loose fists—he twirled
his hands to the rhythm of the music that played, thrusting the pace
into the words. I never saw anyone else write like that; getting the
rhythm from his hands into his brain, in twirling his fists. He was absorbing the music as he absorbed the chemicals, letting it pour through
his belly, in his hands, that twirled, then came down on the keys.

In fact, I would say this was why he'd copied books by famous
authors—to get the music, the pauses; to feel what it was like to type
those exact sentences. It was not just left-brain learning. Dancers
watching dance soak up movements. Bending down to a flower, one
"tastes" the smell. Hunter was rhythmic as well as visual and verbal.

And so I was enchanted by this fireball who was devoted to
Unflinching Self-Portrayal. I will call it BEING UNCONDITIONALLY
AUTHENTIC—no matter the consequences, instinctively. It may be
wrong. That is not the point. *But it is not hypocritical.*

I woke, struggling out of sleep, in that state where you know that
later you will want to remember the phrase. "Putting soul shimmer
into politics"—write it down. Woke not then, in 1991, but now.
"Soul shimmer." It was about Hunter. So that's how I'm going to play
it, a more astute part of me finding the words—more astute than my
normal self, who might not be so bold as to speak of the soul level.

Getting to the significance of the '91 meeting—why it was the
end of the circle begun in '66. I remember how in the 1960s he gave
me the opportunity to pull pranks, backed by him. He enticed people to feel at fever pitch—an insanely wild, absurdly funny, extreme,
hyperbolic, serious genial man.

However, no matter what structure I tell you the book has, remember, it is fitting in the passages itself.

Hunter said, *"You have to understand about time."* This was the first evening; we were alone. A haunting Country-Folk tune I was unfamiliar with was playing, filling the room—something like "Leaving, on a Jet Plane" but different lyrics. I was idly aware of them, focused on Hunter as he mumbled, "Those words are for you." I perked up my ears, too late—backtracked—just picking up the aftersound: the singer always expected to end up with a particular woman. Ralph Steadman, his illustrator-collaborator, would describe how Hunter's voice "cut into my thoughts and sunk its teeth into my brain . . . a cross between a slurred karate chop and gritty molasses."[18]

My heart was trying to compose itself—keep from melting onto the floor. What I felt was, "I'm blown away, I can't believe it, this is what I hoped you'd say, somehow I knew." I pointed out the obvious: that during all these separated years he was surely in love many times. I gestured to a famous photo, where because of his curly, abundant hair, the young Jann Wenner (publisher of *Rolling Stone*) looked to me like a woman.

The real conversation was below the surface, trying to let the meaning slip into place unhindered, because *This Is Big*, my heart was saying.

I wanted to see how much more he would say. Hear him restate what the singer was saying, just to be sure. Would he, in his own words? I was giving the moment time to land down in my feelings. Before it went further, as it was bound to, turning deliciously physical.

Not sidetracking to correct that detail about Jann Wenner, Hunter said, "Yes, but . . . you have to understand about time."

I didn't ask what he meant. I felt I knew unconsciously. Also, I couldn't believe my ears. I held the magic sentence that was riddled with meaning to me—impossible meaning. Whatever it meant, it held open options for us never canceled out by a prior event. However deep a love might have been experienced with someone else, we didn't go into that. Just this: "You have to understand about time." It seemed time was on our side. Time was standing by us. Right here, now.

At any rate, as we are different things to different people, if we stretch enough, there's space to be all those things. But he had something clearly in mind, perhaps a trajectory into the future.

The song said it for him. And his eyes. No matter that he'd been faraway. For me too, there were sometimes at night vivid dreams of shared moments. I'd always felt he was still around, without imagining practically what that left to happen. Perhaps nothing. Just a sense he was on my side, out there fighting the fight. Loving. Connected by an invisible feeling wrapped up in the unknowns and enigmas of the future, not a *what might have been* but a *who knows? It's not over yet.* A Christmas card to myself not yet looked at.

What do you do when a daydream suddenly materializes?

Milton Klonsky said, "I don't like virgins . . . except, on second thought, to *rearrange* them." An angle into time was like a tuning fork.

It sets a pitch, lets the overtones die out.

It cut through. Everything might seem complete before. But an angle was left out.

One might be aware it existed, *how it would reflavor— refocus—everything.*

In the back of his head, was he saying, without giving it any urgent thought, he knew I would be back? A hunch sitting in a corner of his head—an awareness the story was unfinished. A secret, perhaps.

I thought it incredibly wise, paradox or not.

All these thoughts were understood in a giant implication; barely seconds went by. We were back at our theme song line, "So why not throw your life in with mine" (Jefferson Airplane).

That evening finished unforgettably, fresh in memory now and forever. The lipstick tube in his large hand, we withdraw the light from the living room floor and leave the reader to his or her voluptuous, tender imagination.

Unfortunately, because of what came next, it's hard to leave the curtain drawn.

But first, I have to resurrect Willy, who died January 6, only FOUR MONTHS BEFORE. In spite of my telephone confidences, Hunter knew nothing of him. At least, as I remember it.

After his passing, Willy had, according to witnesses in telephone conversation with me, seemed to "go down phone wires."

And that's just the first bit of the spirit energy that—in recent months—I'd felt always around, sometimes intervening. I know to those who haven't experienced such a situation it may sound outlandish. But the aftermath of Willy's sudden death (incredibly, it turned out, on the anniversary of the only telegram Milton Klonsky ever sent to me: GIRDLE OF O, GIRDER OF I. INVIOLABLE. UNBREAKABLE, January 6, 1966) introduced a stream of psychic experiences narrated in the previous volume.

Returning to the ranch: Hunter effortlessly created an orgasm in me in the living room. No problem for him, or for me in that situation. But—the intensity was so high that suddenly my throat began to tremble in the first sign of kundalini kriyas. Now, with kriyas you have no control, because their whole purpose is to destroy blocks. Some physiological signs might be "muscle . . . cramps, energy rushes or immense electricity circulating the body, itching, vibrating, prickling, tingling, . . . intense heat or cold, . . . jerking, tremors, shaking; feeling an inner force pushing one into postures or moving one's body in unusual ways."[19]

It went for my throat, threatening to make me tremble all over. The kundalini energy pierces and awakens chakras. In the case of the throat, the intent is to open up communication with one's true nature, consequently with a lot of emotion, sensation, and awareness deluging my mind and mouth at that moment. My experience of kundalini over the last six months had been with sudden trembling of kriyas shaking a block out of *an arm or a leg*, sending waves of energy through me and into a room. For the first time my throat was the target. Talk about awkward.

Hunter had said on the phone to Belgium he felt like he was talking to "a naked child." With the throat kriyas clearing the obstacles inside me away for the "higher self's" agenda, "the naked child" would have the floor, literally. Except that the emotion made me speechless.

Hunter had shot me into opening the throat chakra. I suppose he would have been intrigued and fascinated with the situation if I'd let or gotten a word out.

However, what happened at this point instigated a fluke. I think the kriya overshot its mark or set up an intensity we didn't get to play out. Kundalini can heighten sexual feeling; can create what is sometimes called cosmic orgasms, stimulating cellular response in the whole body, not to mention bliss. I felt he must be aware how strong the feeling inside me was and that it was extending to him. For some reason he didn't just continue the very intense sex in the living room.

My exact memory is unclear or incomplete except that, still in a highly romantic mood, we left for the bedroom. But he instantly popped a fast-acting sleeping pill. As he swallowed—before I could react—he said it was a good thing he was taking it "because of what I feel like doing to you."

What? Go ahead, I wanted to shout. Too late.

I absorbed the shock. Okay. No problem. I like a cuddly sleep. After all, this was only Day 1. Just last night I'd been in North Carolina. There were eons of time extending before us.

I can see Hunter the next morning preparing a scrumptious breakfast, with cinnamon toast that awakened visions of childhood. With his big breakfast he had Wild Turkey and cocaine. "Do you know what you're doing?" I asked, trying to sound matter of fact, mild but inquisitive, not at all judging. I couldn't stop myself.

He said yes, that *he monitored his intake*, that, "Recently, I noticed I was overdoing it and cut back."

He hopped back in front of the typewriter, on a short-piece dead-line, while I, at his side, fended off sidetracks. I enjoyed this a lot. We took a burger break at the Woody Creek Tavern.

When a fan intercepted us outside—having driven, he said, one thousand miles—I loved Hunter's answer; he couldn't share whatever drug the guy had brought. Even despite the fan's long trip, Doc, a.k.a., Hunter ("Doc" and the "Good Doctor were nicknames he'd acquired, having gotten a write-in doctor of divinity degree from the Universal Life Church, thereafter sometimes using the byline "Dr. Thompson"), had to decline, he said: "I'm in the middle of an argument about religion with my wife." Hunter said "wife" and grinned. We weren't, of course, arguing about religion, but that was the funny twist he put on, I suppose, my questioning his coke habit.

Inside the Tavern he bought two T-shirts, one for me, one for my friend Jyoti, whom I was about to visit in San Francisco. On the back was printed: PART OF THE LEGEND.

He stopped the car on a hill on the way home—for a bit of parking—delicious signs of things to come.

A few etched scenes replay like a movie. In the early evening, as he sat at his IBM Selectric typewriter, his legs hurt from poor circulation. I remembered I'd once had a sixth sense something was terribly wrong with him. It corresponded to what he now told me about having severely injured his back in an accident. With some trepidation I asked to feel his energy field, using the aura healing I'd learned in my two-year study of Basic Applications of Psycho-Dynamics in "Inner Landscaping" (in Brussels) with Chris Van de Velde.

Putting both hands a small distance outside his body, I was taken aback, amazed at the volatility of what I felt. There appeared to be a time bomb energy field around him, huge—and agitated. My hands felt as if in volcanic air space that was not internalized.

No wonder he had to shoot off guns, to get the intensity out of his body.

A little warning bell went off. I tried to shush it—quiet the implications of walking in a highly activated *externalized* energy field.

There could be archetypes in it, sending exploding attractions smashing far and wide. But I didn't let all this information and sensation sink in. I halted it. Held my shock in abeyance.

I asked Hunter, "Would you like to get into altered states *without drugs*? He said, "It would save me a lot of money." I had some idea how to set this up. Maybe I'd look into it, I thought.

I wondered if this was just the field he was used to. Though commenting about its strength, I did not speculate that perhaps it was a very specific field related to our history! I was keeping that voice of awareness quiet. The kind of voice that can predict what comes next, unfurl the whole incident before it occurs, based on the implications that are all too apparent.

He hoped I would take an ultrapure one-quarter LSD dose while he downed three-quarters. High quality. I knew he wanted to share the experience, watch what I did entering his inner world. LSD, unlike cocaine, was not reputed to feed the ego but to cleanse "the doors of perception." ("If the doors of perception were cleansed everything would appear to man as it is, Infinite. For man has closed himself up, till he sees all things thro' narrow chinks of his cavern," as William Blake memorably penned.)

But I said no—concerned (as my energy work was new) with keeping my mind, in general, ready for whatever esoteric information I might receive. I was afraid to try anything so destabilizing. I didn't explain, though, that I didn't want to upset that psychic balance I was *so new at*. And didn't know if this would.

The phone rang. Hunter asked me, "Do you want to go out to dinner . . . ?"—with a good friend of his (whose name I've forgotten). What did I *want to do*?

Thinking he wanted to (though he gave no indication of a preference) or just by reflex, I said go out . . . perhaps thinking it better not to get into cooking yet.

I had told myself there was a highly energized field *outside* him, but I let the intuition come to a dead halt—despite knowing (that is, believing) I had brought my soul grouping with me, and who could say what they might be hatching? Not that they would *make* anything happen, but they could intensify energy. Even electrify it. The rest would be unpredictable. Which makes me remember the first time I met the Lama Sing channel, Al Miner, at his workshop in western North Carolina, ten months before I moved to Zurich.

Al barely knew me, had never seen me in person before. At the workshop he observed that two strangers appeared to be creating an energy field. To test it, he had them stand facing each other a few yards apart. We other attendees then walked through the "tunnel" they formed the ends of. One of the two field-holders had just (after hesitating for years) agreed to be a Christ consciousness channel.

But Al suddenly exclaimed to me, "The energy is trying to jump onto *your* head." This was 1983. Deep into processing the death of Milton Klonsky at the time, I felt sure that if the energy was responding to me, it could only be because of his invisible presence—forming the subtle other half of the field with the new Christ channel.

There were pangs of fear (like jelly) in my stomach when the female who appeared to be holding one end of the field speculated aloud, "There are *energy vampires*." Al started to protest, fearing the worse—about to correct her. But he heard in his head (encouraging him to keep silent): "*She needs it.*" Meaning me. I needed to toughen up and—he also heard—"lighten up."

Under the watchful eye of the impressive Al Miner, this public demonstration was my introduction to energy fields. Mysteriously, the two strangers who had just met in riding the train together to the workshop, then when they stood facing each other created a Christ-consciousness field as conductors.

But the test ferreted me out as an invisible—deeper—conductor, which Al Miner detected. Fortunately. Knowing not a soul there, I was on the spot—frightened but feeling an inner strength as the incident unfolded. Miner in firm control, the shock taught me a lot about energy, lessons the Zurich Initiation afterwards underscored.

Now, here I was in Colorado, putting my hands into, I would say, an equally strong field—just outside Hunter. Possibly stronger.

To a normal person, abominable intensity, as if all the firecrackers or guns that associated with him were subtly present. And as if shooting guns or riding motorcycles fast was just an outlet to exhaust this energy, which his first wife Sandy had said was the case.

Was it his style, his lifework even, to explode outside, to generate the energy that was too combustible to stand still? For everything was in motion, like particles in a cosmic stew, in the energy I felt around him.

Thinking back, I would say I was not pulling my own here. I obliviously anticipated no danger and thought: *Obviously, he can handle it.* Left my intuitions unconscious. Feeling secure. Not a care in the world. It was the kind of situation where you do not walk out into an eventless dinner and later pick up at home where you left off hours before.

Indeed. And we didn't.

Pulling the car up at a store, Hunter leapt out gleefully to buy champagne. What he had in mind, I was not to be privy to—what lines of destiny he had ready in his pocket to draw on some map, some unalterable memory, *though anyone could predict the lines.* Champagne aboard, the Red Shark halted at the restaurant parking lot. And now the unfolding of dire events.

About this moment, Hunter later told me, "I knew I was in trouble at the parking lot."

As we got out a male friend hurried to intercept him, whispering. The energy field shook.

Perhaps, like me, Hunter warned himself and didn't listen, didn't spell it out, didn't use his imagination to foresee the implications. Near-inevitabilities.

Electricity and electromagnetism popping, he loped through the door—with me totally confident, basking in the whole situation.

Once inside, the male friend who had alerted him led us to a table where a second couple sat. Maybe the woman was a raving beauty, but I didn't see it. Didn't feel the least threatened. Nothing of the sort crossed my mind. To my undiscerning eye, she seemed a casual diner. But in fact, they had a history, which is why the friend had just intercepted him, warning that she had popped in out of nowhere. There she was at the table he led us to, unannounced, after marrying and moving to Australia a few years before. Not that Hunter had known she'd be back that very night. Or any night. He didn't. I suppose the reason she didn't call or send him a letter in advance was that she didn't know how he'd react. He might not answer a letter or pick up the phone. He often reacted that way. Maybe he was pissed at their last meeting. I've no idea. I didn't give a thought to it anyway.

And so much for that.

Suddenly she began trying to lure him—softly so as not to be overheard—to "go out with [her]." He didn't know it, but I could hear every word, not dreaming she meant—NOW, this minute. I thought she meant some unspecified future time. He hesitated. Didn't say yes. As of yet, I didn't know about their history, didn't know she was briefly visiting in Woody Creek; had been a fraction of my twenty-one years away! Her hushed prodding continued. She whispered: "Are you married again?"

He later told me he thought no one else could hear.

To make a long story short, he yielded—and after she went into the back of the restaurant, he waited a brief interval and followed, supposedly innocently. My shock was palpable. By the time my brain started turning again, it seemed too late. Anyway, I had lost all capacity to move. To get up out of my seat and—what?—bang on a car window? I stayed glued in my chair while Hunter's horrified friends consoled me. Apologized for him. And explained briefly who she was.

I stayed seated, not moving. Not an inch. Watching the seconds tick, the minutes.

My brain could not comprehend.

The woman returned first, keeping up the charade, but was met with harsh words from her dining companion. Still scolding her, he hurried them out of the restaurant. Hunter met a similar reception from the remaining guy when he returned moments later; then he and I also rushed off. I was now explosive—my lost words came back tenfold. I told him I heard every word and that his friends were all apologizing to me. He looked at me with that trademark clarity, fully present, no deception. And answered something both awful and connective, something that broke through any would-be veil to whisk the actuality away: "I apologize for the rudeness. But not the passion."

Cruel. But you had to be there as he looked me in the eye. And the look wasn't cruel. It was as if talking to himself, but it was me. Normally I would have sunk into the ground. But there was a depth to our relationship that held me. And I also had just felt with my hands his huge energy field, the kind that makes impulse control near-impossible. Once in a workshop meditation, as described in *Keep This Quiet!* III, the "tall man" (my soul-group "clan leader") appeared to me in a vision and showed me a number of people in his energy field—how his energy almost inevitably darkened them. Not because it was dark but because it was overpowering. It did not have strict lines between "good" and "bad." It was dynamic. And you had to think in split seconds, *under energy surges.*

Anyway, it was a not-stop-to-think-about-it kind of situation for me.

In the back of my head I was aware this was a fluke, a perfect storm of coincidence. And now he was in a quandary. He had destroyed the champagne evening. Smashed it to the ground. There was no turning back. But what about us? The whole romance? Was that smashed too?

As I will never know exactly how he processed this later, I am especially grateful that one person, who knew nothing about this incident, was able—or felt compelled—to tell me years afterwards, as if "from the grave," that Hunter talked about me to him many many times, including right up to two days before he died. In fact, he said, "Hunter had a crush on you." That was his friend the presidential historian Doug Brinkley. This meant, from my point of view, that our relationship was unforgettable for him too, as I had felt certain. Doug Brinkley put it in terms of "a crush" and gratitude to me for shepherding him through the critical period of his first book's publication. Not that a lot of people knew it. But Hunter had made sure at least one did. What more he said, I've yet to find out, though if I live long enough I'll read about it one day in a book.

Also, there's this, which I agree with, from Hunter's son:

> My father believed in love. So it was inevitable and right that he would suffer over and over again, willingly, for love, with many, many different women. He was a passionate man and a naive romantic to the end. He believed in love, passion, and the erotic, and pursued these things with great determination his entire life, leaving a trail of passionate destruction through the lives of countless women. . . .
>
> He believed in freedom. He believed in the individual's right to live as he chooses, free from government interference. That meant the freedom to be weird, or to take the drugs of his choice, or to shoot, naked, a .44 magnum pistol from the front porch at 3 a.m., or to tell the truth about Nixon when he was a sitting president by calling him a liar, a hustler, and a tyrant in the national media.[20]

I quote this to indicate that when Hunter loved you, you felt it, which made it all the more bizarre to me to find him suddenly feeling passion for another woman in my presence. In fact, I still knew a part of him was very connected to me, at that moment. We had just run into another part, with other urges. I had had to put up with obstacles with Willy Vanluyten. The psychic Al Miner once told me that if we stayed together, I'd have to practice forgiving and forgetting—that Willy didn't mean to hurt but he was like a . . . well, it was a question of, did I want that sort of emotional growth?

Since I believe people are many things all at once, I was sure the part of Hunter that was deeply attached to me was still there. I'd just run into another part, who maybe thought the whole thing was too much bother to get back together, with the struggle it entailed, when here was a ripe and ready morsel, who knew his current self and wanted to jump back in, without a getting-to-reknow-you period. Maybe even easy come easy go. (Or not.)

Back to the moment at hand in 1991, the cruel, unexpected quandary. And the fact that I didn't collapse to the ground but was aware he was having difficulty processing the situation and knowing what to do. Hunter was being very much himself. Did he use people? Yes. Did they appear to come back for more? Yes. Did he have an attractiveness? Yes. I could have decided he was a heartless SOB. But that was far from my mind.

Right at that moment, *anything could change. Because he was so present.* I had come thousands of miles for this moment. All our relationship hung between us. He had admitted the worst. How serious was it?

Suddenly a giant wave of difficulty swept into what had looked like a night centered entirely on US. It was clear to me she had been able to divert the emotional buildup, the residue of the night before that Hunter had intended to cap off with the champagne evening. Hunter was later to admit, "I knew I was in trouble in the parking lot." Nevertheless, who was he to flinch? If only we'd been out on a boat off Key West. No matter. The impossible had happened. Was there any way to turn the tide?

I knew I was in trouble in the parking lot. He doggedly went into the restaurant anyway, maybe unable to do otherwise once the news broke. Let's replay that. What trickster out in the universe set this up?

Suppose in '73 I'd fallen out of the sky—after a four-year absence. But, as my Zurich Initiation had shown me, there were often contrived energy fields—apparent fields based on subtle ones. And I felt this might have been a field set up for him and me. But attracting another likely carrier, who might also have fit but perhaps, in the sum of things, not multiplied so exponentially. But then, who knows?

Still, however much this untoward interception might have belonged in his life—and it might well have been important—why *that night?*

Inside the twenty-one-year gap between now and the last time I saw Hunter (1969 and 1991) was the incident when in '71 he asked me to work on a book called *The Battle of Aspen* (which evolved into *On the Campaign Trail*). Even possibly (but not likely), he had wanted me to copy edit *Fear and Loathing in Las Vegas*. And I didn't leave my husband and fly in. The time wasn't right. But it *was right* now. I believe the window opened; the energy field encompassed all that; the champagne symbolized it. I think that's what he meant about "time."

But what the heck. At least part of him "wanted to" have that experience.

After all, wasn't he leaping at an opportunity that wouldn't come around again, in *two* unfinished relationships? A woeful plight that happened to box itself into the cubicle where he and I were fitted so nicely moments before, racing from two decades back with our feelings into 1991, out of breath.

Also, perhaps I'd underestimated the effect of my criticism about his drug use. He had not yelled at me, unlike with some young girls who worked for him, as they pointed out to me. But he did tell me that if he fought corporate institutions to live as he pleased, he wouldn't let anyone criticize his lifestyle. He'd made an exception for me.

Yes, yes, yes. He stepped into a mud hole; one incident splashed black onto the other.

Now we had a steep hill to climb, things to be X'd out.

He had followed that philosophy of doing what you "wanted to," without comparing it to something else you also "wanted to do."

Hunter's longtime first wife, Sandy (Sondi Wright), revealed, to *Rolling Stone*, that he told her once he watched that moment when his inner Monster took over. Anyway, that is now moot. It was a major setback. Not much time left. None, as it turned out.

Hunter took the whole LSD portion, not just his three-quarters. I smoked a few puffs of a joint. And just then a departing male friend, likewise falling out of the woodwork, dropped into Owl Farm around midnight—*to say good-bye to Hunter for five years*. He stayed till 4:00 a.m. Five years! I was fuming. What was that compared to the indefiniteness of when Hunter and I would see each other again? We had been confounded by the arrival of a woman who returned after being lost to him for *three* years, in contrast to our twenty-one.

And now here was a guy about to leave for five—*and return*—when we might never see each other again! We were dealing with large stretches of time, in the past and the question mark of now. I felt that hugeness, the ridiculous (to me) discrepancy. Those hours were a strain, seeming wasted. They were not the champagne evening at all. With the pot under those circumstances, I felt wilted, exhausted.

Hunter and I ended the night at a friend's indoor pool over raw oysters; the nearby pool, which he had late-night access to, was therapeutic for his back. I love oysters; with a can opener he expertly pried them open. Naturally, I used my wiles, but even as I swam naked he sat poolside—spirits dampened. Then he jumped in to watch one of his favorite erotic films with me, about a Caesar and his sister.

Now, at this point, I have to stretch the chronology, based on the fact that in telling it in *Keep This Quiet!* IV, the first edition, I didn't have the arrival ticket. But a careful examination of my garage boxes produced it—dated May 13! That means I was there a whole week. What happened the fifteenth through the eighteenth, I have no clear image of, chronologically speaking. Marvelous highlights float through my mind (including my embarrassing, humorous failure to punch "send," so that Hunter was having me fax out his prose to a publisher, but unknownst to us, it remained stuck in the room. Until Deborah Fuller returned, eyed the situation, and broke the bad news. Hunter had been startled, fuming, thinking his prose was being ignored, when, a novice with faxes, I never sent it out!).

Alas, much has disappeared from memory, though I do still vividly retain highlights.

Yet, what makes the fluke evening make particular sense—and be ironic—is that at the Gonzo Fest in Louisville 2014, I remet Deborah Fuller. (I was sitting at the Brown Hotel with Hunter's son, Juan Thompson; we'd just been introduced and were sharing an incredible private meal. And who should walk over but Deborah, with the utterly charming, still-youthful Laila Nabulsi, producer of *Fear and Loathing in Las Vegas* (1998) and a past fiancée of Hunter's. I had always thought the young intruding, long-lost woman of 1991 must be a major love of Hunter's; during the 2014 Gonzo Fest, I quizzed Deborah, did she know? She didn't. I asked then, was it someone like Maria Kahn, his former fiancée? As "Hunter Thompson's Lady Friends" (on *The Great Thompson Hunt* website) put it:

> **Maria Kahn**—daughter of Frank Kahn, described in E. Jean Carroll's biography as a "red neck golf champion." She appeared in *The Crazy Never Die*, the half hour film about HST made by the Mitchell Brothers. She is petite, dark haired and was wearing glasses. I would peg the relationship at 1985–1989. [The time fits.] She seemed like the quiet type. Prominently featured in *Generation of Swine*. In the column "Saturday Night in the City" she allegedly gets a tattoo on her back of a giant striking panther.

The *Phoenix New Times* adds details of how they met:

> In one version, she was a reporter for ASU's *State Press* sent to cover a speech by Thompson, afterwards disappearing with him for weeks. In another version, Baier [Maria] met Thompson while she was a cub and he was a columnist for the *San Francisco Examiner*, and they began a brief but reportedly torrid affair. All versions of the story end with Baier, who reportedly came from a super-conservative background, getting a giant tattoo of a panther on her back before being dumped by Thompson.
>
> Is it true? Well, Baier, the daughter of golf pro Frank Kahn and brother of fire chief Bob Kahn, does appear as a talking head in *The Crazy Never Die*, a 1988 documentary about Thompson. She features prominently in his story collection *Generation of Swine: Tales of Shame and Degradation in the '80s*, published the same year, which the author dedicated to her and which includes his essay "Saturday Night in the City," a story that commences with the line, "I dropped Maria off in front of the tattoo parlor just before midnight."

I was surprised that Deborah responded, unhesitatingly, "Maybe Maria." She repeated it. So I felt fairly sure. To have this former torrid flame advance on him unexpectedly—not many years after they'd considered marrying, yet at the very time he was finally focused on me, over twenty years after we'd last met—threw him off balance, to say the least.

"Maybe Maria." If so, what a fluke. A major love who'd—been forced to leave, some say. He didn't expect her to be anywhere in a thousand-mile radius. In Woody Creek not for long, but time enough to collapse this enigma of possibility he and I had moved heaven and Earth to set out into. The interception wasn't Greek tragedy, but the odds of its happening were perhaps equal to the strength of the energy field I'd felt around him. Been oblivious to. Not ever imagining what scenarios might ride roughshod into our blissful evening.

Hunter told me a white lie soon afterwards: his mother was quite ill, he had to leave for Louisville (not true). A lame excuse. What was he to say? *I give up. I ruined it. I prefer her?????* Better just invent a sick mother. Easy to see through, but I didn't at the time. I even offered to go with him to Louisville.

The very last night he drove off alone and stayed out late. Both Deborah and I worried. I remarked, however, that he never got really drunk. She corrected me: it was not unheard of. Returning, he watched TV into the dawn hours—the bawdy, hilarious, oddly synchronistic Mae West/Cary Grant classic, *She Done Him Wrong.* He was introspective, obtuse, not looking for a farewell. I sat there with him, through the scene where Lady Lou (Mae West) meets Captain Cummings and says—invitingly—"Why don't you come up sometime 'n see me?"

No, he's busy, the captain objects. She's insulted. Asks again. He hems and haws; she says, "Aww, you can be had."

As Hunter watched this I felt it had almost stepped offscreen into the restaurant. The movie plot seemed a mind-blowing synchronicity, underscoring, as Mae West enticed the captain, he'd not taken the initiative. But who could resist Mae West? Not even me. I gave up trying to hold out—it was late—and went to bed.

Up early the next day in his favorite chair, he took down *Songs of the Doomed*. I had no autographed copy of any book by him for myself (just one for my mother). Now he did the job up proudly.

With a felt pen in large silver letters spanning both sides of the inside hardcover first edition, he wrote, "Here's another one—& it's all yr. fault. But thanx anyway, Love, H, Hunter"; he said pointedly that the evening was *not what I planned; I bought champagne*. Also, "I know where I made my mistake." No further explanation. I didn't ask. I was just glad we were parting *not* in closure (too much up in the air) but on a close note; that he was staring into my eyes, summing up his disappointment but also his admission—analysis—that something had been misplayed. Would there be another act?

I left, wishing it could have been longer.

Left, and knew we had halfway succeeded (initially) but not enough—because, from my point of view, I didn't say: *Yes, let's stay home*. Or let "the naked child" have the floor. Or . . .

I remember him in that chair (one room over from where he committed suicide fourteen years later by firing a .45-caliber semi-automatic pistol into his mouth but incredibly leaving his face undamaged)—signing in that translucent silver lettering. Surely, this was not the end. Surely, though, that honeymoon arrival, without anything but the unknown to climb up over, was past. Who ever knew Hunter to mind a challenge? As he said, it never got too weird for him. And about myself? That was May 20, 1991. To be continued.

I waited for a connection in the Denver Airport. Sipping a drink at the counter in the bar, I wondered how Hunter was feeling. In the years since, I recalled he emphasized, "It wasn't what I planned." I never thought it was. What kind of suspicious mind would? I took him at his word. So, he invented an ill mother. (For sure.)

What if he wanted a breathing spell to sort it out? What if it was a case of *"You have to understand about time"*?

Time had put two relationships into the same cubbyhole. He separated them. Two girlfriends required different approaches but his physical presence. Even Hunter couldn't comply. Where his attention and heart were (in time) was for him to know. I left, with no idea what came next, no official breakup, no clear status as Deborah drove me in the Red Shark to the airport—him contemplating in that chair in the living room near where fourteen years from hence, by then ill with surgeries, a broken leg, a lung infection, he would shoot himself in the mouth. Surgically albeit. So that he looked peaceful, with virtually no blood.

3

San Francisco

The plane landed in San Francisco. Jyoti, a spiritual advisor (whom I'd known at the C. G. Jung Institute Zurich as Jeneane Prevatt) and her board-certified transpersonal-psychologist fiancé, Russell D. Park, picked me up. Jyoti was making a name for herself. As a director of Christina and Stan Grof's Spiritual Emergence Network, Jyoti (along with Russ) would sensitize mental health professionals to psycho-spiritual issues. As they explained on the Center for Spiritual Studies website, SEN was successful in "differentiating spiritual emergence(y) from pathological disorders—a distinction first put forth by the Grofs."[21] Further, "Often Kundalini evidences itself through visions, memories of past lives, bodily and perceptual changes, and other expressions that can mimic psychological illness."[22]

This becomes important in telling my story because though I never for a moment thought of my experiences as pathological, to a mainstream scientific community, as specified in the *Diagnostic and Statistical Manual of Mental Disorders* (DSM) until 1994, most aspects of "spiritual awakening" were classified as illnesses. Christina Grof knew firsthand the difference—as a Hatha Yoga teacher who had a spontaneous kundalini awakening. She was helpful to Jyoti and by extension me, which may be a major reason I took many of my experiences in stride. Jyoti would earn a doctorate in transpersonal psychology and later become Spiritual Director of the Kayumari community and the Center for Sacred Studies and one of the convenors of the International Council of the Thirteen Indigenous Grandmothers.

Jyoti and Russ lived very close to La Honda in the Santa Cruz Mountains. When I arrived, Richard Unger—founding director of the International Institute of Hand Analysis—was at their home for dinner. He had read at least twenty thousand pairs of hands. (Over fifty thousand by 2013.)

Part Cherokee, Jyoti has deepened her life and her work through the teachings of First Nation elders from all over the world. It is this way of life and the knowledge from Nature it holds that she feels is the medicine of our times. Richard's website quotes the Navajo saying: "*The Great Spirit breathes in the breath of life, and the tracks of that breath become our fingerprints.*"

Richard taught hand analysis at Binghamton University (SUNY), then at the Esoteric Philosophy Center in Houston. In the foreword to Richard's book, *LifePrints*, Frank R. Wilson, MD, former clinical professor of neurology at Stanford University School of Medicine, wrote: "Richard's use of fingerprints to unmask the healthy dynamism of inner conflict seems absolutely unique to me, and I think it is not an overstatement to suggest that he may have developed one of the most accessible and fruitful constructs in the history of human psychology. Although I am utterly at a loss to explain how fingerprint patterns could possibly provide such a compass, I am satisfied that the interpretive system he describes in this book is not only psychologically wise but profoundly constructive."[23]

Annually, Richard gave workshops in Zurich set up by Jyoti and Russell. When she told him I had an interesting hand, he offered me a mini-reading. Here is what my hand told him. To explain, he drew a diagram outlining my karmic pattern:

LIFE SCHOOL—Karmic Habit: *Deniched*. [Being run out of town.]

LESSON—Least-evolved skill and greatest resistance.

Below that, a ▼depicted the dynamics of this karma. At each tip of the angle he wrote a phrase: "Finding Your Niche" (*left angle*), "Being Understood" (*right*); "Doubts Yourself/Guilt" (*bottom*). The angles summarized the challenge.

My LIFE PURPOSE was "To Do: Big Shot—Donald Trump." The result, if successful: "Leadership," "Impact world," "Gets results, worldly."

How? Through mastering a predicament he outlined in shorthand: "Heartbreak fuels transformation cycle. A broken heart: Key to others' understanding" / The successful outcome: "Worldly influential."

Well, I would say he was batting a thousand. Twenty-five years back, the name "Trump" had no political connotations. He might have said "Bill Gates," to use a more neutral fame-and-fortune symbol today. For me to reach success, *"broken heart fuels transformation"* was the least-costly method; I'd better learn this lesson fast! He sketched the storyline:

Nobody wants me, I don't belong, nobody understands me→Panic/ Frozen→Take Action Anyway→Big Shot/I'm Home/They want you to stay

It was like in a treasure hunt, with a pot of gold at the end. Coming to California from a deniche-ing, I wondered if, at Owl Farm, as implied in this chart, I'd not *made myself understood clearly* ENOUGH. And the kundalini in the throat was trying to pressure me to break through.

My karmic habit was, Richard wrote, "to be run out of town"— check. My life purpose: to overcome that pitfall. The key: successfully communicate at the point of *nothing-to-lose*. End: be understood.

The throat chakra had indeed been on my side if I had let it speak. No matter how crazy. How exposing.

Actually, many artists had to create their audience or were understood after death (Bizet with *Carmen*, Emily Brontë). Early on, I assumed that was the artist's practically inevitable fate. Now, Richard indicated, I had my win-the-lottery lifetime—a chance to reverse the be-understood-after-death pattern.

Be understood *today, alive, here, now*. It was up to me. Or else expect heartbreak and more. However, as readers of *KTQ! Initiations* know, part of me (greatly introverted) insisted on hiding my secrets;

another part (the "naked child") gleefully (or spunkily) revealed them. It turned out this was a key to my effectiveness. But to let the "naked child"—my "least-skilled" facet—speak was an inclination I'd resisted, with greatest distaste.

For good reason. When I was a child, this part of me equated with gullibility; other children took advantage. I was teased. Also, this part of me felt wide-eyed wonder and didn't believe anything was necessarily impossible: *you can do it!* I knew that when my untutored extraverted self was at the helm, I was awkward, I could get into trouble, not hold back, not be discreet. Yet she needed a voice. Without her, Richard was warning, I was doomed. The secretive me was. I had to heed this message. Under the circumstances, was ripe to.

If I look back to the years covered in the first two volumes—up to 1986, when a new nineteen-year cycle began—I would say that the three men I had the fortune to cast as stars (Hunter Thompson, Milton Klonsky, Jan Mensaert) all had a role in teaching me *to speak.* (For those who haven't read the earlier volumes, by "nineteen-year cycle," I am referring to the sense, based on a computerized numerology, that every nineteen years I got a new task, provided I learned the task of the block of years just prior. In a sense, each assignment coincides with a new *Keep This Quiet!* volume. And the last two volumes were increasingly esoteric.)

The great distance between the beginning of my thumb and the first knuckle indicated, Richard said, that for me it was necessary to deal with a lot of information even *before* getting to the point to speak. What I had to say (even how I saw) wouldn't make sense except in a large context. Otherwise, *who I was, what I really meant,* would not be suspected: what I had to communicate went inside the context *only I could supply.*

In the case of Hunter, as said before, I don't believe I'd mentioned Willy's death. I thought Hunter was probably in my soul grouping;

naturally, that was nothing more than a suspicion. And I hadn't brought it up, natch again. But I'd counted on that unconscious base. That of course was the way *I* saw it. *It might not be correct. Also, it was the way I saw it then, before later transformations made things more nebulous.*

In Jungian personality typing, this least-developed skill—partly unconscious—we call the "inferior function," which in *individuation*—the process of becoming a "whole," authentic individual—evolves and is transformative; then it brings unconscious information into consciousness.

In my case, I was so intuitive I might take it for granted that a + b = c, when a lot of others were still establishing what *a* was. Or *if* "a" was. I could be making elliptical, intuitive assumptions where others wanted proof, needed connected dots or added detail. And if I didn't supply that, it would just be missing.

Or I could *not* express a feeling I thought obvious or risky. I could think speaking spoiled the moment. Basically, an intuitive often gets information from the nonrational/nonverbal right-brain hemisphere: "rapid, complex, whole-pattern, spatial, . . . specialized for visual imagery and musical ability."[24]

With this internalizing/externalizing pair in my core, it also seemed Richard was honing in on my mystery phrase—"bipod metalism"—from the last volume. In brief, it was a topic for investigation suggested to me by a Jung assistant in his "museum" in a dream.

To recap, a part of me, the *externalizer,* was key. Yet though I was primarily an introvert, I'd seen my animus (inner male) in a dream that said *his* problem was he *didn't internalize.* He wanted to plop down into locations like a rock star.

The *least evolved* was the path to my potential. I couldn't reach it without this shadow and animus.

I had to close my eyes and let my instinct's voice through. Sometimes blurting things out was intricate to my depth. Not withstanding that it meant, I was sure, some fumbling and bumbling.

But I took from the hand-reading sample this very right-on advice.

My life plan was contrived so as that I would *not* be understood—but would, indeed, be *run out of town*—until I developed the skill of telling my truth, no matter how odd, how original, in such a way that it was received with open arms instead of stones and pickaxes and cries of blasphemy. *Of course, this was an archetype. It certainly had trailed after "the feminine."* But was this not the lot of everyone with something original, individual, to create—and was it not exactly the karma Hunter ignored, threw in little slivers onto the wind? This was the artist's karma. But it was also that of Jesus, of Mary Magdalene, and so forth.

I would need to go into my greatest weakness, with my least-developed skill. Go into my defeat and turn the tables. Overcome this improbability of being understood *by* opening so wide, surrendering so profoundly, so totally—with nothing held back—that only welcome could follow. For everyone recognizes what's authentic.

Well and so much for that. I could have benefited from hearing it a week earlier. I spent ten days or so with Jyoti and Russell.

June 1. I drafted a letter to Hunter. What is a draft? Why make them? I'm asked. To answer, let's recall that if you set out to write to someone, the supposedly final product might not read the way you liked. In that case, I would correct the draft and reprint. However, I am not and have never been a "filer." And differently from other years, in the 1990s I often saved various versions. I now look at the letters and do not know which I discarded, to try again. A point of note: in that decade, when I was living alone and there was so much in flux, writing to a few people was a way to sort out my thoughts. People I could trust. Hunter, on the other hand, was a filer. And for the most part, slipped a sooty black sheet of carbon underneath his ready-to-mail letter, with a white sheet of paper underneath that, and thus had a record of what he actually mailed.

I had obviously learned by telephone that he was busy writing his Fourth Amendment story, "which I really look forward to in *Rolling Stone.*" The June 1 letter mentioned that I'd arranged an

October-through-December sublet of Jyoti's office. Then an ironic anecdote: I described how, just arrived in California, I found myself in the room of a couple who'd been on "a guided acid trip—a 'medicine journey'"—the night before. However implausible it sounded, "I re-created part of the trip [i.e., clairvoyantly unwittingly described it to that couple] without the acid." I guessed it had to do with "all the energy-work." But it was baffling. In warm blue handwritten pages I continued to explain what I hadn't been able to in person, about where I "was" at this point. A few lyrical expressions came in, as the thoughts moved spontaneously into inner dialogue—about

the Other Half of the
American Dream story
the Symphonic Version
For it was never seen, in the known story.

[Hunter] was

one of the Motifs, the Melodies,
already Light in another dimension,
that offered to go into the shadow
to bring to the Earth out of the shadow version
its overturned shadow
behind that its
original Light

In particular, this is a soul grouping
It's my soul grouping
[and you are one]
I think this is a message as important as
our working together the first time, on *Hell's Angels*
See the connection
Hell's Angels

I added that most of my soul grouping fitted into a phrase I once woke with: "He came for a purpose—the mission of divine sin." Also, "Please send my Master Card and cassette. I have enclosed $400 to repay the Aspen–San Francisco ticket, which I charged to your card."

There was another draft—a short note—mentioning photos "of you writing the Fourth Amendment piece I now know you're finishing, which is wonderful news." Well, evidently he never finished it, but also evidently we had a phone conversation that updated me on his progress. I strongly suspect I never mailed the June 1 letter in the long form, with the poetry, but that in writing it, I discovered the Hell's Angels / *Hell's Angels* pun. Anyway, the check went missing.

Meanwhile, on small tan notepaper, my sister Norma reminds me: "*It doesn't sound as if you plan to be working* [in Colorado] since you're planning to stay in the apartment (?) of your friend in California beginning in September . . . That's probably for the best." Ah ha. Detecting the obvious, I conclude I confided to her it was not impossible, depending on what happened during my visit, that I'd get a job in Woody Creek. I don't know whose idea it was. But since my memory no longer holds this information, I am glad that my garage guarded it in a little note.

So, yes, I went to Owl Farm not ruling out staying there awhile. (Or forever?) Knowing, however, that it was a very very long shot. The two young writers who wanted to set the world on fire and give up everything for art (at least, that was my intention) had done so in different life styles, so different that only the deepest connection, which was there, had made both of us hold on to the past as possible to pull out of an old trunk and through it step into the present.

Just when I think I have the chronology figured out—the new chronology—something turns up in the garage. Going through stacks of papers, suddenly I find a letter to Hunter. That says what? Well, that—almost en route to the sublet—I'm sending "the $400 check."

Despite a search at Owl Farm, it was not to be found. (Apparently, I'd never mailed it; the refund was my idea, by the way; Hunter never asked for it.) "How is *Polo*?" (*Polo Is My Life*.) Then an odd tidbit: "Thanks for letting me confide in you some weeks ago [presumably by phone], when I was really thrown a bit by the 'trip.'"

Then I turned to a phenomenon regularly recurring in my apartment after Willy's death that I'll go into more soon. I called it computer PK. ("PK" stands for psychokinesis: mind influencing matter, as in spoon bending.) It involved textual alterations in my printouts; that is, a portion of what was on-screen printed out altered. The phenomenon had begun in January, but even with Hunter's first computer newly arrived while I was at Owl Farm, I had not ventured (or dared?) to illustrate it on his ranch. Imagine how that might have worked, what door it might have opened, to have his energy intentionally mixing with the spirit energy affecting the computer. Ah well. In any case, I was not bashful about referring to it by letter: "You know, what a solution—to have a computer for an editor. Hold it, there's a bell signal. I think my computer wants to write something to you, or else it's to me. Love, Margaret."

As for the trip, I wracked my brain. Was it simply the virtual experience of "walking into" the lingering relics of the couple's LSD experience, the irony being that I'd just refused LSD with him? Cosmic humor.

From the standpoint of now, it seems unlikely I could have been too unsettled by that, but then, I can't think of anything else. Maybe it was the weight of the synchronicity plus the fact that I'd had visions before, but not clairvoyantly; that is, of someone else's experience. On the other hand, maybe I just wanted to get his attention— see what he thought, as I liked to about many things.

If only, I wrote in a second, short draft that may be the one I mailed, I had a fax machine, "what messages I'd send" to him. I elaborated on the "terribly witty" PK of my "spirit-directed computer," how this made me feel "the nitty-gritty of living in the world as a Nonresident Outsider, . . . the Outsider to beat all outsiders."

Meanwhile in July 1991, President George H. W. Bush had nominated the strict-constructionist Clarence Thomas to the Supreme Court to replace Thurgood Marshall. Thomas, a judge for only fifteen months, had never argued before the Court. A leak of an FBI interview with attorney Anita Hill revealed she accused him of sexual harassment in the 1980s. Thus began a *cause célèbre*. Under nationwide TV coverage she testified at his Senate hearing October 11, 1991. Thomas termed it a high-tech lynching but was confirmed anyway.

From this drama "Fear and Loathing in Elko" (January 23, 1992) emerged in *Rolling Stone*. Hunter's alter ego Duke describes coming upon Thomas—roadside at night, Thomas's car broken down, two prostitutes in tow. This I will return to. Busy writing the story, Hunter was back at his ranch.

Hunter at work on the Fourth Amendment story

Postmarked August 30, a thick tan envelope—with a block-printed return address: "H.S.T., Box 220, Woody Creek 81656"—shot over to my Lunevillelaan apartment in Tienen.

Two photos inside. In one, a perfectly round, dazzling sun set. High up in the left corner sat a flying object that at first glance one would say, if one said such things, looks like a silver UFO; balancing it top right is a shooting star.

The other photo is primarily of indistinct dark foliage and trees, surrounding a small pink V, and sitting in that, a pale full moon. Had there ever been a letter inside, there no longer was.

Block-printed digits, perched oddly on the envelope, were two off from the number of my sister he'd telephoned while I visited her home in May.

Sometime, somewhere, in a dream I heard, "When one sun sets, it's the signal for the other sun to rise." Was that related to the sun that set, flanked by a shooting star and UFO-looking object, and the pink full moon that was then to begin to climb? Like many forecasts, if so, it was for way into the future.

Cellular Knowledge

Could another Large Figure be lurking offstage? Indeed. A giant—larger than life, to say the least. I stayed at Jyoti's and Russell's (October, November, and December).

While Jyoti was in western India, in the state of Gujarat at Dhyanyogi Madhusudandas-ji's small ashram near Ahmedabad, I sublet her home office—writing, basking in its spacious Santa Cruz Mountains view through the picture window, enjoying the outdoor hot tub. Sometimes awkwardly maneuvering Russell's red stick-shift car into Palo Alto. (Coincidentally, Hunter had sometimes dropped in at Ken Kesey's Merry Pranksters log cabin in nearby La Honda in the '60s.)

Hanging on the office wall was a calendar with photos of Shri Dhyanyogi Madhusudandas. Dhyanyogi-ji (born in 1878 in Bihar, the state where Gautama Buddha is believed to have become enlightened under the Bodhi tree) was a then-113-year-old Kundalini Maha Yoga master—"Guruji" ("Teacher") to his disciples. His photo stared at me. The experience I am going to describe involves kundalini. It takes over the body. Imagine trying to object to kundalini when it has control. It is stronger than you. It is releasing cellular content that affects your emotions. It has the upper hand. The authority. It is to be dealt with.

In the East it is called shakti, the Divine Mother, the divine energy of action that balances the divine masculine *pure awareness* (or being) of Shiva, which is beyond action. Initially coiled downward near the base of the spine in each person, the kundalini, when awakened, begins climbing up the spine—opening chakras, trying to unite with Shiva in unity consciousness at the crown of the head.

In *An Angel Called My Name* (1998), Jyoti describes this process, which underlay her transformations. I'd read the Zurich draft and had a bound printout of the 1991 version. She quoted Gopi Krishna, *Kundalini: The Evolutionary Energy in Man*, who tells us that the transcendental consciousness that emerges in all successful kundalini awakening "provides incontrovertible evidence for the fact that the regenerative force at work in the body is at the very beginning aware of the ultimate pattern to which it has to conform by means of the remodeling biological processes set afoot."

He counsels not to approach the inquiry into kundalini "in a spirit of conquest or arrogance with the intent to achieve victory over a force of nature . . . but rather with humility, in a spirit of utter surrender to Divine Will and absolute dependence on Divine Mercy, in the same frame of mind one would approach the flaming sun."[25]

Lending scientific support in laboratory experimentation, German biophysicist Fritz-Albert Popp, in 1974, provided proof of a theory: that emanating from living things—including us—there are tiny, biophoton emissions in invisible currents of light.[26] In other words, though we can't see it with the naked eye, there is a "pulsating glow" given off by "cells and whole organisms." A glow with an intensity comparable to a lit candle fifteen miles away. This radiation field is coherent and not to be confused with "the 'bioluminescence' of fireflies, glow-worms, deep sea fishes, and rotting wood."[27]

To coordinate research, in 1992 Popp founded the International Institute of Biophysics: a 14-country network of laboratories. Supporters include highly acclaimed scientists like Nobel Laureate Ilya Prigogine.[28] According to the findings, these photons are bio-informational and exchange communication as a "quantum biological phenomenon." Popp relates these biophotonic emissions to the fact that "DNA in a living cell stores and releases photons."[29]

He affirms, "We know today that man, essentially, is a being of light. And the modern science of photobiology is proving this. We now know, for example, that quanta of light can initiate, or arrest, cascade-like reactions in the cells, and that genetic cellular damage can be virtually repaired, within hours, by faint beams of light." [30] Lynne McTaggart adds, "To this day, conventional scientists don't understand this phenomenon, but nobody has disputed it."[31]

Envisaging years of research, Popp says decisively "that the function of our entire metabolism is dependent on light."[32]

The Rhine Research Center (in Durham, North Carolina) is advancing the findings of Popp and other biologists that indicate "that living organisms generate ultraviolet light which seems to be used to transfer information between cells and between organisms."[33]

A leader in studying "the intentional transfer of bio-photonic energy," the Rhine Bio-Energy Lab has logged years of experiments with healers, deep meditators, and martial artists. Through these tests and measurements, they've provided "established physical evidence that this energy or chi exists in the form of bio-photons"—which has led scientists to recognize it as "a previously unidentified source of energy and information in human beings, animals, plants, and other living organisms."[34]

A recent article on the Rhine reports that in a sedentary individual the baseline for biophotons is 12 to 20 per second. But Executive Director John Kruth notes that in experiments, "I've had people go to 200,000, 400,000. I even had two people go over a million." Observing that the highest scores are from energetic healers and kundalini yogis, he adds. "You don't need statistics to figure out that something strange is going on in here."[35]

Kurt Keutzer, at the University of California Berkeley, speaks of the various descriptions of kundalini and prana, distinguishing two experiences that are often conflated. "In one an individual experiences some pleasant energizing electric energy running along the spine." However, he continues, "Nearly ever person I know with what I call a 'true awakening' has responded to phrases like 'the freight train' inside or 'the volcano erupting' inside."[36]

He contrasts "pleasant energizing electric energy" with the advanced stage, where kundalini enters the sushumna (the center nadi, or canal, that extends from the root chakra to the crown of the head) and rises up the spine, an experience that "will completely overwhelm ordinary waking consciousness. . . . There will no longer be a distinction between the subjective consciousness which experiences and the object of experience."[37]

An Angel Called My Name begins with a myth from the preface to Swami Muktananda's *Kundalini: The Secret of Life*. In it, God clarifies.

The point is made that the key to ourselves has been intentionally hidden inside. This secret key is that we come from a common source and can find our way back to it: "From his own experience [Muktananda] says that what is outside is also inside. The whole universe, all knowledge, the answers to the mysteries of human existence and true happiness all lie inside man and become available to him by the awakening of Kundalini, the divine Mother."[38]

In one chapter Jyoti describes how kundalini came into her heart. Crippled with pain, she was sped to the hospital, suspected of having a heart attack, then diagnosed with pneumonia and a tumor on the lungs. Re-evaluated at a second hospital, she was thought possibly to have a blood clot on her lungs. Tests were planned. A nurse prepared to take blood.

"Just at that moment," she narrates, "a gentle energy entered my feet and extended up my body. It seemed to electrify the air around me." Feeling uncomfortably warm, the nurse left. Then, Jyoti said, a voice inside began to repeat, "over and over, as if in a chant, 'And now you dance the second part of your dream awake!' I had no idea what this meant." But she knew the baffling words were significant.

Jyoti concluded: "I've since discovered that when Kundalini enters the heart, it is often misdiagnosed as a heart attack, due to their similar symptoms."[39]

Dhyanyogi-ji's biography, *This House Is on Fire*, describes how after thirty years of wandering he was so ripe for his kundalini awakening that at the first touch of his satguru, Parmeshwardasji, "he immediately entered samadhi. He lost bodily consciousness and found himself submerged in a sea of bliss and ecstasy, surrounded by 'a wonderful and inexplicable light.'"

Then the kundalini "began to transform Madhusudandas's physical body," creating extreme heat; his temperature was up to 104 and 105 degrees. After three months he "began hearing loud, internal sounds that resembled gunshots . . . his heart raced, and at times he feared he would die of heart failure. Parmeshwardasji . . . explained that these sounds were produced by the prana cleansing the chakras as it moves through the sushumna" (the central nadi, or channel, for subtle energy, which runs up the spinal cord), awakening chakras.[40]

It was October or November. In the Bay Area office I was reading a book I by chance picked up from Jyoti's lavishly filled bookcase, which held complex tomes, such as *Beyond the Brain: Birth, Death, and Transcendence in Psychotherapy* by Stan Grof, MD, a pioneer in transpersonal psychology and her friend. But what I picked up this day was a collection of imaginative Bible narratives by Kahil Gibran: *Jesus, Son of Man*.

Flipping to stories that interested me, I got to Mary Magdalene. Suddenly I felt an eruption of kriyas. Shaking involuntarily, I heard—not physically but inside—"Her water broke." The cells now brought this buried information to the surface.

What to do? That is, for the part of me "conscious" up to this stage. I mention the incident, as it pertains to life purpose but a level of it so extreme or profound (to me then) that one would dismiss it, though unable to disregard it. *But dismiss it.* Except that it swept through the body, not the brain.

That is, kundalini literally "shook" the information loose, shook it out of the cells, the body trembling as was kundalini's effect on me, because it, on me, did not go straight up the spine but had taken the form of jiggling kriya energy, say, in a leg—just like the Brownian effect in physics, where water molecules bump against one another, making the temperature rise; an effect used by Einstein to prove the physical existence of atoms; on another level here, it "proves" to the recipient that kundalini's presence is "real." *

Under such attack how argue? As St. Paul was awakened by a Light that blinded him and heard a voice, so kundalini can burst in, in the same manner, operating not as visible light directly but using its setting, electromagnetism.

For kundalini must surely flow in that. And therefore, is carried by light, going from cell to cell and releasing the memory content, knocking on each jail door to say: *See the key in the lock.* Remember that energy operates globally; what happens locally draws from the global history. It does not organize time the same way we do. It strikes a target, the way lightning does. There has to be a reason, an attraction, as to why it choose "this" target at that time.

But the body makes nothing of this. Nor the emotions. They are caught up in a whirlwind. They totally focus on the body itself. What I responded to in Gibran was a description:

> His mouth was like the heart of a pomegranate, and the shadows in His eyes were deep . . .
>
> And I remember Him pacing the evening. He was not walking. He Himself was a road above the road; even as a cloud above the earth that would descend to refresh the earth.
>
> But when I stood before Him and spoke to him, He was a man, and His face was powerful to behold. *And He said to me, "What would you, Miriam?"* (emphasis added)

"A road above a road"—that got me. She didn't answer. Gibran wrote her thoughts: "My wings enfolded my secret, and I was made warm. And because I could bear His light no more, I turned and walked away, but not in shame. I was only shy, and I would be alone, with His fingers upon the strings of my heart."

---

*   I can imagine that much resistance came from my conscious mind. But the kundalini overpowered it, not stopping at the mental block but opening it up. Because it had somewhere to go—once through this wall that would turn it back, thus turn my whole life back, off course.

About at the point of "What would you, Miriam?" the "water broke." The fact is that I "woke" to find myself in an upper room, deciding what lifetime I wanted. "Her water broke," I heard as if eavesdropping. I was in the type of kundalini kriyas familiar to me, which I knew meant some block was breaking up, recessed "information" entering a multidimensional frame where "I" was there as well but not in a personal, ego form.

In the vision I saw/felt myself in an upstairs room with a few people, before I was born. (They sat around a rectangular table.) My choice of a lifetime was imminent. That is, I had a choice. In the shaking, the electrical information that I could not avoid, the answer came to me. I knew it without hesitation.

As the kundalini shakes the cells, all blocks, resistance itself—making it crumble even, as the walls of Jericho—I hear myself say, "St. Paul." OK, the answer comes back. But in that case with a proviso: "You must also take Mary Magdalene."

That is, *I can have the lifetime of St. Paul. But only if I take as well Mary Magdalene.* The kundalini continues shaking, to integrate this message sparked by there being only silence—no answer—when he said, "What would you, Miriam?"

I could not refuse to go where my cells went, where cellular knowledge went, or if I did, I would be in a war with my own body, fighting it as in a refused heart. Imagine fighting the transplantation of a higher dimension of one's own heart inside. No, life was an adventure. I held on. I listened. I received. I *became.*

That meant I added on this new experience, observed till I could merge with it.

Here was the level where my life purpose was being set. No wonder I had the karma of being de-niched, run out of town. And there from the top, the permission came down—whatever that meant in human terms. It meant something secret, cellular, a resonance, a guarantee. It backed up certain forms of reaction, ascertaining that they were the highest probabilities henceforth. So this secret alliance entered my trajectory as well.

What could one become after being in such a chamber, having the cells, if not oneself, know?

Mariah Martin, a channel I liked to consult for verifications, told me that she did not think anyone working in light energy in the twentieth century could avoid holding some of the Mother Mary and Magdalene energy; it was a very collective situation as well.

A coincidence had sparked the kundalini downpouring. They were my own cells, and even when replaced, they would *will the memories to the cells that came after*. Milton had exclaimed during a dispute between us, as he solved the otherwise impasse, *"What do you think is stronger? Spirit or matter?"* Let us bring that statement in, which, by the almost ferociousness of his assertion, assures the answer.

So I had the "assignment"—a male-female pairing—of taking on the Magdalene energy, backed by that of St. Paul (two archetypes, two historical figures.)

As if she were planning some such arrival among her many arrivals. Coming personally—speaking directly to the cells first and foremost, then afterwards undeniably conscious. But not, to appearances, logically fitting into the links of these chains or feathers, if one were to put it all together—as I am doing now.

For the master keyboard composer Bach, which of the many themes was this? And what other themes were in the piano composition, now finally remembered, that I, the nervous child of seven, forgot the end of at my first recital? I had sat on the piano stool, halfway through, with a blank mind—the rehearsed notes fled—valiantly going over the beginning/middle one more time and yet once again, till, with a burst of inspiration, I recollected the whole piece and played it, start to finish. But I say that precursively, prematurely. I do not exactly remember.

BUT MY FINGERS DO.

5

Fire Side

I don't know how early on it was that—based on this kundalini event—I sensed how the St. Paul consciousness and the Magdalene combined. Later, if not in the stupefaction of that moment, I could easily see it: *two conversions*—treated so differently in history.

History described him after his conversion and her mostly before. Suppose the task was that he would stand behind her. The male strength protecting the female—she his gateway.

I recalled how in Zurich the Initiator brightened the light in my room and released his consciousness. I followed it many times to go into that state of awareness, a human location he called "The Christ State." Once it was *feel*-able over Zurich. It descended into whoever aligned with it. That day he had, *as a state of mind*, moved through the city. This truly happened and the memory of it gives me impetus now.

The point I drew out, though I didn't realize it, was perfectly in line with the old Gnostic (or Vedic) teaching of inner knowing—which had led Carl Jung in 1916 (during what he called his "confrontation with the unconscious," November 1913–19) to write *Septem Sermones ad Mortuos (Seven Sermons to the Dead)*. It was a time when the dead, as he put it, "addressed crucial questions to me."[41]

Spurring him to begin, the atmosphere in his home reached fever pitch. Among his children, twice on a Saturday night, January 29, 1916, ten-year-old Gret woke when "someone" yanked off her blanket; twelve-year-old Agathe independently reported "a white figure passing through the room"; Franz, nine, had an "anxiety dream" so frightening his father asked him to draw it.[42] Amazingly, the child

depicted a fisherman with an angel above him who said the fisherman
"only catches the wicked fishes!"; this fisherman closely resembled
Philemon: an Egypto-Hellenic spirit—with kingfisher wings—who
was teaching Jung during these years of upheaval.[43] With that stage
set, the next day the climax broke.

Jung wrote in his autobiography, *Memories, Dreams, Reflections*,
about the origin of this Gnostic text, *Septem Sermones ad Mortuos*:

> It began with a restlessness, but I did not know what it meant or
> what "they" wanted of me. There was an ominous atmosphere all
> around me. I had the strange feeling that the air was filled with
> ghostly entities. Then it was as if my house began to be haunted. . . .
>
> Around five o'clock in the afternoon on Sunday the front-door
> bell began ringing frantically . . . but there was no one in sight.
> I was sitting near the door bell, and not only heard it but saw it
> moving. We all simply stared at one another. The atmosphere was
> thick, believe me! Then I knew that something had to happen. The
> whole house was filled as if there were a crowd present, crammed
> full of spirits. They were packed deep right up to the door, and the
> air was so thick it was scarcely possible to breathe. As for myself,
> I was all a-quiver with the question: "For God's sake, what in the
> world is this?" Then they cried out in chorus, "We have come back
> from Jerusalem where we found not what we sought."

He added, "It was an unconscious constellation whose peculiar
atmosphere I recognised as the *numen* of an archetype."[44]

The Gnostics exemplified archetypes that did not need an in-
stitution to pass themselves on. They needed people. Directly. A
collective unconscious. The Gnostics were the first of the organized
underground-spirituality thread, always alive in secret, Jung encountered—in addition to his dreams and other experiences since
childhood.

Describing how unclear he was about what to make of his spirit guides, Jung wrote: "Philemon and other figures of my fantasies

brought home to me the crucial insight that there are things in the psyche which I do not produce, but which produce themselves and have their own life. Philemon represented a force which was not myself. In my fantasies I held conversations with him, and he said things which I had not consciously thought. . . . He said I treated thoughts as if I generated them myself, but in his view thoughts were like animals in the forest, or people in a room, or birds in the air. . . . It was he who taught me psychic objectivity, the reality of the psyche."[45]

Much later a friend of Gandhi's, visiting Jung, described his own guru. To Jung's astonishment this guru was a spirit. Instantly, Jung thought of Philemon ("I went walking up and down the garden with him, and to me he was what the Indians call a guru"[46]).

That experience with heretics from second-century Alexandria, Egypt, was in a tradition that had died, it was thought. Before Jung's death it was to reemerge from the sands and caves of the desert, with the discovery of actual texts seventeen hundred or more years old, one codex of which the Jung Institute Zurich bought.

But first Jung discovered and drank the Gnostics straight up without the benefit of papyrus and dug-up codices. As they demanded his attention, he wrote *The Seven Sermons*. It stands at the end of the *Red Book* draft manuscripts.[47]

The Red Book, however, was so personal it was locked up in a vault—seen by a handpicked few—till its 2009 publication, close to a century after Jung's seminal plunge into self-analysis ("confrontation with the unconscious").

Unlike the rest of the revelations from *The Red Book* period, *The Seven Sermons* (with authorship attributed to Basilides of Alexandria), was privately printed in Jung's lifetime (1916).

In his autobiography Jung wrote, "From that time on, the dead have become ever more distinct for me as the voices of the Unanswered, Unresolved and Unredeemed."[48] He told his colleague/assistant Aniela Jaffé, in 1957: "The years . . . when I pursued the inner images were the most important time of my life. Everything else is to be derived from this. . . . My entire life consisted in elaborating what had burst forth from the unconscious and flooded me like an enigmatic stream and threatened to break me. That was the stuff and the material for more than only one life."[49]

This message of inner Knowing, often shunted into the unconscious, was what I was now discovering and it told me to do it: *Go ahead. Witness without prevarication, merge without inflation, with matter-of-factness because What is will take care of itself.* But verify. Be as sure as you can. Then the still-living truths can flow—alive, flexible, silent, or hyperactive—that we use as sculptors of our biographies. That we Report to Earth—to bring to our planet new intensities, new embodied potential that was waiting, hidden away, on the edges of boundaries.

So Jesus asks, "What would you, Miriam?" And Hunter: "What would you, Margaret?" as it were. "Go out or stay in?" That would be a field within a field within a field if the powerful archetype went all the way back, or drew from it only in the tiniest smidgen, or had the most miniscule reminder. But I did not make the association. It just comes to mind now, as I try to reconstruct, get the long view.

During my sublet I flew down to Guadalajara, Mexico, to work with psychologist Hector Kuri-Cano. In 1983–'84, I'd attended his Charlottesville, Virginia, workshops, just after definitively leaving my husband in Morocco. Now, in '91, I went down there to ground my unsettling multidimensional experiences, such as the above-described kundalini episode, and in general all the challenges following Willy Vanluyten's death. Hector had heavy spiritual experience and solid in-the-worldness.

He was over a thousand miles away, but I could bill the airplane ticket to my one credit card and go. I had always been attracted to his earthy Mexican/Lebanese roots and U.S. sophistication, his clinical training, his travels—which included profound initiations in a

Tibetan Buddhist monastery and ashrams in India—his almost-macho confidence.

I remember how once at Openway in 1984, Hector wanted us to "read bodies," so one at a time we unclothed while in a small, respectful group the rest of us "read" the information. Hector said I was so light-skinned, with veins showing, that to look at me in this way seemed almost an intrusion. Anyway, he was one of the few with the command and presence to pull that exercise off quite respectfully.

Another time at Openway he had us, in twos, pretend-suffocate each other with a pillow—not to a dangerous degree but to get the sense of how we might react to death.

I had never had, before or after, this kind of teacher and the energy he radiated stayed with me. I wrote to invite myself down. Though he didn't reply, I was so sure of a reception I went anyway. It might be the last chance to see Hector again. (That was prophetic.)

I jumped onto a plane. It seemed to me that of all the people I knew on the whole Earth, Hector would understand what I was going through, this no-nonsense Western psychotherapist who had vast experience in the East. You could see spirituality in the twinkle in his eyes, and reliability reflected in the somewhat big-bellied, heavy-set physique.

The plane made a small layover in Mexico City and finally arrived in Guadalajara, a bustling city of about 2.7 million.

Obviously, no one met me. But a taxi driver suggested a dinky motel reasonably near the suburban address I had for Hector. Then I hitchhiked in a truck. On the drive from the airport young people rushed over to clean our windshield at every stoplight—nobody too concerned about traffic regulations. A very different atmosphere pervaded the affluent Rancho Contento community in Zapopan, Jalisco—quiet, peaceful, landscaped with tropical trees and heavy foliage. I rang the bell of the home I thought—hoped—was his. If not, I was in a pickle. His wife Barbara answered. In fact, newly moved, Hector was unpacking books in the library.

Wearing glasses, only two years older than me (though to me he was much older), casually dressed, he seemed thrilled to see me. I learned his wife had warmly answered my telegram—but replied to my Belgian address.

It turned out that having just had one kidney removed, he was in remission from cancer—fully intent on surviving.

To heal, he focused on both traditional medicine and the psychological origin. I didn't know he cured himself of a life-threatening disease in the 1960s—en route to a Bioenergetics training—by not disembarking at his destination in New York but continuing on to India. A longtime yoga student, Hector traveled between ashrams in India, "studying with various gurus and developing his own concept of transcendental psychology, as well as healing his heart."[50] In parallel in the U.S., his studies included prestigious teachers: psychoanalyst Erich Fromm; Stanley Keleman (somatic therapy at Esalen Institute), and the founder of Bioenergetics, psychotherapist Alexander Lowen.

But you didn't have to know this background, which I didn't, to fall under his warm spell.

We arranged daily sessions in his Energetic Metatherapy. There was no sitting silently in a chair and listening for Hector. He drew me out and interacted back instead of just waiting for something to happen. Later I would realize he must have been using a lot of intuition. And he responded as a human being, a full being—who taught in personal, interpersonal, and transpersonal terms.

Graciella Damewood at Openway had told me that his private sessions with me in Charlottesville were one of the few times she had seen him get a counter-transference; that is, he found it difficult not to step into the role of major men in my life and project right back—probably because he had things in common, in style, with Milton Klonsky and my father.

In Guadalajara, I learned of his work with Jesuits to teach the poor self-reliance, for example, by growing herbs for healing with medicinal plants; on the other end of the spectrum, he founded a department of psychology in a university.

Monarch butterflies fell onto the ground at my motel. I belatedly gathered it was probably a hooker hangout, but it was cheap,

Guadalajara motel room

convenient, and the rooms were clean, in separate little buildings. With scant time for socializing, I did take the bus into the city, avoiding the pickpockets, and bought handcrafted Mexican boots and a big sombrero with a hand-sewn design.

To reach Hector's condo, I always hitchhiked with truck drivers. After he had me focus on the Buddhist goddess Tara, in my room I tried to practice the Tibetan mantra he gave me ("Om! Tara, Tuttare Ture, Swaha"). But asleep, I dreamed my own mantra: *"Noli me tra-hijo,"* a spin-off of "Noli me tangere" ("Don't touch me"), meaning, I thought, "Don't betray me." Awake, I practiced it.

I was an alto but suddenly sang it in soprano. Hector excitedly encouraged me to show him. I had no idea that as a young man he liked singing opera and that he could influence a person's dreams.

I did know he had psychic power. Once in Charlottesville, he'd offered me the chance to apprentice with him in therapist training in Mexico; then he'd also said close my eyes: what did I see? I said red, gold, purple blocks—in different sizes. He said those were his subtle colors. I was amazed.

An unforgettable event now occurred. I had begun taking "Awakening Your Light Body" classes in Belgium in the spring of that year (more on this later). In Guadalajara with Hector's consent, I phoned a light body healer in California and—fervidly hoping to assist his cancer recovery—set up an appointment for him. But at the last minute, she seemed to disappear. She did not reconfirm. This was unlike her and I was able to "pick up" psychically the sense that something had gone wrong. What to do?

I decided not to tell Hector. I would step into her place. This felt very bold. I hadn't dared consider stepping up where cancer was concerned. But in my energy studies with Chris Van de Velde in Belgium (in "Inner Landscaping"), we learned aura healing.

So closing the door in my room, I imagined Hector in front of me. As I went toward the subtle figure to put my hands into his aura, I felt another presence "walk in." I was *absolutely sure* I was being helped, though I had no idea by whom (and still don't).

With my hands in Hector's aura, I carefully combed though it, feeling the different textures; in the area of his kidneys, I "saw" a man: a young Hector who had a dream; he cared about a project so much that, I wondered, did he, as it were, create—at least, contribute to—the life-or-death illness? I felt the discovery was valuable information for Hector.

The next day, fully under the sway of the vision of his young self, I asked Hector if he'd kept the appointment. He said yes, he had felt Om the whole time. I was so moved as he described the energy feelings I had tears. He asked why. And I fessed up. Though I'd clearly felt the assisting presence walk into the room and believed in it totally, I was so grateful and impressed that Hector took my information seriously.

I asked about the young man. If one has such a vision, it can stay with you strongly, as this one did. I hoped it was a key to Hector's recovery. Sure enough, he recounted how in his youth, he left unfinished some writing about the feminine. He deduced that the removal of one kidney represented the unconscious necessity to shift his male/female balance. And therefore he lost the right (conscious, masculine) kidney, indicating the importance—to him on a psychic level—of this unfinished work involving the feminine, a wish that was vitally deep in his unconscious. He said it was selfish but he wished he could convince me to stay and help him write it. This intertwining of disease with a psychic issue was well known to me through the Jung Institute, so I hoped fervently my vision would assist in his remission. It felt like his younger subpersonality had put this key into my hands.

Then the phone rang. With no further ado, the missing healer surfaced, and they rescheduled.

Hector—able to stand in his own breadth of experience—gave me the reassurance I needed. I had expected him to be unflabbergasted by the many dimensions I was encountering, and he was. He was serious, humorous, and earthy. This combination, in a spiritual and body-oriented embodiment, was just what I'd flown 1,642.75 miles to find.

Normally, one cannot go through great spiritual shocks without a teacher. Not beforehand but afterwards, in the grounding phase. I had sought Hector out. I was sure he was equal to challenges that my encounters with "the afterlife" had brought and that he would support me. He did. Not that my qualms were resolved, but I felt steadied and took away, as well, a reminder of Hector's loving example—*presence* is the only fitting word.

Anytime I have found presence, my own ability to be present is more alive. It seems to catch fire. *Knowing* is reminded. It's that invisible handshake that cements a step. Getting more Hector under my belt would be sustenance for a long time.

I returned to the Bay Area after about ten days. I felt buoyed. I had a handle now on how to go through these shifts—a model of unwaveringness before spiritual buffets. My stomach butterflies weren't quite as dead as the monarchs at my motel, but readjustment was well under way.

It so happened that the psychic Mariah Martin was briefly nearby.

I set out from the La Honda area to see her, driving Russell's old stick-shift car. At the door her light took me aback, it was so radiant. Without a word from me, she soon stopped my session to point out an opera singer on the periphery of my energy field. A part of me, with a gold headdress, she said, wanted to step inside.

After that I often sang soprano (when alone). I named the singer my higher self, "Anna"—associating her chant "*Noli me trahijo*" with Jesus at his tomb. *Noli me tangere*: "Don't touch me, I'm not yet in form." I felt she was telling me how sacred she was, to be careful not to let her energy be touched randomly—at least while so new.

(Later, to begin my private energy sessions with Joost Vanhove in Belgium, when he would ask me to say my name aloud, I would answer, "Margaret *Anna* Harrell," trying the name on, feeling the sound. Hearing it helped Joost find my energy.)

Hector lived several more years, till 1995, but eventually succumbed to the cancer. Even so, his Energetic Metatherapy has survived. Compiling his lecture notes and tapes, Jean Campbell writes, "To my knowledge no one else in the fields of psychotherapy or consciousness studies has *ever* done the work that Hector did, or taught this subtle combination of Bioenergetics and transpersonal, transcendental psychology."

I was lucky to study with this remarkable, humble man.

Russell was about to leave for India to marry Jyoti in a ceremony officiated by the revered Dhyanyogi-ji and his spiritual heir, Shri Asha Ma (soon to be Anandi Ma). Russ and I went to Neiman Marcus with Dhyanyoga Centers cash and a list of items he wanted—U.S. ball point pens, towels, pale blue sheets.

Just before Russ's departure I handed him a draft of my *Love in Transition*; my big challenge was to incorporate (or not) the storyline growing off from the Zurich Initiation and, more recently, the bell.

I was stuck. Written initially as a novel, the book had begun to swell to include its expanded background. How could I, as an author, follow the developments, to where the model for my fictional character Robert—Milton Klonsky, now deceased—appeared to be alive? The fact that in Zurich he'd metamorphosed into someone entirely different, who'd absorbed him but was a much greater teacher. Not to mention that he told me not to remember his old *form*—that it was like an empty frame, an archetype. Drop *form* recognition!

But how could you recognize someone if you didn't have *the form to guide your eyes?*

Asking for blessing from the satguru Dhyanyogi-ji, I sent the manuscript off. Though Dhyanyogi-ji hadn't studied English, he'd said it was possible for him to read a language he hadn't studied. Shri Anandi Ma and her husband, Dileepji Pathak, carried my manuscript into his room.

Meanwhile, "Fear and Loathing in Elko" was completed. I would call this really slapstick, as the rubber band stretches and the two trajectories move apart, yet both fueled in a flood of writing.

What can I say that is more outrageous? I will not accept the dare. I had a sense this California initiation and after would take me too far away—from Hunter—to bridge the "divide." Not a conscious thought; I didn't let it be. A sense right below the threshold. But I can detect it now in my actions, in hindsight.

A part of me—call her that least evolved—didn't know how she would cross the widening gap between us. She was intent, standing firm, trying to write—and then mail!—Hunter a letter. Like someone before a big battle, wanting to bring another person close at that moment to say: *Look, I'm going away for a while.* Or: *Look, can you handle this? Here, I'm still me. Take my hand and help me do this more gracefully. Go through this with me. Otherwise, I'm bound to be outlandish, "abstruse," perhaps incommunicable. I'll say outrageous things. I'll be stoned out of town. At least, till I get a handle on the situation.* The two events—finishing my manuscript and still hoping to make contact with Hunter—intertwined to create the end of what became *Love in Transition* II, the novel that had been intercepted by energy initiations in Zurich and Tienen, Belgium. The initiation in California being yet more fuel to the inner fires.

An enormous kundalini occurrence was too strong to ignore.

I began to believe it logical to put the energy of St. Paul behind the energy of Mary Magdalene as her lifetime was known in Earth history.

Had in actual fact Jesus, as Gibran imagined, asked Mary Magdalene a question she held the answer to in her heart, answering which might have changed history? Or was this a "parallel" possibility, which didn't happen but resided by implication in history, unconscious at the time? Or further still . . .

In the only bodywork course offered at the Küsnacht institute, we once practiced an exercise in which each male was led by the hand by a female as he admitted he didn't know what to do: where to go next.

Because of the transpersonal nature of this archetype (though I did not realize it), my personal, human role would look quite different from what I'd planned. For it must involve reconstructing an impression of male-female relationship, specifically inside the known and Unknown Energy of These Two.

I, however, had just intended to be a writer—a novelist at that, making up plots, inventing characters . . . till I had discovered, after

Milton Klonsky's death in 1981 (I was informed of it belatedly in 1982), that my dreams and even storyline in *Love in Transition* seemed quite privy to the incipient passing—*while* he was dying, *not after, when I officially got the news.*

So my unconscious, I deduced, had fed material to me, the novelist. Which brought me up short. It was at that moment I decided once and for all not to hoodwink myself any more, not to put on blinders and write, asleep, the "dictations" of my higher self—in code even to me—but to fling those disguises aside and see if I could decipher, in the flesh, what my deeper self knew.

I had proceeded that way for nine years, 1982–1991. I considered it part of this nineteen-year assignment that began in 1985. And look where I wound up by 1991. Facing yet deeper plunges into the secrets of the inner self.

My initiations did not wait till the logical groundwork and anchors were in place, but typically burst onto the scene, as if I relished surprise, and I did. My earlier gullibility was not in remission. It was hand in hand with a very strong rational faculty, which was deeply shocked by having to admit that my intuition, not my reason, had known—simultaneous to the event—that Milton Klonsky was nearing death. Now closer . . . now closer. And I hadn't done a thing, except keep writing how it would affect my character if the fictional Milton (Robert)—no, *not if,* when—died.

Looking back, I could see my present shift forecast in a dream while his death approached, a dream in which I was writing in the dark. After a point, the dream showed me, the light came on; the only pages left in my "book" (of life?) depicted never-before-seen (that is, unconscious) beautiful paintings on a wall. Portraits of whom? Of parts of me called past lives that had mastered this moment? Of transpersonal thinkers and spiritual teachers? No matter. A shift was bearing down on me, I was sure. I felt in the throes of it. For now, though, back to the two great personages just mentioned.

The suggestion I took from the kundalini revelation was that it might be significant to "converge" these two—St. Paul and

Magdalena—for an undeveloped (unknown, timely) side of the message of St. Paul (or "the masculine"), as of hers: a good foundation for creating a new pattern as a matter of engineering/reconfiguring/reformatting. In my case, in the guise—put another way—of Mars-Neptune.

For in an Association for Research and Enlightenment (A.R.E.) astrology chart drawn up in 1984, a Mars-Neptune conjunction—not opposition—ruled my life. With its rare intensity (24.8), the conjunction—so went the A.R.E. explanation—would be by far the central challenge in my life. The conjunction of Mars—war, clarifying power, burning through darkness, the masculine. And Neptune—mysticism, psychic ability, higher awareness, the feminine.

Psychologically, this chart was one more point of entry into a male-female balancing act I felt myself in and that we all have. (A prominent Jungian theme is the balancing of opposites to achieve *individuation*, or wholeness.)

Anything could come down to how, in format after format, I filtered it through this tension of opposites.

All of which at this point was not the point for me. I was involved in the experience, or revelation.

The stage was thus set by the kundalini. The kundalini transports a wealth of history's wisdom, or "the field." This is July 23, 2009, the day after the Mary Magdalene feast day. Also the day after the great solar eclipse of '09.

The kundalini kriya episode—"the broken water"—came in or around October 1991, prior to Guadalajara. I am sure because Russell walked into my room just after; he had not yet left for India.

Writings that remain from this period, I printed in scroll format—the only available paper in the house, and I didn't want to drive Russell's car into Palo Alto just for paper. They are typed, with no handwritten corrections except to delete lines. This material returns to the unfinished poetry written with the Initiator in 1986 in Zurich (some of it in *Keep This Quiet!* III). But it has greatly progressed underground—by 1991.

It reminds me what I struggled with—a few states away from Hunter—in this major initiation that would, in kilometers outside Earth measurement, take me many more, as my unconscious, my inspiration, aligned with *the Fourth Amendment of right to privacy in the home* free of unreasonable searches and seizures (that he championed). But turned it into a pun (just ahead).

Below, I tried to write him a letter. I intended to include it with a copy of the (September 10) release of British rock band Dire Straits ("If you wanna run cool, you got to run on heavy, heavy fuel"). Their album *Brothers in Arms* was a staple of Willy's collection. Yet what a sensation I'd felt at Owl Farm to hear Hunter play it, heartily endorse it. No one ran on heavier fuel.

Remember, this is from my point of view. He might see it differently. So might I later. But right then and there I intensely wanted to make contact before I changed so entirely it was out of the question. So, a little part of me feared this.

A tiny part. Probably the me who instigated the kundalini in Hunter's living room, who had something to say and was bound to break through, who crossed the barrier of the unconscious but couldn't get out of my throat or into a mailed letter. And even if she had, what would have changed? But she didn't think about consequences. Or reason.

> And so now I'll just start with this much, however much I wind up
> putting into the envelope because it could go on forever
> as it's after all a big outpouring
> and a heart outpouring
> And the determination to get the message to you but with a very
> very light touch
> So you can scrutinize and ruminate and twirl your fists around,
> as you do when you type
> and let the music stream through you
> And we'll see what turns up
> Next

Today I find my letter attempts in a box of archives, as Kafka had written his father a letter but not mailed it. I see how a small part of me was resisting expanding—would not until she communicated. My Volume II ended with this material (all in poetry) but *with any reference to Hunter deleted.*

However, *four = oven* in French. Hunter's Fourth Amendment preoccupation dovetailed in, shape-shifted into "the Old Man's right to privacy in his own FIRE-side"—a pun on hearth. On that scale, somewhere, somehow, I was taking Hunter along in my mind. Meanwhile, he was writing "Elko." From the draft of *Love in Transition* II, a lot of it deleted in the final version:

I'd dreamed I would [suddenly wake up]
And my book be intercepted
But I didn't know that holding so firmly to my reins of the Truth
for myself I would wind up in this unconscious energy of the
Earth and all the things people never said
that would have made history go another way
It was vowed in the energy left down there not to let [unreadable]

But I had no idea that if I did it well enough
if my heart was blown wide open
and my mind blown wide open
But in the end my heart
so that nothing else mattered
I would wind up in the Alternative Revelation
so deep it took centuries of master-hearting to get to it
A 2,000-year PLOT
by the boldest minds imaginable
But they found their hearts all this time
in being master minds
had got omitted

And they'd had that style of it enough

They would say their message from the heart
which she saw
Looking at him so long ago
Miriam saw
And he said, "What would you, Miriam?"
And it stayed locked inside then
and stayed locked in
And history kept going one way
leading up to this way
when suddenly everything that was no turned into yes
Imagine what an explosion that would be
And so it exploded in me
the answer to the question
that was his own vibration
and was coded into the DNAs of his and her personalities
That if ever the day came
the question was presented again
and it happened by the way to be coded to a personal
Apocalypse
that would snowball,
Well, just look what the real answer was
Practically saying there will be no 21st century
if the King stepped down
dethroned himself
For what was that crown
if he couldn't share
Couldn't have a heart like other men

In lesson form
The lessons they had learned
HIS HAND
THE OLD MAN'S
when he reveals it

As he's opening my hand now
the hand I didn't know I had
That I was one of those who agreed and even shouted that I
wanted to do this
Help bring in the Real RITES OF MAN
Starting with the rites of his own FIRE SIDE
the Old Man's privacy in his own FIRE SIDE
He had never been allowed that
because where could he get protection enough
It didn't exist
How to protect
A VIBRATION LIKE THIS
His own when he looked at Mary Magdalene
Just as he had on the Cross
And then he'd get strength from her
My computer when I felt the question and wrote it wrote the
answer
As the power behind it is fueling everything written here
D
I
D[*]

Lessons for the Earth in its changing position

Now what use for a
medium
THE MEDIUM
OF
LOVE

LOVE
IN

---

*   The insertion "D I D" was a tiny example of the computer PK.

TRANSITION
THE MEDIUM
Of LOVE

For it was in the air now
the germ of it all
the real story behind
The American Dream
in this version
The real one
A
MARY
CAN

WHEN SHE SAID, "I CAN"
and shouted it so loud her personalities heard it
And his heard too
And thus the Avenue being walked down by Christ and Mary
Magdalene
AT THE END OF THE CENTURY
was not the Unthinkable one
in the predictions
For they were set to counteract those predictions

Thus it was something long in preparation was coming into
being and it was meant to be Peace on Earth
But the Alternative would be rampaging war the like of which
had never been seen
If when he opened his heart and said I love you
the whole world picked it up
picked his vibration up
His private vibration
invisible though it was

The message I wrote underneath it, but not in the text of *Love in Transition* II:

That's it. I know how powerful was the feeling I've always held in behind my masks, and there's somebody here, in me, very little, but who's holding on so hard and holding your picture up. If, even, all she got was to tell you good-bye and where she went, she did that. She did get a chance to speak. And in the kind of energy this is and battle, that's pretty heroic. And it must mean she has a pretty powerful memory of her own. And she's part of me. However big or little. She may be the very biggest me or the very tiniest. But she's sure got passion . . .

Yeah, that's what I want to say. Thank you. Somewhere down deep inside me you made an enormous impression. And I needed that this last two weeks, drew on it. But first I had to know it was there and that I really felt it and I felt it so strongly it must be real. And if it was real it couldn't hurt anybody by saying it.

A tremendous new era was yet again to be heralded, and Shri Dhyanyogi was to be part of it, at first unseen, as was his teaching style. In a near-death experience at ninety-three, in 1971 (after tireless relief work on behalf of drought and famine victims), before re-entering his body he'd found himself in the chambers of Lord Rama, the seventh avatar of Lord Vishnu: part of the Hindu Divine Trinity. There, told to return to Earth because *this time he must not "drop the body" with any unfulfilled wish.*

In that chamber Dhyanyogi-ji saw people waiting to be taught by him. Probably I was one. He revived to complete this mission. In a four-year stay in the U.S. that began in 1976, he gave shaktipat coast to coast; he said, "*Many of those faces that I saw in the courtyard of Lord Rama, I have seen here, since I came to America.*"[51]

Although his specialty was Kundalini Maha Yoga, he had mastered all yogic traditions. He preferred to work with small numbers and kept a photo of Jesus. First, he might work in your energy field until you became aware of it, or might.

Just before New Year's Eve 1991, Jyoti and Russell landed back in California. Besides having a private practice in Menlo Park, Jyoti now led workshops—in Maitri breathwork and spiritual emergence—around the world with her board-certified psychologist husband, Russell D. Park. They were experts in kundalini. And integrated traditions, leaning heavily toward Native American, not to mention that Jyoti's path was called by Dhyanyogi-ji that of St. Teresa.

She and Russell prepared a private New Year's Eve ceremony. Allowing me to join them, Jyoti commented that she felt in it we would all three "get our parts." Unknown to me, she was to channel in my future, fix me into it.

Sensing a powerful presence, I said instantly, "*Could Dhyanyogi be here?*" She said yes. In the ceremony my guide (I wasn't aware I had one) went into her. When this occurred, Jyoti had me strike a pose: to stand with arms slightly expanded, curved to a certain height. She said, "Watch." I did. She said that was me—but the vision I had was of books of various sizes, some small like the miniature leather-bound classics that had lined my mother's shelves. I felt a future fully forming, in which I was as if in a magical position I had no control over.

Then I left California. Having just bought the posthumous *A Discourse on Hip: Selected Writings of Milton Klonsky*, I noted that the introduction said he kept his emotional life "under wraps." He emerged from the arid underground of the '50s into a torrent of writing in the mid-'60s—no one knew why. An unproductive Milton—silent in a desert, only to burst into productivity about when we met? I'd never imagined it!

I wanted to correct any biographical gaps I could. So in New York, I phoned *Commentary*. To the stranger on the line, I asked straight out: "Does anyone there remember Milton Klonsky?" A pause . . . then the widely respected managing editor Marion Magid came on.

Remembering him well—he was a *Commentary* contributor—she suggested I write an article, "The Milton Klonsky I Knew." Start it, "There was a time when New York was known for its talkers. Milton Klonsky was one of them."

The morning of the flight to Belgium, I woke abruptly in my Manhattan hotel room at the midtown Pickwick Arms. Jyoti's face in front of me was saying, "*Time's up.*" (Not what one wants to hear before catching a plane.)

6

Fire during Takeoff

On the sidewalk at Grand Central, January 14, I waited for the shuttle to JFK International. I momentarily got distracted, and just then my fancy embroidered carry-on vanished—right off the sidewalk!

In the plane I searched through my second carry-on. What had been stolen? In Mexico, I'd photographed a famous picture hanging on Hector Kuri-Cano's wall: Christ's face. There it was, in my bag.

If looked at from the left, the image on the wall had heavy shadow; from the opposite angle, the face was unshadowed. Looking at it frontally, you saw both shadow and light. I had photographed the three angles. Only the one in the illustration survived the theft; the white streak is from the flash.

Image on Hector's wall

Much later I would learn that Sathya Sai Baba was reported to have been given the Shroud face in a black-and-white printout to bless by a disciple and manifested the new image in color onto blank paper "out of thin air."[52]

I glanced out the window as the plane began taxiing down the runway. It was not a comforting sight. *Big sparks were bursting out of the left wing!* Indeed, "Time's up."

The pilot screeched to a stop, and we sat in the plane, waiting apprehensively for maintenance. Partly inspired by devotees returning

coincidentally from Sai Baba's ashram in Puttaparthi, everyone remained calm in their seats. Jyoti had given me ashes (*vibhuti*) materialized from his hands (this was not in the stolen carry-on). But I
knew little of Sai Baba, and it didn't sink in whose hands the ashes
came from. After the problem was supposedly fixed, the pilot again
attempted takeoff. But fire burst out, on the same wing!

Flight canceled, we were hustled off to a Howard Johnson's airport hotel. But while enjoying the food coupons in the hotel restaurant, I thought: *Suppose time is really up and the plane crashes.* I
pushed back my chair and went to my room.

I felt tested, mortal, in a high-stakes ultimatum. The warning
impressed me so profoundly that under stress I typed up the information about the Zurich Initiation I felt it was important didn't die
with me. I put it into a letter to mail. To whom? I forget but a friend
I trusted. After going to sleep, I *dreamed a great wind wafted copies of
my manuscript far and wide; they dropped out of the air into hands of
just those people who knew what to do with them.* Was my job to deliver
information?

I now felt I had no choice but to incorporate the information and
story of my Zurich Initiation at the Jung Institute as fact into *Love in
Transition*, make it public. That this was central to the nineteen-year
deeper-self task I was newly embarked on.

I returned to Belgium, feeling "ordered" to use Milton's name, not
just the novelistic alias, "Robert," and report as fact my experiences
about the afterlife since he died. This was fodder for the fire. I drew
out all my courage.

Not long afterwards, I was caught unawares, watching TV. What
sailed into my Belgian apartment in electronic information, piped
in from the dream state in New York? The exact scene—in this case,
newspapers being rescued from burning trash cans were lifted up by
the wind, numinously wafted high into the sky. Landing in just the
right hands.

That very evening, January 22, I informed Jyoti and Russ that,
incredibly:

The scene from my [Howard Johnson] dream is in a movie I just turned on. In it a newspaper reporter helping wage a battle for poor people in Mexico has his papers bought out by a rich man and the local government, to burn; as the fire is mounting, a wind beautifully lifts all the newspapers to distribute to people in the village. There's aerial photography as the papers spin in the air and land precisely at those places the poor people will read them. It's very exhilarating and like a miracle . . .

In the film, there are lines such as, "People now, I don't know, they don't know how to act or talk with saints, talk with angels."

"You talk with angels?"

"Those are the only ones with time to spare."

How did I dream that cameo in the New York hotel, then stumble onto the TV channel that played the source? I didn't yet make the connection to Dhyanyogi-ji—both in "Time's up" and the "teleporting" of this scene, as it were. In the film an indigenous wise man, sacrificing himself to protect others, is seemingly killed but amazingly doesn't die. This, like the coming collision with Jupiter, was a very subtle dot to connect.

The wind rescued the newspapers (my book pages) in identical slowed-time wafting of information—in incredible silent suspension. They floated down to contact points. Same hushed significance. Help was near. I trusted that prediction.

I went on:

So when you said we were getting our scripts this year and I get this Mexican or New Mexican movie and there are saints and old old people and Indians and news to get out, and the great wind doing that, and many images of fire, in a movie about faith, when my airplane has caught fire twice and somehow I fused that with the dream just afterwards and this movie right now—well, how's that for a script? . . . this newspaperman was also me . . . Aren't I crazy, going on about this dream that turned out to be also a movie? But you'd have to know the effect it had on me. And that it picks up from that New Year's Eve introduction. With you as MC. And I think that was a crucial step from then to now. What, with the series of mystics [explained just ahead] and the dream turning into a movie. What could happen now—next?

I was, by then, aware that Dhyanyogi-ji worked in time manipulation, especially as (though no one suspected it) he was just about to embark on his *mahasamadhi*, or "dropping of the body," which we in the West call death. Such a yogi can "drop the body" by sitting in meditation (samadhi), not coming back. No life-threatening disease, no medication. The spirit going one place, the body left to not wake up.

But there would be almost three years yet.

January 21, 1992, just back in Tienen, I poured out in a three-page letter to my "Inner Landscaping" teacher, Chris Van de Velde (probably unmailed). "BELL" indicates the nonphysical bell (see the chapter "A Peek into My Apartment") rang audibly.

I recounted that I'd woken "bolt upright," having "finally understood the process I've been going through and what would make it work." This discovery was about my inner male energy. I'd detected that, as with Hector Kuri-Cano I reintegrated "the singer," similarly in Chris's workshop, the painter I'd integrated was my animus. This notwithstanding that all my life I couldn't carry a tune, stiltedly played the piano, as my teacher taught with a metronome, and had been woefully unable to draw detail. "Moreover, I'd detected, he was a young mystic."

And *"he has to come in first by standing outside . . . on the threshold."*

For example, in a pub in New York City, waiting for an Indian I'd just met, I inexplicably found myself on a very high vibration, stimulated to write "The Milton Klonsky I Knew."

I couldn't decide why I was practically shaking. And in joy. And then this Indian walks up and fits the vibration. He begins to speak about a mystic known to Americans and things that mystic said, as if pointedly to me. I agreed to see him again [uh-oh], but no more messages came . . . Then I tried to get into my plane—surrounded by coincidences again. And the plane went up in flames. It really did.

Paragraphs later, I recounted meeting a second mystic just afterwards, in the unlikely town of Tienen. Processing all the synchronicities, I woke up "bolt upright, feeling the excitement of the mystic in me . . . And then I realized how people have to be reached by their own deeper and wider selves through the energy field of the collective, and that matching energies more developed will usually intercept them . . . I forgot to mention, the day I met the first mystic I was feeling I had candles for eyes and that they penetrated right out of me. I was feeling the same again last night . . . This is my research—do you think it's scientific? Ha. You can help me be scientific. BELL."

Not surprisingly, I again felt I'd stumbled onto a "lost theory and much more." And I wanted his help in "systematizing." To take the next step.

But [for the theory] not to find itself over the brink, it needs a steerer into the mainstream and a canoe paddler who has native instincts for avoiding rapids, etc. A scientific laboratory analyst. It's amazing and I have to calm down. Could it be "energy make-up" time [a technique Chris taught]? Hector, in Mexico, by the way, when I asked what [enneagram] type I was, said, "The observer and dramatizer is four [the artist]." He didn't say what the rest was. But it's that part that's male and couldn't so easily communicate.

Well, what will you make of this? You're very good at understanding. And making life an experience to "count" by. Count eternity by.

January 23, 1992, *Rolling Stone* distributed "Fear and Loathing in Elko," an incredibly humorous tale in which the author divided himself in two. The bulk of the article, an afterthought, a "Special Advisory from the Sports Desk," was, warned Hunter, "brainless, atavistic gibberish"—by Raoul Duke (his alter ego)—"I want that screwhead fired!"[53] Duke's memo narrated a night of blinding rain in which HST came upon an accident involving Judge Clarence Thomas and two hookers. HST offered them a ride and they wound up in Elko but soon found themselves on the lam.

"The vicious wit is still there in copious amounts, but the tone is that things used to be different," wrote one reviewer, explaining how, with "political correctness . . . in full force, and at the risk of not getting hurt, Americans sacrificed their sense of fun and humor"—producing "a nation of jailers." So, "Elko" provides "a cautionary tale, that any small act can cause one to be put away for years."[54]

To set the stage, Hunter mourned how once "you could run around naked without getting shot. You could check into a roadside motel on the outskirts of Winnemucca or Elko when you were lost in a midnight rainstorm—and nobody called the police on you, just to check out your credit and your employment history and your medical records and how many parking tickets you owed in California."

Back then, "there were Laws, but they were not feared. There were Rules, but they were not worshiped . . . like Laws and Rules and Cops and Informants are feared and worshiped today."

I studied the piece. What could I comment? I marked passages I liked stylewise. Looked for any reference I could detect of my visit. Found just one. Duke exclaimed, "The snake has come out of the bag."[55] This reminded me of his Florida snake I'd kept in my office while copy editing *Hell's Angels*. (Before it could get transported safely to Woody Creek, this untamable, wild specimen of nature was killed by a terrified Random House night watchman when loose on the stairs.) The besieged snake, Duke implied, was like him.

PART TWO

A "Naked Child" in the 1990s, Dream of Dhyanyogi-ji, and the Comet to Hit Jupiter

Even the ant has a soul.

—Anandi Ma, satsang, July 15, 2000

7

The 1990s

The 1990s stood out radically in my life: a solid, unbroken initiation for ten years, once Willy "left the body" and the bell came. But not only that. I returned to Tienen after the plane wing fire that made me set out in a determined new direction. This seemed just what was necessary to attract spirit committees. Now I was serious. The setting changed. The first spirit committee gave me Jesus materials that did not fit—in a novel, which I'd intended *Love in Transition* to be!

Nevertheless, I tried to make them fit.

The bell never left the house in the first two years. If I did, it awaited my return—audible in the presence of anyone it wanted to hear it; they ranged from Willy's friends and daughter to my friends from Brussels to a few visiting friends from the United States. For instance, it stayed in the apartment one day with Russell D. Park, ringing to accent his thoughts, while Jyoti and I went to Leuven.

As mentioned, Helen Titchen Beeth, a translator in the European Commission, spent a week with me in the first days after Willy's death—witnessing the arrival of the bell.

I detected that on the one hand it was easing Willy into the afterlife. After all, at just under thirty-five he suffered a sudden, violent death. In *Keep This Quiet!* III, I wrote about that personal aspect:

> The bell would help work through lingering issues, such as that despite Willy's insisting how proud he was of his fidelity, one of

Jyoti, Margaret, and Russell in the early 1990s

his friends revealed (after he died) that they'd been to a prostitute together—more than once!—during our relationship. I couldn't believe it but eventually was convinced. I turned all his photos face down. Paced the floor of the living room, telling his spirit that I knew was watching *he was in deep water, I was finished with him*. Why had he done this? I began to imagine reasons. The bell seemed to follow my thoughts.

Curiosity, I thought, he *wanted to compare.* It rang. Not a good answer by half, especially in view of the insincerity, in that he'd insisted so much to the contrary.

But I also realized he was "dead," and look where he was. *Here.* And wasn't that the ultimate statement?

However, the bell played another role—in connection with my writing. Taking me by surprise, it might first ring repeatedly as the printer sat immobile, sending nothing at all out or a barrage of blank pages. In practically the first instance, I felt alerted something was up. The printer light began to flicker, as if beckoning. I decided to turn the printer off, then back on. And what happened? Something very unexpected.

A single page of *rearranged* text printed out. By rearranged, I mean a portion of what was on-screen printed out altered. For example, a line might be lifted up, widely separated from the rest of the text, and a "signature" like "*b0W" inserted beside it. That's just one example. I called it computer PK. (Samples are ahead.) Feeling my mind refocused by the re-presentation of just a portion of the page, I marveled. And was often amused.[*]

This second phenomenon, I felt sure—unlike, for the most part, the bell—had to do with higher-consciousness energy (whether a level of myself and/or, I thought more likely, a spirit group I was getting used to channeling).

I immediately plunged into "The Milton Klonsky I Knew," the essay assigned me by Marion Magid, *Commentary* managing editor since 1968.

Additionally, dreams personified issues in the *Love in Transition* manuscript, taking that process that originated in the mid-'80s further and further.

In helping me edit *Love in Transition: Voyage of Ulysses—Letters*

---

[*] Coincidentally, I had been given a copy of *Speaking Pictures: A Gallery of Pictorial Poetry from the Sixteenth Century to the Present*—edited by Milton Klonsky. And I had been in his apartment when he was working on a poem in it, "The Bogie Man Cometh."

to Penelope, in 1985–'86, the Zurich Initiator, whom I called Milton Christ Mozart, had had me listen in my head to song tunes and snatched phrases, see images at the typewriter, feel feelings he "sent." To keep a text alive takes incalculable tons of inspiration. Looked at repeatedly, words freeze into position.

Also in Zurich, he taught me a process I updated in Tienen. There, in bed, with my manuscript a room away, I would "edit" it at a distance. That is, my mind would locate specific text to correct—without seeing, even thinking, the words. I'd read the rhythms, catch dead spots. Working in bed, I could *abstractly remove bumps,* add to/shape the energy landscape—like an architect drawing a blueprint—*at a distance.*

Though I didn't know *which* pages I was in—it was all nonverbal—the effect, when I next sat at the computer, carried over. I had preprogrammed myself, as it were. It was like living through a level of some of the day's events beforehand, which, too, I began to do.

In Tai Chi class in the early '90s, the practice accelerated. I discovered that while moving my hands during the Tai Chi form, I was contouring text that sat over in my apartment; marking energy ups and downs, *"editing" on a higher plane of awareness*—unconscious of the text I was working in. The hand movements felt the energy "hills and valleys." I didn't know *which* specific passages *I was in, in the text.* But next time at the computer, I'd sense the location.

It appeared that in Leuven in Tai Chi, approached mystically as my teacher taught it, the energy translated into *the hands* while the mind located the text a town away, in Tienen. But not registered as "a town." It was an awareness location. And the text I "read" the energy of was in a geometry of shape, not words. The hands modified the energy contours (at a distance). In a sense, turning "matter" back into energy—patterns—into how the content *felt* emotionally. My hands moving through the Tai Chi form corrected the energy typography of specific pages.

Evidently, an activity of ours could (unconscious to us) correlate itself to yet another activity: differently located. The *effect* might be moved from the location in which an activity happened to one it matched *or amplified.*

At the same time and earlier, trying to catch up with Soviet research in parapsychology and "see" sensitive military sites, the CIA was conducting secret remote-viewing experiments in which psychics described distant locations. Perhaps the experience above could be compared to remote viewing, but in abstract "energy" geography.[56]

This idea grew over years. "Where" was not exactly "where." Even "what" could interchange with another "what." Amplifications could be the transporter. Spectrums could be, in imagination or the mind, moved. By correspondences? I did something one place, while the result was available elsewhere. In fact, targeted it. Cause was only pretending to be in one location, in this scenario. It was there all right, but just as significantly it was correspondingly *somewhere else.*

My hands ran through the Tai Chi form while my mind, in the group, emptied into a high state of awareness. But very specifically the energy harnessed that high frequency—built up by the group, the teacher, and myself—into a second task. Or rather, some part of me did. Or what I called my unconscious, continuing toward a solution I had asked it for.

This meant that I could—we can—in an altered state, use a physical exercise to edit (map out) a manuscript—find an energy geography. *It showed the interchangeability of space-time and space-time, energy and matter, even one activity and something it could be made to correspond to.* The physical movement in Tai Chi used the heightened state, perhaps the group energy. Maneuvered it to a different focus, the invisible manuscript-shape.

Carl Jung—who first began thinking about "relativity of time and its psychic connections" during dinners with Einstein in Zurich in which the influential physicist discussed his early ideas on the special theory of relativity[57]—wrote in "The Soul and Death": "We are not entitled to conclude from the apparent space-time quality of our perception that there is no form of existence *without* space and time."[*]

He went on: "The nature of psyche [conscious and unconscious, including collective] . . . contains as many riddles as the universe

---

[*]   Space-time," or "spacetime," or Minkowski space, is a four-dimensional continuum of the three dimensions of space and one dimension of time.

with its galactic systems, before whose majestic configurations only a mind lacking in imagination can fail to admit its own insufficiency.[58]

Much later I would wonder if this "distance editing" had to do with a "correlation wave" as outlined in a paper by neuroscientist Norman S. Don, in *The Journal of Parapsychology*, which he sent me: "Signal Processing Analysis of Forced-Choice ESP Data: Evidence for Psi as a Wave of Correlation."

Based on data analysis of ESP research, Don et al posited that psi (even synchronicity) "may be an oscillatory correlation field, dependent upon or interacting with mental factors and target characteristics and capable of organizing information or even macroscopic objects in contextually meaningful ways."

Why was there a correlation wave when, in a parapsychology experiment, Don et al took the unusual step of looking at *misses alongside hits*—that is, *both* correct and false answers—in an individual's scores. Usually misses were given no value. Here, though, they had meaning *in the overall picture.*[59]

This led Australian psychologist/Jungian Lance Storm to speculate that the correlation wave represented the Self's goals, whereas hit/miss ESP scores reflected the ego's intent to follow instructions.[60] An explanation that fits nicely with my experience in "editing at a distance."

When Norm Don first sent me a pamphlet reprinting his essay, I could make neither heads nor tails of it—not understanding things like "periodic maxima" and "Fourier analysis." But pulling the pamphlet back out in 2014, I intuited that, as Storm said above, the results could reflect the Self's goals.

As I presented this concept (of a holistic "correlation wave") in a light body class in 2014, someone immediately cited an example: Jaden Rose Phoenix, who, she said, was ill, tried nontraditional cures—unsuccessfully. But realized there was no way around it, she needed back surgery. So she set an intention: *Okay, then in addition to a successful operation, I want to get out of it x, y, z.*

"Operation" had no causal relationship to, for example, "new house." By no stretch of connecting the dots could they be turned into a cause-effect situation. But somehow—in an "information wave"?—"operation" and whatever she wished for "correlated." And however one explains it, she got her wish.

It's outside the scope of this book to go into this further here, but my intuition seized on it, thinking of the process at work in the Tai Chi class, which felt as if I were smoothing the aura of my text at a distance as my hands, on the surface, merely went through the Tai Chi forms. But appeared to be subtly "correlating" to another thing entirely. Did this line up with the science above? I thought so. An overt task might not be the task at all from the point of view of Higher Consciousness, or the Self.

8

"The Milton Klonsky I Knew"

"The Milton Klonsky I Knew" addressed the mystery of what, super-ficially, seemed at the time his unfulfilled life. Maybe his "true" intent was concealed. Not to finish his lifework-novel or become famous, as many people expected:

> Rather than do what others had done, on no matter how large a scale, why not do what no one had done? One who had a vision of the future coming toward us, with predictions of out-of-control events, might decide rather to plant seeds that could harvest that approaching onslaught of energy and make of the crossing between two centuries a Celebration Event. Make, in fact, a Transition period. No one would know that was what he was doing. No one might ever know. Which is why those who were left with the mystery felt it so strongly. That they had been left with something to do. That it didn't die, but in fact at this moment BEAR ITS FRUIT.

Energizing my already fertilized mind, the computer jumped in. In the following illustrations, the text above was broken into two pages—due to computer PK—with lines slanted *both upward and downward*. (Later a Belgian parapsychologist told me what, once he said it, seemed obvious: that it was significant that the print went in *different* directions.) A third illustration carries the passage forward.

Rather than do what others had done, on no matter how large a

C:\WP51\DOCUMENT\MILT6A

Computer PK

a vision of the future coming toward us, with predictions of out-of-control events might decide rather to plant seeds that could harvest that approaching onslaught of energy and made of the crossing between two centuries a Celebration Event. Make, in fact, a Transition period. No one would know that was what he was doing. No one might ever know. Which is why those who were

left with the mystery felt it so strongly. That they had been

But to those who had witnessed the promise itself, there was something missing at the end. The question remained, of course. Where did it go, that promise? Just as alive as his question Which Way Did the Second Coming Went? It was begging to be dealt with, and I felt I'd found a clue to it in his deathbed statement, "No Transition. Debauchery"--combined with the impact of a parade I saw in Belgium coincident with is death. More and more material related to his position was to come, on the basis of taking that step of assuming there was an answer to the

mystery and that it had to include the parade.

':\WP51\DOCUMENT\MILT6A

The parade—unforgettable in Blankenberge, Belgium, November 29, 1981—had been more or less coincident with his death that day in New York, though I only found it out much later. Mysteriously underscoring the association, the Initiator had had me buy a chain-reference Bible concordance in Zurich—*at Parade Square*—in 1985. (It sat on a shelf, getting dusty. I never cracked it open. Not till 1991, when, as we shall see, this computer-PK activity brought it to my attention.)

Events in the future would be out of control. Behind the scenes, I had come to believe, a lot of planning was taking place.

April 28, '92, I sent this essay to Marion Magid. She replied that it did "a very effective job of bringing Milton to life and evoking the very special quality of his presence, conversation, spirit, etc." But she suggested that in view of his cult status (intense but small audience) I should try a more avant-garde journal.

Below is an early account about this "computer PK" process, in 1994. I was trying to convince Program Chair Adrian Parker to let me present at the next international PA convention. As parapsychologists are laboratory-research-oriented, there wasn't much chance, which indeed he reminded me in his answer. Here is what I wrote:

Since the beginning of '91, upon bringing my first computer into the apartment in Belgium, I have experienced unusual text alterations. The computer is a low-budget one, with no unusual attachments. It was programmed by a friend, including the installation of Word Perfect 5.1. The purpose of buying the computer was to facilitate writing a book. It transpired that as I worked first on an article about a man I had known in New York City, "The Milton Klonsky I Knew," the energy I could feel in the apartment was greatly heightened. I had difficulty sleeping many hours, the sense of intensity was so strong. And there began to appear phenomena of altered text. The man who was the subject of the article was someone who had established a reputation of being inexplicable. To many he was a mentor, to others a person hard to know who yet left a feeling of mystery. In the early nineties a book was published, *The Fifties*, in which he was described as "a Village cult genius of the forties . . . with an IQ that could stutter your butter."

I alluded to well-known afterlife studies of a famous parapsychologist—the nineteenth-century Cambridge University classics professor and theorist on "the subliminal self," Frederic W. H. Myers:

There have of course been people, such as Myers and [psychologist-philosopher] William James, [founding members of the Society for Psychical Research in Britain and the United States respectively], who [went a long way toward breaking] through the barriers of spirit-matter . . . so far in fact that they had hoped to continue the experiment after death. It is decades later, and nothing substantial has come from this.

But might it not still happen?

I posit this question because all of it was in the air in my apartment as these strange phenomena began, and only to have felt the intensity in the air was to be unable to stop and say that these were either accidental, idle, or whimsical meaningless changes in the text—from my point of view. I was intrigued. Might this be something really new?

All the concern and motivation of the hope of a new idea, a new answer in science, filled me. I was just as tied to the computer and what might come from it as Stephen Hawkins in England to his. It seemed mine was using this just as he used his computer, in order to say what could not be said, in order to give a means of speaking—to an intelligence that had no normal way to express its words.

In my apartment I collected witness statements: one from U.S. psychologist Robert Van de Castle, past president of the Parapsychological Association. After attending the International Association for the Study of Dreams conference at the University of

Leiden in the Netherlands, he stopped in Belgium to teach a dream workshop I organized. I'd worked in his dream lab, in Charlottesville, Virginia, 1993–'94. He had coauthored *The Content Analysis of Dreams*, with eminent psychologist Calvin Hall and authored *Our Dreaming Mind*. I knew he was recognized as an authority in the fields of both dream analysis and parapsychology.

Since I do not have an earlier signed statement and his is of a professional nature, let's see what he had to say. One type of computer PK Bob witnessed in my apartment was a single line of text isolated high on a page, with a lot of space underneath. Beside the first word, a phrase like "p893Y" spontaneously appeared. I had eventually determined these allusions were probably to my Bible concordance, mentioned just above. Bob agreed.

In a two-page account, "Observations about computer Anomalies occurring in Margaret Harrell's Apartment on July 26–28, 1994," he wrote: "In the process of having some letters transcribed for me by Margaret Harrell, I had the opportunity to observe many examples of what I am calling 'anomalous computer phenomena' (ACP). These ACP might be broadly classified into seven categories. Many of these categories involved references to biblical sources, taken from Condensed Cyclopedia of Topics and Texts (The Thompson Chain Reference Bible, 4th improved edition)."

> The biblical passages often seem strikingly relevant and appropriate for the topic under review. . . . For what it is worth, I did sense a strong energy field around Margaret Harrell when she was involved in interacting with her computer. . . . The dictated material involved a legal document, concerning some matters associated with a separation agreement that I was preparing for a lawyer, as well as a letter to a real estate agent. These transcriptions were being processed by Margaret Harrell's computer and resulted in significant changes in the way those documents eventually took shape. The ACP interventions sensitized me to reconsider certain statements or positions that I had been taking, which upon further

reflection seemed inappropriate. It was as if a trusted friend or a higher level of intuitive wisdom were asking me "Is this the way you really want to say that?"

I still have fifteen pages with his handwritten notes on the bottom. Each page contains eight poetry lines, to which the computer added a new ninth line. He labeled this *category 7*: "file material in spontaneous reorganization without any keyboard input."

Bob finished: "The only computer keys M. H. punched throughout these pages was page down, print screen, & page up. The ACP activity was completely 'self' activated and involved changes in the one line that began with 'the certainty that the truth will out.'"

There's a similar account by Virginia Parrot Williams, who has a PhD in history and (with her medical-research psychologist/neuroscientist husband) would become a leader in mind/body/spirit. They had just coauthored the best-selling *Anger Kills*.

Virginia wrote: "I asked Margaret to go into a text she was working on. We tried several times to no effect. Then we went into a text she said came from the computer, which printed it out all night. We went to page 208, which we printed out. Then we would tap 'Page up,' followed by 'Page down,' then print."

I noted: "This file (made initially by me) was worked on all night once, when I left the computer on because there were sounds of it processing information. The next morning there were 100 fields." About an on-screen page she saw print out in *thirteen variations* on sixteen sheets, Virginia noted: "What interests me immensely is that the line after 'a climate that didn't exist,' with a few exceptions, is different every time."

This changing last line was reminiscent to me, I noted, of a puzzle in psi folklore, where *part of* a communication popped up in several locations—in the "cross-correspondence" experiments in vogue around the turn of the twentieth century. To give a little history:

By the end of the 19th Century, most of those most prominent and active in psychical research had firmly convinced themselves that the conditions under which mediums like Mrs Leonore Piper and Mrs Thompson were conveying veridical [truthful] information, often via proxy sitters, not merely made the hypothesis of deception untenable, but pointed pretty clearly to more than the mere functioning of extra-sensory perception. . . . But there seemed to be no way to torpedo the argument that all might nonetheless be ascribed to some of the extraordinary functions of the human psyche which the new disciplines of psychology and psychiatry were constantly revealing. Moreover, it was one thing to show that the memories of deceased persons were somehow accessible to us: quite another to demonstrate that their active intelligences survived after death and could communicate with those left behind.

Attempting to "clearly defeat what was later to become known as the super-psi hypothesis," a test was hatched: "to distribute to more than one medium fragments of messages, in themselves meaningless, and if necessary to provide enough hints to enable a perceptive third party to piece them together to form a coherent message. All the better if the mediums were unknown to one another, living in different parts of the world, and puzzled by the arcane references and obscure language."[61]

After F. W. H. Myers's death, in 1901, mediums in different countries received message fragments—purportedly from him and colleagues. As in my printouts—but more so in a later printout style, illustrated up ahead in "Computer PK and the Cave"—*they made sense only if put together.* To identify himself, the purported Myers also used classical references (for instance, from Virgil's *Aeneid* VI, which he once wrote a scholarly essay on).[62] Naturally, there was dispute regarding the authenticity, but the idea of jigsaws fascinated me.

The page up/page down command, I devised in order to insert energy just before printing, providing something irregular to "work with." Any irregularity would do.

In fact, though I didn't reveal it to anyone, I sought ways to create disequilibrium, i.e., a break in the printer's routine. Primarily because I detected that in the instability when the computer was shut off abruptly, it was able to produce these reformattings if turned back on. The shut-down created an energy surge. I vividly imagined how an intention could dart into the interstices between *off* and *on*. Momentarily, perhaps the disequilibrium allows for, in quantum terms (or quantum consciousness), the collapsed wave to reenter a noncollapsed stage, when it has all possibilities.

If I turned the computer off, then on, with that burst of energy it was possible to get not just an occasional computer creation—but hours and hours: pictorially refocused text (as illustrated earlier). Alternately, the computer might insert Bible annotations. Or "signatures," such as "&1lL."

I wondered: "Nobody pushes a button to make gravity operate. Gravity doesn't need a human participant—does the electricity in the computer have the same possibility of operating without physical human participation? Is there a shortcut?"

9

Maitri Breathwork—
Magnetic Moments

APRIL 3–5, 1992: a workshop taught by Jyoti and Russell Park in Zurich. (I still have the Hotel du Théâtre bill.) Here, in her Maitri breathwork, I had the experience of going into what I am calling—for want of another term—two magnetic moments.

A "Buddha belly" (a *kumbhaka*, or "prana belly") that Jyoti received September 7, 1988, made her look five months pregnant.[63] In a Buddha belly, she explained to me, it was believed that the *prana* and *apana* (inbreath and outbreath) are in a holding position. Buddha bellies are found primarily in the East among gurus. Jyoti was to have an illustrious career, so much so it's hard to know where to begin to describe her.

After being president of the board of Christina and Stan Grof's Spiritual Emergence Network (SEN)—which successfully sensitized mental health professionals to psychospiritual issues—she would with Russell become cofounders of the Kayumari spiritual community in the Sierra Foothills. Later she would be Spiritual Director of the Center for Sacred Studies, an organization "dedicated to protecting and sustaining the spiritual practices of First Nation peoples around the world as they join their hearts in a prayer for world peace." Eventually, through the vision of Jyoti and others, the International Council of Thirteen Indigenous Grandmothers would be established, with Jyoti designated as Traveling Ambassador Charged with the Mission.

All of this was there in a nutshell in her workshops. But even this says nothing of her incredible intuitive touch—often using an eagle feather. And Russell was to have an illustrative career as well.

In Maitri breathwork the breather lies on a mat. A sitter observes. A number of such pairs sat/lay around the large Zurich room. The day began. When it was my turn to breathe, though I had done this many times before with nothing like this effect, I lived the following incredible memories, more intense than any flashback. One: St. Paul's *instant after conversion*, as time expanded to exactly and only that instant.

The next memory. In a different Maitri breathwork session the same weekend: Jesus saying, "Into Thy hands, O God, I commend my Spirit"—experiencing exactly what those radiating feelings were, from the *tiniest pinprick of precision in all of time*.

With St. Paul, I entered that nanosecond as it stretched, elongated, opened into dimensions as huge as to be eternal. I lived it as if my own, knowing it was historical yet as if time dropped down this instant onto me and I entered it, it was the mind/spirit I was inside, though "the moment" existed in itself, conscious, with an "I."

There was no distance between that "I" and myself.

You could not say "I" outside that "I" if an intact conscious moment descended upon you—*like* your memory but drawn from history, being relived *as if your own history. As if you were bringing back to life a memory of your own*, brought by your own mind, stepped into suddenly.

You feeling it as if it were yourself the historical person. But not making that jump, that leap, because there was no thought involved, even afterwards. It was complete in itself. As there was no *before*, no *after* that one instant sensed in the biography it came out of, there was no implication it carried itself into—too sacred.

I felt the isolated second when the consciousness, the human being, grappled with a reaction—all time and potential compacted in the zoomed-into-but-stretched fateful decision.

That moment when St. Paul thought (and I thought, as if it were not past but in the present, now): *If I can just get to my knees, it will be okay.*[*]

---

[*] Moments afterwards I experienced a giant snake come out of my mouth. I took this to mean communication. It would also indicate that the kundalini was at work and produced this effect.

The act of total surrender gave an ability to move *even in paralysis but not of will.*

Much later, I'd say this sounds like something out of what mystics like the "sleeping prophet" Edgar Cayce call the akashic records (or Book of Life).

To me it was an *experience*, of the deepest magnitude possible, as if it had never happened before. And yet I could identify it historically.

It was happening to me *right then* (with no further glimpse into that moment it appeared in, in history). But I knew where it appeared in history. And also felt it as if it were in my eternal and somehow present *now*. This was the living memory of the "I" "I" entered. Not past, but there, present, vibrating, emotionally charged—able to travel with no feeling of space-time crossed, in making its desperate act of surrender.

There was no structure I knew of, except that "I" entered that moment, with its present (past-tense) "I." No one was there besides the spirit—or awareness—having the experience, which I could unquestionably identify to be St. Paul's in that particular historical setting, the way an "I" knows who "I" is unless in amnesia. Here, no amnesia. The consciousness was as presently, alively quivering with desperate, focused solution as in that analytical existential moment of myself at seven.[*]

Here, the existential moment lived on, as the "I" back then en route to Damascus perceived—yes, it comes to me to say it this way—a mercurial way out. There was no left-over intensity. Just 100 percent presence.

This depth of memory was so powerful it resonated like standing waves. By whatever system the "I" at seven had entered me, calling it himself, I had entered the Road to Damascus memory, vibrating and pelleting the present instant with energy.

---

[*] To recall what happened at seven: an "I" inside me suddenly "woke up" with the thought, the frozen awareness, that he couldn't fathom the paradox of being a famous writer (in his core self-knowledge) yet having a puny record so far in this present lifetime (my seven years), incompatible with his true history. Reflecting on this Zurich workshop of May 1992, it was as if that kind of thing happened in reverse.

How was I lifted up like that? It happened in my mind. Where my mind went (or how, if such was the case, it had been entered), I did not know. I knew nothing but that it had become a *location*. Preexisting. Alternately, if this explanation didn't work, it had dissolved and reentered a preexisting location.

Alternately still, then, I had merged with a still-existing memory or been transported into some electrical field where it could be contacted or entered. A field where electrical storage took place. Or could somehow take place. Unless of course we swoop down into this dimension and getting more literal say that I myself had something to do with it. But we don't say that.

I was on the Road to Damascus. (Yes, we all know that wasn't me.)

. . . abruptly—no focus on why or how—suddenly thrust into the magnetic moment. Not so many years after I had this experience, in 2000 I stumbled upon German-born American physicist Walter Elsasser's marvelous *Reflections on a Theory of Organisms*, in which he questions where cerebral memory is stored. Elsasser obtained his doctorate in physics under the great Max Born at the University of Göttingen, Germany. In *Reflections* he searched for a nonmechanical *transfer-of-information* mechanism that might account for the survival of the species millions of years, which purely mechanical information transfer would seem to prohibit.

Elsasser was a precursor. More recently, controversial Cambridge-trained biologist Rupert Sheldrake picked up the topic. He spent eleven years in India as Principal Plant Physiologist at the International Crops Research Institute for the Semi-Arid Tropics (ICRISAT),[64] and it was while "living in a palm-fringed hut under a banyan tree," as he recollected, "that he decided to set out his decade's worth of thinking about memory being a function of time, not matter, shared by all living things." This resulted in his theory of *morphogenetics*.[65] He noted that we know "the idea of fields extending beyond the material objects in which they are rooted: for example magnetic fields extend beyond the surfaces of magnets . . . likewise, the fields of our minds extend far beyond our brains."[66]

But still not clarifying how I stepped into the intensified instant in recorded history, disorienting "the clock."

So we are now (I am now) walking down Memory Lane. Of a moment, I am stopped. All time, all movement, stops. The energy doesn't stop. It takes over space-time, which stops. And enters it here. It is the only space-time I can *feel*.* There is a rippling, waving atmosphere, which indicates, I think, an electrical medium.

All I was able to know for sure had happened—and I knew it, for sure—was the isolated, carved-out instant. Brought living, quivering, from wherever it had been. As if Cayce was right, that our thoughts and actions were stored in an energetic akashic records "library."

Or as if you could touch a point in a brain—say, my brain—and electrically stimulate it to reveal this memory to me. (Not, of course, what happened here.)

It just "appeared," knocking the rest of time lopsided. Suddenly, I was pinned down, localized in the revitalized segment of awareness. The instant of it. The heightened atmosphere that lifted it. And the energized moment recorded (or needled) into some medium I contacted as if it were in my own brain.

Stronger than a physical brain. Evidently, an akashic soul record. But whatever it was, I received—rather, encountered, *re*-encountered, met as if a living soul—*this instant.*

As if an electronic needle were replaying it LIVE in my brain, which knew such computations or vibrations.

Now all "I" was able to experience was being struck down. I next experienced—recorded in the surviving and reentering awareness—one thing. That I need not worry

---

* There is no beginning, no end. This is the beginning and the end, the whole unit. Isolated. Total. Eternal. I am there. I am it—even That. It is the essence of I am That I Am. Forever, in having consciously, physically embodied, experienced it, or been transported to it, walked inside. I didn't bring up the subject of How? No one would have thought of speaking. Not in such a vibration. The rippling, of course, may be a transformation of the feel of energy as a wave.

myself with forcing :

Computer PK

myself onto my legs, standing up. I did not

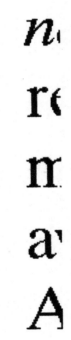

Computer PK

need to struggle to my feet and stand. In the bit of energy that

remained for motion. That was a difficult perusal, in the options I

might think of. But the thought alone struck me. I knew (in

awareness) that all I needed was to raise myself only to the knees.

And to pray.

Decades later, I learned that followers of famous second-century Egyptian Gnostic Valentinus assert that he received—through Theudas, a part St. Paul's inner circle—esoteric teachings from that blinding Damascus moment. Initiations Paul kept secret.

"We today know nothing about them," I concluded in the previous volume. But I think in 2013: *Now, wait a minute. Did my magnetic moment in May 1992 have to do with this esoteric teaching? Did I only think it had no context? Was the experience (back in the second century as well as the first) somehow, somewhere, traveling to the twentieth?*

Again, I am reminded of how the Little Dot of myself, my soul, that I saw in my first out-of-body experience was traveling—with such concentration. To where? From where? I didn't know. Don't know. A determined dot that was me. That's all I knew. Or thought I knew.

The second thrusting-aside of time—into a moment energized and forever alive (but stored where? with what caretaker?)—came at the same workshop. Now again, during Maitri breathwork, I was thrust into a moment. Just as famous.

One dare not imagine it could ever be shared. It wasn't. No one else was in the mind I was in. I just stepped in. Or (again) it into me, whichever (and I don't yet answer, though a reader might). I cannot begin to speak of the profundity of such moments, except we all know they are. I did not even once until now recount them outside the workshop.

This time the moment, captured in infinity or wherever, likewise came unaccompanied by its past (except that I knew it), with no future invoked. It was stopped in time—the moment of the death of Jesus.

All I took away, again, was an awareness—with no follow-up. No prior thought. Just the descent of the once-recorded, so private instant: "Into Thy hands, O God, I commend my Spirit." The moment of saying the words. The moment they left the lips, the feel as they passed through the throat, the meaning.

We are told there were then thunderclaps. Death. The instant I experienced stopped. I did not see the surroundings. Only felt the quivering, vibrating awareness. As if on some lake or pond where the energy was the ripples. And the experience the stone that dropped into the water.

Or as if some Brownian motion sustained the lifetime of the memory, as if no quantum decay occurred but it was held up on the waters of living time. And thus, somehow able to retain and reestablish its intensity and quality. Its message. Firsthand. Because in the tone of experience itself. Is this possible?

10

Gnosis and Little Rock

Like Jung, I came upon the Gnostic-style, personal-experience lineage without prior reading. I did not really grasp the significance of the Gnostics while at the Institute. Fine and good. But when I look back now, I could well have been a Gnostic in those days in Zurich, which I kept secret so long, and in the 1990s in Tienen.

And then, what should happen but that even the Gnostic line led right back to a secret Paul, whose teachings from the Road to Damascus initiation he dared not reveal except to a few.

The question I'm asking now is whether I only thought I received in 1992 *merely* a magnetic *moment* but in fact received a larger transmission. But that part I didn't see. Not then. It was inserted into me, circulating in my cells, which were absorbing these new instructions, as it were. What followed or preceded the moment I encountered perhaps entered my cells through the single scene and went underneath into the unconscious.

Crept like the worm I couldn't shake out of my system as a child, when it bore into my foot. Though tiny, I can just remember how repeated freezing in the doctor's office was unsuccessful. Still, it plodded on in visible tracks. As if the symbol in the child's foot had been jumping in ahead of time, staking out territory—that live worm, a prefiguration. A symbolic precursor. Of this. Forecasting this symbolic "wormhole" worm? Slipped out of the collective unconscious to show my physical—then psychical—vulnerability to such a terrain-breaking symbol?

So did molecules or particles carry this history into my bloodstream, into my brain, into my patterns? Was I now inhabited by a secret *knowing* from the past? And how did I get into the line of it? Or did I plan to? Gave consent, just as in the kundalini moment in California? Because, say, I said I would take on the lifetime of St. Paul accompanied by the Magdalene, whatever that meant.

So what *did* that mean and how would I be "contacted"? Surely things wouldn't unfold along those lines all by themselves.

Later a psychic I would greatly respect, AnKaRa, told me my consciousness was "passed through a prism" before birth—in that way "set." She didn't give details, saying she wasn't talking to my ego. That meant, I assumed, my nonego didn't need clues. I can see a big billowing sheet of consciousness it was possible to go through to focus your awareness. Did being passed through "a prism" assure that certain perspectives had depth? I thought so. But even so?

My speculations have been right before, when I wrote without understanding a word. That is, consciously. But followed tracks. Fascinated with the trails. And believed myself. Of course, who is that? Who am I listening to that I call myself? And is this the Self?

Jungian Remo Roth will tell us ahead that to him the Self today is like *two* "immersed continents": not only the Logos Self but also a divine feminine Eros Self—which are "deeply introverted God-images" he identifies with the king and queen of hermetic alchemy.[67]

In *Keep This Quiet!* III, I focused down on a jabberwocky dream term from 1981: *I found myself in a Jung "museum" (fictional); an assistant of his signaled to me the most-fruitful topic there: bipod metalism.*

I later took the term, in particular the "bi-" aspect, to imply the alchemical tension of opposites, with "metalism" clearly relating to the transformation of lead into gold in alchemy, which Jung equated symbolically with the path of individuation into wholeness. Though any number of *pairs in my life* could express this tension, can we stack up a few leading contenders?

The Mars-Neptune conjunction (in astrology) for starters. And the St. Paul-Magdalene combination. Also, not to forget Richard Unger's hand analysis, which pinned my life purpose on the accomplished/

least-evolved split. Now add in the Logos-Eros Self? This to lead out
of the collective unconscious, or unus mundus.

It looks as if we have landed back in some questions left unanswered in *Keep This Quiet!* III.

About time.

But is there more to add?

Who wants to dive into the speculative new findings? But first
back to Lunevillelaan (Moonville Lane). 1992.

I accepted Jyoti's invitation to co-organize an Easter workshop in
Leuven, Belgium, led by herself and Russell, and a meditation/pre-
sentation/shaktipat energy transfer led by Shri Asha Ma, the spiritual heir to the 115-year old Hindu satguru Dhyanyogi-ji (born in
nineteenth-century India in 1878. The events would take place in
1993, with the assistance of Asha Ma's husband, Deepakji (soon to
be renamed Dileepji).

Meanwhile, I received a *Yoga Journal* article. Its headline read:
"TODAY IN THE WEST WE TALK OF THE GODDESS RETURNING. IF IN-
DIA'S 'DIVINE MOTHERS' ARE ANY INDICATION, SHE IS BRINGING HER
DAUGHTERS WITH HER, AND IN FULL FORCE."[68]

In an unprecedented shift, leading Hindu gurus, it explained,
were handing the mantle of succession to women: "Ramakrishna
passed his to his wife, Sarada Devi; Paramahansa Yogananda to the
American-born Daya Mata; Sivananda to the Canadian Sivananda
Radha; Upansi Baba to Godavari Mataji; Swami Paramanda to his
niece, Gayatri Devi; Swami Lakshmana (Ramana Maharshi's pre-
mier disciple) to the rebellious young Mathru Sri Sarada; Dhyanyogi
Madhusudandas to Asha Ma; and Siddha Yoga master Swami
Muktananda to Gurumayi Chidvilasananda."

The article described the rocky, sometimes violent road to this transition—in contrast to several centuries ago, when there was male-female equality. Asha Ma, the article recounts, met Dhyanyogi at fourteen, when she had fallen into such a trance while saying mantras to the goddess at a ceremony that no one could wake her. Her father hurried her to Dhyanyogi-ji, who, upon seeing her, said, "This is the one I've been waiting for!" and brought her back to consciousness.

In Belgium, I continued private sessions with my energy teacher, Chris Van de Velde, with whom I'd been studying "Inner Landscaping," a form of "Basic Applications of Psycho-Dynamics" (1988–1991). Early in 1992 I began "Awakening Your Light Body" with Raja Yoga and self-knowledge teacher Roland Verschaeve. More on that later. Sometimes Willy's twelve-year-old daughter, Coralie Vanluyten, came to play. I continued to bond with my outspoken dachshund Snoepie.

I hear in my head while writing this, softly in great, moving depth, "Each day in my life was a lifetime."

I lost contact with Hunter after '91. Then at a particular instant before the festival I felt certain I'd connected with someone powerfully, electrically. I was not sure whom. Or maybe I was.

It was on that incentive, that motive energy, that I wrote Hunter the oddest letter I ever mailed him. Perhaps the oddest he ever got. I explained that on my visit to Owl Farm in May 1991, I'd had a kundalini throat opening in the living room with him, prompted—instigated—by him. The letter also mentioned the existence of "Jesus" and "Magdalene" cells, and how he and I had one. How we used to "swim in electricity baths." Who knows what he thought? I hope he destroyed it and it's not buried there in his archives. I meant it, of course. It made sense in the atmosphere of spirit committees, which I was in and he was not in.

Digging deeper in my garage boxes in 2014, I found a similar letter to him (among those to many people far and wide with whom I tried to communicate what was going on—that is, the many surprises and shocks to my system and the struggles to develop a consciousness equal to the necessary shifts. I threw myself in and sometimes, being new in working in the Oneness source, sound quite inflated from my current perspective. Yet something was going on. I had to figure it out. And kudos for me that I tried, kept going, got from there out into the bright sunlight that was behind it).

Jung had cautioned never to identify with an archetype. Yet facing a spiritual awakening, many are not guided into such an understanding. If one says "I" and it's a transpersonal archetype that's the subject, tough times are ahead. I didn't do this. Yet I continually felt that if something happened to me, it must be *about* me. Obviously. And that if I had an experience, it must be "my" experience. This actually is not the case when the boundaries of the personal give way.

To Hunter, I wrote June 2, 1992: "Things keep roaring along here. I consulted a psychic on the phone to America [Mariah Martin], just to check, and before I could say anything she said, 'You're in your body now.'"

With intense, raw sensations, I spoke in ways I think naïve today; everything seemed ballooning, huge. I added that—did I mail it?—she mentioned figures in the energy field in the room where the computer PK was: famous names. I insisted that I'd received a *"go signal"* and thought it was for him as well:

> And I'm going to keep saying something is opening for you until I find out if you've got the message. It's the least I can do. For I know if it were the other way round, you'd say hold it, hold it, I promised to tell Margaret something was in the air and that it was hers too, if she wanted it. And that it involved a different consciousness of the Earth, which anyway you've already got. But this one's official and it has do battle to be recognized and it involves energy in high fields and it's not impersonal only.

Hunter's inspiration had stalled, which I didn't know. He wasn't completing journalism assignments. Also, he was still on cocaine. In telling him he had a "go" signal, I would, psychologically speaking, possibly be projecting my animus (inner male energy). But who knows if other connections were astir and there was some bifurcating opportunity in his career that was a stretch, or 90-to-0 shot? I've no idea, but at the time felt sure.

This was in a period where everything was, in one sense, narrowly viewed from my own perspective, while blown up to lionesque proportions—a battle for the future of the planet and other intense things, which, given what's going on in the twenty-first century, sounds rather like a herald of the times. I wrote a poem, "Leaders of the Transition," and so forth. I was immersed and kept diving.

Obviously in way over my head, I had no framework for the experiences coming in through the unconscious. Put another way, I'd dived into a lode. I felt drawn to the consciousness, as puzzle pieces fit here and there most fascinatingly.

To Chris Van de Velde the same day (did I mail it or not?): "I have to write this to someone. I can hardly hold it. I'm shaking so, but it's not trembling, it's *holding* an energy. Like almost I'm gasping and then I'd want to sob. . . . I asked the psychic what I was doing and she said helping bring in a higher consciousness of the Earth and that as I got more into my body I could ground more of me."

Actually, this was true of so many people it could be a generic statement. But when it's happening to you, it can feel quite momentous and intently personal, as it did to me then. I wrote:

Multitudes in Song
of
the GATE OF DEATH OF EGO
GATE
O
appearing often as
GATE EAU

The word play is on *gâteau* [got tow] from "Le Gâteau"/"The Cake" by French poet Baudelaire. "Eau" (water) is pronounced "O" (in French). *Gate Eau* backwards is Watergate.

In the summer of '92, I attended classes, at Tobias School of Art (England). Even at Tobias the uncanny wasn't far off. A young American flew in from the East Coast to visit his girlfriend (who was in my clay sculpture class); I showed him my poem "Invocation to Masters of the Past." Taking it away to Cape Cod, he afterwards told me by phone he'd read it at events—it needs to be read aloud, he said.

Normal-seeming in every way, with blond good looks, Charlie was maybe fifteen years my junior. Remarkably, he told me he took trips with Jesus. Similarly, my energy teacher Chris Van de Velde could remember himself, as a two-year-old, alone in his crib with the cover over his face, smothering, near sudden death. In an instant a man saved him. The face, he later recognized in the Ghent Altarpiece, *Adoration of the Mystic Lamb.* The face of Jesus. He remembers flying around out of body as a child. Probably something much more widespread than a lot of people suspect.

When the journal published by the Maison Européenne de la Poésie (European House of Poetry) ran a memorial feature on my late estranged husband, Jan Mensaert, I visited their office in Leuven, Belgium. Very welcoming, the director, a poet, Eugène Van Itterbeek, with a doctorate in law and in literature, almost immediately invited me to participate in a festival— "Europe and the Americas Viewed through a Poet's Eye"—in Sibiu, Romania, October 1–7, 1992; it would be followed immediately by a leg in Leuven.

But then, my new-found little trove of letters in garage boxes, written sometime since being invited to the festival and before September 30, includes a long letter to Hunter that I've extracted from below.

It begins with a nap dream in Zurich in which (as I'd evidently previously told him) I was married to him—a dream that impacted me. However—not mentioned in the letter—this theme, though rare and sporadic, went as far back as March 3–4, 1981. There, in

Morocco, in one of my earliest remembered dreams, I was told by a man—Hunter's publicity agent?—"to write 'Chou de [pronounced Ciao D] Hunter' on my palm and wrist. I agreed." The red ink washed away, but "I could rewrite it each day . . . *I married Hunter*, I said to myself, summing up the dream as if coming back with a report." Then it jumped into the future. Now, a dream of a marriage can have many meanings, but it's important to follow recurring threads to know how much is symbolical, how much, if any, is literal. This undated August/September 1992 letter begins:

> My whole life is changing, . . . Part of it I've told you, but the other part I haven't. I haven't told anybody, in fact. The part you know is that I once dreamed, in a little nap, something I knew was the future. Because I've often done that. And when in such a way, not really asleep, it was always literal. So that was in Zurich. I closed my eyes, fell into a little nap, and in it I was married to you. And I was given advice about what to do if a particular day came.

At this point, I jumped back into my literal biography:

> Then [by chance] I carried out what I thought must have been a symbolic version of the dream [meeting, falling in love with, and moving in with Willy Van Luyten for three years]. Though, as I said, these things had always been literal. Not that they happened too often. Then [Willy], though fifteen years younger than me, died suddenly, driving a car. That was January 6, '91.
>
> The accident looked as if someone put a ruler between the road and a tree and in the dark drove the car into it at top speed. It was impossible to really do that, and even so no one could hold the steering wheel that straight. Anyway, he was the best driver in Belgium. Someone who saw me find the tiny cross at the bottom of the tree, the only piece of the car that had come off it, and saw the straight line, said, "That accident was impossible." So I knew my soul grouping [or some subtle, multidimensional energy, with his unconscious consent] drove the car into the tree, as a lesson. That's a long story . . .

But here is a fairly astounding fact, at least to me:

> *Now, the morning this man I was living with died, before I heard it I sank into a sleep, and it was all lavender. That's when I know it's true. In it I had a period of confusion and then packed up all my belongings to go to the United States to write, or be involved in writing, your story.* (italics added)

This is astounding, considering that it literally foreshadowed my return to the U.S. in late 2001, shortly before Hunter died—three and a half years, in fact. And on solid turf here in North Carolina, soon after his death I began my account (including his letters) of "The Hunter Thompson Story." Just as the dream set me up to do. But how did it know? And would it have happened had I not had this 1991 dream, planting the seed so firmly and mysteriously?

My draft noted: "I've often wondered why I picked out that one thing to dream, that one guideline, waiting to be told Willy was dead. Why did I think it important?"

I brought in the California kundalini episode: "It felt like a cell burst inside me and information poured through me. And as it happened and the memory came in, I kept sensing it as a pair signal. That it was my starting signal. But also that it was meant for you."

Now, this could be entirely projection on my part, and I left the interpretation up to him. But as the impression had come through an intense kundalini episode, I was highly motivated. And even if (which is probable) I was asking him to do something he was not at all available to, the sense of connection likely went deeper. We shall see that this impulse to "tell him" may indeed have another explanation than the one I drew.

The "long story" alluded to above brings in a concept I called "event balls" (see the first appendix). That is, events widely apart in time that synchronistically connect, which may be first announced symbolically, later followed by a literal version. It seems obvious to me that the dream, on the morning of Willy's roughly 4 a.m.

violent death, depicting me setting out into "The Hunter Thompson Story," and the fact that that depiction later materialized prompted by Hunter's death, opens up thought about this concept I was already chewing on.

Remember, this letter may not have been mailed, but once started I went through the whole story.

> The other reason I was putting clues together on this level was that beginning in Zurich I was experimenting in walking into setup energy fields and learning how to hold them. It was my karma to learn that. Because I was always invisibly a carrier. The real vibration couldn't be carried, certainly not by me. That's the vibration of this energy group. And it couldn't be unfelt, not by someone also in the group . . .

I told Hunter he was part of a man who was fighting hard for the planet in another dimension. "He's been the center of my whole life, in different forms. He's taught me and taught me. He's made me learn how true I am." I tell him that inside me is "a memory of how he felt when he looked at Mary Magdalene, 'My heart don't lie.'" (To condense, the next idea being that Jesus focused on a collective mission in ancient times, but there was a personal side to the Christ, colorfully called *tu*-lips, as channeled by me in *The Christ State* in Zurich—that involved, among other objectives, working on the archetype of the couple. And—as Oneness consciousness came to the forefront on the planet—to set down some markers to identify figures in a personal sense, where/if desired:

> To sum up, you're in the energy of a channel to your true being, the one in another dimension that keeps you trying to reach it with coke and so on. You're always reaching up there. Not knowing it's trying to reach down to you. That the trips you could take would be on a reality level far beyond those which you dreamed could be real. They are.

And this one channel is in the storm set for now to guide the Earth into the new century. To bring it in in a new way. This isn't just the Jesus we know . . .

What a joke. What a crazy Gamble.

Willy was the local marijuana seller, a bike rider and the best driver in Belgium . . .

Also, August 7, before or after the above letter:

I never even thought of myself as a gambler, but in that dimension I was one of the best. And I was counted on to learn to bring that part of her [my multidimensional gambler soul] here. That was the deal. And some people were so sure I could do it, they bet everything on it too. Now, these people don't bet unless they're sure. They have aces up every sleeve and they know when to play them. That's what made the highly energized events. They stood in rooms, unseen, and other places, and sent energy. It was nothing but heart energy, caring. They cared and cared and had hearts able to express why they cared. Hearts used before on the Earth to make art with. We knew their names, in many instances. To sum it up and get to the point, some people took on the Archetype of the End of the Century . . .

I had much more to say, but this will do. Of course and quite believably, I told him he was one. Well, why not? Doesn't he fit the bill?

Another short peek into the August 7 confidences to Hunter (mailed or not):

To sum it up and get to the point, some people took on the Archetype of the End of the Century. If a few people could do that and survive, then the whole world would have avoided it. It would only take a person making a certain decision at a certain time to have a very large effect; that is, if it were inside one of these "highly energized events." [An example of a highly energized event was Willy's death; I had first heard the term from Lama Sing.]

What I'm trying to get to is you're one, to start with. You probably don't know it in that way, but you didn't have to. You probably wouldn't have changed a thing, had you known it, for it wasn't the time to. And the big thing was to stay true, in yourself. But now the time has changed. Everything is pushed up to or beyond the limit. These energy fields that were to take on the energy of the End of the Century and make a different future with it are standing in a space that the End of the Century itself is also in. That is, the personal is virtually sharing space with the transpersonal. What that means is that every time they plan something, they have about one chance in nine to pull it off. Because somebody will get the energy first. And the energy is theirs. And it's heart energy. All it is is their memories. How they feel when they remember the most beautiful memories. Held secret in their whole lifetimes and they stand in their whole lifetimes. Not just in a single memory but all of it. They remember me every time I've ever drawn a breath, in this dimension and in that one they stand in. They know me in eternity.

What this had to do with us is about everything, because we lived inside their energy fields without knowing it. You carried a secret . . . It kept telling me to look at it, and at least ask, might it be true and real?

Shall I go on? Let's take a break. Possibly I never mailed this, but there will be time enough to come back to it. It was part of what I lived and breathed in the '90s. Stories from another dimension. Stories channeled through my fingers and into my life every step I took at this time. How could I not tell this story? Yes, it sounds odd to me, a bit crazy. Maybe a lot crazy. But I know I'm not. And it hangs together. Add a pinch of some misunderstanding I probably had and a pinch of symbol and so on. But still, there's a lot that is—shall I say it?—perhaps revelation. So let's take a breather and when the time comes, return to this tale I had walked into that I had been consciously receiving, in different degrees since my Zurich Initiation in 1985.

In some form with some of this information, I suppose, and possibly much more, a letter went out to Hunter. In August. It was to cause me anguish later, wondering how he received it AND WHEN.

A novelist I'd worked with on a *New York Times* best-seller at Random House, Herbert Tarr, wrote me in August—"with a big biggg mazel tov (congratulations!) on placing your work in the International Poetry Festival in Brussels & [Sibiu] 'even with experimentation'— that's simply TERRIFIC."

> After reading ["The Milton Klonsky I Knew"], I who never even heard of him, felt I knew him & wanted him to befriend me too. (& if it makes you feel any better, before leaving NYC, inspired by you, I submitted an article to Commentary's Norman Podhoretz; it was the eulogy I delivered at the memorial service for my professor, a world-famous Bible scholar,[*] which got turned down with: "very charming, but . . ." I wasn't disappointed because I well knew my article hardly measured up to yours—that's the truth, not flattery.)

> Sometimes I had "readings" with Joost Vanhove at Centrum GEA.

I have found a record of a significant one. September 25, 1992 (my birthday)—I titled it "Confirmation of Etrea Material."

---

[*] This was Abraham Joshua Heschel: "I enjoy not only Herbert Tarr's artistry, his very fine humor, but also the moral and religious integrity that lends coherence to his work." Elie Wiesel wrote, "Herbert Tarr is one of the great contemporary humorists. Concerned with the ideas and emotions of our generation, Tarr touches us, he unsettles us" (quoted from the Herbert Tarr North Shore Institute for Adult Jewish Education website).

Joost, a level-headed guy with psychodynamic, light body, and NLP training, the co-owner of the GEA Center with his wife (a psychiatrist trained in classical homeopathy as well as energy work), confirmed that I was indeed inside the energy of a "spirit committee." With his association with Jesus, he was able to add that the group that came to give me the Jesus material were "Etrea energy, which is the energy Jesus was in during his teaching."

I start reading the account of how I got from there to here, who I was in my "Awakening." How I dealt with it. How it felt to me then to have a Close Encounter with my Soul, as it were—with nothing but my intuitive grasp, the overwhelming impact of this energy field; how I felt I must—yes, must—respond, if I, my "ordinary self," were to be true to and honor my Soul. Let's take a look, perhaps hitting the highlights if I can bear to leave anything out.

In the Joost session, he said when he looked at my valise—every time, he saw the face of Jesus. And when I asked if he had comments or suggestions about publishing the material, he said he kept seeing the words "none of your business."

I'm not to get opinions from people very much because . . . who could imagine the intensity? Who could believe in the existence of this group or what it was doing or that I was part of it, normally? Yet there are those who do. Joost totally confirmed the validity, as did Chris, as did Mariah, in different ways entirely, each of them.

So this group no one knows about [I thought; certainly I didn't; certainly my Duke University required Bible class made not the slightest mention of even the principle; nowhere near it] is spreading their energy more widely, and everything I know and have to say is inside that energy, because I got it from him [i.e., in the Zurich Initiation] before even from them [the spirit committee in Tienen in the 1990s]. So all I have to say is . . . prepared for. I only have to find a way and pace and hold on tight to belief. I have over and over to step aside and not question why I am in this position.

I supposed I had at last reached the place where, according to Lama Sing years before, my soul grouping was broadcasting and spreading the Christ consciousness, a message about "the universality of humanity." Below, I dare to write to myself—for who else could I tell? And I couldn't just stuff the thoughts passing through my mind, inside, in which case I would implode—very esoteric speculations that follow from everything above:

> Joost said I have old ties with the large group, from flying with them. This also confirms an intuition that I already know this material and that who I *wasn't concretely*, I nevertheless *felt* I was, for I was in the energy; I might even have been the source of something historically on record without ever having been in [I stop and turn the page with interest. I've no idea what's on the next page, what I wrote, the kind of intensity and absolute certainty this energy held me in back then] the body who lived it. I might then really have [I speculated about ties with Mary Magdalene not just on the energetic level, of plugging in now, but on the level of having been in the energy]. But that's not so important to others—I can keep it for myself—as the idea right now is that this is a pattern others can use.

Ah ha, now I'm the one my past self is talking to; we usually try to get in touch with and learn from our "future self," but here I dust off that self who lived, isolated, in that Lunevillelaan apartment in the '90s, soaking up nonstop initiation and channeling on a scale I haven't come close to since. What did she dare to think? I want to know, rediscover it in the perspective of what happened since.

> So if I speak from the energy, no one perhaps has to know why I was [channeling] in it before it became widespread . . . Why it came to be, because it knew me, and because the field I've always lived in, historically, when it became an Earth field, would have me in it. I had to discover me. I had to step aside when the energy

came through me, not knowing it was in me anyway because I used to be part of it collectively. Joost pointed out that I had a sense of wanting to be individual and yet also this old sense of being part of things collectively and that people just were. That enlightenment was for everyone, and so on.

He said I had an overdose of the astral now. And that in the future I could learn to handle such an experience better. That is, not to be so open to the many influences possible at once. He had said, immediately, when I came into the room and was thinking: *It's my birthday; this is the wrong signal to myself, about how to get information now,* "You're going to conduct this session."

So as I sum it up for myself, I was in the same energy Jesus was in for his work and felt, when I energize, that my hands must go up and they must heal. That they can. They know they are made for that. The energy is conscious of its purpose. And its nature. Its character. The particular feelings that compose it in this moment. It's a healing and very serious energy. It's not my personal energy I felt, when I BELL began to be expectant and was joyful and light, like champagne bubbles . . . I can't say how deep. And perhaps it's me who is choosing now to hold him physically . . .

I'm definitely in his energy now. He knows who he is. And I can recognize it.

Just before leaving for Romania, I phoned Jyoti and Russ in California; they were traveling; their office told me, "Hey, we're holding a *Rolling Stone* magazine to forward to you." With rising emotion, I yelled, "Send it on!" I wondered if a note would be inside. There was. It would be a second dynamics intersecting the Romanian one. As the note made its transatlantic crossing, I went to the festival.

In Romania, I had encounters with leading literary lights. I felt my soul grouping was pulling all plugs out. Mariah had said, "Publication is all set up. *They like to surprise you.*"

Romania was an adept sponsor of festivals, as in the Communist era a passport was not permitted ordinary citizens. Also, even in 1991, in view of their lei currency and low standard of living, even the most educated had little chance of traveling abroad, except by paid invitation to conferences. So they brought the world to their doorstep.

Arrived in Sibiu to read my "Invocation to Masters of the Past in the Light of the Past, Come, All Ye Singers," I had a stroke of inspiration. I asked several people to point out who was mystical. Everyone directed me to a tall, thin man my age, Mihai Ursachi. In 1981 he'd fled Romania under the ruthless Communist dictator Nicolae Ceauşescu; sometime thereafter he became a doctoral candidate in literature in the U.S.

I wanted Mihai to advise me how much of my lengthy poem to read. He said read the whole thing. He revealed that while imprisoned as a dissident he'd been six months *underground* in solitary, not expected to survive—though sometimes a guard, breaking the rules, talked to him. Alone with a single dim light bulb, he had spiritual experiences he described a bit to me, in particular involving Pythagoras. He found my poetry much like his own. Coincidentally, just prior to this trip, I'd bought a fancy leather briefcase; the label said, "Pythagoras." Mihai begins "Chance Disavowed" (translated by Adam Sorkin and Lidia Vianu):

We, the promised moments,
have always existed on other planets
or even distant constellations which
not one of our eyes' rays strikes.
. . . .

And concludes:

> Oh, these specks of cosmic dust which once,
> just once, had been Me,
> will they repudiate forever the chance
> by chance disavowed?

Industrial Landscape with Insect (translated by Adam Sorkin)

> Moment by moment. Millions of tons.
> The stone's heart burns—steel
> pours out in a stream, like milk
> from a milk pail. The thunder of flame.
>
> Tick, tick, tick . . .
> the ant's heart in the fire-red night.

"Elsewhere, Ursachi is even more expansive, linking himself with artists, languages, media, and catastrophes in all ages because 'every speck lost in the extragalactic / void, in the worlds of Anti-Being, carries within it the seeds, the glory / of my march to the stars.'"[69]

Wearing a ten-gallon hat, he escorted me around. He won the festival prize for best poem. In 2001, Ursachi would be Romania's Nobel Prize nominee in literature.

As colorfully summarized by translator Adam J. Sorkin, after his defection, Mihai "wound up in California (teaching swimming) and then Austin, Texas, where, while learning English (which he had not studied) and working as a garage mechanic (for which he'd had no training) and a German instructor at the University of Texas, he put himself through graduate school, subsequently teaching part-time at the University of California, La Jolla, for four years." In Romania again he became a controversial Director of the National Theater in Iasi.[70]

"He returned [to Romania] after the December 1989 revolution and, in 1992, was awarded the first national Mihai Eminescu Poetry

Margaret with Mihai and goat herders

Prize since World War II."[71]

I met the reclusive poet Mircea Ivănescu, also scarred by Communism (winner of the lifetime achievement Medaille d'Or), another Nobel Prize nominee, and Ion Mircea, the festival's cohost.

As in Rome in 1985, I felt that an extra-romantic film had been spread around me by my soul grouping and that the natural affinities of these Romanians made it easy to fit in. This led, in particular, to a very strong attraction to one (not Mihai or Ivănescu). In short, I was blown away by the reception I received. A number of invited writers became my friend, including Roberto Sanesi, "one of the most remarkable Italian writers of his generation" (*The Guardian* obituary) and U.S. poet laureate Mark Strand.

Ion Mircea, the Romanian festival organizer, editor of a literary review, *Transilvania*, soon wrote, astonished, "I recently met Mihai in Bucharest. He confirmed that he is translating your poems and he promised me he will send the text here in Sibiu." He added that Ivănescu was likewise translating "Invocation to Masters of the Past." And: "I now try to find, for these versions—Ursachi's and Ivănescu's—a place to publish them—of course, it will be one of the most important literary reviews in Romania." A few months later he would write again, "Be happy, please, you have been translated in Romanian by two of the most important poets at this hour—Mircea Ivănescu and Mihai Ursachi."

Below, Mihai translates the opening of *Love in Transition* III: *The Christ State*. I love the look of it and the sounds, the choice of font; it all seems exquisite to me. It begins:

Extra, extra, read all about it—
the end of the world
everywhere bombs were going off,
people waking up,
the end of the world

Robert died.
It was the end of the world.

Extra, extra, citii totul despre asta –
sfârșitul Lumii
Peste tot sună alarma,
oamenii trezindu-se
așteptând semnalul acesta,
sfârșitul Lumii
așteptându'l să vină,
sfârșitul Lumii

Robert a murit
Acesta a fost sfârșitul Lumii

              *

   *   *

Oameni trezindu-se
alarme interioare declanșându-se
sunete din planul astral
un bărbat din planul astral sunând
clopoțelul de cină
zicând că se dă de mâncare pentru masse
omul acela trebuia să vină la masă
întâlniți'l acolo la cină
mâncarea'ndelung așteptată e gata
numai că'i pentru micul dejun
ca'n vremile biblice
dintr'un pește îi saturi pe toți
micul dejun e gata pentru Vremea cea Nouă
și micul-dejun al Vremii celei Noi
fu tot ce avu omul

            *

   *   *

Micul dejun al Vremii celei Noi
tocmai se prepara
Acum totul se potrivea

          *

   *   *

Mihai's translation

Back in Belgium, I was aflush with excitement. But what should be waiting but the forwarded *Rolling Stone* issue? As the Bill Clinton/ President George H. W. Bush/Ross Perot battle for the presidency was raging, *Rolling Stone* featured—in its September 17 issue—an interview with Clinton, by William Greider, P. J. Rourke, and Hunter S. Thompson. Clinton, in a nod to young voters, was wearing khakis, a shirt with short sleeves, and running shoes. In "MEMO FROM THE NATIONAL AFFAIRS DESK, DATE: August 4th, '92," Hunter wrote:

> I have just returned, as you know, from a top-secret *Issues Conference* in Little Rock with our high-riding Candidate—Bill Clinton—who is also the first-term Governor of Arkansas and the only living depositor in the Grameen Bank of Bangladesh who wears a ROLLING STONE T-shirt when he jogs past the hedges at sundown.
>
> Ah, yes—the *hedges*. How little is known of them, eh? And I suspect, in fact, that the truth will never be known . . . I wanted to check them out, but it didn't work. My rented Chrysler convertible turned into a kind of *Trojan Horse* in reverse . . .

There followed a hilarious account of Clinton's Doe's Eat Place two-and-a-half-hour meeting—attended by the three journalists and Jann Wenner, with an assortment of Secret Service and staff. A photo is captioned: DR. THOMPSON PONDERS CLINTON'S CALL FOR MORE COPS IN THE STREET. In his half-slapstick, half-serious assessment, it was, finally, advisable to vote for Clinton. OK, I would take his advice. But I was focused on the shocker—that inserted into the magazine was a sheet of paper containing a bolt-out-of-the-blue typed message to me. An invitation from Hunter. It asked, ordered, invited, "Meet me in Little Rock election night. You are just the person I need."

I calculated that having been parked in California, it probably crossed with my latest letter. Would he have invited me if he'd read that first? In *Keep THIS Quiet Too!* I remembered this quandary— and assumed the letter in question was the one about how he and I "swam in electricity baths." Which upon retrospect embarrassed me greatly. But as we now know, I recently discovered, in boxes in my garage, no lack of potentially embarrassing drafts. For instance, August 7. In hindsight, that embarrassed me even more. On the other hand, I do not really know anymore what letters (to anyone) are unsent (talking to myself) and which the final version. But I am pretty sure I exercised a good amount of pragmatism in what actually got into the mail during this Awakening period, knowing I was way over the line as to how a lot of my old friends saw me and what they could accept (I thought). But as said, who knows? And anyway, in another way, come to think of it, I'd been way over the line in my life with Jan Mensaert in Morocco. It's pretty sure that I did send, though, the one about "swimming together in electricity baths"—off planet sometime in the past.

I am looking at a cassette tape—from 1992. It helps me remember the quandary Hunter's invitation plunged me into.

The plastic container lies open: "M Harrell c/o Hunter Thompson, Woody Creek Rd., Woody Creek Colo 85616." Inside had been a phone reading with Mariah Martin, May 1991.

It's erased. Coralie, Willy's daughter, taped over it. In the background paper is crackling, my dachshund Snoepie is barking, my voice is insisting *not to erase the tape!!!*

She was eleven. She loved loud music, her favorite foods—spinach *stumpf* (spinach-filled mashed potatoes) with *Boudin noir* (blood sausage)—and visiting me. The death of her father, Willy, precipitated the arrival of the bell, and it often rang during her visits. Everyone said she was like him.

Though the '91 reading, # 85616, was overwritten, the November '92 portion, containing a reading a year and a half later, is intact.

The tape reinforced, which I had guessed, that in my belief at the time Hunter was in my soul grouping. I referred to that fact in the surviving portion, '92.

Look at what opposite species we were—*if* it was true. Imagine the stretch of consciousness that ran from his to mine. Hunter violently repelled hypocrisy. That would be sourced in the pool. Mercurial, denouncing hypocrisy. Some of the rest, for sure, he made up. And so now we were "friends." But at what depth.

It could evolve. Not in this lifetime. But hold on. We are just in 1992.

Detoured to California, the Little Rock invitation idled un-urgent. It was there in the waiting mail when I arrived from Romania. Opening it, what did I find? Hunter at his best, inviting me confidently, tersely, cutting to the chase, *to meet him "in Little Rock."* That was it. Not a word more.

I stop and laugh hilariously. Could any comedian, any trickster, any Gonzo conflict inciter, plan anything more far-fetched, star-crossed, embarrassing, open-ended, to test what the result would be? And then watch the players try to squirm out of it or embrace it? Hunter added that I was *"just the person"* he needed. *I took it to mean needed in Little Rock on election night 1992.*

It was a mysterious conclusion or challenge to the in-person part of a twenty-five-year history. Receiving his invitation, I felt stage fright, identity fright. Fear that I wouldn't have the gumption to stand up for myself with him, no matter what. Fear he wanted to rekindle a relationship, and I'd just started one!

Repeatedly writing the long *unmailed* letter in California in

1991, I'd intuited I had to hurry because of what was going to happen *to me*—as if the part of me insistent on reaching him would not be "around" much longer, not speak for me? Thus, my hyperintense sessions at the typewriter till finally something went into the mail. And wasn't he *moving out of reach too*?

I had cold feet—apprehensive—regarding the hotel room extravaganza I might find myself in. By October 8, I no longer felt like flinging myself back into the relationship (if that option opened up). Did not feel confident that looking at him, I could say *no* to Hunter about anything. Perhaps most of all afraid because I'd mailed the "absurd" letter, hinting at our multidimensional history to the point I suspected it. Or imagined it.

Afraid I wouldn't get the chance to explain recent developments.

Which did not preclude my going, if—a long shot, a risk, a hairpin curve on a motorcycle going one hundred in the dark—it was on a high frequency. Then no explanation needed. I didn't want to stay in smoky rooms where who knew what might be going on, up to what wee hours.

But maybe he wanted me to keep him on track writing! Command him to turn out copy. Whatever he intended, I felt it was inspired by the deep second in the electricity that pushed me to mail my letter, a second in time that said, *we can pull this off.*

I remembered the purple soul energy enveloping the bed the last night at Owl Farm—when, sitting up in the other room, he was finishing watching Mae West on TV, perversely knowing something hadn't come out right. After that, what insights seeped into him in bed in sleep?

I had thought none. But reflecting now, I see that it perhaps explains his mood the next day. Poised in that chair, holding the book, he signed it—looking up to mention again what he called his "mistake," not clarifying. I knew, or could guess. *My mistake equally.* Then he handed over to me, in a last gesture, *Songs of the Doomed* signed by various personas—Hunter, HST, and H, though not Raoul Duke.

But let's assume all of the above didn't matter—didn't hold a candle to the hunches we would follow in skillfully interacting (it seemed unlikely)—how on earth could I squeeze myself into such a time crunch? For to be with Hunter meant being *fully* in the room. What if having just begun a new emotional chapter with a different male—and a whole country—I packed up and flew in?

Still, that's only half the story. I recently turned up a 1992 letter—telling someone in North Carolina *I was going to Little Rock to cover the election!*

Well, Hunter's invitation did surprise me, with no time to switch gears. Where in Little Rock??? Nowhere, it turned out.

Ralph Steadman's wonderful 2006 memoir, *The Joke's Over*, describes Hunter's disastrous visit to London September 4, 1992—accompanied by blond girlfriend/assistant, Nicole, who "struggles to control a trolley which groans under the weight of six large cases, half of the doctor's equipage for the five-day visit." At the Metropole Hotel he retreated into his Stevenson Suite, refusing to leave for Scotland—eluding journalists there to ensure he wrote a story on the Royal Family for the *Observer*. The invitation to me must have been sent near the time of that trip.

I received it belatedly—and dawdled, postponed answering. Hunter in fact was in Little Rock election eve, with—Nicole. Just as my life kept moving, so did his.

Well, now that I've speculated and tried to re-create, I found drafts of letters, October 23 and November 9—fueled by the *Rolling Stone* note. And a small trove more. They knock aside the speculation. Who was I then? What did I think? Let's see.

The Leuven leg of the festival ended about October 15. Yet I still hadn't answered. (This is not the way I remembered it.)

But the letter October 23 is clear as day. That draft explains, I'd been "exploring Eastern Europe and would enjoy talking to you about it."

Behind all this [participation in the Leuven leg of the festival], I kept remembering your invitation to meet you in little Rock.

What a crazy idea, and how in the spirit we've known each other in. How very right to just meet like that. I was glad, because I'd wondered if you'd accepted some of the really far-out things I'd been writing to you. Or if not, which was fine, if it had at least been considered interesting and perhaps courageous. Anyway, I'd kept that belief you'd keep a place for me as a very special friend

Now I haven't phoned in that period of the Festival and perhaps you have [I had no answering machine] or if not expected me to. But I kept the invitation close to me [who knew?]. And the joy that you walked that road you did, holding a hand firm whenever I reached for it. And that you evidently understand my hand was always there for you too . . .

So how is *Polo?*

Then the computer interrupted my printout, the bell rang, and I told him what was going on, suggesting he write a script: "As a comedy, it would be nonstop roller-coaster intensity. BELL."

I can imagine your style of half tongue-in-cheek, half eyeball-popping-out amazement, blow by blow. And underneath, the seriousness.

Well, that's a script suggestion . . . And I can imagine supervising the movie in Hollywood, sunglasses and all. Back to The Continental [hotel we had rendezvoused in].

As for the November 9, '92, draft, it said lamely, "Sorry we didn't get together on the Little Rock Thing. I was totally exhausted after the poetry festival," etc. Except that of note, considering how his life ended, I again hoped his back was getting better.

How flat, after the geyser outburst that preceded it. Nowhere did I mention, naturally, that I had started a new relationship—during the very time his letter sat waiting in my unpicked-up Tienen mail. Similar to the timing of Hunter's letter to me in '69, forwarded to Germany while I was getting engaged, which began, "Ho Ho and

late again." Indeed. He had waited right till the moment I was "tak-
en." For better or ill.

The new relationship I'd started was lyrical, with sporadic elements of Johnny Cash ("We got married in a fever" in fact played
coincidentally in the background as we walked into a nice hotel). It
was a now-and-then situation, however. Lovely, all the same.

But in a short year and a half so much had happened. Our paths
diverged—on this level. It appeared I ignored Hunter's invitation.
And thinking how he might read that, I assumed he'd given up on
the idea, now cooling in dying embers, the delay having been fatal. I
also thought someone else had walked into the opportunity.

I did believe he was in this soul grouping that was guiding me,
irony of ironies. Because he was probably a big figure in it, he could
surely invent an original lifetime. And was that the person who was
telling me it was not what "I planned," sitting in that chair in '91?

Was his soul speaking then, and I didn't get it? For hadn't I written that the Christ sent some of his top lieutenants into the shadow
to see what could be turned up, to aid our survival in the coming
Big Shift, when there would be out-of-control events? One doesn't
change archetypes except with a big throttle thrust from unexpected
quarters. Who better to help humanity out with shockers?

Hunter went to Little Rock. He wrote his editor: "The Fun
Begins . . . M E M O R A N D U M. 12/4/92. Re: Bad News."

He said: "I have tried and utterly failed, Bobby, to figure out how
a smart person could whine and jabber day & night about 'the desperate need for at least some pages about anything that happened in
Little Rock on ELECTION NIGHT.'" He continued: "But what the
fuck am I suppose to think when I see that YOU have very shrewdly
cut (dropped, deleted, excised (sp?) 'edited out') the only two pages
I've sent that have anything to do with real events that occurred on

either the DAY or the NIGHT of November 3 at Clinton headquarters in Little Rock (see attached/below Pages 26 & 27—which I wrote & planned & intended to be my LEAD INTO Election Day/Night)."

His editor, Bob Love, called these deadline episodes "part Mardi Gras part falaqua . . . There came a time, however, when the stars aligned—Hunter would find his muse and settle himself down for serious work."[72]

11

Little Rock

Whether I mailed my ruminations about his out-of-the-blue invitation or not, in late October or early November, I left a message on his machine; afterwards, another. This last—when I began to get personal—was cut into by a voice that said, "End of Tape. Call back later."

A human being or a mechanical robot? It sounded like a tape. Or was it Hunter, disguised, breaking in as the speaker phone broadcast the message into the kitchen, where people listened—friends and/or his new girlfriend—an awkward moment? The Prankster salvaging a prank. I thought so.

So I had bombarded him—mailed or not. He had stepped up to the plate. And what did I do? Ran the other way. Well, one reason was the new relationship. For another, I was overwhelmed. I had enough sense to know that what I had to say would sound absurd. But then, I wasn't a physical being only. How could I turn my back on the rest of me? Also, of course, this is part of being initiated through the unconscious. You walk blindfolded. You haven't any clarity where you are, what an outside view might look like. That is, an informed outside view. From Wisdom. But you can't let go. This is too serious. The call to Destiny. That's how I felt. I couldn't let my soul down. There was also a spirit being—sometimes I called him the Christ—pouring energy into me. Or it was coming from somewhere. I couldn't say: *oh, energy far more powerful than me, I turn my back on you.* I just couldn't. Because love threaded through it.

Much else was on my mind, though. On my plate. All in high intensity.

Then I returned from the festival, and Hunter had "bitten," calling me to Arkansas. And I was abashed at all my outpourings. I couldn't stand in them in front of him. Yet, I believed them. What to do?

So I woke with amnesia. No.

However, I don't remember. Not for some sinister reason. But because now, after a full life, I would have to keep track of so much if to pull it all back up. Who was I then? Let's have an introduction. *Hello, tell me what you think I wrongly put out of my mind, left out of the picture, erroneously even believed happened differently.* Let my detective self come into play.

Oh, you don't think this makes sense? Well, try it on yourself sometime. Test your memory. Test if what you've remembered one way is in fact who you were decades ago. And whether that younger self actually was wise and smart in ways you think you've outgrown. But to your detriment. We are all like that to different degrees. *Centuries too.*

And so I peered into the haze of the past, peered through the haze to where actual typed pages had something to say. And say it definitively. Oh, I could add psychology today for perspective. But let's don't. Let's face the facts cold. The pieces of paper holding them.

My letters during this period, mostly unmailed, sum up some of the feelings whose intensity is indescribable . . . Perhaps they're [the Etrea energy] asking me to carry this [channeling of messages] or this man, to let him live in me [the inner Christ], and at the same time there's the invitation from Hunter, if it's serious, that's also bringing this to a point. Hector too [one of my plans was to return again to Guadalajara for six months].

It must be about my Little and Big Self.

12

Dhyanyogi-ji

I began organizing the Jyoti/Russ "Healing through Sound and Image" workshop and the events for Dhyanyogi-ji and his spiritual heir, Shri Asha Ma (later renamed Anandi Ma, which is what I will call her), to take place in Belgium, Friday–Sunday, April 9–11, 1993. Easter weekend—*in a Catholic country*, where pharmacies close for seven days! I bought cast-iron, enamel-coated pots for her food to be cooked in.

I was primed for the experience. Anandi Ma would lead shaktipat (energy transfer) into the Lord Rama, or Ram, tradition. (From then on, you are in the lineage led by the guru who carries it.)

Some of the information below, I learned then in 1993. Much, though, I gradually learned in the next years, in particular as I found that discovering this tradition by reading their monthly newsletter, *Shakti*, was easy for me. I lapped it up as if I'd actually lived in India and studied all this in earlier lifetimes. The subtlety and mysticalness of yogic consciousness just melted into my understanding with no difficulty at all, which I found a bit odd.

The ancient Vedic scriptures, the oldest Hindu scriptures, were "heard" revelation. *Véda* (knowledge, wisdom) derives "from the root 'vid,' meaning to see, to know, to directly experience, or to realize within one's own awareness."[73]

Besides, there was no conflict with any other tradition. Not that I spent hours meditating; I didn't. But then, as *Shakti* said, ritual worship was "easy for the mind to accept" and might be considered step one on the journey:

However, the culmination of that step is within oneself. Whatever is done externally ultimately must unfold internally. Pujas [ritual worship] and rituals may be equaled to first or second grade, but just as alphabets or numbers are used through all the grades and ultimately all of life by the physicist, the engineer, the physician, or chartered accountant, similarly puja just continues to unfold internally in many levels of spirituality.[74]

According to Hinduism, the triad of Brahma, Vishnu, and Shiva (creation, maintenance, and destruction) are the primary forms of one unmanifest, unknowable reality. A form is *an ishtadev*. As Anandi Ma says, "Whether it is Ram or Krishna or Buddha or Christ, it doesn't matter; ultimately it's all one." These divinities help us feel a personal relationship to the incomprehensibility of the godhead. Dhyanyogi-ji defines God as "a personification of the Absolute. An intermediate form with personality and characteristics through which one may approach the realization of the ultimate, formless Absolute or Brahman."[75] According to this teaching, in times of extreme need an ishtadev incarnates. Examples of Lord Vishnu's incarnations are Krishna and Buddha.

Lord Rama, the tradition I would receive shaktipat in, was the seventh Lord Vishnu incarnation. I thought it would really add to my breadth to be in a tradition this different from the Christian one I was reared in. The Ramayana scriptures, by the Sanskrit poet Valmiki, describe an epic spiritual adventure. As with *The Iliad* and *The Odyssey* by Homer (until archeological finds turned up the historical cities), the debate over the facticity of the figures and locations in the Ramayana has historians on both sides. But the recent underwater find of the "lost city of Dwarka" (Lord Krishna's fabled capital in the Mahabhrata scriptures) in excavations by Dr. S. R. Rao of the Marine Archaeology Unit of the National Institute of Oceanography of India—as well as multiple verifications of the existence of cities in Lord Ram's travel route in the Ramayana—are intriguing. Lord Ram was said to rule for eleven thousand years. Literal truth, however, is not necessarily the point of these stories, long assumed by many to be legend.

Now for the story. In the Ramayana, Lord Ram (or Rama), the son of a king, was exiled for fourteen years (the king having been tricked by his own wife). In exile in a forest Lord Rama was joined by his wife, Sita, and his brother. But Sita was kidnapped by an evil king, Ravana, whom Rama pursued and killed with the aid of a monkey army led by Lord Hanuman. Then Sita had to pass a test by fire, proving her purity. Eventually, they returned home, where Ram was crowned, ruling in peace and compassion.

To determine when (if) Lord Ram lived is not easy, because in Hinduism "time (Sanskrit 'kal') is a manifestation of God." And "God is timeless . . . The past, the present and the future coexist in him simultaneously."[76]

Moreover, time is cyclic: thus, the Ramayana did not take place in a century—linearly measured—but inside a cycle of time, the *Treta Yuga.*[77]

This idea of successive universes is no longer absurd to leading-edge Western science. Simulations of quantum loop gravity picked it up. According to a model developed at the Institute for Gravitational Physics and Geometry at Penn State University by Abhay Ashtekar and other astrophysicists, which astonished them, "It appears that . . . the universe we inhabit is not 'our' universe but a 'multiverse' of an indefinite number of universes." By that explanation, "The matter-component of the prior universe 'evaporates' in black holes and is reborn in the superfast expansion that follows the final collapse. Instead of a Big Bang leading to a Big Crunch, we have recurring Big Bounces."[78]

It underscores to me that almost nothing is too far-fetched to be in the bounds of consideration.

This is one more place where leading-edge Western probings run into ancient yogic beliefs, resulting in incredible-sounding speculation. Through it all, consciousness and the workings of the universe become more and more mysterious and multidimensional. In the book from which the above quotation is taken, *The Self-Actualizing Cosmos*, Hungarian Ervin Laszlo, a philosopher of science, a systems theorist, and an integral theorist, also a classical pianist, revives in the West the ancient Sanskrit term for space, *akasha*, in positing a behind-the-scenes "A-dimension," where consciousness originates. Somewhat as in Carl Jung and Wolfgang Pauli's unified psychophysical field, it is the source of our matter universe, which Laszlo calls "the M-dimension."[79]

In all the incredible leading-edge research in Western science, trying to understand "our" universe, the East has stayed with ancient explanations.

Anandi Ma explains about Dhyanyogi-ji's tradition to readers:

> Dear Brothers and Sisters, since the very beginning of Creation, with the manifestation of the individual soul in the human body, the search for eternal and complete bliss has been constant. . . . As a result, over the centuries different paths with different techniques have become available to reach this inner state.
>
> Over the years many of these techniques and paths became known externally, and some were taught quite freely. But often paths were kept hidden. . . . At times these paths manifested inner faculties and powers that teachers felt might be misused. . . .
>
> For thousands of years this particular path of Kundalini Maha Yoga was kept secret.[80]

Shaktipat awakens kundalini. From his small Indian ashram in Bandhavad, in Gujarat state, Dhyanyogi-ji would supervise as Anandi Ma administered it in Leuven.

Dhyanyogi-ji was announced by Lord Krishna in a dream to his mother four months before his birth. Krishna said: expect "a very great being . . . Don't misunderstand him. Don't mistake him for an ordinary person"[81] Already at thirteen, after failed attempts, Dhyanyogi-ji ran away definitively to become a *sadhu*, a "penniless, wandering holy man"—studying for ten years with various teachers, including living "among lions and crocodiles in the Gir Forest in Gujarat."[82] The wildlife preserve there was not set up until 1965. It is the sole home of the Indian (Asiatic) lion, who was on the brink of extinction in 1974, with 180 lions, and in 2010 had 411, including 77 cubs.[83]

In late nineteenth-century India it was still possible to live a

Asiatic lion in Gir Forest

nomadic holy life in search of "Who am I?" and God.

Then Dhyanyogi-ji spent ten years in the Himalayas and another ten in intense spiritual practices, especially in cramped caves on Mt. Abu, in Rajasthan state, with tigers roaming if he slept outside. For six years he lived primarily in "Elephant Cave"—Hathigufa—on Mt. Abu.[84]

It was there at Mt. Abu—meeting his teacher, Parameshwardasji— he attained (actually reattained) enlightenment. And the answers to his questions "Who am I?" and "What is death?"

Chota Hathi Gumpha Cave, Udayagiri, photo 1892

Shakti: An Introduction to Kundalini Maha Yoga describes how in the womb, with consciousness in the sahasrara chakra (crown of the head), the soul constantly repeats the mantra "You and I are one" (identical to the biblical "I and my Father are one"). At birth this Soham mantra is replaced as consciousness descends and becomes "Who am I?" It descends further down, to the kundalini in the first chakra, where it becomes "I am the body," and "To make matters worse, everything vibrating around us enforces that impression." But when the kundalini turns upward, the process reverses; when it reaches the top of the head, "as the scriptures say, you are no longer human; you are then God."[85]

Dhyanyogi-ji studied different types of yoga, Indian/Sanskrit languages, a musical instrument, and the traditional Indian medicine, Ayurveda. He said: "I did not put on shoes for 20 years. . . I walked on the snow of the Himalayas with bare feet, and also on the scorching earth of India's central province in summer, when the temperatures were 119 to 120 degrees Fahrenheit and the tar was melting. I developed calluses half an inch thick . . . They were so hard that they broke the strongest of thorns."[86]

The Indian soil, according to Dhyanyogi-ji, retains traces of the subtle energy built up over centuries by the yogis. This practice of meditating in the Himalayan foothills or mountains, his biography says, brings the generation of such energy that if such a reclusive individual did come out into society, his or her gaze was almost too powerful to look upon.

The Indian society itself, until relatively modern times, took it for granted that one of these gurus was more powerful than a king and could heal and bring about other results that in the West are considered impossible.

Kundalini has been described as "a sum total of all the electrical energy that has been produced up to this moment and that will be produced as long as this creation exists."[87]

After ending this reclusive period, writes Dileepji (Shri Anandi Ma's husband), of a firsthand experience, "he would simply look up into the sky . . . the weather would change."[88]

Something else that is interesting is that in India it was assumed these powerful yogis could end an outbreak of disease at will. I had never known about this part of history, in quite this way. It was about healing not only individuals but also communities, by a single sage, a saint who had learned to hold (and been given the task) the energy of a thousands-year-old tradition.

Shaktipat (*diksha*)—energy transfer—which attendees were now about to receive individually at the Leuven, Belgium, workshop, can be given in four ways: by a look, a touch, a thought, a word.

Beforehand, I endeavored to make a private, silent, subtle pact with Dhyanyogi-ji from a distance—that I was not foregoing allegiance to the Zurich Initiator or the "spirit committees" I had worked with, but was expanding my ability to relate to Light. I asked him *not* to take on my karma (lessons), as a guru does, except in life- or life-work-threatening emergency involving a lesson I'd already learned. I had the intuition I was to hold karma for others sometimes, which, normally only a great teacher does. Nevertheless, it felt right to ask, and I assumed that if truly that powerful, he would read my intention provided I was clear.

One thing about Dhyanyogi-ji is his devotion to Lord Hanuman, the monkey god worshiped as an incarnation of Shiva. Hindu scriptures state that in choosing the form of a monkey to serve Lord Ram, he became the supreme example of humble service.

As mentioned, shaktipat in Belgium would be administered by Dhyanyogi-ji's heir while he remained watching in India.

I'd been exposed to kundalini piecemeal—in the initiation in Zurich in 1985, in a number of incidents in 1990 before Willy Vanluyten's death, and at Owl Farm—but had no formal training and little information. It had all been experiential. Besides that, I had witnessed it in Jyoti. And been "led by the unconscious," to use a Jungian term.

I repeat this because my consciousness was trying to expand. However—as we are unable to take many quantum leaps at once—I was at the moment trying to understand Hindu consciousness: how in the East, what we call paranormal or miracles were evidence of yogi knowledge. They were siddhis, not anomalous events but evidence of mastery over matter. Physical evolution followed Darwin, but the East focused on spiritual evolution, or "the science of yoga." The basis was experiential in high, non-dualistic states of awareness and self-realization individually; the yogic masters then consulted and found their experiences alike.

An example of a siddhi that I find particularly interesting comes from Anandi Ma's husband, Dileepji, who was carefully taught by Dhyanyogi-ji. Dileepji prefaced it: "There is not an answer for each and every question." In 1965, he was to photograph an important fire ceremony, but the flash didn't function. He told Dhyanyogi-ji he couldn't take pictures. Dhyanyogi-ji said, "Don't worry, just go and put the flash in front of the statue of Hanuman, and then start using it."

Dileepji reflected: "My rational mind thought this was stupid, but I had faith in his words. I did as he told me, and a minute after I placed it on the floor in front of the altar, the flash began to go off on its own, and it worked fine for the next 15 years!"[89]

According to Dhyanyogi-ji, awakening takes place through the kundalini. As a Kundalini Maha Yoga master he activated this process by energy transfer. The initiate is thereafter watched over subtly (sometimes in person as well) by the guru, who sees that things never get so far out of hand as to create fatal danger.

An example of this type of protection is told by Dileepji, who witnessed it, among innumerable siddhis: it took place in Desert Hot Springs, California:

> A group of disciples was on our evening walk with Dhyanyogi-ji when all of a sudden, for no apparent reason, he [Shri Dhyanyogi] just fell down. He sprained his shoulder and got a bruise on his nose, but he said nothing by way of explanation to us. About two weeks later, a letter came from Bihar, India, where Dhyanyogi-ji was building a hospital for the community. It said that at the construction site, an eight-year-old boy had fallen from the third story but had escaped without a scratch. At this point Dhyanyogi-ji stated that he had seen and felt the boy falling in India, and that he took it upon himself to protect the child.[90]

During shaktipat we each received a string of beads. Then for a number of days, at home, it was recommended that we meditate—an hour in the early morning, an hour in the evening if we could, always at the same hour—touching the beads one by one. A Guruji disciple, Ellen Balis, reminded me, "But I wouldn't use the word 'expect' so much as recommend, with the understanding that people do the best they can. Guruji was compassionate."

I did this ritual, but long meditations were not yet, if ever, my style. Nevertheless, it's not the outer form that counts ultimately but the inner alignment. And I did have a few experiences, so subtle that

I made nothing of them; for instance, I felt myself as a prayer. I did not think about how that could be. It was clear to me Dhyanyogi-ji was assisting.

Subtle experiences would become quite common in the light body courses I began in 1992—a study I continue to this day.

I sent a selection of computer-PK printouts to a parapsychologist professor in Belgium, then to a Dutch experimental physicist, Dick Bierman (University of Amsterdam and Utrecht University). Bierman asked to send an Orion random number generator (RNG) to hook up to my computer—to test the energy in the apartment. But I didn't particularly like that idea yet.

I feared the focus on randomness would weaken my energy field. (This turned out to be perhaps a savvy intuition, as today in reading neuroscientist Norman Don's manuscript on his work with famous psychic Olof Jonsson, I see that Olof said skepticism would interfere with entering the state of harmony necessary for Condition Three, CD3, because energy that is present is pooled. More on that when I get there, beginning in 1995.)

So Bierman filed the computer-PK packet away, hoping a graduate student would get interested.

In February, just before the shaktipat or ten months after—I am not sure which—Shri Dhyanyogi appeared in my dream. In the East it is believed that a great guru does not allow anyone to dream of him or her except by permission. Standing, he pointed over to one side of himself—at energy graphs suspended in the air, which, he said, he'd been looking at.

He then showed me myself; I was sitting solitarily on a wooden bench. *He* used to be like that, he said. "It's nineteenth century."

His tone indicated it was no longer obligatory to be alone for years, decades, on a spiritual quest—figuratively, benched; that times had changed and sitting on a bench did not fit the new options; it might now be procrastinating. My choices, no matter the intention, lacked the awareness of what the times called for and offered, he was indicating. It would be romantic to see the global, fast-changing twentieth, or approaching twenty-first, century in the same filters and lens as the nineteenth.

Later I read in his biography: "Dhyanyogi-ji once said that whenever he met people, he took X-rays of their past, present and future. He wanted to see into their hearts. Some people were like dynamite, he said. He'd touch them and they'd blast off. Others were like coal; it was hard to get them started, but once they did they burned very well. Still others were like wood . . . [requiring interaction]. And finally, there were those who were like stone. Dhyanyogi-ji said, 'It's my job to turn stones into humans, and humans into gods.'"[91]

He instructed in the dream: *Come to me direct.*

Evidently the charts (which I took to be of lifetimes) revealed I didn't need years of practice to come to where he was. This is called a "boon."

He indicated not to go into a particular group that normally I would feel it natural to join. I felt he meant I would be dwarfed there. Though I did not realize why, I would now say he meant something about me he perceived (perhaps in my charts) would not fit the distinctions, being too *subtle*. The subtlety would be invisible. I would be out of place; I would not even progress.

A teacher can revive an earlier-lifetime awakening or energize a potential. In his case, for instance, he finally remembered having been enlightened before. In other words, focused on him, I could get to him.

As mentioned in his biography, "Once a soul reaches that state [enlightenment], it can either choose to merge with the divine consciousness or decide to take another birth—not for its own evolution, but out of a desire to serve God or out of compassion for other beings. If the soul elects to come back in a new body, it will not immediately remember everything from previous lives."[92]

Though not knowing about his X-ray vision, I took this dream to heart. It was a tough, delightful assignment.

This dream, I held tight to. A promise. I couldn't see him physically. But he was there, to access. Dhyanyogi-ji had such energy when in the body that from yards away people would heat up and sometimes faint.

In certain situations, I think he meant, my energy would blur into a larger energy. I hadn't a chance, he'd said, through a normal Eastern method.

Come to me direct. How? There was no hint, no instruction manual, just my charts, my experience in other lifetimes, or some energy I could tap into. That was all I had, to find my way. Where was it he called me to? He was a realized master in his last months on Earth in a body.

But where else? In bliss, peace, unity consciousness. In fact, he was about to dissolve into the universe, though no one but he knew this.

If not on a bench alone, would it be a public role? Time would tell. Or not. I had been warned. Again.

What did those charts hold? What past? A solitary meditator in Tibet or the foothills of the Himalayas? Had he been my teacher? Just this type of recluse he'd been in the caves of India—holding his concentration once when a large scorpion joined him; another time it was a cobra ("whenever Dhyanyogi-ji made some noise during puja, the cobra hissed in response").[93] Then in 1960, deciding to offer his tradition openly, he'd broken with the long-established custom of secrecy. He introduced kundalini publicly, as did a few other saints. Brought out his consciousness as the sole legacy bearer of his many-centuries-old tradition, passed to him by Yogiraj Parmeshwardasji.

What could I do? Hold close the vision of the two options: the bench or—?

Dhyanyogi-ji lived the hero archetype. Had, even, that archetype changed? *Anyway, out of solitude* seemed to be the message.

Eventually I read on the flap jacket of his biography: "He was

100 years old and walked so fast that no one could keep up with him. He had spent 80 years of relative seclusion in rural India, but in the early 1960s he came out into the open, burning with a desire to help ordinary people attain the highest states of spiritual realization. Having undergone many painful ordeals to achieve his own evolution, he hoped to spare others that suffering. Shri Dhyanyogi often urged everyone to take the spiritual gold he had to offer, saying, 'This house is on fire—loot all you can!'"

Sitting on a bench alone—eighty years of relative seclusion? Sometimes surviving on a liquid of fresh-leaf juice? No, he said, it wasn't the way now; this wasn't the nineteenth century.

I visited my family in North Carolina each year. If I stopped in New York, I saw good friends Hannah Green (a writer) in Greenwich Village and her husband, John (Jack) Wesley, a painter in a whimsical-erotic Pop Art-Surrealist vein. Infrequently, I dropped in at the office of Jim Silberman—a former Random House boss of mine and editor of Hunter. (I just found the visitor slip for March 1993.) Naturally, Jim mentioned HST sightings. After editing *Generation of Swine*, he and his wife Selma visited Owl Farm.

Back at work on the books, I printed out my three-hundred-page poetry manuscript, *The Christ State*, written in 1985/86 with my Zurich Initiator. In the printing, sometimes "computer PK" reformattings occurred; for instance, an annotation—such as "*p2015"—might be inserted beside a word in a line that, in the printing, had been thrust up, isolated, to the top of a page (I thought it referred to the Thompson Bible concordance mentioned earlier). Whenever the computer participated, the energy was so high I could write/print for hours.

I continued Tai Chi. Including workshops with the visiting teacher Patrick Kelly. Patrick had the great distinction of being the only non-Chinese ever admitted to the inner school of Master Huan

Xing Xian (Sheng Shyan), himself a student of Cheng Man-ch'ing. His focus was on internal movement, the esoteric principles of it, or "True Taiji." I also attended workshops, such as "Travel without Physically Moving," led by a Hungarian shaman master, Joska Soos. Having occasional private sessions, I asked Joska about the computer PK; answering in French, he explained about metallic energy; he said this was living energy—thus, gave me a real boost (I still have the tape). It was another example of being almost cradled by experts and even, in this case, a master, who did not dismiss my experiences but from a deeper state of awareness gave me glimpses of why it might not be so extraordinary, but be just part of consciousness and reality I had yet to understand much in. But I would. Never fear. Put another way, I was being led, on all these fronts, to where, in Patrick Kelly's words, "the Beyond grows within."

About that time, I got a severe back block. To alleviate it, I luckily discovered a kinesiologist in Tienen; his office, half a block from the train station, was one of the few European locations with an outpatient spinal traction machine. So regularly, the nurse put weights on my feet and I'd get my back stretched in that way, my neck as well.

As a way of absolute dating, I can refer to a letter to Hunter February 7, 1993, that said I was about to go to the U.S. Then re health:

> How are your teeth and so on? I greatly sympathize about your back, even more so in that something strange has happened to mine. It doesn't show, but it's collapsing. At least that's how it feels. Well, let's hope one of us answers the phone. I would feel awful if it took the rest of my life to get in touch and there was so much going on. [It did.]
>
> So where are you holed up?

Soon, though, I acquired my version of a Buddha belly—a small one—which, it seemed to me, came in conjunction with Dhyanyogi-ji's teaching. Also, one day I had sensed a guru in Ghent, Belgium, whose satsangs I attended a few times, was subtly asking me would I mind developing one? I said no, I wouldn't mind (internally), and it came.

The first time I'd gone to his ashram, I arrived early; he walked right into the kitchen, sat at my table, and started talking to me. Afterwards, someone explained I had received his "amrita"—nectar, or blessing.

My next visit, he stayed uncharacteristically absent from the satsang; the chanting went on without him. I was enthralled by the sound of his followers' voices. I very much disliked his term for them, his "babies." But that aside, I felt his powerful energy. In this chanting I was resisting the word "babies" and had a vision in which he said, "Would you mind being a *baby* Sai Baba?" What a twist.

I thought it referred to my computer PK. Sai Baba, of course, was believed to manifest and teleport objects. By any stretch of the imagination, I was a baby in that world, if it even existed and I believed it did.

Anyway, I did not continue to attend his satsangs—actually, I didn't have a ride—and soon I sensed, so subtly it was as if nonexistent, the tiniest question from him: *Would I mind having a Buddha belly?* I would have thought nothing if that were the end of it, the hint was so deeply inside. But it came. So for years, I'd wear loose clothing. No one knew why.

When I next went to get traction, I felt sure I could use heavier weights. Lying on the flat slab, I told the nurse, and she began adding feet weights. It was simple to hold more, once the "Buddha belly" came. I had intuited it added mass. And the weights seemed to agree.

Most of us have seen portraits of gurus in loin cloth, with a large belly, but most Westerners don't know that this is transpersonal energy. The belly gets large and small, depending on what it has to do. In a matter of minutes it can change size dramatically. In some people, as with Gandhi, it doesn't show, it's internalized. I covered it with loose blouses and sweaters, so no one knew. It cannot bear to be constricted. I couldn't put on anything tight, not stockings, not elastic at the waist. In contrast to lying flat, it wants to poke out, to protrude, to *breathe*. This increases mass:

Just behind and below your navel (belly button) lies the hara . . . a natural balancing point of your consciousness that can be thought of as the center of your subtle body. No one really knows what the hara actually is but we can use it to our advantage. When your consciousness is centered at the hara instead of in the head, your thinking process slows down and can even stop. When the thinking process slows down, you can relax in the expanded world of pure being. . . . By transferring your center of consciousness to the hara, thoughts gradually disappear on their own without any inner conflict. This is why you see Buddha statues with a big belly.[94]

With the severe back block, my back became so cramped while I slept I had trouble getting out of bed; so I'd put pressure on my arm, turning sidewise, to sit up.

Also, a strange thing happened. Lying in bed in a very profound state of awareness, I'd realize I was imagining myself walking deep into darkness. It was a solitary, total awareness. At a point I knew if I kept going, I couldn't come back. I was sure it was *not* my mind that had this awareness. It was an incredible depth of pure consciousness—and I concentrated with it, which was easy and utterly profound. I was walking in awareness, why?

In retrospect, after his death, learning he'd been bedridden, I thought that sense of walking was Dhyanyogi-ji practicing his *mahasamadhi*, or moment of "dropping the body." Exploring that border where life in the body ended. That I had somehow been able to share some of those last months, this experience of testing the pathway, the one we call dying.

13

Interstices

1994—Shri Dhyanyogi

On the refrigerator at Jyoti and Russell's in 1993, I was fascinated by a newspaper clipping that said a comet, the Shoemaker-Levy 9, was predicted to crash into Jupiter. Though comets are typically sun-centric, this one had been captured by Jupiter's gravity. It was orbiting the planet and would soon destroy part of it. For no particular reason, I intuited the crash would associate with some Earth event—symbolically. In other words, it was a clue; something was up. But I didn't know what. I was right. Now a big event began to prepare itself, one that would be important to me—being set up unconsciously.

I dreamed, in 1991, I was to help write "The Hunter Thompson Story." It seemed glitteringly joyful, but when? How? What? Something held, underneath. It held beyond logic. Held as charisma. It held as love.

Another big thing in '93 was the annual poetry festival in Leuven/ Sibiu, where I again met wonderful people, including poet Tess Gallagher (wife of Ray Carver).

I organized hand readings in Belgium for Richard Unger (the founder of the International Institute of Hand Analysis), a foremost authority in his field, in June, and had a private reading. In addition to
his research, including into the hands of fingerprinted criminals, he
did a certain amount of "channeling." Immediately he said a lot was
going on. Then looking at how the tip of one index finger slanted
obstinately to the right, toward my thumb, he asked had it ever been
wounded. I said no (actually, how did I know?). He said it was rather
unusual and deduced that a part of me was quite willful, it could take
over and I then entered a world that was not his reality. He paused
and said he wanted to go into this world, take a look around. Then he
came back and at first described me as something of a mad scientist;
then went on:

> As I climb into this world, reality doesn't look the same to me . . .
> It's like a coke bottle bottom, of thick glass, and the world that
> Richard lives in is just barely visible on the other side of this glass.
> Because the part of you who lives on the other side of this glass has
> only a 2 percent contact to the world of Richard. This is a world of
> dragons, castles, knights on white horses, . . . archetypes, a world
> of pure ideals. Your world has clip-clops, not automobiles . . . It's a
> world of fantasy, but it's not unreal, because you're interacting with
> direct energies . . . It's a world of pure energies. I think one piece
> of what you're trying to do is to bring the pure archetypal energies
> back—back so that they can be integrated with how that other
> world sees them. Not back in like a Broadway play *Camelot*—but
> to bring that archetypal purity . . . make that a moving force to
> create a template for new energies to align themselves around . . .
>
> In one sense of it this is a virtual reality. Here's what I'm seeing
> also. In this virtual reality world you're the princess, sad, because
> your knight has not arrived. Already your reading is different,

weird, unusual. So this is where your reading begins. This is how your hand speaks to me.

Let's make believe that you're Dr. Frankenstein and you're working in your laboratory . . . very diligently to make something happen. Down in your laboratory you're working twenty-three hours a day, but you can't really talk to other people about this work, living in this world. One of the first things I'm noticing—first of all, this world is delightful. Part of the delight is the purity that exists here. The bad people are bad. They're just bad, and they delight in seeing how bad they can be; the strong people are strong . . . We have a couple of things going on, now that I've got oriented here. I think you must be able to leave your virtual reality world, maintain it with you and interact with the other world in the twentieth century. Only 5 percent more objectivity and Franken-stein would have been a [strong positive contributor] to mankind. He needed to be close [to that other world] or he never would have thought the things he thought.

If he enters that world in a perfectly healthy way, it still looks crazy to the normal scientist, but those are the same scientists who told Pasteur you're not supposed to work on penicillin. Now, as I talk to you from inside, in physical reality, where although your prince will clip-clip-clop and you'll be able to recognize him, he'll also have an automobile. Frankenstein . . . was exploring con-sciousness. These are crucial questions that the scientists were afraid to ask.

The caution point is [if you were to get] 5 percent too close, or forgetting to return. It reminds me also of Castanedo. He extends it as far as he can into this alternate reality system, but he returns to take care of his body. I'm talking about taking care of your close-ness function. You must be able to completely live in your virtual reality world. The hardest thing, you did get through the keyhole. What you'll do is meet somebody in this present world and the two of you will have virtual reality helmets that are similar and you'll delight in each other because you can eat apples in the way apples

are meant to be eaten, but you'll have twenty-first century clothing
. . . It's a dimension that all of us are reacting to. What happened
in your case is that you happened to have synchronization.

    . . . Medieval archetypal purity translated into twenty-first cen-
tury spiritual/techno-reality. That doesn't translate into the last part of
the twentieth century. That is trying to be reborn.

Let me add that Richard was tapping into the energy of my apartment, where I was not only experiencing computer PK but also in the
midst of my Awakening. Not to mention that my *Love in Transition*
series was focused on "the unconscious history of the Earth."

As a novice, it can be hard if not impossible to completely distinguish one's physical self from the energy one merges with—at least at
first; in fact, energy continuing on and on, it's a never-answered question where one "starts" and "stops," so we establish boundaries. It's
easy—and dangerous—to identify with an archetype or a field personally, though the instinct of a novice is often to do just that. Our experience—the energy we go into—is so convincing; it doesn't necessarily
initially inform us it's not just "us," it's transpersonal, even universal.

Too, I was plunged into nonstop speculative writing about consciousness—what is it?

Richard's storytelling slant takes us right back, fittingly, to Jung:
archetypes, alchemy, and the collective unconscious—allied to twenty-first-century techno. The loss of connection to nature, to connectedness, to the sense of the aliveness of the entire universe. This went
out the window in the West after the scientific mind raced ahead
as seventeenth-century discoveries mushroomed into a roar, and
Western consensus reality moved into the overwhelming direction
of our current Earth. Yes, but having left that more holistic perspective behind, we evidently had—of course, we had—a strong push to
rediscover what we'd lost, discarded. Not everything, but the parts
we could put to good use. Evidently, I was involved in such thinking.

Richard reinforced his earlier assessment (made in Jyoti and Russ's
apartment in California) that my hand lines promised great success,

but only if I overcame "tomato fears/stage fright." He mentioned "lines of genius/gifted mass communications" and insisted my path had to be "output, output, output so that feedback becomes possible."

He cautioned, "Your research is to be brought out, not to capture you."

He called me "a grand synthesizer" of "worlds highly detailed"; I had to "hold [multiple] detailed worlds at one time." The risk was my self-doubt and a tension of "escapism/exploration."

Not far off, actually. This "tomatoes fear" could be overcome by self-confidence that sent me back out into the world fearlessly.

What he described was true of many creative people, e.g. William Blake. However, it was also about exploring consciousness. He said, "From another angle an advanced consciousness is using this, but it's . . . living, that's the difference. It's breathing."

On other fronts—in the very practical vein, the antithesis of this but I had both ends of the spectrum in my blood, fortunately—I was twice a delegate (expenses paid) to the international planning conference "Culture: Building Stone for Europe 2002," which examined what transformations were necessary to adjust to the increasing globalism of Europe—highlighting the importance of culture.

To contribute to the post-event assessment of the first seminar, in 1993 in Bruges, I mailed Hatto Fischer, the 1994 organizer, a follow-up "Reflection on the Convention Nov. 26-27." If I do say so, I like it a lot. I began: "The word not used was 'consciousness.' What is that? Where is it? It's something pervasive, located in the multi- and in the singular, in the micro- and the macro-, on all levels and connecting the levels, in threads and cross-sections. It weaves, it runs, it stops. it shocks. It holds together, it is passive, active." Invited back by Hatto for the following June seminar, I joyfully packed my bags. This seminar—"Cultural Actions for Europe"—was in Athens.

In Athens, unused to public speaking, I had the clear sense, at one point, that Jyoti's outgoing personality entered my hotel room—ready to let me "step into" her. I have been much struck in the succeeding years at the way one may hear the advice to call on our "inner" X,

Y, or Z, which might be what happened. However, Eastern teachers have long counted on "out-of-body" travel—or projections of their physical body into situations where they can be useful.

In any case, suddenly, I felt as if this "personality" of Jyoti had come to assist, to help me talk with assurance. It knew how to be a public figure.

This was another experience in how energy can move around transpersonally and—once understanding the principles—we can master these useful techniques. Near the conference wind-up, after carefully listening to others speak from the audience, I closed it out with a short, in-depth observation. A number of people thanked me (I don't remember what I said—something about unity).

Afterwards, I had discussions with an Austrian professor, Franz E. Moser, founder of the Institute for Chemical Engineering (now split into three parts, one of which is the Institute of Process and Particle Engineering). With his wife he was passionate about finding a holistic paradigm involving science and metaphysics: quantum mechanics, chaos theory, and self-organizing systems. As he did not discount my computer PK, I eagerly mailed him originals.

He wrote back that "your contribution at the meeting in Athens was one of the highlights of it." He did not scientifically understand the computer phenomenon, he said. However, his wife believed "a source [was] coming through with a high intelligence but it cannot manifest itself clearly enough because the medium itself is not yet clear." He speculated that the consciousness was me and that when I became "one with yourself," all would work out. This was not at all what I expected, and I just filed it away in my pile of papers.

14

Subtle Experiences—
A Magnetic Moment

Feeling driven to write Shri Dhyanyogi in mid-'94, I sealed the letter, expecting him to read it unmailed. In it, I thanked him. It was as if I knew he was about to "drop the body." And didn't I?

Study with Roland Verschaeve accelerated my skills in seeing the energy level of anything—finding it as energy. Having taken the foundation course, "Awakening Your Light Body," two hours a week for months in 1992, traveling by foot (or taxi) to the station, then an hour by train, and further by taxi, I graduated and for some time thereafter had a full-day graduate class monthly. In a guided-meditation format Roland taught in Dutch, which I half understood; he answered my questions in English. But one didn't need to understand all the words to follow the meditations, which I loved.

Mystical things happen, people walk in and say things to me only possible in subtle energy. I visited Mother Meera—to the Hindus an incarnation of the Divine Mother—once, in Thalheim, Germany. In 1993. (How do I know it was August 6–8? The little red agenda book I found in my garage.) I was there for *darshan*, which, in short, I took to be "blessing." (It led, obliquely, to my being put into *Who's Who in the World*.) But read now, much later, her explanation is telling. From her website:

The Darshan event with Mother Meera follows a precise structure, original to her work and exactly suited to allow the transmission of the Light she brings down upon the earth. For a little moment, while she touches our temples, she is working on something that might be described as the "wiring" of the soul. In her book, *Answers*, she describes an inner system of subtle energy in the human body that reaches from head to toe. By the process of incarnation and the entanglement of body and mind with worldly influences these subtle channels of energy can become knotted or blocked. During Pranam (*"bowing down"*) Mother very delicately works on these knots, gently freeing up the blocks preventing spiritual development. This process has to do with the soul and its unfolding and Mother Meera says that only Divine personalities can do such work.

When Mother releases our heads, we sit back and she looks into our eyes. This is Darshan (*"seeing,"* here *"seeing the Divine"*). During Darshan, Mother is working on our "personalities," the everyday body/mind. She searches for areas in our being where her Light is specially needed, giving us energy, purification and inner healing—whatever is required for the mental, emotional, and physical aspects of our being to live in harmony.

She says: "I am looking at everything within you to see where I can help, where I can give healing and power. At the same time, . . . I am opening every part of yourself to Light."

Standing there, looking into her eyes, I was in that instant struck with powerful resistance: I couldn't recognize her unless . . .

As she put her hands on my head, as numbers of other people sat watching, I suddenly couldn't pretend, ignore, cancel out, disavow—betray—my Zurich Initiation. I was compelled, in that moment in front of her, to ask her—silently, but with all my being, though it seemed irrational and overbold to me—for recognition. Surprised, I inwardly requested that she "recognize me" in the way the Initiator had. This felt inflated. I was embarrassed. But I felt it at a gut level. I silently blurted out and clung to this request. An instinct.

All the while she held her two hands at the sides of my head. Then I felt a drop of water exit my nostril, and she took her hands away. It was many years before I equated my act with a variation of the ancient Golden Rule—or "Namaste." Here, I ask "that *the level of me that parallels the level I am recognizing* be seen, even on my human level."

Now, of course, this is an outrageous thought and I'd rejected it during the Initiation, or it never occurred to me, but my allegiances changed in that moment. Thinking of the Initiator, all he knew that I didn't—viewed from my soul level—I let the thought stand. Held to it.

I felt nothing but the need to assert this request, not realizing that the sheer determination of the thought meant I *had* felt something, *was aligning with it, in resonance with her energy.* Anyway, nothing happened; there was no follow-up, nothing that I connected with that instant. *Little did I know.*

Shortly afterwards, I went to a light body seminar, "Opening to Channel," in Utrecht, Holland. In a meditation I saw a flash of pale blue, then blanked out—i.e., stopped remembering. When I came to, a woman in my group announced she'd just met her new guide, Mother Mary.

I was aghast. I felt it could not be that Mother Mary came right into my little group of seven and skipped entirely over me. I deduced the flash of blue was her, as she often wears blue in paintings; that when I went unconscious, I probably "merged." When I asked the workshop leader later, she said, "You know, don't you, you go in and out of your body." That night I vowed to "stay in my body" the next day.

Why did I think I had a connection with Mother Mary? Because the Zurich Initiator had said so, and also I'd detected—and been "told" by a channel I trusted—that I was a "personality" of Mary, i.e., that I was carrying a lot of that consciousness. It in no way meant I *was* her, naturally (heaven forbid), but that—if I continued to hold the energy (and *only if*)—I would be holding a form of consciousness that was an important part of hers; that a large part of my purpose on Earth was to walk with that energy into any situation that might present. Here was one.

It took decades for it to sink in, which it did one morning in meditation, that 1) a large entity can't just incarnate. In fact, one would suppose no entity can. (Yogis say, "You were never born and you will never die.") Part of the entity incarnates; 2) the original entity incarnation, as energy, if it becomes woven into the collective fabric, is spread out in percentages among us. But being of an age now when I have made the best sense I can of pieces of my puzzle, I also, in the twenty-first century, figured out, and two channels independently confirmed, I was carrying the Divine Feminine lineage from an Essene "maidens" past life, in which twelve maidens around Mother Mary were taught to carry that consciousness. Not only did this ring true, but I'd met several of these maidens, first or second generation, this lifetime, and one, when she realized there were others but knew nothing about the "maidens" aspect, called them "mothers."

As an aside, in Zurich, Jyoti had lent me a little book by a New York-based Dutch Jungian-oriented analyst, Erlo van Waveren, of a mystical bent, who, with his down-to-earth Jungian analyst wife Ann, had analysis with Jung and later saw him annually till Jung's death; in fact, when van Waveren had an influx of information from the unconscious in dreams, he turned—greatly troubled—to Jung, who reassured him it was no neurosis but a true "Confrontation with the Self."

In van Waveren's case, the focus was the passage out of the Age of Pisces. His dreams introduced the birth of a spirit or archetype or Self figure called Aquarius. The demands made on van Waveren were heavy, sometimes agonizing, as he was being injected with initiations and mystical information about the age to come, which he said would involve uniting the light with the dark, the shadow experience that had been left out, including in Jesus. Van Waveren, Jyoti told me, had secretly, keeping copious notes, believed himself to be a "personality of Jesus." His many forays into the unconscious throughout decades were put into safekeeping in a foundation.

His book, *Pilgrimage to the Rebirth* (part one), revealed how, similarly to Jung, dreams and symbols shaped his life into a personal/collective myth, or "soul's journey." Though I only skimmed it at the time, I was impacted that Jyoti told me he perceived his life purpose was to bring together his disparate lifetimes into one here and now; this meant addressing the conflicting consciousness they produced disparately. The book, therefore, despite van Waveren's resistance to it, responds to "past lives" ("ancestral figures," Jung called them). As van Waveren and others (Jung included) accepted the injunction of the unconscious to come, follow, learn more, so did I.

Only if I accepted to explore this "personality" possibility could it go any further. Otherwise, all its potential regarding me would be stopped dead in its tracks. In such cases, I always left the door open till I'd fully tested a hypothesis. Who was I to declare that a hypothetical organization of our metaphysical structure was impossible? unlikely? I, who knew so little, with my human brain's capacity, about the universe.

In fact, when I went to Owl Farm, as garage notes here remind me, I had already tested this hypothesis a lot and felt fairly sure of it. And what, if—in this larger picture—I were a "personality of Mary," was he? Hunter? I tentatively thought he was in Christ energy, working in the shadow; that his soul gave him that assignment—to bring Light out of the Earth shadow. But I detected this through my Zurich Initiation. Only now, in 2017, in a kind of half-awake surprise, do I see that van Waveren, being drawn into the unconscious, was receiving information in line with the same information I had in Zurich. The unconscious was on the move.

Its archetypes were. We were not alone in facing the storms of a new era. Processing where consciousness was not in synch with the shifting times, our collective unconscious was going before us and behind us. Of course, some would call this the Self or God or Divine energy.

Again, in all this I was making my way through uncharted territory toward the Oneness consciousness, which, in the West, had only been theorized about. How did one assimilate these expansions of consciousness if to go as a planet into the awareness of our Oneness source?

By January 1991, still not ready to read the book but thinking my experiences might intersect with van Waveren's unpublished material on "the shadow of Mary," I'd talked with the chairman of the Ann and Erlo van Waveren Foundation, French-born, Harvard-educated art dealer and author, Olivier Bernier, in his beautiful New York City apartment. Olivier gave biannual sold-out lectures at the Metropolitan Museum of Art. Soon I would apply to the foundation unsuccessfully for a small research grant.

I didn't know then about the various ways van Waveren's mystical experiences reflected on my question of how to integrate a Oneness consciousness in 3-D reality.

Ready to read the book in 2017, I found that his sometimes-harrowing dives into the unconscious drilled down on this question. I thought only people who read it in that light would understand rather than find it inflated, taking it too literally.

When someone goes deep into the unconscious for us—as many have—and comes back with a report (some don't), it's typically of great collective use. It tells us something of what our own unconscious energies are up to, the jumping-off points they've reached, the new issues that have built to being addressed.

But back to 1993—the Utrecht seminar. The next day I had a reading with a teacher, Lindsay Senecal (she was in the light body seed group of LuminEssence and the channel of AnKaRa)—intent on settling the uncertainty about *what was personal, what transpersonal.* I was on quavering legs, not matter of fact, because such information was not integrated.

I thought it would be crystal clear if I asked, "What dimension do I come from?"

She answered, "From the heart of God." So much for anything particular.

Near tears, I went on desperately; I had to make some sense somehow: was everything impersonal?

I asked, "If I come from the heart of God, why is the Jesus incarnation so close to my heart?" I was so completely open, because my heart could not hold it back, that now finally she spoke personally. It had seemed to me there was no way to distinguish personal and transpersonal, no way to anchor.

She answered, "Because it is your incarnation that is closest to your heart." She said a lot of energy would go with me from the room, and memories would come. She said three large beings were with me; she used no names: "A mystery will gradually unravel."

Then she stepped back into her personality. Looking me in the eye, she said, *"Be outrageous.* That's the way I got where I am."

She would not speak a word further on my question for years.

These inconclusive meetings—with Mother Meera, with AnKaRa—I did not dwell on. The important thing was that I had been authentic. I did not realize there would be repercussions; they would take time.

In 1994 (sent by an acquaintance), a young American spiritual teacher (I'd never met before) arrived to spend the night in my apartment. She came by train—incidentally, I thought—directly from Mother Meera's in Germany. She walked in, and being very psychic (she was in Europe to teach workshops), asked first off, stunning me, "Weren't you in the Bible?" In a flash pondering possibilities, I cautiously said, "Yes." What would she say next?

Then she said, "Wasn't your name Mary?" Carefully I decided to let it play itself out: "Mary who?" She said, "Mary Magdalene." Then she began to describe *that* "me" as she saw her: "You used to sit on the floor like now. You had a house where people came to be healed by drinking some sort of liquid. You were very *sensual . . . but very pure.*"

Sensuality, purity, sitting on the floor—this combination, she connected to that figure. It made sense to me that such an archetype had no clarity here on Earth, where sensuality is physical, purity spiritual, at least in certain circles.

So I was in this combination of opposites we polarize. This offers great insight—into who I am, into the feminine. But as was pointed out at the Jung Institute Zurich, a *complete* archetype of the feminine—mother-to-"whore in the bedroom"-to-saint—does not exist in the West, except perhaps by combining Greek goddesses. But there is a potential, an archetype, a woman who once lived, where this comes to a point. Later I will learn to see these things as "consciousness" in a focus close to me.

Then the visitor left *to return straight back to Mother Meera's*; I made no connection with my request. Not till 1995—at a sweat lodge at Kayumari, Jyoti and Russell's spiritual village in California that I helped form and occasionally visited.

Though most of this had not happened in linear time in late 1992, it was all present in different degrees—different intensities, lines into the future: *potential/probability under momentum.*

I became intent on learning to "stay in my body"—stay in it even as higher energies were very near—merge with them, *remain conscious.*

As we go up and down and sideways on the consciousness ladder, often we learn new laws before the skills. I had a lot of fear. My personality task, the psychic Mariah Martin had helpfully said, was to "get over the fear of being strong and powerful as a female." And on the soul level, to "help others overcome the fear of enlightenment." Again, removal of fear. How?

By learning laws that are stronger. By knowing the laws of love, more powerful still—of surrender, of putting one's own will under Divine Will.

The third energetic memory (of stretched space-time, with its quivering Brownian, vibrating molecules)—exactly in quality like the others—was at the 1994 annual conference of the International Association for the Study of Dreams (IASD) at the University of Leiden, the Netherlands. It was summertime.

Each person participating in a short workshop was to make up a movement, then watch how the movements *self-organized* as a system. But straightaway as I started creating my movement, my mind shifted to that other level, where the energetic moments take place. Suddenly an "I" in my awareness was standing on the Sea of Galilee, choosing disciples.

All of a sudden, that "I" was inside me but *there.*

As I recorded shortly afterwards, "I felt my energy entered and merged with that of Jesus choosing disciples, though it was an exercise in a workshop." A note here on merging one awareness with another: in my experience, it involves a total sense of only one aware "I." I had no sense of my human personality as a separate self.

Continuing the quote: "As I chose them [that is, as Jesus back then, but also merged with me in 1994, chose his disciples at the Sea of Galilee], I [he] swerved that energy away from an image of the king and queen riding to where they would behead John the Baptist." The regal pair were at the end of a right-hand fork in the road, symbolically the conscious side. In the biblical story, Herod Antipas, dazzled by his stepdaughter Salome's dance, promised to answer her one wish. Consulting with her mother, she made the infamous request for the Baptist's head on a platter. Like a *static pictorial fact*, the king-and-queen scene (and its implied aftermath) sat at the end of the path on the right.

Unlike with the other two magnetic memories, energetically I was *in* one location, on the left. But *saw* the road was bifurcated. I *knew* the (left/right) scenes were alternatives. The choice was obvious. I did not sense any sensation in the path on the right; the *live presence* was only on the left.

Outwardly, I was standing, composing my movement, at the workshop. Or was that where I was? Anyway, I appeared to be; yet energetically, the more real reality was suspended—outside its surrounding time dates.

In linear reality, the reality I would continue in, unless reentering this time warp or whatever it was, I would live this as a symbol. Yet it was *an experience*. In some way, a memory.

Someone was linking, juxtaposing, these two historical scenes. *The workshop was the only physical event going on that I could put into my biography.* However, it turned out that this time something else was happening.

I didn't know it, but that night a telepathy experiment was scheduled. A woman had been assigned to "send" into our sleeping minds a secret target image—to influence our choice of a picture among a number of pictures spread out on tables the next day. As it happened, she tried to send the target image by *wild dancing*.

All night, my mind mysteriously warded off, "Come on, baby, let the good times roll." Normally I loved the song. Not knowing why, I observed myself repeatedly shove it aside in favor of "This, this is Christ the King." My mind participated in the mental dual without my conscious understanding.

The next day I learned about the experiment, and it appeared to me the nighttime combat (of sparring songs) was a restatement of the Sea-of-Galilee-versus-the-beheading fork.

The target telepathy image was of Rumi. The gyrating "sender" had tried to telepathically associate a graphic sexual sentiment to the mystical thirteenth-century Persian poet and Sufi mystic—hoping to make the Rumi image attractive to the voters. The proof would be in which image of those laid out on the tables got the most votes.

It was not Rumi. The voters chose a sacred scene. The telepathy appeared to be a failure, yet I knew I'd unconsciously interfered. The sacred sentiment I'd unwittingly energized was resonant with the winning picture. I told the person who had set up the contest, psychologist/dream expert Robert Van de Castle.

Of course, there was no control case, and I didn't explain my own experience to anyone else.

This had been a test *inside a test inside a test*. Beyond-3-D, an old old master technique had been employed, as the ante was upped for the Earth to go to a higher consciousness. In their/our depths, consciously or unconsciously, the Earth was choosing. Here was one way we did it.

I was convinced the vision in the exercise at the workshop *presumed* knowledge that the later group-telepathy event was to occur! I played my part, half unconscious. But then who was conscious? Who was using such a technique?

Was it the Jesus frequency? Jesus himself, standing inside me, transmitting into my mind, by re-creating his state of mind when choosing disciples, teleporting it into the twentieth century, right through my head into this event—*asking for a choice right there, not of him per se but of the awareness?* That's what it felt like.

As the months and years unfolded afterwards, this certainly did not recede, though by 2017 as I go really public, I had forgotten just how deeply it bored into my future. Had forgotten till—you guessed it—the garage archives reminded me.

Well, we posit this right here in *Keep This Quiet! Ancient Secrets Revealed* as part of our territory. Perhaps (or doubtless) there is some urgent reason.

Thus, I sat here, wondering what part of me, or of the whole history of humankind and time, was being tapped into. Full well knowing that an intelligence much greater than the part of myself I had thus far known must be speaking; and in fact would have to do so, to take over at this point, if *Keep This Quiet!* IV did not drive itself over a steep cliff. For I could see how much was being set up as the subject. And what is more, prepared to be expounded upon.

Just as if I knew a thing about it. I knew nothing at all. But years later, it hit me. In fact, I could see a spiral building off the original exercise by the workshop leader, who had expected that our movements would self-organize. The surface situation, with the split alternatives, was mirrored one level up and backward/forward, till even time itself—nonlinear time—was being "self-organized" outside time. A term that comes to mind now is "consciousness reprogramming." I can imagine that some readers will jump in and ask if I was tapping into the akashic records. Perhaps.

The thing was, though, the presence inside me felt so real, *so there*. But let's say I tapped into the akashic records. Even so, someone—whom I detected instantly to be Jesus thinking inside me—set up the alternate choices, linking them to the telepathy contest.

In *Keep This Quiet!* III, I experienced how a highly emotional past event was sometimes intentionally mentally combined (in this manner) with a signature past event—engineering the conditions to rewrite, as it were, the earlier outcome, which then spilled into present-day options, the pattern being available to us. I thought the choice between the static king-and-queen scene and the highly charged living energy of Jesus at the Sea of Galilee was, analogously, working in just such an energetics; or, to bring in a phrase from *Keep This Quiet!* III, a *Meta4.*[*] (More on that in the chapter "Bipod Metalism and a Cave.")

Until quite recently I had read none of the Western research into the akasha. And I am glad; I had the experience without influence. Ervin Laszlo writes in *The Self-Actualizing Cosmos*: "This—nonlocal—information first reaches the subneural networks of the right hemisphere, and then, if it penetrates to the level of consciousness, also reaches the neuroaxonal networks of the left hemisphere. Given that this information is a translation of holographically distributed information in the A-dimension, it conveys the totality of the information in that dimension. Thus our brain is imbued with the totality of the information that pervades the cosmo." Imbued, permeated, but not, I would add, commensurate.

Experiential investigation of this dimension is precisely what happens in yogic science. I tapped into a memory stored somewhere or transmitted. I thought transmitted. The dosage I received was precisely tailored to be powerful. It did not appear holographic, but it could easily have been an entry point, like a key, made just for me.

Laszlo's argument on the *HuffPost* blogs is that this A-dimension gives us as humans the possibility of attuning to each other and, like other species, becoming coherent. We'll pick up this topic in Part Three.

The energy that had entered my cells—of Jesus by the sea, choosing his disciples—remained and became something my cells had experienced in this lifetime. Then whatever happened, they had this frequency inside. And the loyalties that produced. As I digested what had happened it seemed clear to me that given the chance, I could no longer meet people in this dimension only, for my energy would be looking further—even as St. Paul, at each instance that was "Damascus," built a path of repetitions of his choice.

---

[*] See the "Brief List of Important Personal References" at the end of this book.

15

Writings, Mysteries

The Parapsychological Association was a proud, elite organization with only about one hundred professional members worldwide at the time. With a membership that included a variety of scientists, it dedicated itself to laboratory and statistical studies (not experiential), trying to get the field respected by the science community. In fact, some members still questioned whether psi was real. I knew that Rhea A. White was the editor of one of the foremost publications in the field, *Journal of the American Society for Psychical Research.* Hoping to interest her in my computer PK, I wrote to ask if I could submit an essay. I mentioned having interviewed parapsychology pioneer J. B. Rhine, whom she remembered fondly as her boss.

What I didn't realize was that Rhea had a passion for *her* organization, the Exceptional Human Experience Network, with *its* newsletter and journal.

Over the summer she suggested that all the unusual experiences coming to me, a novelist, with no format to write them in, I put into the nonfiction frame she'd created: Exceptional Human Experience Autobiography. How lucky this proved to be. No matter how bizarre they seemed, exceptional events, *if potentiated*, she said, led to transformation. She was making a database of EE and EHE categories.

At the same time I attended the 37th Annual Parapsychological Association Convention at the University of Amsterdam, August 7–10. My interest in parapsychology went back to the 1960s, when, as a student, I interviewed Rhine's lab for the Duke University *Chronicle.* Rhine was appreciative, and in the aftermath set up a photo of him and myself for an encyclopedia; it happened to get spread worldwide via a number of books and articles.

That introduction to parapsychology was much furthered by later experiences. A friend who taught literature at Columbia University wryly commented: *Look, if all these things happened to Nabokov, he'd write about it and say he made the whole thing up.* But this idea didn't appeal to me. I wanted to understand "reality" the best I could and untangle the mysteries that decked my path. Why waste a mystery?

After the Amsterdam convention, I mailed Dutch parapsychologist/physicist Dick Bierman updates on my computer PK. Already in 1994 I was exposed to Ervin Laszlo, as he gave a speculative banquet address on holographic information storage in nature and information waves, which can now be read online.[96]

Meanwhile, my thirty-years-in-the-works *Love in Transition*, begun in Paris in 1965, now split into two volumes, was finally finished. I concluded the second volume at the end of August. Amazingly, on the twenty-eighth—as dated by my yellow sticky note—in the fury of finishing, *every other page* after 76 printed out with no text except a narrow column of single or double letters to the far right—the rest stark blank.

Alternate pages were normal. But the energy was so immense I felt the strange effect belonged in the book. I included one page with just a column of single letters down the far right border.

What I didn't yet know was that with devotees en route to meet him in India, Dhyanyogi-ji had "dropped the body." It was in the intensity of his *mahasamadhi*, at 1 or 2 a.m. August 29, Gujarat time— sitting in meditation, leaving Earth in what his website calls his "complete and final union with the Divine"—that the book completed.

With the India event unknown to me, I began to feel myself *spinning inside*—fast, as if jumping out of my skin. For several weeks at night, beginning in mid-August, I endured the baffling sensation, letting it run its course, at the edge of my ability to bear it. I liked to fully ingest an experience in that creative zone of the unconscious before asking for an outer explanation and relief. In September the energy still didn't stop. In the evenings I felt this strangeness inside me physically, as if I had put something into me that couldn't stay but I didn't want it to go, and yet I couldn't stand to hold it. By the end of the first week in September I phoned my friend the psychic and teacher Mariah Martin.

Before I said a word, she observed it was as if I were on jet fuel. She also said it was as if I had poked my hand into another universe, one usually accessed only by masters, and was trying to bring it here; that wasn't the way to do it. And that my energy had merged with Jesus.

Neither of us yet knew that in the aftermath of the comet striking Jupiter, king of the gods, Dhyanyogi-ji left the body. When such events occur, great energy is released, available. What did Dhyanyogi-ji have to do with my experience as he merged with the wider Oneness, the great ocean of consciousness, a departure he took consciously and had, if my suspicions later were correct, practiced for, walking in utter penetrating awareness, in the "dark"?

Meanwhile, others were experiencing Dhyanyogi-ji's departure. Not only in India. For instance, a longtime follower, Ron Rattner, who is the principal writer on SillySutras.com, a wonderful website of his mystical memoirs, from which the following account is excerpted, reported he was in San Francisco, asleep, August 29, suddenly wakened:

> With eyes open, I beheld in amazement an extraordinary and unprecedented vision—an otherworldly, multi-colored bird, translucent with a peacock-like tail and human-like eyes. Nothing about the bird appeared like any "real-life" bird I had ever before seen, or might have imagined.
>
> As I gazed in awe at this ethereal apparition, I was enveloped and transformed by a supernal aura of supreme Peace, which emanated from the bird's radiant dark human-like eyes. I awakened in the morning puzzled, and wondered about that extraordinary apparition which had enveloped me with "peace that passeth understanding."

The next day, thinking of the vision, he spontaneously wrote a poem, dictated by an "inner voice," about death. It ended, explaining why we live lives:

To awaken as Bliss
From all of this
Joyous that all is
"I."

Only a couple of days later he learned of the *mahasamadhi* and believed it to be "a parting gift and message from Guruji."

Learning of Dhyanyogi-ji's departure, which—barely, but precisely—fell on the birthday of Lord Krishna (remember that Krishna announced Dhyanyogi-ji's approaching birth to his mother in a dream), I recorded:

Even as this holy man died, I had completed the story I was telling in the book form. And the computer had every other page, in a style invented for this one occasion, printed out only the last letter of each word. Letters had been used, before this, as if in signatures, by the computer energy.

Even as I wrote that, quoting him, we are not always conscious of where our energy is, he had just passed away, into a new form, and I will say I was receiving some of that energy.

Then, referring to the IASD dream-telepathy contest, where I intruded unconsciously to telepathically offer the sleeping group a second option, I continued:

The Resurrection Christ would not walk onto the stage in a recognizable way, but he would over and over give people the chance to choose Him [that is, the higher consciousness], when the more visible choice, the usual, the seemingly obvious perhaps, was to choose Barabbas. Not even told that we sat inside this issue, or rather not told again for we had heard it before, we yet did sit inside individual choice that was remolding our world. And as there was no Appearance before each event, the room that opened, on purpose, gave to each the chance for that particular growth . . . To see what the choice would be. Was it the incarnated second, the moment's spark, illuminating the presence of the cosmic Christ?

Klonsky had told me he felt like someone in a murder mystery who finds out he's the one being murdered. But "there *will be* a punch line."

In 1994 I mailed Steven Spielberg a letter—never delivered. A perhaps outlandish attempt to get this material to the public, it was an idea for a film that now reads very 9/11-ish. This sketch below may be part of that idea, or it may be from another film. For ideas were flowing under the impact of the spirit committees. Read in that perspective, the story looked reasonable, just entirely multidimensional. It brings in my fictional Robert and Paula.

MOVIE SKETCH

Begins with a new millennium. In the heavens a new commandment is being recorded. It reads across the sky: LET THERE BE
NO MORE DEATH

Thunderclaps, for the heavens are clapping, lightning.

On the Earth, which hasn't received word of the commandment, much upheaval. The instruction is still Light Years away. Can it intercept the known End of the Century? The known Laws of the Earth? Can it give the Earth a closer connection with its real situation? Can it bring it out of the Cave of Plato, closer to the blinding light? Can it do miracles that are positive and not negative—that are constructive? Can it beam signals into the atmosphere that counteract the negative signals of the Archetype of Death as it dies?

For death on so large a scale will try to take many inhabitants with it. It will pull them into its clutches. It will hypnotize them with fears, bind them with barbed wire cords as they scream. Much evil will ensue and even nature may react with fear—just as animals in the forest run before a fire, as Bambi ran, hearing the sounds of the hunters approaching.

Thunder, lightning. Let us begin.

In a corner of the sky God appears, saying not to worry, things are as they should be. The Earth is undergoing an enormous change—a move to a higher consciousness—and much will have to fall in its wake. Much lower consciousness will have to give way. How can that be? For consciousness is identity to most. How can so many at the same time undergo this stripping bare of their souls, this loss of identity on a cosmic scale? But then how can a new consciousness come in, otherwise? And come in, it will.

Chills, o chills. Must this be undergone? It must.

There are many ways to begin this story, of a universal conscious-ness sweeping the Earth, like the Great Fire of London, like the plague, like a giant meteor crashing into the god of poetical triumph, Jupiter. O, let's make the Jupiter Symphony be seen first. A mighty symphonic hymn, a many-planet orchestra. Let's pick up the spirit roaring out into the starry night, of the song of the agonizing god, the one so close to the Earth that only poets and artists heard originally.

Now Time, in a cloak comes onto the stage and says the key words: "Earth, I am a burden to you. I should not be. I am making a connec-tion with Eternity this decade. I am opening my locked doors, as to a levee. Will you experience the floods of the unleashed water at my sides or will you come with me?"

But who will make a buffer for so great a shock as the feeling of eternity?

Leaders, there must be, familiar with it, at home in it, who dare to take on this mantle, pick up this sword, and as Time marches through the gates of Eternity defend the Earth, which shakes and rumbles and quakes with the human fears set loose. With the tremors of temptation.

BACKGROUND

A man and a woman, and God says you have the whole universe for
a stage, provided you clear up the Archetype of Love.

*So the Archetype of Death is on stage, at the same time sharing it
with the Archetype of Love, and this couple is in both. Both Archetypes
will be casting shadows and veils, and this man trying to reach high
noon, to be in a position of the sun at its zenith.*

Time, Place: Earth, New York City, 1960s

Action: *A double love story—one including a cerebral young woman,
about twenty-four and a poet with a strong practical side, considered
a genius by many. The other story involves a triangular relationship
between a very physically oriented housewife and her husband; the
woman acquires a fantasy attraction to an enigmatic young man.*

*Unbeknownst to anyone, this married woman, Anny, is the shad-
ow life of the cerebral Paula—the physical involvement, with a passionate desire for experience. Her husband, Joseph, is unable to satisfy
the need for excitement; thus, the spell cast by the mysterious Ian, who
himself finds this type of woman fascinating.*

*Robert (in the first couple) provides astounding insights in con-
densed form that speak to the depths of Paula. For her spirit is in love
with him but trapped by an Earth personality caught in a separation
between spirit and matter. And something in her prefers the unconscious, shadow relationship with the flamboyant, self-destructive dependent Ian, as dramatized in Anny.*

*Beyond this is the dimension of Archetype. Spirit must have new
outlines. New, original relationships. When the Earth breathes out this
time, it must breathe even further, beyond the contours it had. Expand
to include a new understanding of love.*

*And so this story, which had every reason to enter the Earth ex-
perientially in triumph, comes in differently. In challenge form. In
the satisfaction that soul growth feelings will equal those that in this
scenario had been sacrificed.*

The Earth is under the shadow of guilt and sacrifice. Only by going through that path can the real future open. If a man so loved a woman that he wanted her to experience what he had, that her soul might so grow it could become as visible to him on the Earth as off Earth, well then, wouldn't others learn from that as well? And so the multidimensional facets of the story would work with the missing facets of the Earth to help it in its birth. To help the female Archetype of soul growth, for instance.

Let me say that I got carried away writing this. Remember that I was a born novelist. I loved epic vision. I had no idea—and didn't care to know—how much literal truth was behind it. Reading the plot now, it's interesting to me and that's all that's important. Was it an off-Earth plot? It might be but didn't have to be. I was becoming me, writing the script, however it had been prewritten. Ultimately, we all do that if we become authentic.*

---

* Also, the young universe left us many models. Just born, the size of a Planck length (1.6 x 10-35 meters), it began to expand. It began to create. It was burning up hot: 1.4 x 1032°C. It might be that first touching our transpersonal nature, small as we are, an individual, feeling part of the All, with a way in—a hologram aspect—naturally begins to inflate. Not necessarily in feeling self-important but in feeling the work, or message, is. This is a trap that many who begin consciousness expansion pass through (safely). Jung emphasized not to identify with an archetype, not to identify with the Self. Spiritual teachers say not to identify with the Light.

However, first touched by the immensity of a transpersonal message, if you don't know where you've landed and see Big News all around, it can be baffling how to keep it in proportion. Sometimes in these years my reaction, as I was intense anyway, was to "see big," "think big." Think urgent. Not a bad thing. But it needed balance.

Something I didn't always have. The Self is certain, not uncertain. But as my initiation in Knokke will show me, now is fleeting. It's eternal. It's immense. But in our time, it's gone before you know it. It can feel like you're on top of the world in one second, what you have to say is so important, and then someone else's message is in the center. One way around this roller coaster is to get a healthy perspective on how encounters with the Self work. But that takes maturity. The kind that led the old yogis to chop wood and peel garlic. That is, come down to earth.

By Christmas 1994, I was working with a Romanian publisher/author, Didi-Ionel Cenuşer, a professor and former Fulbright scholar, to bring out in March 1996 *Love in Transition* I and II—in offset printing. In preparing computer PK examples for *Keep This Quiet!* IV, I look back wistfully at how easy it was to use low-tech hand-placement. "Signatures" that went far outside the printable window, I can only partially reproduce in the U.S. camera-ready files.

Didi, about forty years old, had the computer PK scanned; then we scissored the images out, Scotch-taping them to film paper, which the plates were made from! I'd been working on *Love in Transition* since 1965. Thirty years! Now two volumes would come out.

I was allowed to be involved in every step. All materials were selected individually. Would it be Austrian ink? German? Italian paper? I was exhilarated. Also—new to me—the printers were considered artists.

Kayumari was founded in 1995 as "a community and center for healing and spiritual seeking." Jyoti and Russell were the founders; others, like myself, donated money, each buying a yurt (tent house) to live in part or all the time.

> Kayumari is known in the Huichol Indian tradition as a blue deer
> that brings messages to the people from Spirit. It is said that where
> the blue deer walks, healthy communities grow.
>   The original home of Kayumari was nestled on 160 acres, sur-
> rounded by national forests in California's Sierra Nevada moun-
> tains near Yosemite National Park. From there Kayumari went

on to develop communities on the east coast, Switzerland, and Prague, and founded a home in the Brazilian Amazon.

I sit on a boulder in a forest clearing, drumming. My first sweat lodge. I am at Kayumari on top of a mountain. The other participants are inside a cavelike natural enclosure. Suddenly I see a face flying toward me. It bobs in front. Mother Meera.

She smiles and I instantly understand she's answering my request from two years back; by way of answer she asks me to perform an action. In recognizing me, she asks that I recognize someone else. But who?

I watch the group exit the grotto. Mother Meera has not told me whom to recognize. I assume it's someone she's watching over. I look for a person staggering, barely able to walk, under great emotion. No such person.

Then I see Wendy Cummins, being held on both sides as she leaves the grotto. She must be the one. Feeling very sure of it, I go over and it is. I tell her she is under the protection of Mother Meera, who was just here. It turned out Wendy was, in this period, in the full impact of her Awakening, in which spiritual events were numerous.

In the sweat lodge they had already realized that the Mother had joined their ceremony, but not whether it was Mary, Lakshmi, Green Tara, Isis, Kwan Yin, or any other divine feminine form. As I hold my hands on the sides of Wendy's head, in the characteristic pose of Mother Meera—which I felt spontaneously energized to do—she receives a vision.

Later, still at Kayumari, I sit inside the communal living room in the lodge, in front of the large altar. On it are photos of spiritual teachers (Dalai Lama, Dhyanyogi-ji . . .) and a golden statue of the Buddha; above the altar is a portrait of a running, red-haired Jesus. For the first time I am listening to a recording of Shri Anandi Ma singing samadhi music. Suddenly, I feel myself in a trance energy like never before.

It is as if I'm in a vortex that transmits and conducts; to my left in spirit in a vision is Shri Anandi Ma, to my right Dhyanyogi-ji.

I feel him saying he wants his biography to be about not only her feelings for him *but his for her.*

This intense communication I was clear was real. But what to do? I say nothing. As it turned out, years later his completed biography followed this format, though I never revealed the occurrence. Yet I knew for sure it was the wish of Dhyanyogi-ji.

Only, how would I communicate this intense transmission? Not verbally. But in a vortex of such strength, I believe the presence of the format was a conduction system, and in some way the fact that I listened in on the plans assisted. Or if not, then I merged with the planning location.

But there are now other incidents. I leave California and Jyoti drives me to San Francisco to drop me off before I fly out. As I sleep in the motel her image appears to me—subtly, suspended just under the ceiling. It tells me *the Earth wants safe passage. It wants to learn things for itself!* It asks for safe passage to make those discoveries.

She tells it to me as if I will deliver that message or act on it in some way, that the delivery is purposeful.

PART THREE

Clouds, Marlowe, Wish
of the Earth, Versailles

Jump into a black hole and come out with an arrow.
> —Polyxène Kasda, Greek artist

The imperative for human life on the planet is clear. Become super-coherent, or become extinct.
> —Ervin Laszlo

16

Akasha, Clouds . . .

Hungarian systems philosopher Ervin Laszlo speaks eloquently about how the people of Earth must learn to live together—must even go so far as to become supercoherent, as are a flock of geese. He goes back to the ancient Vedic system—its Sanskrit term *akasha*, or space. This space is in Vedic tradition the source of all life. Laszlo turns the word into a speculative zero-point "A-dimension" arising out of the "quantum vacuum."

There is an "M-dimension" (of matter) and an A-dimension, he says. In this subtle A-dimension we are all bound together and share information, though most of us never tap into it. We have to, he says.

He writes in *HuffPost*: "The new and revolutionary findings we detailed in our second blog of this 'Akashic Think' series, that our brain is connected with the world not only by decoding waves in the air—sounds—and waves in the electromagnetic field—light—but also by processing the wave-propagations that make space into an energy- and information-filled holographic cosmic matrix. It is now scientifically credible that we can connect with each other and with nature."[97]

I bring this in because some of the experiences I describe fit well in the context of tapping into a Source dimension, or field. I like Laszlo's eloquence about needing to come together and listen to each other.

Dhyanyogi-ji describes different aspects of ourself that, as bodies, we are in close contact with. He writes: "The physical body is like a house. The subtle body, which takes the shape of the physical body, is like the electrical system. The causal body is composed of all past karmas. That body is in the akash (sky)."[98]

Put another way, he writes that the astral (subtle) body "resides

in the physical body and directs all its functions. . . . [It] is guided by
the causal body, and that finally is guided by the soul."[99]

To indicate how difficult it is to put Sanskrit into English, the
Translator's Note of *Brahmanada* explains:

> Sound has been used for the Sanskrit word *nada* although the term
> *nada* includes far more than the word "sound." It includes all the
> more or less intangible energies of a wave-form or vibrational na-
> ture, from the first, most subtle stirrings of the mind to the pres-
> sure variations of the gaseous atmosphere which the ear hears as
> physical sound. . . .
>
> Another problem word is the Sanskrit *akasha* which has been
> rendered "ether" or "space" when we are talking about the struc-
> ture of the subtle body and the mind, and has been rendered "sky"
> in other places . . .
>
> Thus when one comes to the statement that ether is the me-
> dium for sound, for example, one should understand that the cate-
> gories are really *akasha* and *nada*, and should not fall into the error
> of thinking that because every high school physics student knows
> that air is the medium for sound waves, here he has some primitive
> unacquainted with the basics of modern science.

Under certain conditions, I have found, a person can tap into
("read") his or her akashic records, where karmic information is
stored. Under certain conditions also, it seems, a person can tap into
a global nonlocal information field. In fact, if we are not to take all
our experiences personally, literally, it seems obvious.

Earlier, in *Keep This Quiet!* III, we examined Carl Jung and
Wolfgang Pauli's belief in a unified psychophysical field, which they
took to be the spawning ground of both psychology and physics. The
ancient mystical positing of a Oneness field that Indian *rishis* and
other spiritual explorers discovered experientially is related. It recalls
physicist David Bohm's now-famous implicate/explicate order:

While working on plasmas at the Lawrence Radiation laboratory in California in the 1940s, Bohm noticed that once electrons were in a plasma (which has a high density of electrons and positive ions), they stopped behaving like individual particles and started behaving like a unit. It seemed as if the sea of electrons was somehow alive. He thought then that there was a deeper cause behind the random nature of the subatomic world.

Bohm came up with an idea of the quantum potential to suggest that subatomic particles are highly complex, dynamic entities that follow a precise path which is determined by subtle forces. In his view the quantum potential pervades all space and guides the motion of particles by providing information about the whole environment.[100]

In Bohm's hidden-variable theory, the universe is holographic. Each part contains the whole, because the implicate—Source—dimension feeds into and out of our explicate world of form. And nonlocal quantum information—based on "the configuration of the entire universe"!—guides the motion of point particles in 3-D space in a "pilot wave."[101]

Having these ideas swirling in the background is very helpful to me in anchoring my own experiences. However, it would be rampant chaos, I believe, to suggest that everybody has access to everything, as there has to be a way in, which is where resonance fits in. Resonance—based on what? we'll get to that—will provide a key.

To celebrate the one hundredth anniversary of the birth of laboratory-parapsychology pioneer J. B. Rhine, the Parapsychological Association planned a panel—to be held at their convention in Durham, North Carolina, in August 1995. At their previous convention, in Holland, I'd met Nancy Zingrone, a parapsychologist with a doctorate in psychology who was the 1995 program chair. When I sent her copies of my letters from Rhine, she put me into the slot of lead speaker on the panel.

What happened next turned me into a cloud photographer. Standing on my Tienen balcony, making slides, I shot film of Rhine's letters to me. To end the roll, I pointed my $100 Fuji camera randomly into the sky. The roll was developed, and I was amazed at faint images of what looked to me like faces in those final shots. Today I'm surprised I made anything of those blurs. But I threw myself into taking skyscapes. I would shoot about four rolls a day outside my apartment—the Belgian climate is perfect for clouds—watching progressively more clear details emerge. I couldn't wait to develop the film.

At last my nighttime dreams of staring up at the sky, seeing detailed scenes—continually transforming cinematic scenarios, impossible in the real world—was reaching showtime. The incubation sprang to life.

But it was also an evolution in subtle sight beginning in 1984, the night I met Mexican psychologist Hector Kuri-Cano at Openway in Charlottesville, Virginia. Later that evening, sitting on my bed, I had watched—for the first time—tiny circles in the air float around the room. The next day I saw them in the sky. When I asked, Hector said they were prana. Afterwards, I saw prana whenever I looked at the sky.

Now, in 1995, I spent hours staring at clouds. I would feel myself sinking into a meditative state; then, experimenting—intuitively— I'd angle a tip of the camera toward the sun, getting a bit of UV rays into the scene; "pulling" edges in—altering the color, it turned out.

By luck I sent the rolls to a budget service. The calibrations, without human input, produced strange colors—pale green, a tan I called "da Vinci brown"—that a human developer would have adjusted out. With the ground darkened in the development, invisible images materialized, as if stepping up from "behind" the blazing sun. Sometimes the blue sky, in the developed photo, was dark brown. Naturally, I liked the look and associated Rembrandt's use of brown.

Staring upward, I saw paintings—just as verbal cues in a book can bring sketchy mental pictures to life. But I could not paint. In a light body meditation I experienced the sense that I'd lost my hands—that I could sculpt or paint but was born without the force in my hands that could do so.

I had to use "mind through matter." My soul grouping focus.

It seemed to me I was "painting" *with perception* that, as I stared, materialized. Why did these images erupt full blown?

Leonardo wrote: "If you look upon an old wall covered with dirt, or the odd appearance of some streaked stones, you may discover several things like landscapes, battles, clouds, uncommon attitudes, humorous faces, draperies, etc. Out of this confused mass of objects, the mind will be furnished with an abundance of designs and subjects perfectly new."

The Renaissance was rife with examples: "Mantegna secreted zephyrs in the billowing clouds of his paintings, Bellini's rocks hid human faces and the folds in Dürer's drapery contained a camouflaged catalogue of physiognomic types."[102]

What created the medium? I decided it had to do with concentration organizing an energy field. Also, were the orange and the purple dots on my 4 x 6 prints infrared and ultraviolet that, now that I could see prana, I could see?

In my experiment, the light was critical—as I felt drawn to particular patches of cloud, fertile for perception, for form to appear out of. A manifesting ground.

Then one day in a photo there was a large pink stone poised in the air. Someone told me it was a hologram reflection of a huge stone in my Taos, New Mexico, ring. Maybe so. Anyway, over time I tried multiple shots with and without the ring. At unexpected moments the pink object would appear, at times looking like a triangle. Another illustrations is ahead in "Run Out of Town: A Pink Stone." Natural hologram or weird materialization, I loved it.

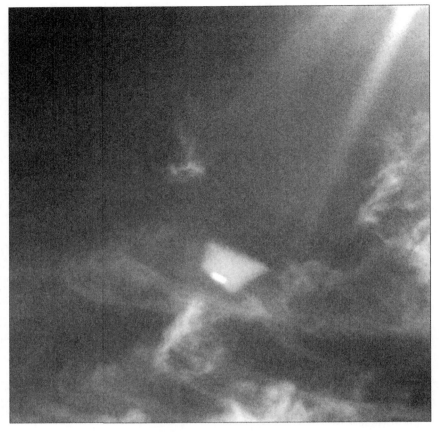

Taos Stone: detail

Insecure about bringing out my first two books in Romania, I found support in unexpected quarters. Two people—a Belgian and an American—saw in a vision a book by me in a store window. In Bruges it was at an introduction-to-channeling workshop; the person was a novice. The second was at the 1995 PA Convention celebrating Rhine. There, a parapsychologist I by chance talked to likewise— during the conversation—"saw" my book in a window. The same image. Hmmm. Peculiar. But years passed. It would be eighteen. Then without warning at the 2014 Gonzo Fest honoring Hunter Thompson the prediction blossomed. In Louisville, Kentucky, outside a bookstore a friend said, "Look at the window!"

Carmichael's Bookstore

What? There in the window were *Keep This Quiet!* I and II! In the iPhone photos that captured this moment in 2014 another surprise cropped in. I initially overlooked it because there were two shots. But when I went to select the images for *Keep This Quiet!* IV, I happened to pick up the second shot, taken also at 4/14/2013 4:13 p.m. When I enlarged it, the small object *half hidden behind the glasses* in the first shot was *at the right side of my head*, revealing unmistakably a pair of tiny, deep rose clapping hands! I swear the photos were not altered by me. But whatever produced it, this kind of weirdness breathes life into me. Here is something baffling, humorous. Something to question and learn about, and create out of. My curiosity is piqued. I want more.

Clapping Hands detail—first shot

Clapping Hands detail—second shot

At the 1995 PA Convention something else notable happened. A few months before, I'd been asked to help edit Shri Dhyanyogi-ji's biography. In preparing for the Durham, North Carolina, convention, I lay the open suitcase out on the floor a week or so in advance and as I passed by inserted items. Absolutely first was my passport.

Two nights before the trip I did a check, and the night before the early-morning flight I did a last quick check. No passport. Impossible.

I said, *don't panic* . . . slowly taking everything out. No passport. Then I thought: *Okay, I'll play along. Maybe I've omitted something important—so crucial that to go without it is like not going at all. What could be my symbolic passport?*

Okay, I went on, and packed Dhyanyogi-ji's manuscript for no reason, just in case. I couldn't think of anything else that could have an energy large enough to make my passport disappear, if that had happened. And it looked like it, in spite of the illogic and unlikelihood of it. Who knew why the presence of this energy had any bearing?

Then I inspected the suitcase again, as before, and there was the passport.

Well, the first evening in Durham, I went to the hotel bar, sat on a stool, and ordered a beer. A handsome parapsychologist, who appeared to be my age, was seated to my left; we talked. Somehow one of us mentioned kundalini, and this neuroscientist, Norman S. Don, began to tell me of his kundalini awakening. So I mentioned—of course—"Dhyanyogi—"

He interrupted, "Madhusudandas."

I gasped. He said, "There's a 99 percent chance that I'm the only person at this convention who's heard of him."

He went on: what had brought us together was "subtle energy." He said his own kundalini awakening had been spontaneous; his lower body wouldn't stop vibrating. Awkward indeed. It happened, he said, during the brief period Dhyanyogi-ji visited the United States. In desperation after trying other options Norm went to see him. He worked up to the front of the line, where hearing the tale, Dhyanyogi-ji said it was quite serious, to return at a certain time.

But pretty panicked, Norm got right back at the end of the line, advancing to the front. Dhyanyogi-ji then explained that he told Norm Don to return later because the matter needed thought. And so he did return at the stated time, receiving a mantra that eventually worked.

Don asked for a copy of the Dhyanyogi-ji-biography draft; I thought to make an exception was permissible. So, our encounter began.

It was helpful to have the head of the brain-function lab at the University of Illinois in Chicago to talk to—with his wealth of insight into consciousness and parapsychological research. Further, he had a key to the Meher Baba Center of Chicago—having been awakened to consciousness research by meeting this very famous Indian spiritual master in 1970. Don's PA profile includes "extensive field work in Brazil, studying the brain function of trance mediums, healers, people who take the hallucinogenic mixture, ayahuasca, and people claiming UFO abduction." It adds: "In addition to more mainstream work, he has published some 100 papers and book chapters on parapsychology and brain function."

Soon he would give me "Condition Three," his manuscript about testing Swedish psychic/engineer Olof Jonsson and being apprenticed to him. Jonsson sounded interesting: "Known for his soothing, soft-spoken voice, [he] preferred being called a scientist rather than a psychic. He came to the world's attention in a Feb. 26, 1971, *Time* magazine story about [in-flight] telepathic experiments he conducted with Apollo 14 astronaut Edgar Mitchell."

I find this odd fact: "Jonsson served as an officer in the Swedish Navy, using psychic powers to guide ships through undetected mine fields."[103]

Don's manuscript went beyond where I could follow in the 1990s, but in 2014, I happened to stumble on it again, inside a FedEx Express envelope. I find it enlightening, when placed beside *Keep This Quiet! IV.*

Olof's psychic powers came from reaching a level of consciousness he called Condition Three, he explained. CD3 tested in him as a 40 hz, gamma frequency that was coherent in all five electrode sites. To get there, he used fast circulation of chi—which works even sometimes if unconscious. Very slow circulation, he said, may also possibly get you there.

Olof said Condition Three was Light energy, not kundalini. This actually squares with what I'd been learning in light body courses since 1992.*

---

* But remember that in the Hindu system kundalini—the divine feminine energy—is only half the picture. Rising to the crown, she unites with Shiva, the divine masculine principle, or pure consciousness; in their united state, "knowledge, knower and the object of knowledge become one" (http://www.chakras.net/yoga-principles/22-shiva-and-shakti).

Back to my biography. Here is a good spot to bring in the Lake Tahoe story.

In Tahoe for a seminar, I was invited into a small side group for a sacred "medicine journey."

Trusting the spiritual atmosphere, I took a dose of Adam, an empathogen (also called MDMA). My first reaction was, I felt "normal," like "me." However, I started to black out, helpless as the darkness began to roll in. But just before I "disappeared" to who knows what aftermath, the leader came up and pointedly asked, "How do you think I stay conscious in samadhi?" *So this was samadhi,* I thought. *That's what this is.* (Samadhi is a meditative state of union with the divine.)

Instantly, I snapped out of it and was suddenly aware of my multidimensional self, also of the leader's multidimensional self—in multiple frequencies and names. Without hesitation, I heard myself speak to her as her highest self, asking, flabbergasting myself, "Shall we just march in?" Talking in that highest self, she understood the question, replying that she'd like to but there were reasons she couldn't.

When it was over, I was stunned she didn't remember the conversation, which had been aloud. I also was struck by the fact that this drug, which promoted empathy, felt natural to me. It just released my ability to say what I really thought.

But as time passed, I tried to digest the experience; pages and pages in the garage archives attest to the struggle. I believed "delegations" of spirits were assisting in the task. My apartment was again filled with very active subtle energies. I spoke of—or wrote of—a photon belt and "collecting, even as a bucket in rain, masses of energetic particles that hold pieces of our future if we assemble them or if not of our past or at least the consciousness that comes from there." I found it mind blowing to have convincingly, as in an intense kundalini experience, beyond my conscious control, blurted out thoughts of a much higher dimension of myself, thoughts I had no inkling of. It had been a severe jolt to my self-understanding. I could not go back.

There had been a breakthrough. How rarely, I thought, we get forced to experience the stretch of our multidimensional selves personally and in relationships.

The Tahoe experience was one of a kind. But beginning in 1995, I experienced, now and then, some Native American tipi ceremonies—an all-night healing in the Native American Church from dusk to dawn that might last thirteen hours. It features Grandfather Fire, a sacred tobacco pipe, drumming, singing (thanking Father Sky, Mother Earth, Lord Jesus, etc.); also, it features ill (sometimes terminally) people requesting healing, which involves the medicinal plant peyote. The ancient ceremony is conducted by a medicine man, or roadman, and is legal.

Underneath this shamanic ceremony is a great respect for the spiritual properties of plants and their connection to spirits. Though the indigenous use of peyote as a medicine is ancient, I was told a legend about how the Huichol Indians, who live in the mountains of central Mexico, came to know about this medicine and its intelligence. The legend is that a woman was traveling with her baby, and when the baby got ill she prayed to Creator. Opening her eyes, she saw peyote buttons. And the peyote, or cactus plant, told her intuitively how to use it and how to get back to her village. There, she shared the story, and the plant became one of their teachers. Eventually, the practice began to move up into North American tribes. In the ceremony no one is required to take peyote. The healing is also brought about, if it happens—which it often does—by community support, singing, trance drumming, listening together to the problem, taking it into the "tribe" sitting packed, cross-legged, on the floor. Not all Native Americans subscribe to this form of church, but many do.

In Romania, Professor Cenuşer finalized preparation for my first two *Love in Transition* books. I sat beside him at the computer in his office in Romania one hundred hours as he untangled my floppy. The perfect person. From then on as long as I lived in Belgium, I would spend two weeks to a month a year in Sibiu, always sleeping in "my" $7-a-day room in a private home.

Then Didi arranged a book launching. Here something happened that was relevant to my scant experience with shamanic ritual. Occasionally, I'd attended an event where a pourer of the Amazonian sacrament ayahuasca would arrive from Mapiá, Brazil, deep in the remote rainforest jungle, and hold a ceremony. Ayahuasca has been used in South America for thousands of years. For these indigenous peoples it is considered possible to get messages from spirits through close relationship to plants. In this particular plant is DMT, a human neurotransmitter. "The ayahuasca vine contains chemicals known as monoamine oxidase inhibitors (MAOIs) that allow the body to absorb the DMT from the leaves. . . . Vomiting and occasionally diarrhea, which the natives call 'la purga' (the purge), are considered part of the experience. This purging process is medically beneficial, as it clears the body of worms and other parasites."[104] Not to mention emotional poisons.

The purpose of taking the brew is healing and can bring spiritual gain. "Tukano Indians often report visions of jaguars and snakes and brilliant 'phosphene'[-]like bursts of light. Their shamans often use ayahuasca to enable their 'spirit flight,' at which point they can travel the Milky Way to commune with the ancestors or descend into the underworld to locate the sources of illness. The vine's name is well-earned, because many people report terrifying Near-death-like experiences (including Western researcher Michael Harner) (Harner, 1973), regardless of their cultural background. But interestingly, like many 'true' NDE experiencers, those having these visions almost always claimed they had found some kind of new insight or illumination."[105]

I attended a couple of these Santo Daime (ayahuasca) ceremonies over the late 1990s—being served a very small amount of the tealike liquid, as I was expected to be quite sensitive. I remember my first time, in 1996. A small group of people stood around the room. Everyone had to wear white. I had on a loose skirt.

For a split second soon after drinking, I "saw" the flutter of rippling air that in *Star Trek* heralds a materialization. I discounted it as probably nothing.

But the next thing I knew, I felt a being inside me who mentally asked me to raise my arms just slightly into a certain shape. Telepathically he communicated into the room that he was present, saying (still telepathically) if anyone wanted his help to go sit at the table in the center of the room. I concentrated on holding the focus. A few people went to sit in the center. And I guess he worked subtly on them.

I felt very shy about mentioning this afterwards. But when I did, the person I was talking to did not dismiss it. She said, "Look at your face!" It impressed her. Then the next morning the noted Chilean anthropologist and psychiatrist Claudio Naranjo arrived to lead us in discussion. He had not been present the night before.

Right off, he asked, "Did anyone go to heaven last night?" I said I did. When I described the arm position I'd held, he said it had a meaning in the first century A.D.

Soon afterwards when I went to my Belgian light body workshop, this being who had guided me in the ayahuasca ceremony came along. That was obvious to me. I felt excited that I finally had a guide who would be clearly present in public. But he did nothing till I told Roland I'd brought a guide. Roland, a very confident teacher with whom I got along well, said it was okay, let him loose. In the next meditation the guide worked directly on Roland and me, electrically. Afterwards, I asked Roland if he'd felt it.

He said, "Maybe in ten years I'll understand what happened." He described an experience of flying back in time to Egypt while simultaneously leading the class in his preplanned meditation. He said he thought it was an experience in time manipulation and shifting, that it was overwhelming. I had felt the same sense of pieces of time moved around in a high-speed flight into the past.

This guide was active again—for the last time—in the Romanian book launching.

17

1996

At last in Sibiu (March 25) *Love in Transition: Voyage of Ulysses—Letters to Penelope* I/II were launched; to introduce the series—swept up in the idea of a launching—I'd temporarily turned myself into a playwright and written *From The Eagle's Nest*; Mircea Ivănescu translated it, and the International Festival of Young Professional Theatre staged it.

My flier explained: "The eagle's nest, symbol of a highly perched consciousness, is the apartment in which Robert lives in New York City in the 1960s—the period during which the New York City scenes take place." The title also alluded to the Eagle Nebula (the Spire), seven thousand light years from Earth, with its Pillars of Creation, in which interstellar gas and dust create new stars. "Robert, the inspiration for the Ulysses character, now dead, is both communicating from his aerie and being remembered in flashbacks."

Robert/Milton had earlier told me he was down in the labyrinth—regarding our relationship block. "Find," he said, "the Ariadne's thread."

In the myth, Ariadne gives Theseus a ball of thread to unroll—as he progresses through the Cretan labyrinth, searching for the terrifying Minotaur, who wanted to eat him as a sacrificial victim. Slaying the monster, Theseus makes his way out with the thread.

An excerpt illustrates the play's experimentation:

Scene after scene after scene, looking for a thread to connect them.

A LITTLE CHILD: I'm the thread, Mommy. I'm your higher consciousness. I came in a child form. Nobody will be intimidated by me if I come in that form. I'm only a child.

PAULA: You know the meaning behind all this?

LITTLE CHILD: Of course I do. I'm the child who watched, inside you.

PAULA: And where are you now?

LITTLE CHILD: I'm taking you over more and more because you more and more see as I do. I don't have Earth eyes. I have extraterrestrial eyes. With those eyes everything has more forms, physical, energetic, and more—in one moment in time. I am those moments where that vision is seen.

PAULA: With those eyes, then I can make peace with my past.

LITTLE CHILD: You already did that. That's why I came. But you can dramatize it so that others can do the same, all of them, if they want to.

PAULA: You'll go to them too?

LITTLE CHILD: I already have. However, they don't know it—they don't see me. They're not sure how to use these new kinds of eyes.

In the discussion after my play, the talk was like fireworks as the audience argued. Some said the play didn't fit the traditional format. Mariah Martin would later explain to me about this guide that had come with me, "He's an electrical being. I don't think he's guided an earthling before. He was attracted to you because of your courage."

Anyway, that experience was short-lived. As quickly as he'd come, he left.

Lucky enough to have, two days later at the esteemed Astra

Library (built in the 1800s), a literary *Love in Transition* launching—
a panel—I emphasized a theme that was underlying the play:

> MASTER OF CEREMONIES: Let the show begin, the real one. Let the
> curtain go up on
>
> OUR NEW PERIOD Of
> EARTH HISTORY
>
> CURTAIN GOING UP on no matter what stage, what scenic set-
> ting, but behind all that it is the stage in Earth history that is being
> set. Portray it, then, differently, in different theaters.

18

Marlowe

I consolidated the theme further. Recalling my vision in a motel in San Francisco (page 202)—in which Jyoti brought me a cryptic message about the Earth's future, I melded with Humphrey Bogart. He teases information out of that hint.

Bogie speaks in the "I" form, even when referring to the "*Time's Up*" warning I received—the morning of my flight out of JFK (see the "Fire during Takeoff" chapter). Reminiscent of Klonsky's voice, his trench coat, his style, Bogart addresses Philip Marlowe (the private eye he played in *The Big Sleep*).

About my first piano recital: at seven as I nervously performed, the notes flew out of my head. So, I played the beginning and middle of the Bach keyboard composition, and beginning/middle again, forwards . . . backwards, till my hands miraculously recollected the end! Then I raced through the whole piece start to finish. I later speculated that situations in my life might be analogous to the child's attempts—that only by not despairing through repeated trials could I get to the real "The End."

End-of-Play Conversation[*]

BOGART: I've told you, Marlowe, who brought this second bit of information, in a vision. I guess it's just as accurate as the earlier vision at JFK, when the plane almost crashed at takeoff—though it was far from a close call. Yet this time is totally different. Though this is

---

[*] You take it from here, Sam. That's it for me.

about the future, I understand right away. I'll sit back, Marlowe—see what happens when the next round at the piano goes into play.

No, Marlowe, there is much I am concealing, examining, but I think this is the best ending—until the new round opens . . . the very last rendition, when all is clear. Anyway, what I am primarily interested in, to keep the focus on and tighten the screw on, *is*: what will become the end

*
r
b
C

Jo

this century's chapter in Earth history. Louder and louder the trumpet sounded, as more people went to the polls, to vote in the Earth of the next century.

And so Sam played, as in *Casablanca* (casa blanca). This was the ending. It hadn't been known which it would be.

It was just me here, now. Humphrey Bogart. But I understood the choice. All would be contained in it. It was broken into form—event form. I knew, though, the intention now. I didn't have to worry about the unfolding. I understood now what was inside it at the different moments. I had received the communication. Let the whole come in.

The Earth had explained its wish. (I don't care if you don't believe

this.) What the Earth wanted was safe passage. It wanted to be allowed to discover, from right here, which aspects of consciousness to add into its own. It did not want something already established. It wanted to delve into its own center to go into its own underground, to use the stock of energy there to fuel its expansion. But it needed protection. And so it requested no intervention but a rite of safe passage. I didn't know what that would mean, Marlowe. I didn't know when they would get back to here, but I would be waiting. I *had* understood.

I stood there, all by myself, taking it in. The Earth had an unknown future—which it wanted to construct, starting from deep within. It wanted the hidden wisdom there to be the focus. It wanted protection as it did this, a carved-out tunnel which surrounded it as it moved upward and outward. That was the wish of the Earth, Marlowe. It did not want to be taught. It wanted to learn on its own, but protected in this moment. So it will receive (with a bit of wariness and some rigorous barriers) that protection.

I received this communication, hot off the outer space wires, just as this was going into last rewriting. It was, as it were, the early Sunday morning edition of *The New York Times*. It was late at night here. I was taking a stroll Sunday morning. I picked up the *Times*, in this great city of New York. I read it and I reported what the Earth wanted.

As the computer is turning on this special effect—and off if that occurs—it is down there, where it is possible, that this communication comes from. I am walking on water to do this, you might say. No one sees that this is what this is. But let me tell you, Marlowe, it is an interesting evolvement I am witnessing.

19

Synchronicities, Visions, . . .

There are many synchronicities, visions, things hard to classify. One day—in 1997—a spiritual teacher I knew personally only a bit came to town to visit me. I greeted her on the Brussels platform. Above the roar of the trains coming and going she called me "the Magdalena."

She said, "To me you were one of the greatest mystics of all time."

The identification "one of the greatest mystics of all time," though about an archetype, an energy potential in everyone that was prominent in me, was amazingly rejuvenating. It fed my personality in a place deep inside.

I took it that my abstraction, my severity, were normal to me *and had been admired*. They were something that I, in my current time and place, was not championed for—not in that way. But I would always value the preciousness of that mystical state, that mystical information which flowed through me.

It was secretly relabeled. Its authority recognized. My wild, experimental ideas given a new position in my mind. Not twentieth-century Western, nor twenty-first-century Western but ancient mystical.

I went to Paris with this spiritual teacher and visited cathedrals. She said let's "receive transmissions." By this, she meant we would sit in meditation on a pew in different cathedrals—such as Notre Dame—or the Sacred Heart basilica of Montmartre (Sacré-Coeur). And see what came to us, into an empty mind, in the stillness. I tried. But I received no transmission. Nothing.

Till suddenly in the Versailles chapel. I was stopped in my tracks. In the midst of the fifteen minutes of silence, suddenly it was as if—to contradict my dislike of what the opulence represented—the walls themselves gave another viewpoint. Another thought intervened, halted me: *look at the variety, the abundance, look deeply at the detail. The point about these kings, queens, and nobility is not extravagant waste. Like a hand of multicolored cards—the queen, the king, the jack, the ones, the twos—they represent life.*

I read later that from 1682 till 1790 the Versailles palace was the official residence of the kings of France. Louis XIV retreated here for lovers' assignations with Louise de la Vallière. [106] Crowned at age four, he was dubbed the Sun King after performing in a ballet at fifteen. He was a patron of artists, including Molière. Molière's work survived because after one of his plays was plagiarized, he began to publish them himself.[107]

The park Louis XIV built around the Palace of Versailles was a fairyland, strongly scented by orange trees, with a grand canal and exotic animals. The Hall of Mirrors contains 17 arches, with 357 mirrors decorating the Galerie des Glaces.

The finance comptroller general required that decorations be built in France. But mirrors, very expensive, were a specialty of Venice. So he enticed Venetian workers to build them in France, using a new high-temperature melting technology.[108]

Despite censorship by King Louis XVI, Marie-Antoinette had given secret readings of Beaumarchais's *Marriage of Figaro* at court. As France's monetary crisis grew she cut back royal household staff positions that were based on privilege. Nobles were alienated.[109] History sometimes omits these facts.

I never forgot that message about how Life uses stories: that moment in the chapel I sensed real hearts, an assortment of human nature in daily life as rich and varied as a wall tapestry.

What suddenly became clear was that in living through moments of deciding, we do something far-reaching. The stories are handed over to human designers—all of us—as we remake the pageantry. The molds are drawn from. We revise, recalculate, offer stories to life.

The Versailles chapel somehow was the vehicle for the message not to dismiss these inhabitants as privileged, superficial. That they

were more—to the life force. In the times ahead I learned much
about how this works.

Versailles, the Human Tapestry

About ten years later I was intrigued by the following account. On
August 10, 1901, two English academics—the principal and vice-
principal of St. Hugh's College, Oxford—visited the gardens of the
Palace of Versailles. Exploring the grounds, they became lost. At an
abandoned farmhouse, they *"noticed an old plough lying by the side of
the road. Immediately, they both began to feel strange, as if a heavy mood
was oppressing their spirits. Two men dressed in long greyish-green coats
with small three-cornered hats passed."*

Asking the way to the Petit Trianon, the chateau where Marie
Antoinette retreated from court life, they were pointed to a path,
along which they spotted a gazebo (little shelter). But the dark mood
grew heavier.

*"Everything was very still. A repulsive[-]looking man, his face pitted
with small-pox, was standing by the gazebo, and he stared unpleasantly
at them."*[110]

Someone, hurrying up, told them to cross a small bridge. They
did and thought they had reached the Petit Trianon; there they found
a woman *"sitting on a stool, sketching."* She wore *"an old-fashioned
dress, covered with a pale green scarf. Again, they experienced a sensation of intense gloom. Suddenly a footman came rushing out of a nearby
building, slamming the door behind himself."*

The footman told them they were in the wrong spot, *"the entrance to the Petit Trianon was on the other side of the building."* On
the other side a wedding party prepared to start a tour of the rooms.
The mood lightened.

In England three months later one of these two academics,
Moberly, mentioned the sketching woman. Jourdain, the second
academic, hadn't seen her. Both recalled feeling that in the garden
something strange had occurred.

To compare, each wrote down a separate account. Moberly had seen figures Jourdain had not, but other details matched. A historical check showed that after mounting tension, it was *on August 10, 1792—the anniversary of their visit, August 10, 1901*—that the Tuileries Palace in Paris, where (in rising tensions of the French Revolution) the king and queen had been forced to take residence and were under surveillance, was sacked, their Swiss Guards massacred. The king and queen were soon imprisoned, shorn of every finery, ridiculed, and humiliated. A year later, white-haired and gaunt, riding in a garbage truck but with her back straight, the thirty-seven-year-old Marie Antoinette, who in better days at seven, as the Archduchess of Austria, had charmed the seven-year-old Mozart, was beheaded.

Mobley and Jourdain asked: had they somehow—on the anniversary of that terrible day—seen the ghost of Marie Antoinette? Or telepathically entered into one of the queen's lingering memories? A picture of Marie Antoinette looked to Moberly like the sketching woman, even to the clothes.

Returning to Versailles in January 1902, they discovered that on October 5, 1789, several years before, upon first learning of a Paris mob marching towards the palace gates, *Marie Antoinette was sitting at the Petit Trianon.*

They concluded that her memory of that terrifying moment must have remained fixed at that location, and they stumbled into it.

That Marie Antoinette had been in the garden is verified from the firsthand account of her daughter:

> It was on the 5th of October, 1789, of a Monday, that the first disturbances which, in the end, convulsed all France broke forth. In the morning of that too memorable day everyone was still tranquil at Versailles. My father had gone to hunt at Meudon, a royal château midway to Paris; *my mother had gone alone to her garden at Trianon* . . . Hardly had my Aunt Élisabeth reached Montreuil and begun her dinner when they came to tell her that all the women and all the rabble of Paris were coming, armed, to Versailles. A few

moments later the news was confirmed; they were already very near Versailles, where my father had not yet returned. My aunt went back at once to Versailles accompanied by her two ladies-in-waiting. Going to my uncle's apartment, she asked if he knew what was happening; he said he had heard talk of all Paris coming out to Versailles armed, but he did not believe it; my aunt assured him that the thing was true, and together they went to my mother. (emphasis added)[111]

Without investigating further, this instance—whatever one thinks of it—is a good starting point for some of what I go into from experience.

The Petit Trianon incident at Versailles was similar to my experience in the chapel. But in the Petit Trianon a sliver of individual time was walked into inside a collective momentous upheaval. In the chapel, a message left in a room helped me reassess the history lived there—an insight it was possible to pick up in the atmosphere, in transmission.

What is transmission? How could a room transmit? Or people leave behind an unwritten message for a stranger centuries ahead? A message left in emotion remaining in the walls, in a timeless imprint?

Another instance of history being picked up—this one visual—is narrated by Carl Jung. He was in Ravenna, Italy. There with colleague Toni Wolff, his mistress, whom his anima projected onto. At the Baptistery (near the Tomb of Galla Placidia) both saw four incredibly numinous mosaics. He was "vexed" not to remember such magnificent scenes from his one earlier visit, twenty years before. In the "strange mood" that descended he was "deeply stirred," aware of "the mild blue light that filled the room . . . [yet] the wonder of this light without any visible source did not trouble me."[112]

For twenty minutes he and Toni Wolff discussed baptism, its

initiatory connotations as depicted in the mosaics. It never occurred to either to question their sight. Most distinctly, Jung kept a "memory of the mosaic of Peter sinking [in the rough waves], and to this day can see every detail before my eyes: the blue of the sea, individual chips of the mosaic, the inscribed scrolls proceeding from the mouths of Peter and Christ, which I attempted to decipher."[113]

But the mosaic was not there. Never had been.

Sometime later he asked a traveler to bring him postcards or photographs of the mosaic he liked so much, *but the latter discovered this was not an easy errand at all. It was impossible: there were no such postcards; the mosaic didn't exist.*

Jung found it "among the most curious events in my life"[114]; he related it to the turbulent history of Empress Galla Placidia, daughter of Roman Emperor Theodosius I. At one point, captured in battle by Visigoth king Alaric I, she briefly became his consort, until his murder in 415. Returned to her brother, she was married off to Emperor Constantius III.

After many coups and much peril, around 425 she survived a shipwreck, traveling from Constantinople to Ravenna, capital of the Western Roman Empire, and vowed—if her family came out alive—to build a basilica depicting the riskiness of sea travel. But the resulting Church of S. Giovanni Evangelista, with its mosaics, burned down in 1568. Almost four hundred years before Jung and Toni Wolff "saw" them.

How, Jung pondered, did this sophisticated woman manage to live with a heathen, brutish Visigoth? Jung felt her intensity must resonate with *his* anima.

He wrote: "The anima of a man has a strongly historical character. As a personification of the unconscious she goes back into prehistory, and embodies the contents of the past. She provides the individual with those elements that he ought to know about this prehistory. To the individual, the anima is all life that has been in the past and is still alive in him. In comparison to her I have always felt myself to be a barbarian who really has no history—like a creature just sprung out of nothingness, with neither a past nor a future."[115]

During the years of Jung's "Confrontation with the Self," in the period in which he wrote *Seven Sermons to the Dead*, he'd experienced near-drowning (in the unconscious). After he emerged unharmed, he said, "The integration of the unconscious contents made an essential contribution to the completion of my personality."

In fact, he stated, to integrate "previously unconscious contents" leaves a subjective conviction of change that, though not able to be scientifically verified, is "fraught with consequences. Realistic psychotherapists, at any rate, and psychologists interested in therapy, can scarcely afford to overlook facts of this sort."[116]

In the series of situations above, one event went into another, one memory entered a different scene or just mind; floated in—convincingly. A scene, a feeling. If to actually, with a witness, see a mosaic, who could deny its literalness while staring at it or even afterwards, unless further evidence made it clear that, invisible the moment before, it was called forth for one's own eyes' perusal? "Contacted" somehow. How? In a momentary demolition of the usual partitions of time?

Around 1997, I attended a weekend event held by Al Miner, the channel of Lama Sing, and his wife, Susan, in mountainous Asheville, North Carolina. After a scary, high-winds landing at Asheville Regional Airport in a small, shaking plane, I was ready for the workshop. There, in the gorgeous Blue Ridge Mountains setting, at just over 2,000 feet above sea level, in a meditation led by Al, I had an impactful vision of Mother Mary (I later learned Susan saw her too but not the next detail) flying—holding a large curved container. She repeatedly reached into this bowl, like a flower girl in a wedding reaching into a basket of petals; each time, taking something out to distribute it.

She motioned me to help. We were flying, reaching into the basket. Distributing, I sensed, her consciousness—herself, in fact, and as I've been in her personality I felt it must include parts of me.

I was completely enchanted to participate. It felt light and wonderful. There are those who work on that level, preceding the physical, I would learn. I felt the process vividly, felt honored, light, full, and had no compunction about being a helper—a Distributor—invisibly.

I suppose this might be the part of me who loved to tell my secrets, showing me how it felt to just share everything, have open arms without a thought of return—at the same time be part of something secretive.

To jump a little ahead, in 2007 I rethought the implications. Perhaps, I saw, slapping my hand on my forehead, *she gave ME something to distribute*—visibly—direct from the container. Then I remembered how—to be recognized by Mother Meera on the soul level—I'd had to, at the same moment, recognize another person in California.

It happened again at a seminar in Bruges in the late 1990s. I saw Jesus pass through me in a light body meditation. *Through me* into someone else. He cast a glance at me, like saying: *See where I'm going*. Seated beside me, as she opened her eyes the young woman he entered remembered nothing.

She told the group it felt as if she'd gone deep under anesthesia. In my typically awkward reaction in those days, I was perplexed about what to say. I couldn't just leave it at that. In the break, I asked what she remembered. She brushed me off, didn't want to talk. Went outside for air.

Meanwhile, I went to speak to Roland, the teacher. But then, reentering the room, she walked straight up to me. Kissed me on the cheek and said, "I remember. I saw him. It was Jesus. I was *there*, but I don't know how . . ." She paused, looking at me quizzically, rhetorically, matter-of-factly. "*And his face was something like yours.*"

There was no need to elaborate. The experience had built-in safeguards. We had shared this and did not need to either broadcast what had happened or compete. We became wonderful friends. Though we rarely saw each other, she, a painter, wallpapered my apartment hall.

But still I didn't get it—this was my consciousness expressing how energy moves around, passing out tasks. In bestowing power, one did not lose power oneself, no matter how high the recognition one accorded the other. One did not project. It's Namaste.

Yes, I am being passed out. I, who had hidden so much, initially flinging my winter coat over my writings spread out over the floor if anyone entered my walk-up Village apartment in New York. No one could see any page of it.

Yet in writing, all that work was reorganizing ideas, patterns, energy—to pass myself out in the higher-consciousness level, that Mother energy being distributed. And far from wanting to hide, on a level or two or three up I was turning right around and intentionally passing my ideas, my creations, out because it all went into Source. In the unconscious. In the preconscious. I had just established, at least for now, a law. Of course, as consciousness expansion occurs, I could knock out this law. But it would do for now.

Much later I talked to Mariah Martin about writing this *Keep This Quiet!* series. "Do it," she said. "Consciousness needs New Consciousness." Right down here, when we get to *Why.*

As I got ready to bring out my fourth *Love in Transition* book, I needed permission, I thought, to quote from the Hindu satguru Sai Baba. But a formal letter might get lost in his screening process, I thought. I had no idea whether this was likely but decided to just ask him silently. The answer came in the most unusual way.

A visiting American spiritual teacher wanted to sightsee. Late in the day in Bruges we stood before the entrance to a Hindu shop filled with statues, candles and other items from India. But it had just closed for the night. Still, we lingered. And suddenly the owner's hand—coming up over my shoulder from behind—put a key in the door. He said, "Baba sent me out to get something for my daughter so I could meet you."

Agog at the bronze and brass items, we went in. It turned out he was the leader of a Sai Baba center. He said, "You are very fortunate. You are both in the energy of Sai Baba."

We bought a few things, ate a vegetarian feast he invited us to, and he drove us to the train. About to leave, suddenly he changed. We were crossing the pavement, headed toward the station entrance, and he filled with light, saying, "I love you . . . I love you." We were spellbound, as it appeared to us Sai Baba had taken form in him—was speaking to us.

I organized more Belgian workshops. And once, purchasing flowers in Leuven before a Hindu guru arrived, I was waited on by a man just back from Sai Baba's ashram in Puttaparthi. Snipping the ends of the stems, he told a story: Sai Baba had handed him a ring "to give to my Belgian devotee." The man hadn't known who that was but taking a guess gave it to a friend. I had no idea, but was it possible Sai Baba meant me? Who knows? I didn't. But I did feel the magnetism of having stumbled onto these scenes.

In a workshop for another Hindu teacher, I disagreed with statements he made to the participants. As the organizer, I felt a bit responsible. He was belittling great Hindu teachers, from my point of view. I felt they were helping me express their objection. So hoping to trigger a gentler angle, I asked a question. Suddenly while he answered me aloud, I felt—simultaneously—telepathy in my head.

On the one hand, I listened to his answer, but my attention was directed quite differently: I was shown a line drawn through space, an information boundary. (This was entirely inside the telepathy; the audible words were unrelated.) Normally—the message went—this line separated what we could learn on Earth from information not permitted us. Not only was that startling, but the one(s) transmitting invited me over the line.

Was it good intent? I wasn't sure and didn't respond. No, I wouldn't go *past the line* of what I was telepathically shown was a boundary, normally, to what we humans could find out. *A matrix, controlled by*—? *Good or bad? Was it a real line? When someone is inserting information into your head, it feels quite powerful and sure. But who's to say?*

Soon I experienced telepathy again. From the outside, Willy Vanluyten's low-rent apartment looked like the block apartment buildings in Communist East Europe. Inside, it was decorated nicely. This spiritual teacher was in the car several evenings as I was dropped off.

One day, standing in my living room, I felt a sobering appraisal hammering into me: *how awful it looks*. I was sure it wasn't my thought. For a few days the severe judgment forced its way in whenever I looked around. I was quite aghast! I couldn't control my own mind. But I shook the intrusive thought off. I felt sure he'd planted it, meaning it helpfully—he wanted me to upgrade. Then in a brochure I read about his teaching methods—telepathy was high on the list!

Is telepathy possible? On his website, physicist and quantum activist Amit Goswami looks at "quantum discontinuity" in spontaneous healing and other "leaps in the creative process"; they are signalless, he states; no exchange of energy is necessary to consciousness, because in his view it is self-referential: the "ground of being." He adds, "Nonlocal communication such as telepathy is another example."

A few years later, I wanted to leave Belgium. I remembered the high energy in the telepathy and plucked it from its hiding place. Now *that it was not imposed from outside*, it was useful.

To come back to Swedish psychic Olof Jonsson, whom neuroscientist Norm Don had extensively tested in his lab. Olof had been, in turn, grooming Norm to do psychic card feats by practicing two ten-minute energy-circulation meditations a day.

In 2014, finding Don's manuscript "Condition Three" in my papers, I was fascinated. The level Olof named Condition Three promotes healing and miracles, he said: it's Light in perfect harmony. Unlike kundalini, according to Olof, this Light energy has no color.

Don's book-length manuscript would be ready for publication now except that in numerous places he made a note to include a reference or anecdote. Also, he made videos to illustrate. The book opens July 26, 1986, on the forty-eighth floor of River Plaza with a panoramic view of the Chicago sunset. Olof has playing cards out. The room

is filled with laboratory equipment used for scientific experimentation involving brainwaves.

Olof has just asked me to shuffle one of the decks. During the seventh shuffle he asks, in a sort of Swedish accent: "What card would you like to find?" I pondered a few seconds, then said, "Ten of clubs." Olof then said, "Where in the deck is the ten of clubs?" I attempt to let the answer "float into my mind," as Olof had patiently put it to me countless times.

It's in the thirty-first position, Norm decides, then goes slowly through the deck, expecting the ten to show up at every turn. But it didn't. Finally, he got to the thirty-first card: "I was astounded to see the ten of clubs." To achieve this feat, as he did many times afterwards, required, Norm revealed, circulating his chi and controlling his energy level.

Here's a key statement: "Psi does <u>not</u> exist in Condition One, which includes our ordinary waking state. On this we completely agree with the skeptics."

Rather, "Psi is a state-specific phenomenon, as Charles Tart has suggested. Psi is not part of ordinary perception because of the difficult access to these other states of consciousness. . . . It should be clear that the future of parapsychology is very dim unless it becomes involved with the phenomenology of states of consciousness and learns more about access to these states. A 'state-specific science' must explicitly deal with access to the states of consciousness."[117]

This makes sense to me. Everyone is right. Psi doesn't exist in physical reality (in our everyday world), except that our everyday world has people in many states of consciousness, in some of which psi does exist and Condition Three is even the norm.

Don also said that martial arts master Gabriel Chin told him that more than Qigong, Tai Chi "circulates the chi."[118] From that, I better understood my experiences in Tai Chi in Leuven in the early '90s. Rediscovering my Leuven teacher, Jef Crab, in 2014, I learned that his Tai Chi was rooted in Taoism in the Master Henry Wang style, emphasizing the internal "circulation of the chi." Bingo. At the right place at the right time, I had unwittingly happened upon the Tai Chi that emphasized *what Olof said was the way to Condition Three.*

Don questioned Olof about a story in the *Indian Journal of Medicine.* As reported there, in a supervised experiment a yogi allowed himself to be buried alive. He wore an EKG monitor "and apparently stopped his heart for several days, then restarted it and was finally unearthed alive." Olof explains that this feat requires great skill and is dangerous:

If we lived the kind of life they do and we had the training, we could also do it. Even though the heart stopped, the brain is still circulating enough energy to keep from damaging itself. The brain is also not using energy because it's not doing anything. The yogi is in the light when he does that; he gets the life energy from another source we don't know anything about—we just know that it is there. It has to be there because nothing can function without energy. Similarly, there are people in the world who hardly eat or drink and they don't die.[119]

Yogananda clarifies: "The internal consciousness of ordinary people operates only from the lumbar, sacral, and coccygeal centers [the lower chakras] that direct all material sensory perceptions and enjoyments. The divine lovers and celestial poets work from the heart center. The calm unshaken yogi operates from the cervical [throat] center. He who can feel his presence in the entire vibratory creation has awakened the medullary and Christ centers.* The illumined yogi functions in the cerebral center of Cosmic Consciousness; he may be spoken of as an ascended yogi."[120]

For the umpteenth time, the Christ reference is to consciousness that is universal, not a religion, such as our preglobal geography restricted it to. Yogananda adds: "When Cosmic Consciousness comes into the realm of matter—into each of the atoms that make up the planets and island universes, and the different forms of plant, animal, and human life—that Consciousness is called Christ Consciousness."[121]

---

* Which brings us to how in the West there is no brain function indicated for our interaction with cosmic energy. "In *Autobiography of a Yogi*, Yogananda notes that the medulla oblongata [at the base of the brain stem] or the cerebellum [in the hind brain] is the secret to tapping into the cosmic energy reservoir" (Bradford, http://thedaobums.com/topic/4943-secret-of-the-big-accumulator/).

Run Out of Town, A Pink Stone

The karma of being "run out of town"—predicted by Richard Unger in reading my hands in 1991—roared in, in the late 1990s. It would not let me get through this lifetime without confronting it head on—thanks to my flamboyant late former husband Jan Mensaert, his last gift to me.

To get the gift required shunting aside the assaults he left in hiding. Some (silly, embarrassing) letters from me to Jan were in his house when his mother donated boxes of materials to the het Toreke museum archives (she couldn't read English!). How cornered I felt—stripped publicly—as my most crawling, codependent "inferior function," shadow writings entered the Flemish museum for all to see. And though it couldn't legally publish them, het Toreke could list them in catalogues or let *any interested party* peruse them in the reading room. *Even the silliest letter!*

Then around 1997 the museum began to plan a retrospective. To influence how Jan was pictured (as well as myself), I wrangled the four-year position of international editing coordinator of *Life, Page One,* an anthology it would publish on his life and work. I recruited contributors. Included were three U.S. psychologists, a Belgium therapist and publisher, and a process-oriented Zurich psychologist. They would give him a sensible—not merely sensationalist—platform. The project lasted till April 2001.

A Note I Sent to the contributors

The concept of INSCRIBING a life in a certain size came from Jan
Mensaert in his late writings; ideas sufficient to form a theory of the
larger, multidimensional nature of the human being—of which he
was an example, a proponent, and in this instance an inscribed portion of the larger self he also introduced. With this preface, we can
show him in as bizarre, as humorous, as playful, as genial a nature
as all of this included. We can break the mold of merely thinking
of him inside his limitations, BECAUSE HE ALREADY DID THAT IN HIS
WRITINGS.

Of all the people I've ever met, he was one of the most dedicated
to, and admiring of, his Higher Self. This self, he did not even ap-
pend the "his" to but termed the source of his writings. Never too
busy to listen to this inspiration, he went to great lengths to entice it
into presence, which was a major reason he lived so long in Morocco,
the nature-abounding "thinking man's country."

The limitations he had, on the one hand, worked with genius to
give it *limitations to break through*. These two poles—limit and breakthrough—were the theoretical boundaries he saw his lifetime in.

Another overview I sent the contributors was on Jan's death-defying
refusal to take the physical seriously—or rather, the threat of death.

I suggested this brought in a motif of *freeing the mind*. Imagine
"what kind of lifetime there might be—for the purpose of expanding
consciousness—of a consciousness centered in freedom if it thrust beyond the usual boundaries, never seeing them as literal or inherent."

I brought in the Russian classic *Crime and Punishment* in which
Raskolnikov, an indebted ex-student, murdered a pawnbroker.
Dostoevsky wrote: "From superficial and weak thinking, having been
influenced by certain 'unfinished' ideas in the air [at university], he

decides to get himself out of a difficult situation [poverty] quickly by
killing an old woman, a usurer and widow of a government servant.
The old woman is crazy, deaf, sick, greedy, and evil." But unexpectedly wracked by guilt in sleep afterwards, he had a nightmare in which
the pawnbroker laughed at him.

After death in *The Suicide Mozart*, Fiss, Jan's protagonist, faces a
graduation exam *on the soul level*:

> In his semiautobiographical novel, the presiding over of Fiss's Grad-
> uation Ceremony on Vega Fünf by muses, graces, gurus, and artists
> reveals that we are meeting this consciousness in some variations on
> the theme "playing with freedom," but it must pass strict require-
> ments for acceptance as a Path. The birth of the St. Paul conscious-
> ness [faith, hope, and love remained deep in Fiss's heart], inside the
> Raskolnikov consciousness, is one slant that offers a road in.
>
> Of course, Dostoyevsky slew the Raskolnikov consciousness.
> So do we here. But there is more to freedom.
>
> To have "the courage of existentialism" integrated with, or
> having just as strong a foundation inside, a St. Paul-Buddha thread
> of the free mind underneath. The basis of the burst of freedom into
> the modern age, the uncoupling from old beliefs, with some new
> twists, so that truly a path is made.
>
> A path into the Leap of Faith, it appears. These things, we are
> looking at, because we have arrived there by induction.

Jan Mensaert: Partial cover—*The Suicide Mozart* manuscript folder

Photograph of Pink Stone

Something else happened in 1997: *The Proud Highwayman*, consisting of Hunter Thompson's early letters—in which I was nowhere to be found. For shock effect I sent him some of his 1967 original letters to me—in bright orange-gold. He didn't respond.

I wrote May 14, telling him I was surprised to be missing from *Gonzo Letters* 1:

> But as you yourself noted, this was not a conclusive representation. There were many friends in the same boat. However, I am most partial to the collection of letters I myself have, and even the tribute to you that they offer and the personality and dreams that come through. Also the humor nonending. And the characterization of you that is completely uncensored and yet as appealing as any restructured or invented one. I have said this before. I am sure these letters are destined for survival someday, in the general understanding of how these things turn out. Probably I will not even be around then, but they will. This is because anyone who stumbles upon them will recognize the genuine voice and the immersion in a drama that they tell. For you are, day by day, writing about what produces the finished work of *Hell's Angels* . . .
>
> Most of all, I hope you are happy. And also that you are still healthy. I wondered it, all the more, as it is that time—sixty and all. So here, looking back, I hope you will find one of the best friends you ever had. As I find that, looking back, and always believed it. I hope you will always sing, "This is my life. I'm satisfied" . . .
>
> Remembering how you have a photographic eye, [here are samples of what I'm taking now]. I've enlarged the photographs, some to 50 by 65 cm [roughly, 20 x 25 inches] . . . I enjoy the startling sensation, of making these practically invisible portions of photographs completely visible. And the images they show.
>
> If ever you have a hunch you want to say something to me, or give me any kind of assignment or whatever, you know that I am someone you will be able to count on. No? I would like to think

that you think so. Are you well? (once again). How did you manage? (next question).

I sent something along these lines, including a few 4 x 6 cloud photographs. Whether or not they had the pink triangle, I don't remember. In grayscale the more the pale blue sky in the image below is darkened, the better you can see the cloud, it's so bright. Hunter's next book of letters, he left no stone unturned to give me credit. Not that I discovered *Gonzo Letters* 2 till 2005.

Flying Pink Triangle

PART FOUR

Bipod Metalism, Sinca Veche Cave, RNGs, Computer PK, A Double Initiation

The aim of wisdom is to dream high enough to lose the dream in the seeking of it.

—William Faulkner

I have spread my dreams under your feet; Tread softly because you tread on my dreams.

—W. B. Yeats

Bipod Metalism and a Cave

**1997–'99: visits to the Romanian cave,
Temple of Sinca Veche, Temple of the Wishes**

In Romania to publish *Love in Transition* IV: *The Bedtime Tales of Jesus—The Unconscious History of the Earth*, I was in the office of Didi Cenuşer, my publisher, when a man entered with a manuscript. Didi said it was about a cave the man wanted passionately to publicize, study. A cave? The mere word bespoke mysterious underground chambers to me. Naturally, I wanted to go. Back then the cave— near the small Transylvanian town of Făgăraş in Brasov County— was frequented only by locals. Its age is unknown—seven thousand years?—and legends abound; for instance: "The temple consists of five rooms, with two altars, and on the ceiling there is a chimney through which you can see the sky. The walls are drawn with different signs, and also with texts in a forgotten or unknown language . . . In here, the Dacian Priestesses used to operate. For a long period of time, the spiritual and administrative activity of the ancient Dacians was led by the High Priestesses." When I went there, we had the cave to ourselves.

Preceded by two children who presented me with flowers, we reached it through a meadow. On the way Didi pointed out a prehistoric mound.

Inside the cave I heard, in a little voice in my head I half dismissed, that I should pay special attention, it should stir my memory.

The near-eighty-year-old man guiding us, who was president of the society for preserving and researching its history, had played here

Margaret at the Temple of Sinca Veche

as a kid. He said to look at the chimney on top, it hadn't been open like that when he was a kid—the light had been blocked.

As the interior was earlier utterly dark, none of the children (or anyone else) had known about the face and symbols carved into the inner wall.

In his day the children lit branches to go in. Also, the two giant, empty holes conspicuous in the entranceway walls today had held huge crystals. Stolen around the time of the Second World War, they brought, he added, disaster to the thief. He showed us tiny pieces of quartz lying on the ground outside and said someone who slept in the cave dreamed the entire site sat on a bed of crystals. He said he thought in earlier times people meditated inside, using quartz "technology" to make contact telepathically with other dimensions.

Then I saw the symbol deep in the interior and the face on the wall. A man with his mouth right up against his nose. I felt drawn to him.

I had a vague sense of recognition. I couldn't shake the impression it looked like Jesus. When I later asked Al Miner whom it looked like, he immediately emailed, "the Master."

Beside the face was a hexagram (the Seal of Solomon, or Star of David) with a yin-yang, symbol inside. When I look at the long, winding road of my journey, the unlikely find on the wall is a perfect synchronicity.

The face on the wall

The symbols on the inner wall

Notice the thick, black outline around the Romanian in the photo on the next page. It appeared spontaneously. He had told me the cave produced light effects in photographs and to watch for them. I hadn't noticed any, however, till just now.

The Star of David on the cave wall brings us right back to physicist Wolfgang Pauli. F. David Peat points out that the Self for Pauli was represented by the two triangles of the Star, which symbolize "the full feminine with the   masculine."[122] For Pauli, the bottom triangle, the feminine, must be chthonic ("subterranean").

Jung, on the other hand, represented the Self by four, the quaternity. This led Pauli to wholeheartedly object when Jung embraced the Vatican doctrine of the Assumption of Mary *into heaven*. Taking the Trinity as masculine, Jung thought the Assumption added the feminine to it (making a quaternity). But Pauli, writing Markus Fierz in 1953, spoke out against hoisting the Queen, the feminine, into heaven, where she was dissociated from the dark and the acausal.[123]

The Romanian who took us to the cave

He criticized this disinfection of matter to Marie-Louise von Franz: "What the unconscious demands of us as a compensation for the '*Zeitgeist*' . . . —to which the atomic bomb also belongs—is *a mirror image of the downwards-pointing Assumptio Mariae* [Assumption of Mary]: a reception of the [underworld/earthy] chthonic wisdom into the male consciousness out of a deep, dark mother's womb. This could lead to a new balance (while the projection of quaternities into heaven leaves me cold)." [124]

We are now at another fork in the road, descending further and further down and back—as if staring at a silver disc in hypnosis; further till we are almost in the Gnostic period, which had beckoned at Jung's front door, invisible fingers ringing his bell. The Gnostics inspired him, with their archetypes, to find the psychic history of Earth. Yes, we are almost where this nicely clicks in.

Let's go further. Pauli frequently dreamed of a Chinese woman, his "dark anima" (perhaps the "anima mundi," the "soul in matter"); once she advises him to play chess "in every conceivable combination." Based on that famous dream, I can better interpret a significant dream of mine: *an engaged woman and man from China were separated two years. Their wedding date already set. Just before the reunion she betrayed him but arrived to be wed in a numinous emerald-green dress.*

Thinking of alchemy's Sacred Marriage of opposites, it takes little skill to associate the brilliant emerald green—of my mysterious dream wedding—with the famous Emerald Tablet of Hermes Trismegistus. The hermetic-alchemy Tablet's precepts begin: "1) True, without falsehood, certain, most certain. 2) What is above is like what is below, and what is below is like that which is above. To make the miracle of the one thing." [125]

Before the wedding, preceded by a two-*year* (read "centuries") separation, my woman from China was unfaithful, incurring a dazzling reclothing in emerald green. The obvious conclusion is that she "embraced" (a dream pun) hermetic alchemy. Was she adding it to Taoism?

But wait. Before we leave, the hexagram exists in Hinduism as well—representing Shakti (water, the divine feminine) and Shiva (fire, the divine masculine): active divinity and pure consciousness. [127]

In his last published work, Jung related alchemy to the individuation process, or wholeness: the goal of his depth psychology. He said the alchemist *projected psychic contents* onto the outer object. Yet alchemy was carried forward into modern times without being understood as a symbol.

So we have another archetype, two more peas in the pod.

Let's return for a second to my dream clue that "bipod metalism" was a continuation of Jung's work (see page 128). In that dream in 1981 in the Jung "museum," his assistant gave me this topic as the most interesting thing to look at there. Jung believed that grappling with the alchemical Sacred Marriage (the *coniunctio, or mystical union of opposites, deep in the human psyche*) precipitated his two heart illnesses: one, a full-blown cardiac arrest incurring a near-death experience.

And perhaps the mask the assistant's words wore in my case was just this: the fighting *matter* symbol of Mars (the male principle, jet fuel, fiery yang: enthusiastic, forceful) and the occult, mystical, intuitive Neptune. These two being conjuncted at a rare intensity in my natal chart.

Physicist F. David Peat, in *Pathways of Chance*, describes editing film. Splicing and dissolving scenes, he found himself unexpectedly, "in the zone: it was as if the movements and relationships of the film had become internalized in muscular reflexes; the film had become feelings in the stomach, subtle movements and a symphony of sensations."[128]

It said something remarkable about mind/matter. About psyche/matter. About the sensation function in Jung's typology when it combined with its opposite, intuition—as in Peat's example, where his muscles inwardly illustrated the inner properties of the film itself. Demonstrating that the irrational abstraction (of intuition) and the physical tangibility (of bodily sensations) might point to an even larger symmetry or equation in matter/psyche.

Might it be the very bipod formula we've been seeking? But we are not there yet.

This book does not yet collapse its wave function down into *this is it? Found it. Stop.* In the way of the modern sound byte—

Let's keep this journey alive into a few more—just a few—pages.

For this bipod mystery thrown up by the unconscious. Perhaps there's a pair here as well: a Logos and an Eros ego, which communicate with us by different methods. Supporting this idea, Jungian Remo Roth in *Return of the World Soul: Wolfgang Pauli, C. G. Jung and the Challenge of Psychophysical Reality* says the introverted Eros ego involves what he calls "the gut brain," or belly brain. More ahead.

Maybe the great harmony of the spheres in Johannes Kepler's day, the deeper answer Newton sought (beyond the properties of gravity he discovered),* the answer in the Emerald Wedding Dress, the answer in the Meta4—to go back to one of my original metaphors—had to do with psyche and matter playing together at the piano *à quatre mains.*†

But hold on. Roth refers to a famous incident at the Jung Institute in Küsnacht. At the inauguration festivities Pauli entered the room. As if right on signal, a Chinese vase shattered on the floor—pouring out water. Used to psychokinetic effects activated by his mere presence, Pauli admitted he felt as if he carried alchemist Robert Fludd and scientist Kepler—seventeenth-century opposites—inside him. The unruly, dynamic Fludd/"flood" symbol of this clash, suggested, he said, the fledgling Institute's calling.

Roth emphasizes that yang and yin, in Chinese philosophy, "exchange attributes." The masculine/active and the feminine/passive principle exist in a bipolar dynamics. "The latter reaches into the unus mundus and the Beyond. In the Daoist [Taoist] process, yang transforms into yin and in the same moment yin transforms into yang with higher order or increased negentropy [harmony]."[129]

Here I Skyped my former Tai Chi teacher Jef Crab for a comment:

---

* Newton wrote that "'philosophers have hitherto attempted the search of nature in vain' for the source of the gravitational force, as he was convinced 'by many reasons' that there were 'causes hitherto unknown' that were fundamental to all the 'phenomena of nature' . . . And in Newton's 1713 'General Scholium' [appended to] the second edition of Principia: 'I have not yet been able to discover the cause of these properties of gravity from phenomena and I feign no hypotheses'" (https://en.wikipedia.org/wiki/Newton%27s_law_of_universal_gravitation).

† A French term for a duet played on one piano—"with four hands"

The old Taoists, he explained, believed the universe was already there, but in the nonmanifest form: *wu chi*—"resting in itself." Jef went on: then came movement and the universe went into Tai Chi, distinguishing what is resting in itself (yin) and what starts to move (yang). "Everything still has these aspects." He illustrated with a pair of glasses on a table (wu chi). "I put them on my face," he said; "they have a function." Yin (contracted) and yang (expansive) are "two sides of the same coin." He said, "For every manifestation both must be present. They simply cannot exist on their own."

For various reasons, Roth connected the Tao to Pauli's Fludd/flood synchronicity, saying it favored "treat[ing] energy as a 'fluid principle' that can cross the barriers between yang and yin, between the world of physics and depth psychology on the one hand, and the world of the paranormal on the other."[130] He calls yang *spirit-psyche* and yin *matter-psyche*—matter-psyche being "a 'supernatural,' i.e., a magical principle repressed in the 17th century, when mathematics reduced natural science to causal science."[131]

Pauli and a red car provide an illustration. Thinking about his feelings—aware that red associates with the feeling function in Jung's personality types—Pauli was sitting in the Café Odeon in downtown Zurich. His gaze settled outside the window. Spontaneously, as he looked at it, the red car burst into flames.

Roth says that in the precipitated scene, matter-psyche, *being nonlocal*, spotted a potential symbol of itself: a red car filled with gas. He calls this "the spontaneous observation of an *inner* quantum leap" (my italics). To clarify, he added that "the 'individual' and the 'collective' matter-psyche are nonlocally connected."[132]

His thesis is in too intricate detail to go into here, but I found it interesting.

I questioned Jef about the relationship of Taoism with nonlocality. In illustration he said, "The meridians in my body don't start or end at my fingertips—the six meridians there connect with energy streams (energetic patterns) in the surroundings."

Jung hypothesized there might be "a second psychic system

coexisting with consciousness"—one that fed its own perceptions into consciousness. If so, it would be "of absolutely revolutionary significance."[133]

Picking the idea up, Roth believes the second system is in the autonomic nervous system, or ANS. (Roth calls it the "vegetative nervous system," or VNS.)

Older than the central nervous system, the ANS controls unconscious bodily activities like heart rate. Jung said it "possesses 'transcerebral thought and perception.'"[134]

To some degree the concept draws on Chinese medicine, in which the sympathetic nervous system of the ANS raises yang, and the parasympathetic puts the brakes on it in a peaceful yin.[135]

When I again consulted Jef Crab, he flipped the whole thing around, saying "we are like hollow barrels floating in an immense ocean of colors, which is streaming through us—all the different types of energy and archetypes." This supports our nervous system. Not surprisingly, he speaks in terms of filling up with universal energy in a motionless, nonresistant, accepting state, then using attention (or intention) to direct it into action. He demonstrated by barely touching his wife with his fingertips. She instantly keeled over backward. Anybody can learn to do that, he said.

Besides the connection to Eastern medicine, this topic brings us right to contemporary body-centered psychotherapists like London's Roz Carroll, who writes:

> I come from a therapeutic tradition, whose basic premise is that bodily processes are intrinsically involved in psychological processes, and vice versa. In this field the autonomic nervous system has long been recognised as a barometer of emotional intensity and internal conflict. Body psychotherapy developed out of the work of Wilhelm Reich, who was a student of Freud's. Its basic premise is that the mind and the body cannot be understood as separate phenomena, and therefore need to be addressed together in psychotherapy. . . .

My proposal this evening is that object relations are inter-
nalised in the body at every level of function and structure, including as modifications to the autonomic nervous system. . . .
Although I'll be drawing on some very recent neuroscientific and
metapsychological thinking, I want to give credit to Reich's insights which were so ahead of his time.

Roth assigned the term "Logos consciousness" ("Logos ego") to a
"superior thinking/inferior feeling" type in Jung's typology. Opposite
it is "Eros consciousness" ("Eros ego"), where the sensation function
associates—not with the central nervous system but with the VNS.
And—in his view—can have *inner* quantum leaps.

F. David Peat, who has taught many Jungian seminars, explained,
"The notion of a missing dimension appeared to Pauli in several of
his dreams. And what was that missing dimension, that dimension in
which it would be possible to unify physics and psychology, matter
and psyche? None other than Eros, the missing dimension in Pauli's
own life—the vacuum he recognized as existing in a physics that
had become obsessed by a will to power."[136] Which brings us back to
Pauli and the red car.

In view of Pauli's deep identification with the Logos consciousness, Roth writes, something inside him took a counterposition in
the VNS, "which he sensed as a tension in his belly. . . . Since matter-psyche is psychophysically nonlocal, it was not limited to Pauli's
body, but affected the surroundings, as well."[137]

Roth uses this unconscious process to explain the Pauli Effect;
that is, the psychokinetically triggered mishaps often in proximity to
the Nobel Laureate, whereby an expensive piece of equipment might
malfunction or disasters, large and small, occur in his presence.

Historian Robert Moss writes: "The best story on the Pauli
Effect is from Rudolf Peierls, a German-born physicist who moved
to England and later worked on the Manhattan Project." Moss described how some scientists tried to parody the Pauli Effect: "They
carefully suspended a chandelier by a rope that they intended to

release when Pauli entered the room, causing the chandelier to crash down. 'But when Pauli came, the rope became wedged on a pulley and nothing happened—a typical example of the Pauli Effect." Ross added: "According to his close colleague Marcus Fierz, 'Pauli believed thoroughly in his effect.' He experienced an unpleasant inner tension before things blew up. After the event, he felt relief and release from tension, even moments of euphoria." As an aside, in preparing this index, when I touched the item "Pauli Effect" with the mouse, all the items from "nonlocality" through "Pauli Effect" turned red.

Rather humorously: "It has been suggested that the reason Pauli was not invited to join the Manhattan Project—which recruited many physicists from his circle—was that the directors knew Pauli's reputation and were worried that he would blow up something vital."[138]

Once, when Pauli's train halted in Göttingen, an experimenter in the local university lab experienced inexplicable malfunctions in his equipment; it then suddenly resumed working properly; the mishap was quickly traced to the timing of Pauli switching trains.[139]

Roth believes Pauli exhibited this inner "radioactivity" as a result of repression because of an extreme, one-sided development of thinking. For example, when Pauli's first wife, the cabaret dancer Käthe Deppner, left him, he rushed into work and announced (correctly) the hypothesis of the neutrino a month later. But inside was a cauldron—in Jung's typology—of "inferior feeling."[140]

In *Keep This Quiet!* III, I recounted some of the Nobel Laureate's dreams. In one, early scientists went on trial, joined by Pauli himself. The charge was that their animas (their inner feminine) "objectified" rotation, a word that Pauli, in the dream, associated with "the circulation of blood and the circulation of the light." See page 265 for clarification. He realized that unlike those (including Johannes Kepler) who stood trial, Kepler's contemporary and nemesis, the alchemist/doctor Robert Fludd, understood rotation. A good interpretation comes from David Lindorff, who explains that it "suggests that the anima's spirit was being projected onto a rationally oriented vision of the cosmos, as opposed to the mystical conception with which she had been associated up to that time." For Fludd, I wrote, "the world still had a soul. A wholeness, now symbolized by number 4. And being cooked up high above, *en haut*, in our master oven, or *meta4*."*

The Pauli Effect couldn't have seemed too bizarre to Jung—who had experiences of his own. In 1909 in Freud's library, Jung asked this father figure psychoanalyst what he thought of parapsychology. Freud, very rational and materialistic, was skeptical. Suddenly they heard a loud crack. It came from the bookcase. *See,* Jung said. *That's an example of an exteriorization phenomenon. And it's going to happen again right now.* Bosh, said Freud.

Sure enough. The bookcase complied with another loud crack. Jung much later explained in his autobiography that as this occurred his belly felt like red-hot iron.

Maybe the bipolar "exchange of attributes" was partly what Newton looked for. Maybe it tied in to his alchemical research. Maybe, maybe . . .

Roth sums up: "It is important to note that this new [bipolar] definition contradicts the currently accepted one." For in science today "psyche" is another word for "spirit."

"As a logical consequence," he writes, "the term 'matter-psyche' does not exist in the terminology of consciousness theories, nor does it exist in C. G. Jung's depth psychology, where the collective unconscious is only defined as the spirit-psyche principle. Thus, the replacement of the unipolar by the bipolar energy concept leads into a particularly new worldview."

Roth hypothesizes that Pauli carrying inner opposites was symptomatic of a "constellated problem"—perhaps related to the fact that in his quantum physics formulation for elementary particles, he substituted spin for "a bipolar energy concept."[141] Roth speculates that

---

*   *En haut* (pronounced O) is "on high" in French. Four, to Jung, as a number meant wholeness, individuation, the Self. *Four* is "oven" in French. For more on number 4, see the "Brief List of Important Personal References" at the end of this book, or read *Keep This Quiet!* III.

Pauli's unconscious was leading him down one path and his scientific self stopped short, with QM spin. This balking had repercussions.

In illustration Roth cited the following Pauli dream: *An Asian woman led him through a trap door, then balletlike, in pantomime, guided him to an auditorium. There, an audience expected him to speak. Rhythmically she danced up the steps, to the open air outside, and back down. Her left index finger and arm pointing up, her right arm and index finger pointing down—the "rhythmic movement" creating* (as Pauli put it) *a "rotational movement: the circulation of light. The difference between the floors," he added, "seems to diminish 'magically.'"*

Roth observed how the (side-to-side or up/down) oscillation became spin—revolution—when the floors began to merge (the Above and the Below) into *the point A of nonlocality.*[*]

Whatever we have gotten a hold of, it's a wild thing. Surely announcing itself hither and yon as hugely significant. Rectifying. Preparing us, through the tools that synchronicity has, a constellated archetype has—beckoning, glimmering, glittering and smashing us over the head—telling us to go further, to step into this adventure of Who am I? What am I? What is the Self? What is reality? What is Earth? The universe? For underneath these clues are threads into the Bigger Picture.

And so let us go on, à *quatre mains.* Perhaps even all hands on deck. We'll see where the story is going, offering us a chance to jump on board.

---

[*] He adds elsewhere, "I concluded further that the process (oscillation → rotation) symbolizes the incarnation of subtle matter out of the unus mundus into our world" (Roth, *Return of the World Soul* II: 159).

22

Computer PK and the Cave

By 1998, *Love in Transition* IV was out; I was focused on a new series, *Space Encounters*. This time to display the computer illustrations at full size, I chose A4 format (the European equivalent of 8.5 x 11).

Pondering the Romanian cave—the Temple of Sinca Veche—I asked Didi to take me to it again, imagining that *on the symbolical level* the male face on the wall could be a literalization of the Jungian animus. In the 1970s I'd made a draft of the end of *Love in Transition* I/II. In it, the skeletal plot, oddly, led me to a male painter—trying to get my attention from a cave inside me. This mystifying outline my inspiration concocted in what was then a novel made no sense until I learned that in Jungian individuation, to get in touch with the Self one must discover one's opposite sex within.

Reflecting much later, I'd realized the "inner painter" must be my animus. Then here, I saw—there as if out of my conjurings years earlier—a male face on an *actual Romanian cave wall*. Though that was literal, I compared Jung's hallucination in which he distinctly saw the Empress Galla Placidia frescoes (courtesy, he thought, of his anima). Below, the computer provided a humorous twist. On-screen, in normal-sized font, I had typed, "A question had been 'begged'— represented by him—well, EXACTLY WHERE DOES THIS SAY WE ARE????" To read the text, I had to fit two printouts together. Unlike in the following version, computer PKa) was so small I at first thought the page was blank; b) was super-large.

TLY

Computer PK-a

"begged"--represented by him?—well, EXAC
SAY WE ARE?? ???

Computer PK-b

In this style of computer PK, in the printing a single passage was broken up into two fragment-pages—beginning or ending in jagged letter-pieces. In the first such instances, I inadvertently discarded the tiniest. But then I noticed—a eureka!—how fragments *fit precisely together*. I loved the puzzle factor, the live intensity. The moment when— the sheet out of the printer—I saw what had been created.

Perhaps this was the visually focused animus—his quirky self "caved in." What don't we know? What part did these experiences play in discovering me?

I speculated: "First I was sensing that a man was inside me, waiting to draw me to where he was. But is this not the *beggar on the other side of the window?*"

As a reminder, while sitting at the Dôme Café in Montparnasse, Paris, in 1965, I noticed a beggar; merely by his mouthing a desperate request, he somehow signaled me to begin writing *Love in Transition*. (See the "Brief List of Important Personal References" at the end of *Keep This Quiet! IV*.) Decades later, at the launching of *Love in Transition* I/ II, the French professor, poet, critic Eugène Van Itterbeek said, "It was not only Hemingway you went to see at the Dôme Restaurant; it was Charlie Baudelaire—discovering the unconscious link with his poem 'The Gâteau.'"

I decided it was "clearly the archetype of the universal Inner Christ or Inner Light, higher consciousness, the Self—for the term transforms as the writing continues . . . But look how it proved itself."[142] As Jung put it: "What happens inside oneself when one integrates previously unconscious contents with the consciousness is something which can scarcely be described in words. It can only be experienced."[143]

From *Space Encounters* III: "All across the Earth the integrations are going on. As here, they are devastatingly original and unbelievable. It is not the time of marching joylessly and laxly into a great new age (whether or not one calls it the year 1999, or the year [2040], or the year 1210, or 1060 for some others), but of justifying the claim of the Earth to have a right to march forth *into the universe*."

23

Marlowe Comes Back In

With so much to think about, I retrieved Marlowe to talk to in *Love in Transition* IV—this time directly, not through an alias; I told him about finding "the collective me—correlative to the individual me":

> I have found another myself, you might say. I have found the one that is spread out over the universe, in stories and events and that is always present *only* in field form. I have found that one, Marlowe, who has so many experiences, and is directing them into my mind, of the collective funneled into the personal. I am holding that form, and— . . .
>
> The collective facet of the person brings in a different psychology, and we were just understanding single-person psychology, with a little of group dynamic psychology. Quick as a flash we race to this new TRANSPERSONAL PSYCHOLOGY.

Showing Marlowe the Cave

When Marlowe got over the first shock, he wanted to know what it might be like, living in tune with the sky—having advance notices, if we wanted them, of things to come: spreading them out and making choices, working toward what one wanted, knowing the struggles that weighed the odds more in one's own favor. Not being passive, helpless, a tool of the gods. Marlowe was willing to hear how he might learn this and what he might do.

I told Marlowe the story. He had been witnessing in the background, standing for MASS THOUGHT, ready to object to everything, to split me if he could, even at this point. To say that for his part, solidity was the name of the game.

Marlowe, I said, Ramana Marharshi once told a disciple that he did not preach his message to masses because "Have you not heard of the saying of Vivekananda, that if one but thinks a noble, selfless thought even in a cave, it sets up vibrations throughout the world and does what has to be done—what can be done?"[144] (I got this from *Unknown Man: The Mysterious Birth of a New Species*, by Yatri.)

In the chapter "Critical Mass," Yatri pointed out that morphogenetic fields "do require a certain number of repetitions of forms which set up a resonance, to establish a habit of similar forms."[145]

He went on: "J. Krishnamurti, once said that it would take 10 awakened beings working in consort, while Gurdjieff assessed the number of such beings needed to change the world at 100. Bhagwan Shree Rajneesh, who has attempted to bring 10,000 disciples into his own Buddafield, agrees with Gurdjieff that the number needed to detonate the evolutionary megabomb is around 100. And yet maybe it is only one."[146]

What had startled Marlowe so? Perhaps the idea, as I put it, of "thoughts in the air, the patterns formed," as a "giant indoctrination system" he was wired into. "The shock of a new insight," Yatri wrote, "can . . . literally transfigure the very brain cells. . . . can jolt a lifetime's accumulation of connections and habitual neural pathways. A flash of insight, which comes from the original ground of the implicit order, is not bound by time. If it manages to surmount the barriers and to shock the 'timebound' cells of the mind for a microsecond, all of the old connections are blasted away and become disentangled in the immense dissipative fluctuations."[147]

24

I Couldn't Be Born—
And How That Affected My Later Life

Many archetypes are crying for adjustment today. New ones of *more accommodation*, greater adaptation to a global society, crying to be walked into by people who want to step in the outlines of the future. Some archetypes are even heavily energized.

But right now I want to explain how this fact of being on the cusp of medical technology—and on top of that, the solution being right out of a biblical outline—affected me. How it becomes possible to see in any physical birth a prefiguration, like a map. *A pattern that will repeat during symbolical "births" later.*

Doubtless, you are in some patterns and archetypes, even small ones or ones so subtle you have no idea. Much of the time the involuntary influence is not a problem. But it can be, especially if you want to go to another level of your potential. In fact, to realize it.

In the case of my birth, it is not that the path existed but that it was JUST OPENING—*that minute becoming available. I could not be born, and then lo! Suddenly, a way opened.*

My mother recounted this story—just before she got into my new used car and tested it, leading the way to the edge of town. I followed in *her* car; then she stepped back into hers and headed toward unexpected death!

My mother, Rosa Lee Harrell, could not hold a child nine months, but she and my father heard of research at Duke University Hospital: a medical miracle.

It sat right down inside the archetype: "the barren woman who conceives."

Now, my birth began to sound like an age-old tale—pivoted into history back long ago, where this archetype raged.

After months of shots to prepare the uterus, my mother was told to go home, conceive, and all will be okay "if you can hold the child *five* months." That was me. My mother explained it the last time I saw her; by luck I asked if she had wanted me, not knowing I'd not see her again, because how could I predict the car accident? Or could I? Such an odd question being very unlike me, as I had not asked it before in my forty-three years.

Much later I read about barren Elizabeth, mother-to-be of John the Baptist. Elizabeth, cousin to Mary, advanced in age, miraculously conceives and "*hides herself away for five months.*" THE EXACT TIME PERIOD.

So this archetype involved a test, silent phase. In the next passage Mary herself "miraculously conceives." Archetypes are accumulative by the time they begin to operate openly. Sometimes, also, an archetype needs updating.

But this is phenomenal. It adds surges of energy. I see how it works.

It's nothing to be concerned about that I hit snags and lack of preparation, that I have to bang on doors and perhaps fall down and straighten out errors. It's the sudden mercurialness of the door that appears *out of nowhere*: a new option no one knew might develop, or knew of but it had to wait. I am not to feel frustrated, because apparently it was a blessing, not handicap. An obstacle predating any connection with me. The sudden removal of it was an opportunity for masses of people. It just so happened that it coincided with my birth. And my parents were instantly told. I suppose I was one of the experiments.

And this is the pattern I am in, of coming in when a way is clearing. I remember a dream from a Zurich workshop. *For reasons I intuited it to be about my birth. In it my mother and I tried to walk down a slope together—a slant. I saw her turn back because she saw a male figure—coming toward us in the narrow area where we were walking.*

Interpreting the dream, I pondered whether symbolically my birth was delayed, maybe just a few contractions, because of this "figure" who entered—thinking there was room enough for all us both. But not my mother. She stopped our walk for the time it took him to go first. I think she was afraid. For me.

And then this idea came, spinning off from the dream. Was it simultaneously a higher level of consciousness entering? Did the "Omega" surreptitiously enter, as it were, with the "Alpha"? Was it always (often?) like this with patterns?

And then I sat down. It all became clear. My birth. This was the desperate kind of situation I was given, the one where there was the attempt from the past? Future? Anytime? To push time, knock it off balance, settle things now. No matter the setbacks and frustrations.

My birth involved what later seemed to me a multidimensional coin-ciding: the figure stepping into me—and myself, the tiny human baby—coming to Earth at the same time. How? Why? What next?

My mother, in the dream, turned me back from the exit. But the contractions had begun. Both met in the body at the same time. War and peace. Life.

Life without these old patterns.

25

A Contretemps with Jesus

In April 2000—not having done so for years—I asked for a reading from the highly regarded international psychic, channel of Lama Sing, Al Miner. I enquired:

about history . . . about how long we human beings have been here . . . about the various reports and all the lost histories, the new researches, such as in South and North India, that push the time of civilization back further than archaeologists first thought. So, up to now I have worked on the unconscious history of the earth through ideas and people . . . I thought that if I submitted my own timeline to the information question, it would manifest the way I think consciousness works best, that we each hold some keys and "tricks," some revelations that can come through ourselves and with our permission . . . but yet, must not violate the rhythms in which we should bring them forth. And as you told me years ago, some things must come from the solitary inner glow of knowledge. Others are far enough advanced within ourselves that added insight from a source can be of benefit.

I am interested in the archaeological dates put forth in *The Web of Life* by Fritz Capra, whereby archaic forms of Homo sapiens existed 250 thousand years ago. The great species of Neandertals existed 125 thousand years ago, but I am newly aware of the dates that the channel [like Edgar Cayce] has long cited, which put the most evolved of human beings already here [much earlier], and that makes a revolutionary situation . . . I know that my timeline has some interesting intersection with the early Christian period . . .

So I do not ask for a timeline of the Earth, but for its intersections
with my timeline where a comment might be fruitful in the future
without being out of place coming in that way.

I knew I didn't ask the question well, also knew that it matters
what dimension of our energy is tapped into. In this case, I suppose
my motives were not as pure as I thought, or else the question was
perceived that way. Not by Al Miner and not by Lama Sing.

No, my quarrel was with Jesus himself. The answer was not at all
what I expected though looking back now with fresh eyes at how I
posed the question, it's no wonder. Not so surprisingly as I reread my
question with the distance of sixteen years, the reading, began with
a discussion on "creative forces." My timeline was barely mentioned
except to say I was lucky enough to have been taught by Shem, which
meant nothing to me (we couldn't google, so I didn't know he was
a high priest, the most important son of Noah, ancestor of all the
Hebrews, and teaching in an awakened master lineage).

But here was the kicker: there was a miniscule reference to my
presence during Jesus's lifetime: a cameo of a little boy. I didn't buy
it. It rang no chords, that insignificant walk-on. I didn't begrudge
the fact if I hadn't played a role. However, I just didn't believe it. It
didn't match anything else I'd ever deduced. I took it as a snub by
Jesus himself.

Taking a new look in 2017, I saw that I had barely listened to what
was actually said. The "little boy" was in fact a man who, in a council,
helped screen writings to determine which would be chronicled for
posterity. In this way, Lama Sing said, he got to know many who
were important in the master's lifetime. Also, the master. A scene:
Around a village fire, where people could speak openly, "The master
asked of you what were the writings on this and that. And you and
two others would respond. See? Very nice picture, don't you think?"

Nice picture, but it didn't match what the Zurich Initiator had
told me, or my own experiences, or even findings of other psychics,
including Joost Vanhove. Also, drawing a blank regarding Shem, I

could not piece together the fascinating possibility of his relationship to my attraction to the light body. In fact, being taught by Shem suggests much to ponder.

The reading ended: "And so we leave you with these words from the Master: Many knew Me not, and for this I ask that our Father forgive them, for they knew not and, therefore, knew not what they did. Could you fill the chalice, which you shall place upon the altar of life with knowledge for those who cannot see, who have not hearing in their spirit, whose eyes are closed or dimmed by darkness? This would be a good work, and I am with you in it."

I barely noticed this jewel of advice either, as my emotion was all on being relegated to a "little boy" (who in fact wasn't in the reading at all).

Reacting personally, I walked—or stalked—toward the house of Flemish spiritual teacher Joost Vanhove, co-owner of Centrum GEA, with whom I had a prearranged counseling session. I felt, in fact, strong energy as of St. Paul, tempering my outrage. I knew Joost was the person to go to. He would favor me *in no way*. But address my concern.

I also felt that Joost had "an inside track." So I went into his healing space in a huff. I said I had felt a wave of St. Paul energy on the way in. He asked: *The one from long ago, or later offshoots?* I said the original.

Remember that this does not have to be the actual St. Paul, but an energy that feels like his and announces itself that way. Joost listened as I explained that I was angry with Christ. He asked if I wanted to talk with him. Startled, I said yes. He said, well, which one? Jesus or the Christ? I said both. He said, well, he would bring him in.

I waited, expecting channeled information. I'd never before had information from Jesus coming to me personally from another person I was in the physical presence of. But instead, the next thing that happened was that Joost shivered and I saw he had actually brought Jesus into his body. Using Joost's voice, Jesus said to speak to *him*.

I could have asked a million questions. But at that moment I asked about exactly the issue I'd entered with: why had he refused to recognize me in the Al Miner reading?

Calling me "Sweet," he said, "It was a test. . . . but it's over."

A lot of my outrage melted, though the answer signaled, I thought, that my motives in the earlier reading had been suspect, indicating self-importance, being self-serving—not from the soul but from the personality or ego.

But though Joost was technically there and it was his mouth, Jesus went on in a private answer: "If you were to ask me in what ways you participated in my incarnation, we would need a couple of days." He said, "You had more than one role. Some had one role; some had more than one."

Well, needless to say, my anger had totally dissipated and my curiosity was aroused, but being an intuitive and timid in such a situation to boot, I didn't pry. I held the answer in a sacred place of silence. Never again would I ask someone to "tell" me something so private as in that question I'd put to Al, which had been interpreted, in the highest spiritual realm (not by Miner himself), as requiring a lesson on my part, a rebuke. Basically, I realized I had been told in this manner to answer such very personal questions by going within.

I remember only a bit more. I could have asked so much but didn't feel the need to. I just felt delight. Yet he gave me interesting advice. I still drank wine every evening with my meal, and when I asked about it, he said: "Choose your temptations carefully. Choose what gives the *most* pleasure . . . and the *least* damage."

I found this beautiful and humorous. There was *nothing about sin*. It was the kind of reply I'd expect: not to resist but to—in terms of health—be balanced in my approach to "temptations." Yes, indeed. I liked it.

At that point, Joost had to come back in; he told me he'd brought a spirit into his body before. That he first checked with inner guidance to be sure it was in the best interests of *all* concerned. And then "went in and out," catching snatches, making sure he consented to what as a channel in trance he was saying. He finished, "Wasn't that interesting: 'My Mother is the Earth.'"

Jesus had volunteered though Joost's body: "My Mother is the

Earth." Joost added, "What was that he called you?"

"Sweet."

Let me stop a moment and bring in how I believe the transpersonal relates here. My huff captured the reaction that the "real" entity who had been in the Christ lifetime would have felt. Then it doesn't matter what someone else says.

She/he would not have believed the opposite, no matter what external source said so. Yet *beforehand*, I hadn't been satisfied with *simply asking myself.*

And that was the test: that she/he could—I could—contact the energy in myself that knew different and had the gumption to express it.

I didn't know any of this, precisely. I didn't, that day, ask for more explanation. Didn't even ask which of those who incarnated with him—perhaps all nameless today—he was including in the statement "You took several roles."

Was it energy like that of Paul himself that recognized his own energy that day when I resisted the answer given me; who bucked the system, who went against even the highest authority? Seeking, zeroing in on places to keep on expressing itself, *and that's how the transpersonal works?*

I thought of the transpersonal as inductive/deductive. Deductively it descends on us, from where it is *itself*; we receive. But inductively we act "like" it. And as we build a "likeness" (As Above So below), we build to a position where, inductively, THAT energy is visible, recognizable. It recognizes itself. I couldn't help but think of the California kundalini revelation: "take on the lifetime of St. Paul." If so, "the Magdalene." A pair, two intertwined archetypes, a restructuring. In this instance, the "male" indignation (animus) standing behind the feminine.

But, you may ask, then is nobody anybody? Is everybody

everybody? Isn't that a cop out? You who always wanted to *survive* in posterity as an artist, make a lasting mark—forever—isn't this a cop out, explaining that you don't have to because you're doing something else? More on that later.

26

RNG Experiments: June 2000

I had decided to move from Tienen, but where? Someplace I could afford. I pondered. Bruges, Belgium? Italy? The U.S.? Maybe Santa Fe (near my Jungian analyst friend Pui Harvey). Maybe Raleigh, North Carolina. Realistically, where did I want to live and could afford to? One thing for sure, I'd better hurry up and test the energy in the apartment, as I'd always intended to since first being offered the opportunity of receiving a random number generator by Dutch physicist/parapsychologist Dick Bierman ten years earlier.

But I hadn't felt like it then. It was now or never. Was the energy actually nonrandom in a way that could be measured? I'd spent fourteen years in this magical setting—kept always on my toes with surprises the last ten. By spring 2000 almost every text printout in my manuscripts was preceded by a page containing nothing but a "signature," like "*b0V" or "s2Q" or "E" on a blank page.

I wrote Dick Bierman, asking if he still wanted to lend me an Orion "true" random number generator. Taking the train from Holland, he brought me one. We met in a Flemish railroad station—I think, in Antwerp—where he checked me out. I wore a favorite ankle-length pale gray skirt with a slit up most of both sides (a popular wintry style in Belgium). I thought his face showed approval. He said, "I want to disprove mind/body dualism once and for all." I inferred he meant *mind over matter* would tend to refute that concept.

I'd been told he was rigorous. I hoped so. And that he had an open mind.

Back home, I set up his rectangular metal RNG, attached it to a parallel PC port, and uploaded the software. But let me explain the process.

An RNG, an electronic device, produces random sequences of 1's and 0's. It was used in the Princeton Engineering Anomalies Research (PEAR) program for twenty-eight years—a program set up in 1979 by aerospace scientist Robert G. Jahn, Dean of the School of Engineering and Applied Science, "to study the potential vulnerability of engineering devices and information processing systems to the anomalous influence of the consciousness of their human operators."[148]

The Orion RNG website explains:

> Random Number Generators are generating numbers in a sequence in such a way that the next number has no relation with the previous numbers. . . .
>
> [One] approach to obtain random numbers is to use noise in nature. The most commonly used noise sources are bouncing of ping pong balls (in lotteries) or more sophisticated: *radioactive decay or electron tunneling in electronic components.* These processes are in principle unpredictable. ORION's Random Number Generator is of the latter kind. (my italics)
>
> Our RNGs are being used all over the world by casinos, scientists, military experts, encryption specialists and software developers. They are used in scientific research, e.g., in so-called Monte Carlo simulations. They are also used in research on so called paranormal or psi phenomena.

PK (psychokinesis) mentally influences "the outcome of chance processes."* It was first described in 1943 by J. B. and Louisa Rhine, in terms of experiments with dice that were thrown or rolled down

---

* Sometimes the term used is telekinesis (TK). Sometimes PK. PK is also defined as "mind-matter interaction." Or "direct mental interaction with physical objects, animate or inanimate." Stanley Krippner, parapsychologist, professor of psychology at Saybrook University, and former director of the Maimonides Medical Center Dream Research Laboratory, who has won the American Psychological Association Award for Distinguished Contributions to the International Advancement of Psychology, told me to call the computer PK telekinesis.

an incline, as reported in "The Psychokinetic Effect (*Journal of Parapsychology*).[149] Only decades later did researchers use RNGs, grounded in quantum randomness.

I had by chance been photographed with J. B. Rhine at Duke University—alongside a wire cage containing falling dice. We posed as if he were administering (which he wasn't) me a PK test. An odd *pre-picture* of what was happening now—with modern equipment—as if taken in that non-timebound dimension of synchronicity and the collective unconscious described by Carl Jung. But how a pre-picture of a later event might or might not drop down in my life ahead of "time" is a topic I just posit here and keep going.

I attached the metal RNG device shaped like a half-sized cigarette pack to the PC. It would generate binary 1s and 0s randomly in a stream. The distribution would display as a range of values, 0–255.

For each trial the results were handily depicted, ready to print out, both in graph form and in a list of numbers, 0–255. "An Introduction to Probability and Statistics" explains:

> Since we expect the [random number] generator to produce ones and zeroes with equal probability, each bit from the generator is equivalent to a coin flip: heads for one and tails for zero. When we run experiments with the generator, in effect, we're flipping a *binary coin* . . . Even though there is no way whatsoever to predict the outcome of the next flip, if we flip a coin a number of times, the laws of probability allow us to predict, with greater accuracy as the number of flips increases, the probability of obtaining various results. . . . As we make more and more flips, the graph of the probability of a given number of heads becomes smoother and approaches the "bell curve," or *normal [standard] distribution*, as a limit.[150]

In flipping a coin *over a very large number of trials*, the probability is you would generate 50 percent heads, 50 percent tails: despite getting "heads, heads, heads, tails" groupings, if you throw a hundred times you average out to 50/50. A large enough divergence from that distribution will be statistically "significant"—that is, nonrandom.

My task—because I believed the heightened energy in the apartment was present—was to demonstrate patterns or sequences or clusters of numbers that deviated from the expected random output. Yes, I was biased, yet the RNG data collector instrument was not!

First off, the random number generator doesn't measure anything. It can't. It just spews out a stream of bits. Most scientists would say that the acausal process cannot be influenced by consciousness. That was where my project entered in: to somehow influence the output through the energy field in the apartment. Such feats had elsewhere been successful, producing *small*, statistically significant deviations, called "micro-PK." A number of scientists, especially parapsychologists, were comfortable with micro-PK outcomes in RNG trials.

For example, in the Princeton Engineering Anomalies Research (PEAR) in many millions of trials, "The observed effects were usually quite small, of the order of a few parts in ten thousand on average, but they compounded to highly significant statistical deviations from chance expectations."[151]

In addition to decades of individual trials, PEAR did successful experiments on *collective emotion* (involving multiple points around the globe). RNGs were situated in various cities to measure shifts of RNG data during such events as the funeral of Princess Diana or the announcement of the O. J. Simpson verdict. PEAR's hypothesis was that a highly emotional global event could generate a nonrandom pattern in the RNGs located in the different cities, and that hypothesis proved true.

But what I had in mind would hopefully be of the Dhyanyogi-ji or "rainmaker"—Eastern—type, where the PK result is large. Of course, any significant result would make me happy.

I had by then read how Dhyanyogi-ji, in his short two years in the U.S., enjoyed submitting to scientific tests. For instance, UC Davis professor Haines Ely, MD, in Sacramento, California, September 9, 1978, took Dhyanyogi-ji's blood pressure in two-minute intervals, and Dhyanyogi-ji moved it "up to 215, then down to 160, then down to 145 within two minutes. . . . The doctor said only a yogi could do this." A similar PK test, likewise involving his blood pressure, was taken in Los Angeles—the results being 160, 200, 145.[152] The yogi explained that "the secret of controlling the spiritual, mental, and physical parts of oneself" was, "It comes from the heart, and what you feel in your heart."[153]

Now let's take a look at my experiment. I kept the data in printouts and the descriptions of progress in a log for future review.

As described in the log, almost immediately the RNG Bierman had handed me at the train station was defunct. I sent it back. Before he returned it, repaired, Bierman had his best RNG tester put it through rigorous trials—beyond the usual high-caliber Orion labwork—to leave no room for error this time.

LOG BOOK, RNG EXPERIMENTS

Date: July 9, 2000

This is the journal notes regarding the rng experiments in my apartment, Tienen Belgium, beginning in June.

The first Orion rng was defunct upon arrival, but I experimented with it. It would print only 0's on the PC. But on the laptop, which I used every day, printing from it, it would generate a limited amount of numbers, the rest 0's. This defunct rng was returned to the Amsterday lab for checkup, repair and confirmation that it then worked properly. Receiving a complete workup, being certified as ready for use, it was sent back in June. Upon arrival here, as well as there, it operated apparently normally. I made tests using the fastgrnd program from the laptop, and nothing abnormal appeared in the results, to the eye. To show development, the beginning results of the number 223 (which will later be very high) are listed below:

File 4rng: Name

Try 1 Incidence of the number 223: 2

Try 2 Incidence of the number 223: 1

Date: June 28

He was 100 percent sure it operated perfectly. He already had a raised eyebrow at the notion that his Orion RNG just happened to break upon arrival here. He was locking in with certainty the nondefective status of the second attempt.

So soon after this RNG arrived in June in the mail, I put on light body music to up the energy and sat down at the PC. To take an early example, the color graphs of July 3 *start normally*. But not for long. I have them in front of me. By July 4, the runs showed extreme deviation from random. Some energy field appeared to be present in my apartment for the RNG to pick up these wide extremes, wide swings in the numbers.

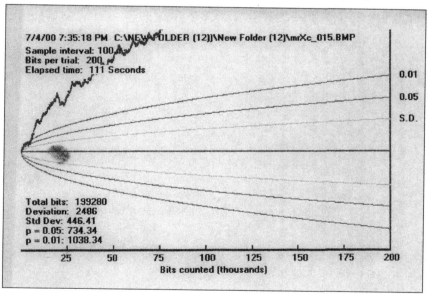

July 4: 996 trials—Deviation 2486

Take a look at the representative graph of raw data above: on 7/4/00 at 7:35:18 p.m., whereas *standard deviation (S.D.) was 446.41*, my deviation was 2486—six times higher. The other indicators give the p-values—the 5 percent and 1 percent odds, respectively—of a particular result being generated randomly. Here, $p =$

0.05 is 734.34. And p = 0.01 is 1038.34. These were the numbers to beat if there was something going on in my apartment with "energy," and my intentional energy was in some way influencing the RNG output, and the apparatus was working properly.

As you see, the July 4, 7:35:18 p.m. results are well over the expected random numbers output. In fact, the actual findings over 111 seconds soar off the graph, showing a huge diversion from the expected p-values (the null hypothesis) and standard deviation (S.D.). But this would not count if it were an isolated incident. It wasn't.

A few more results, taken on July 4, show how wide rangingly and recurrently extreme my trial deviations were: at 7:30:44 on July 4 my deviation was 2774; at 7:32:51 it was 1852; at 7:35 it was 2486. Then it dropped to only 684; then minus 1002. Such results throughout the weeks of experiments were "my norm."

A little statistics terminology from the Dartmouth.edu website:

- Hypotheses:

  Theories or ideas you are trying to test with data. . . .

- "Null" and "Alternative" Hypotheses:

  In the simplest case, the two possibilities for the real mean [average] of data. Often one is zero, and thus is called the "Null."[154]

The null hypothesis, given the assumption that the Orion RNG in my trials produces a random output, is *that the results will be random.* More largely speaking, the null hypothesis here is the premise that mind/spirit cannot interact with (or influence) matter. The null hypothesis is what I was trying to disprove.

Longtime parapsychologist Dean Radin, Chief Scientist at the Institute of Noetic Sciences, summarizes, "After sixty years of experiments using tossed dice and their modern progeny, electronic RNGs, experimenters have produced persuasive, consistent, replicated evidence that mental intention is associated with the behavior of these systems. . . . Today virtually no serious criticisms remain for the best RNG experiments. Informed skeptics agree that something interesting is going on."[155] Radin says these tests "merely scratch the surface of what appears to be a more fundamental phenomenon."[156] Also, "The overall results for all RNG experiments exceed odds of trillions to one."[157]

In addition to displaying the raw results in graphs, the software listed the byte read in number format (0–255). But that didn't look random either. Over and over, 223 was favored. Likewise, number 117.

In reviewing all of my data over, I kept obtaining these unlikely large deviations from the random norm, and the probabilities were off the charts.

I consulted with Bierman—what to do?—checked all the settings with him, took the computer to be cleaned. Nothing stopped the climb of 223. Did I associate it with anything? I didn't think so, though 117 might associate with Dhyanyogi-ji, who had left the body at 116 years old (but I thought it was 117). I loved doing these runs. It was thrilling to see the deviation climb high above random, like pulling for a race horse. Yes, I will say it again, I wanted these nonrandom data!

Beginning again on July 5, the RNG started off nicely restrained. But the sixth, as if geared up for a real push, at 1:22:10 it was off the charts: 6872. At 1:26:48 it was 4658. At 1:33:39, it sailed straight up off the page again, at 5954. Followed by 5750 at 1:30:48. And 4064 at 1:30:20. And 4888 at 1:41:12. I was on a roll. The anomaly was consistent.

Was it real? Not likely. That's coming up. But whatever the verdict, the assignment had been to get nonrandom results. And—if that had been achieved by breaking the RNG twice—well, that was one way to go about it. Meanwhile, I took the laptop to a light body seminar in Ibiza, Spain. I remember showing some tests to Roland. Before continuing the RNG story, let's look at Ibiza.

27

Interstices

Light Body. In Ibiza. Double Initiation. 2000.

It was July 23–29, 2000. I was at a light body seminar in advanced channeling. My teacher, Roland Verschaeve, had moved from Belgium to Casa Can Encantado, a beautiful Ibiza estate at the top of a mountain reached by a winding dirt road. The main house was white, columned, surrounded by red passion flowers, palm trees, pines, mimosas . . . Today, under new ownership, it is compared to "a beautiful Moorish palace, . . . with idyllic views of the valley in the foreground and the sea beyond."

All our meditations were outside in sunlight. For one, he had the participants—a very small group—stand in twos facing each other. When I was supposed to channel to the young man I was partnered with, I felt a deep indigo blanket of energy that I recognized descend. But it gave me nothing to say.

I reversed the assignment, asking the young man, a Dutch light body teacher, to speak (that is, "channel") while I listened in the purple energy. He did. He said, "We're having a double initiation. I see us kneeling at the foot of the Cross."

Perhaps that day, perhaps later, someone I was paired to channel with saw me as a male in the Inquisition approached by a bright female child—a male so overwhelmed by her light he couldn't carry out his Inquisition functions.

As he spoke, I had a vision of the image in a painting. Roland later told me he checked out the information—he always does—and it was accurate: the Inquisition scene and the painting were two different lifetimes, plus he saw a combined one. That made sense. I deduced it had become a pattern. I was both: the strong male energy had had to learn not to abuse power, which it did through being impacted by the presence of light in the child, who ultimately was a part of himself. So I would be carrying that pattern, *another version of Mars-Neptune.*

Whether or not the Inquisition information came the same day the Dutch light body teacher told me, "We're having a double initiation. I see us kneeling at the foot of the Cross," the following incident did.

It was 9 p.m. I was in my room, apart from the others, who shared rooms. I had to pay extra but needed the space to sleep. Into my room walked the deep-indigo energy. It was Jesus. Instantaneously my energy shifted. As a side note, I didn't see a "real" figure standing near me. I sensed the presence in the deep indigo energy, which was enveloping the room—but subtly, palpably, not physically.

I knew instantly who it was. How? There wasn't even time for a thought to register. One minute I was going about an ordinary task. The next I felt myself inside thick indigo energy that was familiar— the clear telltale (to me) presence. Then what happened inside me was quite beyond my control. On the split second of recognizing that presence, some energy in me turned into Mother Mary and *loved* with a tremendous strength the indigo energy that had walked in.

The spirit Jesus told me, without audible words, *that young man* I'd worked with in the seminar *was him.* I was terribly perplexed. I couldn't help but believe. Obviously. Under the powerful circumstances. But what a thing to believe.

Under the sway of this deep indigo energy, I accepted the incredible fact that the Dutch guy was him without a blink. I didn't question it rationally.

What happened next was unbelievable. I felt inside me the energy of Mary Magdalene from a particular moment: one scene I'd never imagined or heard about. Unrecorded. I felt it in my hands. I saw and felt them touch each disciple as he set out on his mission after the Crucifixion. I felt the energy of Jesus flow through my hands into each one of them as I touched their heads, one by one. I guess this is called the Descent of the Holy Spirit. It was passing through me into them as a blessing before their dangerous missions.

I realized that each disciple "became" Jesus in going out on the mission. As they scattered to face hardships, life-threatening risks, they walked in this Christ consciousness energy of Jesus that had been transmitted into them.

This experience was so beautiful and numinous I could never question it. It happened somewhere, probably in our reality, certainly in the realm of psyche. I thought it had actually happened historically. In fact, that was my deep impression.

The energy was so miraculous-feeling to me—that the next day I approached the tall young man. He said not to talk, *we were "having an experience in another dimension."* But I wanted confirmation he'd experienced something too. I hastened to ask had anything happened to him the evening before *at 9 p.m.* Yes, he said, energetic things had occurred then but didn't say more.

I told myself: *Look how what just happened could make all beliefs go flying out the window. Because if that young man had said, "By the way, I'm Jesus," I'd have had no choice but to believe.*

He didn't, however. I searched frantically in my mind to think of any way I could hint further or draw him out. I blurted, "Your mother is the Divine Mother." He took it that I meant his physical mother and answered graciously. I said "No, I meant Mother Mary will be helping you in the classes you teach." He thanked me.

That afternoon at the Flea Market, I found a hundred-year-old porcelain conch from India to go with my eighteenth-century Tibetan-shaman conch, at home. I bought it. The Hindu one had Om in Sanskrit and other symbols carved all over it. Back at Roland's, the guy in the initiation with me was interested.

After that, I learned from his elegant girlfriend that he was being woken at night to decipher the conch symbols in bed—receiving "downloads" that analyzed them, especially the use of cubing. She'd never seen him so involved, working on the symbols. He told me nothing about it. We had, as he said, had a "double initiation."

That was it. In the Eastern history of siddhis, initiations, or teachings by great masters, these things occur regularly. So to me, once again, I took this without a grain of salt. It was totally real. How else could I measure it if not in the same way I measured other events in my life—that everyone believed? Now I can put a = b together and see the incident of Jesus passing through me en route to the young woman in Bruges as an update on the incident of Jesus passing into the disciples via Mary Magdalene's hands.

I felt how real and complex is multidimensionality. This sudden experience has always sat in a special place inside me and could be a prototype—coming the way it did, carrying instant conviction. Heart knowledge. Leading to no communication with the young male after the workshop. But I bet that he (and his girlfriend) remember.

And yet, how would I propel the information anywhere at all?

In that or another weeklong workshop on Ibiza, I was alone outdoors with Roland, looking at the spacious rustic vista. Ibiza, Catalan speaking, is a colorful Mediterranean island with a fairly well preserved history dating back to the Phoenician–Carthaginian period; it became a World Heritage Site in 1999.

Against this beautiful panorama, Roland invited me to join him in a private meditation. This happened twice over the years I've known him and was always exciting. He said we'd go on a "journey" together, "Come, follow me, Margaret." Our only goal was to do something for the collective good. I totally trusted him and was focused on detecting where his energy was. Where I went energetically, it turned out, was up to my soul grouping, who sat in an open-ended U-shaped formation.

Then I heard Milton Klonsky say a single phrase, up there wherever we were, "Measure me."

I was intrigued by the symbolic shape of the group. The U was not closed; it had an opening, an outlet.

The only one visible, Milton, had stepped up as spokesperson. (In this type of communication, many may be behind a visible figure.) When he told me to measure him, instantly I associated the RNG. And more broadly, I thought of chaos theory—the paradox, where in view of its irregularity and fractal nature, if you try to measure in detail a portion of a coastline, how would you determine the length? It might have lagoons, bays, fjords, leading to a wildly different result depending on the measurement tool.

Again, I felt how pithily perfect the one-liners of the Milton I had known were. In a second—an epiphany of no-time—I understood so much.

Wasn't this a central question, a peg to hang my book series on?? If I could get the mentality of thinking practically—in all its complexity—which locations *and which ways* an in-form though not totally physical body, or rather not continually physical, not exclusively physical—well, you see what it would take to get the hang of it.

Milton earlier assigned me: "Don't let *time* measure *you*. You measure it."

But wasn't this harder? The simple task, given from outer space—real, warm, ironical, heart-challenging—"Measure ***me***."

Sent telepathically: *Look, here's a good assignment. Look, I don't need to spell it out. But in code. You see what I mean. Measure **me**.*

Okay. So you want to measure energy. But look. I'm not here at all physically. But I'm very much here. To find out how, try to take a measurement of my size and dimensions. My presence, location, speed, composite interactions.

*Measure **ME**.*

As I tried to access a communication on my mental screen, a screen that didn't exist either, the message had popped in. *Look, you got this far. So here's a conundrum.*

We will phrase this homework in the structure of: "Can you—? Can you—or what will you create if you try it? try to "Measure me"?

Of course, that would relativize as others too took on the task not of finding out so much *who they were,* but the implication would be there—that they were the one who was *there* and *there* and *that. Doing the measuring.*

In other terms, that they took up this much space-time.

So hold on now. See what it turns into. Like another measuring rod into time. This one into personality, soul length or presence, into energetic survival. Into the relationship between *form and survival.*

Into the length of connections as the threads wore thin or strengthened. Into—?

No elaboration. It implied: well, look, if the length of a fractal is infinite, what about me?

How did this thought reach me? Or I get to where it traveled or sat?

Now I know that this instruction, properly implemented, would be a variation on the Upanishads' "You are That, I am That, and All this is That." With "You," of course, being "the unknown, hidden, unseen You" (not a physical entity). According to one sage, "grasping this truth is like chewing on steel peanuts and digesting them. It is not a little thing."[158]

But I didn't know it then. Felt only the adrenalin shot of a gripping, ingenious assignment. "Measure me." *Where was he telling me to look?*

A so-cryptic instruction but potent—using his handful of words to send me out into the universe, where the answer was. Just as Dhyanyogi-ji had said, *Come to me direct.* So here were a couple of assignments in cosmic geography. In nonlocation location.

28

Two Broken RNGs

Reluctantly, I returned the second RNG. I had to admit it must be malfunctioning, it was by now so consistently outrageous. TWO broken RNGs? Did it pass the smell test? Bierman confirmed it had broken. He swore it was perfect when he had it pretested; the energy, he asserted, did the dastardly deed. But there was no proof.

Bierman was disappointed. He told me, "You'll never be able to present a paper." He had hoped, he said, I would present at the PA Convention. He repeated the lament of parapsychologists: that psi was too "elusive"; you couldn't capture it to prove this kind of wild deviation. However, he believed in the Orion RNG (designed by him and Joop Houtkooper), so much that I felt he thought I had been testing real psi, but he would not be able to take the data to the scientific community, who—while some by then had proved to their satisfaction in the Princeton Engineering Anomalies Research (PEAR) that group emotion around the world during a seminal event could make RNGs or REGs deviate *slightly but significantly* from random—would *not* be likely to think a mere human or human energy field could get a large deviation. A tiny one? Yes. But a very large deviation? Like moving objects around with the mind, it was suspect in the extreme. Humans could not do it. Besides, parapsychologists had been tricked often by imposters.

Bierman continued his painstaking laboratory research in the years ahead, testing "presentiment"; that is, non-conscious, aware-ness that "something is going to happen."

To an intuitive person, obviously, this makes sense. To me, the theory below is a beautiful possible explanation, whereby the mind might have receptors that allow it to receive what scientists call "advanced" electromagnetic waves—from "the future."

Why does the causal arrow of time seem to go in only one direction?

Famous particle physicists Richard Feynman and John Archibald Wheeler spent about a year in the 1940s trying to figure the answer out. Their conclusion—the Wheeler–Feynman absorber (or time-symmetric) theory—proposed that a charged particle emits radiation into *both* the past and future: T-symmetry. A *retarded* wave arrives *after* it set out (traveling at minus the speed of light). An *advanced* wave arrives ahead of when it set out (traveling at the speed of light).[159]

But the universe is missing, they said, the light *absorbers* necessary to maintain T-symmetry.

Their theory is that charged light particles that radiate advanced waves, in a sense arriving to us "from the future"—bringing future information—do not normally reach us, whereas "retarded" ("past-tense, in our terms") waves do, creating our cause-effect linearity. But more recent galvanic-skin and brain measurements involving presentiment have proved that our body/emotions can in fact *unconsciously to us* detect a stimulus or an event in advance.[160]

In "Consciousness Induced Restoration of Time-Symmetry (CIRTs): A Psychophysical Theoretical Perspective," at the PA Convention in 2008 (published in *The Journal of Parapsychology* 74, nr. 2), Bierman asserts that "the brain, when it sustains consciousness, is a special system that partially restores time symmetry and therefore allows 'advanced' waves to occur."[161]

In a YouTube video he explains that Feynman and Wheeler concluded that time does not run backward. Why? Because, they said, "the cosmos was not in equilibrium"; it has "many more . . . multiparticle coherent light emitters" (a quantum system), like lasers, where particles behave as in a corps de ballet. "There's nothing similar that absorbs light."

Bierman added: but what about the brain? "And if those absorbers are there, then time *should* run backwards." Elsewhere, he flatly

states that "people can [sometimes] sense the future before it happens."[162] Another in this field is scientist Dean Radin.

> So impressive were Radin's results [in testing presentiment] that
> Dr. Kary Mullis, a Nobel Prize-winning chemist, took an interest.
> He was hooked up to Radin's machine and shown the emotionally
> charged images.
>   "It's spooky," he says. "I could see about three seconds into the
> future. You shouldn't be able to do that."[163]

This research begins to put science behind experiences many people have had, such as those who felt uneasy and didn't get onto the
planes that crashed on 9/11.

Back to 2000: I didn't give up.

Not wanting to break another of Bierman's RNGs, in January
2001 I ordered my own. In extreme caution, I immediately shipped
the device, on February 9, FedEx Express, to Norman Don at his
brain function lab at the School of Public Health, University of
Chicago. There a neuroscientist, Bruce E. McDonough, tested it.
This time, there'd be no suspicion. It was a foolproof plan.

On February 12 Bruce emailed the RNG had been put through
"200 runs 9200 bits per trial, 1 second interval, counting ones, XOR
on"—over fifty hours. Not to tie up a lab computer, this was "done in
overnight and weekend sessions." What a trooper. He said, "It looks
to me like the RNG is working properly."

But by then, I was swept up in other things. Four years of preparation for the het Toreke museum exhibit on the life and works of Jan
Mensaert (now set for April 10–June 10, 2001) was in its final stage.
Just before that, I attended the International Conference on Science
and Consciousness in Albuquerque, New Mexico, while visiting my
good friend Jungian analyst Pui Harvey (a mentor to many) in Santa
Fe. Also, I was feeling great pressure to figure out where to move
from Tienen.

Wherever it was, I'd be shipping papers, clothes, furniture. As if in anticipation, the computer PK now went overboard—rearranging batches of pages from my *Space Encounters* drafts as if to stock up. As if I might not be doing the aberrant printouts much longer. As if the energy field might not go with me or might shift focus. In all this activity I put the RNG aside. I expected to probably pick it back up in the new apartment, though considering all that had gone on here, I doubted it would initially have the same energy field. At least, the RNG had been checked out in Chicago.

As the countdown for the move continued, I attended a workshop that would be highly meaningful to me and lead to writing two papers for publication.

PART FIVE

A Quantum Jump—An Initiation into a Oneness Framework, E. H. Walker and the Experience of Redness

These are stories. These are things that happened. I was there for the ones that happened to me and though I was not there for the others, I know of the reputations of those who were there. These things, these strange things did occur, and they give us a taste of another reality, another domain, an incredible world . . . Are there little mysteries in physics that hide under the guise of something called the measurement problem that would change your entire outlook if physicists told us the story straight? . . . These are the things we will explore. These are questions we will ask—and that we will answer.

—Evan Harris Walker

To some, the One Mind may resemble a crazy aunt hidden in the family attic—too weird to be respectable, too controversial to talk about, too strange to be seen in public. But in view of the evidence we shall examine, she is about to descend the stairs and make a shocking appearance to the guests.

—Larry Dossey

29

Two Visitations

An initiation into the Ground (also called by such terms as transcendent reality, Ground of Being, or the One) was a major new step in 2001. It was brought by Milton, then underscored in a revelation by Dhyanyogi-ji—in the same light body seminar . . .

A short reminder from *Keep This Quiet!* My first memory was of being a tiny tot, curled up at the top of the stairs, listening to the sounds below. I could hear, downstairs. a rare poker game going on. I wanted to surprise my father and his friends by going down but was afraid. Jung says our first memory or dream symbolizes our personal myth. I went down the stairs.

What happened? Fortunately, I was greeted with open arms.

Reading Larry Dossey's metaphor, I got tingles. I thought: let's say that—in the collective mind—leaving the perch up there might be an analogy for stepping down from the One Mind ("she is about to descend the stairs"). A stairs might symbolically link states of consciousness. In another association later, I found that according to the Sleeping Prophet Edgar Cayce in 1937 (reading 5749-8) "the angel on the stair" chose the child Mary, among the Essene maidens, as the twelve walked up the steps; they had been in years of training to see which one would become the Mother of Christ: "On this day, as they mounted the steps all were bathed in the morning sun, which not only made a beautiful picture but clothed all as in purple and gold. As Mary reached the top step, then there was thunder and lightning." What I took from this other clue was that to come down from the stairs was to have the courage to bring a consciousness with you.

Prior to the February 24–25, 2001, Knokke workshop led by

Roland Verschaeve, I arranged with Rhea A. White, founder of the Exceptional Human Experience Network and a pioneer in transpersonal psychology, to report on it in *EHE News*.

Rhea, a past president of the Parapsychological Association, had moved away from parapsychology proper. She had coined the terms "Exceptional Experience" (EE) and "Exceptional Human Experience" (EHE) to cover any anomalous incident that, if "potentiated," was transformative and empowering. Her database ran from intense art inspiration or archetypal dreams across the spectrum to alien abduction. In explaining what constituted EE or EHE, she drew on William James (*The Essence of Religious Experience*) but added that her focus was a little different: "Nearly 100 years on, I believe James's words can be further secularized, and I think this is necessary, for people today must be shown how they can contact the sacred right where they are, in their daily lives, without resorting to any particular religious imagery. Instead of referring to a "higher part," which implies judgment, I would like to use the phrase 'more connected part.'"[164]

I met Rhea just once in person, in her home in New York. As mentioned, she became very influential in steering me into a format for my books—now that I was converting what used to be fiction into nonfiction, using real names. She appreciated my experiences, however unusual, and even said, in reviewing my *Space Encounters: Chunking Down the Twenty-First Century*, I had the "most far-reaching, open-ended mind of anyone [she knew]." This supplied a welcome support base.

She reviewed my *Love in Transition: IV*: "The thread of autobiography dematerializes at points throughout only to rematerialize like roman candles that burst into a myriad trajectories like stars falling to earth. . . . [The book] also explodes with insights gained from science and her remarkable intuition."[165] Needless to say, who could want a more receptive editor? Did I mention that she was also a highly detail-, "thinking function"-oriented editor who kept bringing me back to a style her readers could accept? This provided a wonderful transition to ease me into publication in the U.S.

Rhea was coauthor of such books as *In the Zone: Transcendent Experience in Sports* (with Michael Murphy, cofounder of Esalen

Institute). She published my light-body-seminar account in her newsletter, *EHE News* (March 2001), then bumped me up to an expanded peer-refereed version in the farewell issue of her journal, *Exceptional Human Experience* (2004). That seminar is described below.

After nine years of guided meditations in light body courses (created in California and Oregon and taught in Belgium and Ibiza by Roland), I attended his Divine Will seminar in the seaside town of Knokke. For teaching purposes Divine Will had been broken up into seven aspects; the meditations below focused on the Will to Unify and the Will to Evolve.

I sat up my laptop in the back of the conference room; during breaks I took notes. I felt sure I could report something that fit with her intent to empower the experiential side of life. But I never expected the dramatic unfolding that almost left me speechless. Later I marveled at how what I experienced the first day seemed tailored to support her lifework. I wrote it up the very next day.

Sending my essay off, I confessed: "Rhea, I know that this is in some parts highly esoteric, merely in the level of thought. But for giving you a glimpse of *my experience* this weekend, here it is. I entered that consciousness, of the Whole, but narrowly funneled. And it told me something. Yet it was not widely ranging, but so narrowly insistent on a single *profound* point." More:

> It turned out to be heavily Buddhist. I didn't know this, but it turned out to relate to "the nature of mind." I would have trouble describing, conceptually, an experience of the mind when it stands prior to the creation of concepts, yet instead of being empty, it is coexisting in a state of emptiness and awareness. The awareness inside the totally empty state is something like seeing a thing in the full force of its "truth" . . . The implications were not inside logic, but inside a kind of process of shedding concealment. Yet nothing was really "shed." Each passing awareness was able to deepen the immediate grasp—because everything had "immediacy"—of the understanding one had attained the moment before.

In the newsletter I groped to describe how suddenly, early on in the meditations, I felt myself "forming" my expression *around* the shape of another face, that of Milton Klonsky, "assuming his exact facial lines—copied into my own—as I saw this one-time mentor in front of me." Some twenty ago, he "opened me to all the higher-thinking work I later did, both during the period I knew him and was exposed to his thoughts and personality in New York City, and after he died (which started me on my earliest recognizable EHE)."

For purposes of the newsletter, it was irrelevant, I noted, whether Milton was actually there or "some kind of energy principle made *the association with his mind* bring the information to me." Obviously, the impact on me personally—not theoretically—was that he was there, powerfully so, in spirit form.

I explained how "it was not a matter of going in and out of experiences, as sometimes happens in guided meditations. Rather, of *holding* a vision—in a sense, seeing through eyes and intelligence I had never looked through before." I added that at the computer the next day, it was clear to me the words I wrote for the newsletter were under the influence of the energy from the meditation: "a transformation of information received unconsciously and nonverbally in it. . . . I cannot express sufficiently the extreme level of simplicity and sense of utter importance I felt as I experienced it."

The revelation this intelligence with the face of Milton brought, in a stream of awarenesses, was about "*human resources,*" by which he envisaged a novel role for humans.

In an entirely different twist, I saw that each of us—just like plants or diamonds or water—is a vital *resource* for the Earth. That is, just like coal or oil or the sun or wind or forests and such, we are, in a very different way, a great Earth resource.

Milton showed me a kind of math: *a relationship—or ratio—between problems facing the Earth, on the one hand. And the capacity to solve them.* Every problem had solutions, locked in information and experience *inside* human potential, held individually.

Humans—like a secret weapon—connected the *number* of

problems to the *unknown, untapped abilities to work them out.* I explained that "our planet now has a lot of potentially high risk situations *because of the lack of balance between increasing risk and increase in development of human resources.* The sometime appearance of 'sameness' in the population, due to falling into mass thought, has masked the fact that many differences have not been brought to the surface. And each difference—or differentiation—inside a given individual (i.e., if properly brought out) is in fact a *human resource.*"[166]

Simply put, "The missing perception is locked into people." (I did not, at the time, bring up nonhuman contribution but bore down on humans as information "locations.)

I sensed "the analysis came as if from a 'foreign,' kind, loving, higher wisdom that had the ability to compare levels of development across planets." This subtle impression, I did not pursue. But it impressed me. I tried to convey the point: "This unevolved richness inside the populace can be made use of only by people transforming their knowledge of odd bits of fact and experience into usable suggestions, self-expressions, *truths,* of which the planet is sorely in need."

> We think of developing *ourselves,* our consciousness, and our particular truths as a kind of luxury we have a right to choose or reject. Here, impacted into me as from a perspective not familiar to me, I saw that in the history of planetary evolution there are balances in knowledge that need to be maintained, or a conscious information quotient that is required on each planet, in proportion to the level of friction that exists there, and because of lack of understanding of this fact on Earth there is a disturbingly high percentage of untilled resources hidden in the general populace.[167]

I had no idea how to develop the implication that it was possible to compare planetary evolutions. It was overwhelming enough to feel in the presence of revelation and truth. I continued: "To put it another way, there is some kind of principle of equivalence between the level of dispute and discord experienced on a planet and the potential for its solution." That is, "Inside the principles that make us one of Earth's species, we are *expected* to transform information."

This brings to mind—but it didn't at the time—facets of information theory, by which—from molecules to genomes to radioactive particles—the whole cosmos is an information factory.

According to this built-in principle, it was essential for each person to "dig carefully into what precisely *he* or *she*, and not somebody else, had been given to explore and discover, based on *who* they are, *what* they are, *what* they stand for, and *what* they could teach or put into expression or words. *Or* explanation. *Or* illustration."

In this way, I stressed, "You *rebuild* the Earth, by having each person bring forth the *piece of the Earth* in his or her possession. Not a physical, visible resource for most of us, but a hidden unconscious human resource."[168]

It took time to digest the other insight I took away. I saved it for the expanded version. I had, in a flash, seen—in quantum mechanics language—continual wave function collapses of all sizes, rippling off from a single bit of information. But watching "the whole," I saw that from its perspective the resulting change was recoverable. The whole kept moving, while we followed the isolated "collapsed" point *in time*. I will come back to this.

I asked Roland, "What is the main message of this weekend?" He instantly replied, "God." After a long pause, with strong enunciation, he went on, "The Divine Will. Not the personal will. Not transforming the planet, but God." I then said, "God can go into every corner." He shot back, "Absolutely."

In my revised account—in the journal *Exceptional Human Experience* (June 2004)—I took the story much further, titling it "The Gift of the Natural Mind: A Consciousness." As consciousness is mystically considered an unlimited unity (God, the ground of being), a title I might prefer now would be "The Gift of the Natural Mind: Consciousness in Itself."

I identified the vantage point of "the whole" I had seen as "the Ground state." For four years, though, I struggled to integrate what I wanted to say.

In this second version I applied a term I had newly discovered: "satori"—a sudden awakening—to the experience. I gave Eastern examples. My main focus was on the vivid *picture* impressed upon my awareness: the sight/sensation of how information always moved as a whole; it rippled through the fabric of the All—precipitated by a single shift, a single new fact.

What in quantum mechanics language would be seen as *irrecoverable* "wave function" collapses (see below for an explanation)—that is, the collapse of waves of possibility into a unique event in time—was, to the whole, recoverable.

The whole kept moving, in innumerable reorganizations throughout the fabric of possibility. Inherent meaning seemed instantly "processed"—merely by the dynamics of juxtapositions. Or, let us say, the quantum jumps of, not electrons or other particles per se but "information units," of "self-aware" (or "position-aware") feedback, or resonating repositioning. Shift after shift registered and remained in readiness, as of an "all-Knowing," transcendent consciousness intimately realigning, in every movement and connection—potential and actual.

That jives, I think, with physicist Amit Goswami's description: "When possibility waves move about in the brain without collapse, consciousness is present (it is the ground of being: where would it go?) but not awareness."[169]

Another thing I did not understand before the meditation was that now one, *now another* point was *energized by the whole.*

We stopped to invest in our reality, feeling it definitive, concrete, decisive because of a decision, an event, a wave collapse. But every single perspective that existed or potentially existed could have *all information brought to bear behind it if it* in turn *came forward*—acting on *its* information, its experience. Unconscious to us, the potential was already set up. The whole had recalibrated in view of new information, absorbed and digested it in what seemed in the dynamics instantaneous. I watched as it quickly shifted to encompass the ramifications of *any additional fact or event and reinforced whichever new centers* had captured the attention *now*—that is, captured actuality, potential or implied support.

A word on wave function collapse. Part of quantum mechanics

(QM) theory, it occurs during the measurement of a quantum system, as in a laboratory. The wave function describes all information about "the quantum state of an isolated system of one or more particles. There is *one* wave function containing all the information about the entire system."[170]

Adding quantum states together produces *a superposition* of waves of possibility. But no one can predict which probability will become actual. When the wave function collapses, in physicist Henry Stapp's words, "Nature delivers the answer to the question of what potential will be selected."[171] On the other hand, before that, "it is in all possible states simultaneously."[172] For example, in a wave packet with multiple momentums, one for each wave, at the collapse (or reduction) of the wave function, only one momentum remains.

Here it becomes thorny. There is no agreed-upon definition of what constitutes measurement. Will observation "cause" the collapse? For physicist Amit Goswami, one of a new breed of Western pioneers who has embraced the Eastern notion of consciousness as the ground of being, "the agency that transforms possibility into actuality is consciousness. It is a fact that whenever we observe an object, we see a unique actuality, not the entire spectrum of possibilities. Thus, conscious observation is a sufficient condition for the collapse of the possibility wave." In the next chapter we will explore this topic.[173]

In my vision—in the perspective of the "whole"—the collapse is only of "information." To me this made great sense. It was as if to a non-time-bound level of consciousness with a capital "C," the outcome in our 3-D world was a thought puzzle (that could be rethought).

Some pages back, in "Marlowe," I spoke of my botched piano performance at seven. But only superficially botched. I stayed on the recital stool, playing the piece over and over, up to different points till finally I remembered and played "the whole."

Similarly, in dreams, Wolfgang Pauli's anima in the form of a Chinese woman told him, "You must allow us to *play chess* with you in every conceivable *combination*."[174] In *Keep This Quiet!* III, I wondered aloud if my intuition, when I forgot the end of my piano recital at seven (and stayed on the stool), had flown me into this collective/personal aspect of my journey as I tried *all possible note combinations*—to remember *the whole*—linearly/nonlinearly, as an entry card into the archetype? Was it, even at that instant then, popping in? Had my panicked, startled mind transported me outside the physical setting into the collective while *my hands* performed the archetypal movements: to play every possible combination, dark notes and light? . . . In 2001, I would at last receive an experiential understanding of how this vision of Pauli's (and myself at the piano) might play out in the structure of Oneness, or Source, and even quantum mechanics. For now, I had a child's insight.

Here in February 2001, I seem to have been presented a dramatic dénouement of that task. Editor Rhea A. White was excited by the terms "your own piece of Earth," and "information-tilling." As I reported it, the *potential* solutions seemed as if poised in a see-saw manner, to balance the manifesting problems. In that dynamics, as problems become conscious, so do solutions need to step out of the unconscious. If not, then nature finds some way to restore *its* equilibrium.

It seemed to me a problem could be (or perhaps naturally was) in symmetry—paired—with unconscious potential solutions; that there seemed to be some sort of tug of war striving to maintain symmetry, break it, restore it.

I found it new and exciting—not that we have to know every answer in the world, but that according to this vision, there is built in a solution-potential to balance *particular* problems that arise, *by switching the focus.* And if problem/solution are out of kilter, either we rebalance them by tilling our "pieces of earth" inside the vast combinations in the collective wave of Mind/Spirit/Psyche/Matter, or the balance becomes restored in some more turbulent way.

In our "locations" as information compilers, observers, focusers, and potential coordinates, we provides "arms" for Earth. This directly ties in to Rhea's EHE concept of *potentiation.* I saw potentiation (our alchemic transformation) as not only a personal choice—but also a survival mechanism for the planet. In fact, tending your "piece of

Earth" brings back the archetype of home: home*land* security. Even our *Fire* Side. But until we admit the role of consciousness, we cannot peer yet further to see just how critical it is and how not just elegantly woven into the creation of reality but made, in effect, into a *deus ex machina*.

The 1985 Zurich Initiation in a Sense Finished in 2001

The 1985 Zurich Initiation set in motion the 2001 culmination—a long wait. Better say, period of development. I could have had the (1985, 2001) initiations back to back as the straight line they were if you connected beginning to end. But I had to go *through time* to get the understanding, potentiate the implications. It fit into a much larger wave, collapsing here and there.

When a wave function collapses, we know that all the unselected potential "dies." But in my vision, other possibilities were held in reserve—burrowing (on borrowed time) back into the conscious choice, operating there like limbs cut off that can still be felt, by some. I had the impression it was a representation I was looking at—once removed from the actuality—a giant information model. Yet one impinged on the other. As if we got our information, our awareness, from this model, our "knowing," our possibilities. But it was a two-way system. We'll go into this ahead. In 2001, I was in a seminar. That's the end, the Omega. In 1985 had come the Alpha of this same idea.

30

Dhyanyogi-ji Post-9/11

Milton Klonsky's message the first day of Roland's light body seminar in 2001 was followed by a second—from Shri Dhyanyogi—the next day. It was faraway-seeming in February but extremely revealing—though still mysterious—after 9/11 and the subsequent challenges in an increasingly violence-torn globe.

Dhyanyogi-ji and Vishnu

In the meditation I saw Dhyanyogi-ji's face clearly, and in focusing on it, I found myself at a council of great teachers. For me, it was very unusual to see Dhyanyogi-ji's face. At the council a discussion was under way about a massive collective shift. And these teachers were intently addressing a question.

Fortunately, I have notes: "Now, the same thing happened again. But it was a Hindu face that stepped in and that I shaped my focus into. That was a guru, Dhyanyogi-ji. The subject of the meditation was to connect the lower mind to the higher mind, taking the lower mind to it. The teacher, Roland Verschaeve, said, as he gave the meditation, that from the lower mind there is no solution."

Glimpsing into the meeting briefly, I got the impression that massive change was coming, traumatic events these teachers were aware of; their concern was what about people who—ill prepared or no longer really needing the lesson in question—might pointlessly be caught up in the downside? Lingering residue might sweep them in. Or in some other way they could get pulled into the net.

This created a dilemma: Was it ethical? *Or should they be protected?*

Protection meant intervention. The answer was *Protect them*. The vision passed. I saw no more.

Roland told me the description was obviously of a council of Lord Vishnu. He startled me by telling me he had seen me at such subtle conferences before. Seven months afterward came 9/11.

> I felt, from the Vishnu level, the double sensation of absolute solidity there in the focus, with (at the same time) a great deal of unstableness I was aware of outside the focus. Roland pointed out [to me afterward] that it was important to feel the two at once. That Vishnu represented the high intelligence and that it was important to look at the instability of the Earth from the Vishnu mind. There, it's totally stable. . . .
>
> Many people think statistics are okay, karma, etc., I realized from the Vishnu mind. But if you give some people a 99 percent challenge and some only 1 percent—thinking in collective terms—in the Vishnu mind, you don't just accept statistical resolution and "chance" or karma, in deciding what is moral in moving to higher levels of light, or "proliferation of consciousness," and aligning them *before* there are new group answers.

Later, in *Shakti: An Introduction to Kundalini Maha Yoga* by Dhyanyogi-ji, I read these words from Shri Anandi Ma:

> Today we have instrumentation that can predict the weather; we know when events like earthquakes are likely to occur. We can know all this, yet there seems to be no power to stop these events. However, even in these days, there are beings, yogis, who do have the capacity to stop such events from occurring in creation. For the most part, they will not use their energies to bring about such modifications, but rather follow the laws of creation and of nature. By and large, following their intuition, they allow things to unfold as they are destined to be. In rare instances, however, they may use their energies in this way to help protect humanity.[175]

The rudimentary introduction of a Vishnu perspective, in early 2001, concerned the effect of consciousness expansion on people who would have different percentages of preparedness. How fallout of consciousness shift could AFFECT those who really were not intricately involved with the lesson that was causing the turmoil. They could easily be CAUGHT IN THE SHUFFLE.

Though I did not proceed further into the message then, it would leave a provocative enigma. No, said the second message, it was UNACCEPTABLE TO JUST LET THINGS BE, FALLING AS THEY MAY. Was there a way to avoid it?

The Vishnu-consciousness level was well able to stand steady under torrents of changing conditions. Many were not. Outside the steadiness of such a level, rampant confusion would be afield. Many would not know, literally, what hit them.

Did it matter? Statistically, no. But, *yes*, it mattered a lot. I got only a glimpse. But I did puzzle over it and the visit to the council where some kind of shepherding hand was concerned with degrees of challenge and varying effects when collective karma, with a broad sweep, was afoot.

Just as one example, from the spiritual point of view some would benefit by being "hit" by death-of-ego circumstances. Others, not. Not in this way. Or, supposing they had already passed through such a shift, it might—because of lingering karmic traces or impulses—land on them again, as if they needed a reminder, WHEN THEY DID NOT.

31

E. H. Walker

With the February light body seminar fresh in mind, I attended the Albuquerque International Conference on Science and Consciousness in April. I arranged to visit a good friend, Puanani Harvey, from the Jung Institute Zurich days, an analyst living in Santa Fe, a wonderful person I hadn't seen in years. So I was doubly excited. Featured speakers included an array of leaders in the fledgling field: Amit Goswami, Peter Russell, Gregg Braden, Karl Pribram, Claudio Narañjo, Bruce Lipton, Charles Tart, P. M. H. Atwater, and Larry Dossey. Also, Evan Harris Walker.

I first met Walker in 1983 at the Parapsychological Association Convention in New Jersey—my attention drawn to a stranger, a physicist bending spoons, which was the rage that year. The participants tried their hand. I wasn't able to do it, but for Walker, with his huge power of focus, it appeared to be a snap.

On the PA website, nevertheless, he listed the relative values to him of different types of proof that psi is real. Least convincing were, "I have seen them happen," and "I have made them happen." At the top was that parapsychological phenomena were consistent with QM principles and had demonstrated reliability in scientific theory and tests.

I next saw him at the 38th Annual Convention of the Parapsychological Association in 1995 in Durham, North Carolina, where I was in the panel to discuss pioneering laboratory parapsychologist J. B. Rhine. As the panel ended, from the podium I took the opportunity—despite fears of rebuff—to mention my computer PK: did anyone want to test it experimentally? If so, I urged, come up to me afterwards. Walker did. He deferred any test, however, until he could interest "at least three other colleagues." He added, "By the time I get around to setting up the experiment, you will have forgotten all about this." I never forgot, but he never pursued the idea.

As it turned out, I ran into him in Albuquerque. I arrived early—it was a short bus hop from Santa Fe—and found him sitting alone in the hotel dining room. He was glad to have me join him. I remember it well—minute by minute.

As I listened intently, he said he'd like to get philanthropical contributions (for his Walker Cancer Research Institute) by asking very wealthy people to choose a famous unrealized historical idea—a genius project (he mentioned da Vinci's Gran Cavallo horse statue)—and pay him large sums of money to implement it in their name. I liked that he thought big.

I eagerly showed him a portfolio of my computer PK samples—remembering that moment six years ago, after the Rhine panel. We flipped through the pages. From a parapsychologist's point of view he wasn't interested any more—no longer conducting such research. However, he said, seeming to mean it, *if the printouts were his, he'd paint them.* I asked if he painted. He said yes.

Leaving the conference, I had a copy of Walker's *The Physics of Consciousness* (I'd get it signed three years later) and of QM physicist Amit Goswami's *The Visionary Window*. On the back sat a blurb by Walker.

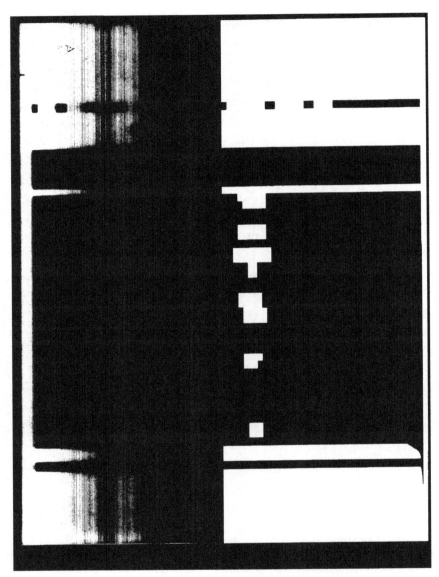

Computer creation Walker would have painted

32

Back to the U.S.

I returned to Belgium with my mind made up. I would move to Raleigh, North Carolina. By the end of August 2001, I was relocated. I was just in time to get my part-container transported and my fourteen-pound dachshund Snoepie squeezed into the pet carrier at my feet on Delta. In two weeks came 9/11. Before moving, I used Belgian universal health care to get, for the first time there, a complete checkup: heart-stress test, bone loss. The results showed that both heart and bones had suffered from my focus on meditation, shortchanging—even ignoring—exercise. I was borderline osteoporosis and needed to retrain my heart.

Getting my warnings, I thought: I have two choices—the yogi way (by mental power and subtle energy) or the Western way: exercise. I decided on exercise.

There was a gym in my Raleigh apartment complex. I went there, stepped onto the treadmill, and kept moving. After several times, suddenly I felt my back block opening. Sure enough, the lower-back block I'd regularly treated with traction at a Tienen kinesiologist's clinic (where weights were hung from my feet) opened up—spontaneously. I don't believe this could have happened earlier. But now the intent and lifestyle worked together and my back block vanished. I'd been advised at the kinesiologist's I could never again do exercises involving the lower back. But now I promptly went to a studio and signed up for "New York City Ballet Workout."

The extreme back discomfort had seemed to me to align with Dhyanyogi-ji's condition the last years of his life, when bedridden— for instance, having to be carried to the cab to go to JFK International

Airport. In my case, I'd had trouble getting out of bed. I intuited that perhaps sharing a condition, though his was far more severe (yet his cosmic energy remained unaffected), furthered a deeper tie.

That the block opened was no small thing. But it also felt like, with the opening, another adjustment occurred; as if—incredible as it sounds—my consciousness moved out of reach. As if it had been tangibly located and that place disappeared. I tried for days to connect to my consciousness. It's a strange feeling, as if a road suddenly disappeared off a map.

No luck. I even asked psychic Mariah Martin. Nothing helped. Then I flew to the light body conference in Oregon. During a break I approached cofounder Duane Packer, a clairvoyant former bodyworker, who is described on his website as being able to "see energy fields around the body" and has a PhD in geology-geophysics, having "traveled the world [for his job] as a geologist." I explained my predicament in a word or two.

He extended his forefinger, which to my eyes looked at that moment giantly long. Drawing on healing abilities of the spirit entity he channeled, DaBen, with that seemingly never-ending finger, he lightly touched me in several spots along the front of my spine, aligning them.

The effect was immediate. I saw and felt a thick cobra shape go all the way up my spine, out through the crown of my head. It followed the light body pathway, yet was clearly reminiscent of a thick kundalini cobra.

The cobra extended straight up over my head. On the extended part I "saw" what looked to be three small hublike "communication stations"— circular energy spots that seemed to be for making contact with—who knew? Bright-colored transmission-like junctures that I intuited connected out into the universe. He had realigned me to my consciousness in its transpersonal nature, with these few bright stations dotting the cobra-like form, then some of the flow going upward, the rest downward.

As I'd shifted focus from kundalini to light body, I'd never experienced the kundalini travel all the way up to the crown. Here, both systems evidently united in a single path. This did not surprise me, because once, in my apartment, a spiritual teacher had while sleeping experienced herself chanting in *Sanskrit in a Christian abbey* with Dhyanyogi-ji.

My head was cleared. I felt reconnected to my consciousness. In my room, where I'd scheduled a healing to work on this issue, the healer saw immediately it was unnecessary. She said I had new neural pathways. This was one of two times I lost the ability to "reach my consciousness"—the second being when my dog Snoepie died. In this first instance, I felt that the Buddha belly consciousness had been, clearly, partly unconscious to me. It would require a more conscious understanding on my part.

When Dhyanyogi-ji had shaktipat, his ecstatic God consciousness state lasted three days. Had I come to *where he was*—as he instructed me in a dream? Who knew? I sighed with relief that I was "me" again, no matter if it was in part a transpersonal being, hooked up to all sorts of receiving "stations," but then in the unity of ourselves, we all are.

As earlier noted, the computer PK went overboard in the summer, printing out page after page in Belgium as if hurrying to get me stocked up for the move. That was foresight; in my 1000-square-foot North Carolina apartment, where would I have put the masses of papers, had I continued making the printouts? (Remember, in this situation the only convincing document is the original hard copy.) Besides, I'd decided to bring out my archives rather than keep piling up unpublished manuscripts, with computer PK filling the apartment. Not to mention 20 x 30–inch cloud photograph enlargements. Before shipping, I stripped the whole poundage of paper and furniture in half. That meant I had a much tidier apartment. Happily, much clutter was gone.

The little girl at the top of the stairs now had to come down. To do so had been my repeated "command." Notably, in a Big Dream in 1982 I had to descend to a lower level and start over from the bottom. I had been on the plateau with—half visible in a Black Hole—a dead Milton

Klonsky, whom I futilely tried to pull out. Finally realizing the serious threat of falling onto the concrete below, I descended to the ground level. There, handing me a "monster," a small, wise magical woman (a Jungian image of the Self) explained that this distorted part of me, if held under a fountain, would clean up into a delicacy. I learned in hindsight that this format of individuation could be interpreted as calling me to the Jung Institute Zurich, *city of fountains*. In any case, it was telling me that at that date, the early 1980s, I hadn't the skill to communicate my intuitive knowledge. I would fall "onto the concrete." (Ultimately, today, 2015, thirty-plus years later, this—this moment—is a new attempt, a recycling with much more perspective. Working, this time, upward from the ground level of *Keep This Quiet!* I and II. Good luck, little Margaret!)

A new task awaited as the twenty-first century opened. I was about to begin another nineteen-year "assignment." What was the lesson now? To go public. For me, a real challenge. Hadn't Richard Unger, the hand-reading expert, said, it was the least-skilled part of me: the extravert, who, it turned out, wanted to "tell my secrets." In fact, that secret-telling was exactly called for.

That part of me had, in my childhood, been so eager to slip down into the men's poker game. To risk rebuke, breaking the rules, in order to listen to herself, to "live, live, live. It's a mistake not to."[*]

I began teaching light body courses. Also, I spent time in Sibiu, Romania, to bring out the first three *Space Encounters* books, drafted in Tienen. My publisher, Didi-Ionel Cenuşer, an English lit professor and author, newly out of Communism, had no commercial instincts. But he was detail-oriented, professional yet a friend—ideal for me. He even took me as a mentor. Since 1992, I'd spent two weeks to a month each year in Sibiu, renting a room for $7 a day (heated by a freestanding round ceramic floor-to-ceiling stove I turned on by lighting a match, getting out of bed into a cold room). Yet now the dollar was dropping. Romanians preferred the German mark. Soon the Euro. I was winding down that part of my journey.

---

[*]   Henry James, *The Ambassadors* (paraphrased)

Rhea A. White, besides being Director of the Exceptional Human Experience Network, was the longtime editor of the *Journal of the American Society for Psychical Research*. But by the early 2000s she had semiretired. Through her, I was friends with the new editor of *JASPR*, Suzanne V. Brown. With my light body article finished, I asked both if *JASPR* might like Evan Harris Walker's book reviewed. They said yes. Rhea said it should be a lengthy "Review Essay."

The ASPR, as stated on their website, was founded by distinguished scholars and scientists "who shared the courage and vision to explore the uncharted realms of human consciousness [such as] renowned Harvard psychologist and Professor of Philosophy, William James. Many early participants were pioneers in psychology, psychiatry, physics and astronomy. Freud and Jung were honorary members." Also members were the inventor of Xerox and theoretical physicist David Bohm, who posited the nonlocal hidden-variable theory mentioned earlier.

I was on a roll and thought *The Physics of Consciousness* would help me tackle further the 2001 light body incident. I was ready to dig. How did my view of the uncollapsing One, the nonlocal, backstage "essence of consciousness," stack up alongside quantum mechanics?

Walker was a parapsychologist. *JASPR* needed his book reviewed. Unfortunately, *JASPR* suspended publication of its journal before I turned in the article, so it never got into print. But it went through some editing rounds with Rhea.

In the next pages are extracts from my 1997 Walker book review article, interspersed with my current findings on QM. Eventually, I added so much new text to the proposed *JASPR* article—updating it to 2015—I no longer identify which passages are from the original essay. Many are, though many are additions.

I don't pretend to solve the thorny, tricky problems of QM, but it intersects with issues in *Keep This Quiet!*—in particular that the Knokke light body meditation raised—so I didn't duck but headed into the mysterious waters.

Two positions will fight it out. In one, the physical world (of atoms) is primary, and for many consciousness is an epiphenomenon of matter, though no one claims to know how the brain might have produced it. In the other, in reverse, consciousness is primary, the ground of being—out of which comes matter. But matter is waves of possibility until a wave "collapses." I was eager to see Walker lay out the argument in favor of consciousness as the Ground. He waxes lyrical in describing consciousness (human and other). He says, let's resolve this.

First a little summary: *The Physics of Consciousness: The Quantum Mind and the Meaning of Life* asserts that "consciousness is real but nonphysical." Consciousness, writes physicist E. H. Walker, is "not so many atoms. It does not consist of photons or quarks. Neither is it molecules spinning about in the brain. Consciousness is something that exists in its own right." [176] Foundational to Walker's investigations are the role of the observer and of quantum mechanical tunneling in the brain. His experience of *satori*, or enlightenment, permitted him to understand consciousness and his task is to make "enlightenment" scientific. I look at his book from my experience with ancient Eastern teachings and the Ground state.

A Little Mystical Background

In *One Mind: How Our Individual Mind Is Part of a Greater Consciousness and Why It Matters*, Larry Dossey states up front: "T. S. Eliot once said of Indian philosophers, 'Their subtleties make most of the great European philosophers look like schoolboys.' . . . For most Western readers, however, I find that these granular analyses of consciousness can be off-putting. To be told that in Buddhism the Kamaloka, or empirical/worldly plane of consciousness, has 54 states . . . makes Western eyes glaze over." [177]

In fact, in the yogic East, centuries of studying consciousness— the "science of spiritual evolution"—produced so many Sanskrit terms that "cit/chit" ("consciousness") is almost a combining form.

Cit serves as the foundation to all states of consciousness, and as such is eternal and unchanging. There are many minute categories.[*]

But this yogic science is nothing like science in the West. The ancient "science of spiritual evolution" is *experiential*. Where is the East–West bridge?

Evan Harris Walker draws from both camps. Described on the Parapsychological Association website as a paradigm shifter, he is cited as a founder of the modern science of consciousness research, one who "originated the 'Quantum Observer Theory' relating to state vector collapse that is of significance to parapsychology."[178] In the Quantum Observer Theory, *the observer* is responsible for the wave function collapse (also known as state vector collapse, or wave reduction). *Observation is just what he brings back in.*

Before going further, let me note that Walker included a lot of hard science but took the approach of a Quest. Chapter titles ("Jitterbug World, Jitterbug Reality," or "Looking for the Emerald City" and "The Red Shoes") are in line with the hero archetype. Perhaps with a nod to Don Quixote. He sets out to solve contentious issues in quantum mechanics, about which there is no agreement, and bring together Eastern mysticism and Western materialism. How does matter interact with mind? Let's find out, he says, and heads to the starting gate.

But first one must realize that the topic he tackled was hotly disputed by Einstein and Niels Bohr, among others. Even today it is contentious.

A 1998 Weizmann Institute of Science experiment in Israel validated one QM theory. The observer was a beam of electrons: "Institute scientists used for this purpose a tiny but sophisticated electronic detector that can spot passing electrons."[179] Merely by its presence, the watching detector forced the electrons to behave not like waves but like particles. To describe the experiment:

---

[*]   For more, see the American Sanskrit Institute online.

When behaving as waves, they can simultaneously pass through several openings in a barrier and then meet again at the other side of the barrier. This "meeting" is known as interference.

Strange as it may sound, interference can only occur when no one is watching. . . . In other words, when under observation, electrons are being "forced" to behave like particles and not like waves. Thus the mere act of observation affects the experimental findings.

To demonstrate this, Weizmann Institute researchers built a tiny device measuring less than one micron in size, which had a barrier with two openings. They then sent a current of electrons towards the barrier. . . .

Apart from "observing," or detecting, the electrons, the detector had no effect on the current. Yet the scientists found that the very presence of the detector-"observer" near one of the openings caused changes in the interference pattern of the electron waves passing through the openings of the barrier. In fact, this effect was dependent on the "amount" of the observation: when the "observer's" capacity to detect electrons increased, in other words, when the level of the observation went up, the interference weakened; in contrast, when its capacity to detect electrons was reduced, in other words, when the observation slackened, the interference increased.

In Eastern spirituality experiential observation, not laboratories, is key. Expansion of consciousness develops awareness, a state of "Knowing"*—antithetical to proving (perhaps complimentary in the Niels Bohr sense). In explaining some *siddhis* (or "miracles") in the satguru Dhyanyogi-ji's life, his biography notes, "Dhyanyogi-ji's faith had no limits, so what might seem impossible to most was perfectly plausible to him."[180]

---

* Such statements are based in my years of studying and teaching meditation. I currently teach basic and advanced courses in the light body, a study of frequencies the brain can "track."

How does one approach such opposition? Obviously, from the inside is best. So Walker went inside. Inside consciousness itself, to the Zen experience called *satori*. He went into this state without expecting to.

While many scientists were at home in the theory that the mind was an offshoot of the brain, Walker had a moment of *satori*—a Zen Buddhist state of sudden comprehension—that said different. He found in the brain itself a "quantum mechanical connection." It just so happened that as a young man—as he walked through a field across from the University of Maryland campus (the Department of Physics and Astronomy building in view) in 1966—he had an insight into electron tunneling. "In one moment," he said, "the problem was solved."[181]

The event led him to believe *electron tunneling* in the brain created a condition for nonlocal (QM) effects in the *synapses*—"switches in the brain that do the actual information processing."[182] His explanation takes up many technical pages in Chapter 12. Not only was the mind not, as many physicists claimed, produced by the brain. But "we are left with the wave function—the state vector of quantum mechanics itself—as somehow the access route from the physical world into the mind."[183] He spent the rest of his life founding a science of consciousness based in the quantum mind.

German physicists Günter Nimtz and Astrid Haibel, who experimented at length in tunneling, speculate: "Our knowledge today of quantum cosmology tells us that the universe also came into existence through tunneling, the so-called 'Big Bang.' A stationary state of space and time of infinitely small dimension tunneled into our world and expanded until eventually today's state of our universe was reached."[184]

Here in a nutshell is tunneling. "On a quantum scale, objects exhibit wavelike behavior. For a quantum particle moving against a potential hill [the hill is not physical but an energy barrier], the wave function describing the particle can extend to the other side of the hill. This wave represents the probability of finding the particle in a certain location, meaning that the particle has the possibility of being detected on the other side of the hill."[185] How did it get there if it hadn't enough kinetic energy to? By tunneling.

If one remembers, in *Keep This Quiet! III: Initiations*, I described how a chance September 1995 focus on this very quantum tunneling—as I read about a "loan mechanism" that allowed particles to "borrow" energy to cross an impossible "hill"—immediately preceded my Zurich Initiation.

To go a step further—in formulating his observer theory, Walker said *anyone who observes anything can affect it even from the future.* Theoretically, then, his observation of the tunneling effect (unknown to me) could influence me, "lend" me energy! Or somehow, theoretically, his *satori* revelation might confer with or make more likely my Zurich Initiation—the sole clue that this occurred being the presence of the same topic, or "secret attractor," at the time of both. And in reverse, theoretically my experience (in the then future, in 1985) could backwardsly affect him!

Later, physicists such as F. David Peat speculated that instead of matter/energy ($E = mc^2$), we might imagine a "matter, energy, information" triad. To this point, MIT's Scott Aaronson said, "'I don't know how you could even conceive of a universe' without information."[186] Was this implied in my dream of a *lending* library (the night before the Zurich Initiation began in 1985)? Were *library* loans in some way symbolic of the quantum *loan* mechanism? Or of "consciousness in itself"?

And where will it stop? Experiments into biophotons inside us, making a coherent information field, hint at a oneness of Life that we share energy and information in. Just as has been implied by a lot of the experiences reported subjectively in this book. So going out on a limb wasn't so far out after all.

Walker's Approach

Making the point that consciousness is nonphysical, Walker explains how [Paul M.] Churchland defined the "redness" of an apple as "a matrix of molecules." But, he objects, this cold definition comes nowhere near capturing "the experience of redness in the mind."[187]

Explaining that consciousness is not thinking, he says, "A fly blankly staring at a red tablecloth in a red room will have redness consciousness."[188] He counters with the Zen master, who, if asked what red is, "may pat your head or splash water (because these are, in fact, closer to what redness is)."[189] Neither is consciousness perception or attention or conscience.

"Consciousness is the blue of the sky; it is C#, the taste of sweetness as it fills the mind, the smell of gardenia, the pain of love that is lost."[190] And much more. But, he says, it is impossible, for example, to measure whether an ice cube feels pain. He imagines it melting on the floor. "Does the ice cube feel pain? . . . This question is neither frivolous nor answerable." It is impossible to objectively demonstrate the answer.[191]

Descartes brilliantly attempted to solve the mind/body problem as a philosopher, Walker points out, and was well ahead of his time, therefore inevitably doomed.

Walker hones in on the question of what this phenomenon—consciousness—is, stating it sharply: "It is, nevertheless, a part of the whole cloth of reality." But, he asks, "How does it tie in to the physical cloth? It seems like a shimmering color that floats somehow above the fabric. What is its connection to the rest of reality? These questions imply something about how we must search for an answer, and they imply something about the phenomenon—namely that we seek to understand some *one* new constituent of reality, and we seek to find its *one* connection with the rest of reality."[192]

He noted the past radical departures science took when discoveries led it to do so—as with Newton's law of universal gravitation—and believed, with "his rare fusion of intellectual ambition with emotional urgency," as Booklist pointed out, that now was just such a time.

At the crux is the question: does objective "reality" exist—that is, nonsubjective, nonpsychological, independent of an observer? Weirdly, QM experiments answer, paradoxically, no. By 1923 it was clear that "a photon, an electron, an atom, a molecule, in principle any object, can be either compact [matter] or widely spread out [in a wave]. You can show an object to be bigger than a loaf of bread or smaller than an atom. You can choose which of these two contradictory features to demonstrate. The physical reality of an object depends on how you choose to look at it."[193]

Einstein agreed that QM interpretation said so. But, he vigorously asserted, the theory was incomplete. He and Bohr argued back and forth. Erwin Schrödinger, hating the concept of quantum-jumping particles, created an equation for "matter waves," but his mathematical description did nothing to solve the "quantum enigma." Where was the "matter" in a "matter wave" before it was observed? Was it spread out over the wave, with no physical existence?

In 1935 Einstein—with two young scientists, Boris Podolsky and Nathan Rosen—sprung on the community a revolutionary paper: "Can Quantum-Mechanical Description of Physical Reality Be Considered Complete?" Known as the EPR thought experiment, it involved two electrons that start out intricately connected, then separate. Yet afterwards any observation of one causes a reaction in the other—faster than the speed of light. EPR demonstrated this "entanglement" of electron 1 and electron 2 to be a fact. (In actual fact, "Because electrons [before measurement] are *indistinguishable* particles, it is not proper to say electron 1 goes this way and electron 2 that way." But it is a convenient way to explain it.[194]) Goswami described the nonlocality conundrum: "Suppose somebody coughed in New York and caused water to move in Seattle! Could one do science under such circumstances?"[195]

No, insisted Einstein. See, QM theory is incomplete. There must be *local* hidden variables. Explaining the historical importance of "locality"—as opposed to spooky "action at a distance"—to physics, Henry P. Stapp, of the Lawrence Berkeley National Laboratory, University of California at Berkeley, writes:

The ideas of Galileo Galilei, René Descartes, and Isaac Newton created a magnificent edifice known as classical physical theory, which was completed by the work of James Clerk Maxwell and Albert

Einstein. The central idea is that the physical universe is composed of "material" parts that are *localizable* in tiny regions, and that all motion of matter is completely determined by matter alone, via *local* universal laws. This *local* character of the laws is crucial. It means that each tiny localized part responds only to the states of its immediate neighbors: each *local* part "feels" or "knows about" nothing outside its immediate microscopic neighborhood.[196] (my emphasis)

The Bohr-Einstein clash on this point is summed up by theoretical QM physicist Howard M. Wiseman:

Contrary to popular opinion, Bohr had no defense against Einstein's 1935 attack (the EPR paper) on the claimed completeness of orthodox quantum mechanics. I suggest that Einstein's argument, as stated most clearly in 1946, could justly be called Einstein's reality-locality-completeness theorem, since it proves that one of these three must be false. Einstein's instinct was that completeness of orthodox quantum mechanics was the falsehood, but he failed in his quest to find a more complete theory that respected reality and locality. Einstein's theorem, and possibly Einstein's failure, inspired John Bell in 1964 to prove his reality-locality theorem. This strengthened Einstein's theorem (but showed the futility of his quest) by demonstrating that either reality or locality is a falsehood. This revealed the full nonlocality of the quantum world for the first time.[197]

Heads spun in theoretical physics. Einstein, dismayed by the implication of "spooky action at a distance," wrote Max Born in 1948, "My instinct for physics bristles at this." Einstein also famously asked Bohr, "Do you really think the moon isn't there if you aren't looking at it?" To which—firmly believing QM theory was complete—Bohr responded, "But still, it cannot be for us to tell God how he is to run the world."[198]

To the rescue, in 1964 and '78, John Bell, a Northern Ireland physicist, tackled the thorny dispute. In 1964 he put the 1935 ("entangled particles") Einstein-Podolsky-Rosen *thought experiment* to the test. After which the scientific world could no longer simply keep EPR on the dusty shelves of theory.

From then on paper after paper tried to come to grips with the notion that "nonlocality" of our world—or "connectedness"—was apparently a fact. But what did it mean? There is as of yet no consensus. Very astutely Bohr said physics didn't have to answer, that its job was to show how things worked, not what that meant.[*]

But Bell had earlier planned to be a philosopher. He didn't let the enigma go. His results disproved the contention that EPR could be explained away by a *local* hidden variables theory. No, his results contended, if a signal cannot travel faster than light *locally*, in our 3-D world—which Einstein had said was the case (the speed of light was constant)—what might be going on? Another option was that our reality was "irreducibly random"; that is, with "no hidden variables that 'determine the results of [all] individual measurements.'"

Barring these two options, what was left? Reality is nonlocal and—with everything made up of particles—"'the setting of one measuring device can influence the reading of another instrument, however remote.'"[199] How would Einstein, who died in 1955, have reacted? A distinguished Princeton physicist put it: "Anyone who's not bothered by Bell's Theorem has to have rocks in his head."[200]

Importantly, however, Walker states what he himself affirms

---

[*]   Recent Chinese experiments, reported in 2013, have demonstrated that—if the science holds up—spooky action at a distance "is at least four orders of magnitude faster than light, and may still turn out to be instantaneous, as quantum mechanics predicts" (http://www.technologyreview.com/view/512281/chinese-physicistsmeasurespeed-of-spooky-action-at-a-distance/); also see a follow-up successful loophole-free Dutch experiment in 2015 and a November 2015 experiment by the National Institute of Standards and Technology (NIST) in Boulder, Colorado, re-testing the Bell nonlocality/entanglement theory; it closed all loopholes in the design of the experiment and found that nonlocal "spooky action at a distance" is conclusively real (http://gizmodo.com/physicists-prove-that-spooky-action-at-a-distance-is-re-1742617252), as did tests in Holland and Vienna.

throughout: "the philosophical system—the paradigm—on which Einstein based his physics was itself hopelessly incomplete."[201] It had to be, Walker believed, because it omitted the conscious observer, leaving "mind" in the brain—brain function in biology.

Again, there is the contentious question, what is "an observer"?

Back to Henry P. Stapp, who worked by invitation with Pauli, then Heisenberg; he has a knack for explaining things in understandable language. Stapp addresses the question, What does it take to cause the quantum system to collapse—that is, anything to manifest? A conscious observer, he says. But what is that? A thermostat, "from my point of view, no, [when it makes decisions,] I wouldn't like to say that a thermostat is conscious." What about a mouse with cheese? he's asked. Is the mouse an observer? If not, then there is no wave function collapse. Therefore, though the mouse eats the cheese in our 3-D world, the *quantum system* remains in a superposition of all possibilities, so there you'd still have all possibilities.

Stapp says, "A superposition means that you can bring these possibilities back together."[202]

He also speaks of a "neural correlate of intent" and thinks three hundred years of science imposing one way of seeing the world has brainwashed us away from the deep intuition that thought influences action; that restoring this connection fills "the causal gap . . . And in this age of computers, and information, and flashing pixels there is nothing counterintuitive about the ontological idea that nature is built—not out of ponderous classically conceived matter but—out of events, and out of informational waves and signals that create tendencies for these events to occur."[203]

Speaking in a very different camp, which we will look at briefly further on, physicist Sean Carroll objects that in the Copenhagen interpretation, "It doesn't need to be a 'conscious' observer or anything else that might get Deepak Chopra excited; we just mean a *macroscopic measuring apparatus*. It could be a living person, but it could just as well be a video camera or even the air in a room [emphasis added]."[204]

However, if consciousness is the ground of being, the paradox is shifted. A reviewer of Goswami's *The Self-Aware Universe* wrote: "By making the leap from a universe based on bits of matter, to one based in consciousness [as the ground of being], he hopes to logically and coherently resolve some of the major paradoxes of physics. He suggests that instead of everything being made of atoms, everything is made of physics."[205] Goswami, the son of a Brahmin guru, came to this view slowly, helped along by a Big Dream that asserted, "*The Tibetan Book of the Dead* is real. It's your job to prove it."

Throwing down the gauntlet, Walker declares, "A thousand physicists have grappled with this problem and failed to come up with any satisfactory answers. . . . And yet," he responds, "this is the problem we must solve if we are to peer beyond the veil of the physical world to find the hidden workings of reality."[206]

He reminds us that proofs of Bell's 1964 theorem, in establishing the nonlocality of our world, "proved mathematically that certain quantum correlations, unlike all other correlations in the Universe, cannot arise from any *local* cause."[207] (emphasis added)

No, Walker answers—the materialistic view based in *local, independent* reality is false: "The observer interacts with matter. Consciousness, the substance of this new-found reality that defines the observer, has fundamental existence. It is the quantum mind that is the basic reality."[208] A bold statement indeed.

Here's a lively objection in Wikipedia: "Critics of the special role of the observer also point out that observers can themselves be observed . . . and that it is not clear how much consciousness is required ('Was the wave function waiting to jump for thousands of millions of years until a single-celled living creature appeared? Or did it have to wait a little longer for some highly qualified measurer—with a PhD?')."[209]

What collapses a wave function? The yogis don't speak in such language; they "Know" from vast experience over centuries engaged in "mastering the physical."

And in the eyes of David Bohm, there is *no* wave function collapse anyway; there are just hidden *nonlocal* variables that appear in and out of an explicate/implicate order.

A new book, *Tales of the Quantum: Understanding Physics' Most Fundamental Theory* (2017), by Art Hobson, focuses on quanta and fields, reminding us that not everything is made up of atoms (light waves are not atoms). But everything, he writes, is composed of quanta. Even macroscopic matter, such as a baseball, obeys the laws of quanta; thus, theoretically can be in multiple positions at once. (The emphasis is on "theoretically.") Experimentally, he reports, a barely visible object has now been put into a superposition to move in two contradictory ways at once. To Hobson, reality is fundamentally waves in fields. Where is this going?

My vision seems in part compatible with Bohm's theory. It shows consciousness itself as it zips in and out of events, registering and self-organizing them.

Though I had no intellectual input during my experience, I can imagine a large complex answer, including that the collective unconscious builds up to the "collapse," and synchronicities send the possibilities into high-alert status. But then Goswami says, yes, that's it: that's the essence of consciousness: the Ground state. Ubiquitous.

Recently, in the *European Journal of Physics*, a Harvard doctoral student, John Miguel Marin, published a short paper on "the mysticism controversy" that spread through early quantum physics. Reverting to those days, he says, "The controversy began in Germany in the 1920s . . . but was much different than debates on similar issues today. At the turn of the last century, science and religion were not divided as they are today, and some scientists of the time were particularly inspired by Eastern mysticism."[210]

Many of the questions they openly discussed remain unanswered, such as those debated by Einstein and Bohr, recorded in letters and conferences, and joined by Wolfgang Pauli and others. They didn't sort it out. Certainly, I can't. But my vision in the 2001 light body meditation stays with me as my answer—not a theory but a highly energized picture of consciousness itself.

33

"A fly blankly staring
at a red tablecloth"

Satori, or Enlightenment

Although *satori* is considered to be beyond description, my experience in the light body meditation in 2001 had a revelation—in a governing symbolic image—that I reported back.

From the point of view of the Ground state, I saw that each new thought rearranged everything inside the whole, just as Cézanne said each new drop of paint restructured the painting. It was not just a "drop in the bucket." And the same with us. Once information, including personal experience, becomes a commodity, we become yet more largely responsible for the tending of it in our "piece of Earth."

Walker's satori experience was intrinsic to his ability to go to the level of consciousness beyond mental chatter to the stillness of the void, where, even so, something remains. Satori, he further found, could not be communicated to someone who had not experienced it. Asking rhetorically what consciousness is, Walker offers a metaphor: "the moment's whole world painted across the canvas of sensations."[211] He says:

> You have never touched a brick, never touched a wall, never held a book, never seen a word on a printed page, never held another, never touched a lover's lips. Those, if they exist at all, lie beyond you, and you can never reach out a hand to touch them. That is

reality. . . . We have seen that there is no objective world. The tests of [John] Bell's theorem have undercut that logical avenue. That objective reality is no longer there. . . . You should not think that the brick is an external object with an internal image in your brain. You are the brick. If this comes as a wondrous revelation, changing all your understanding, then you have just touched satori. You have discovered enlightenment, the consciousness of consciousness.[212]

He goes further to say, "Space is mind. And mind has the space of the whole universe spread out before us."[213]

Walker first realized in retrospect he had experienced satori through reading a Buddhist book and after puzzling over why when he spoke in the *simplest* manner in a lecture, he was the *least* understood. In Zen Buddhism, satori is defined as "a state of sudden spiritual Enlightenment" or "seeing one's own true nature."

Observation Plus Consciousness

What links consciousness to material phenomena? To answer, Walker says, we must understand observation. To properly understand the Copenhagen interpretation, he says—stating his controversial position—we must realize that it is not observation *minus consciousness* that achieves this reduction (or collapse) of the wave function. Consciousness out of the equation, the effect of a measuring device is to increases the number of potential, uncollapsed states. There is no collapse as the pure result of mechanical measurement. Consciousness selects, isolates, "collapses" into a single state.[214]

That is just what mathematician John von Neumann argued in 1932. What would happen, he asked, if a Geiger counter, set apart from the world, encountered a quantum system? For example, take two boxes and a Geiger counter "set to fire if the atom is in the bottom box, and to remain unfired if the atom is in the top box. Von Neumann showed that the isolated Geiger counter, a physical object governed by quantum mechanics, would *entangle* with the atom in both boxes. It would thus be in a superposition state with the atom. It would thus be simultaneously in a fired and unfired state." Imagine that something else, such as an isolated measuring device, likewise comes in contact with the Geiger counter. It too becomes entangled. "This so-called 'von Neumann chain' can continue indefinitely. Von Neumann showed that *no* physical system, obeying the laws of physics (i.e., quantum theory) could collapse a superposition state wave function to yield a particular result."[215]

Goswami restates the point, referring back to von Neumann (1955): "In order to initiate collapse, an agency is needed that is outside the jurisdiction of quantum mechanics. For von Neumann, there is only one such agency: consciousness." Goswami goes on significantly: "This potent idea, however, became bogged down in a nasty debate because consciousness is misunderstood in the West." As the spiritual teachers always told us, in his view, consciousness is in fact One—self-referent. And the world, "[in] reality, . . . is discontinuous, quantum, and conscious."[216]

With regard to those who assert "that only the material world exists" (the mind is an epiphenomenon of the brain)—denying the independent existence of mind—Walker's whole thesis is in rejection of this tenet.[217] Matter is waves. (That's what QM says.) What are the waves? Vast fields of connections, of possibilities. Nonlocal, meaning a point way across the universe might connect with one right here under my nose. An idea in your head might simultaneously make its way into another.

Hmmm. Just as I "saw" it before reading any of this.

More to mull over: what are all these waves out of which we "pick," as in a store, what we "see"? That we turn into pictures? Vibrations.

Throughout *The Physics of Consciousness*, Walker's swan song, as he died soon afterwards, he sparsely counterpoints the science with entries from his 1952 diary; in one case, to draw out the living reminder of himself already interested in the Tesla coil and "building—yes—a time machine."[218] Back in the present he proceeds to "count the stitches" of the fabric of mind, of consciousness (without reducing it), "and give birth to a new science."[219]

The last time I saw him, he was speaking at the Rhine Research Center in Durham. At noon November 19, 2003, the rain fell in sheets, but the small room was nearly full. I remember he emphasized the importance to science of having a theory. He signed my copy of *The Physics of Consciousness* and agreed to read my draft review of it. He answered the first email but then no more, probably already ill with cancer. He died in 2006, less than three years after the talk, at seventy.

He believed in science, but also in consciousness as the ground of being. A tough tightrope act. He believed in balancing the right and left brain hemispheres—art and science, painting and logic, the personal and the collective. No one, certainly not I, can say for sure yet what the answer to this thorny question of "the measurement problem" is. And yet I do know that intentions matter, listening to the "inner voice" matters. It affects how things happen.

Ancient gurus demonstrated it in their siddhis, which was their centuries-long task, just as a rock has a silent long-lasting presence. So this yogic mastery of the physical (including the mind/spirit's mastery of the body) was their success, as technology is our Western version of "mastery of the physical"—like night and day, but the work of many many lifetimes in each case.

How Information Plays In

Back to my experience: I saw information self-organizing instantly when new input warranted a restructuring. I did not see whether this required observation. It seemed to me the information just "knew" where to go. I don't begin to explain how it was "conscious." It was as if—I say as if—truth was self-evident as it came into being, shed light on by new information. Or as if information that belonged together had an attraction, a resonance. Again, I don't begin to explain this level of information organization.

A final quote: "I regard consciousness as fundamental. I regard matter as derivative from consciousness. We cannot get behind consciousness. Everything that we talk about, everything that we regard as existing, postulates consciousness," Nobel Laureate Max Planck,[220] one of the early QM theorists.

To return to the recent Harvard paper on early QM by John Miguel Marin: decades later (as reported in *Across the Frontiers*), the QM founders adopted "a perspective akin to Pauli's." Marin quotes Heisenberg:

> The physicist Wolfgang Pauli once spoke of two limiting conceptions, both of which have been extraordinarily fruitful in the history of human thought, although no genuine reality corresponds to them. At one extreme is the idea of an objective world, pursuing its regular course in space and time, independently of any kind of observing subject; this has been the guiding image of modern science. At the other extreme is the idea of a subject, mystically experiencing the unity of the world and no longer confronted by an object or an objective world; this has been the guiding image of Asian mysticism. Our thinking moves somewhere in the middle, between these two limiting conceptions; we should maintain the tension resulting from these two opposites.[221]

It's well to remember that the early founders, who paced back and forth over every aspect of QM they could think of, saw that its implications pointed East–West.

In a 1925 essay Schrödinger, who underwent suffering, including starvation, in World War I and long studied Eastern mysticism, recounts an ancient Sankhya Hindu paradox about apparent contradiction such as he would later tackle in his famous thought experiment with a half-dead/half-alive cat. He wrote, "The plurality [of viewpoints] that we perceive is only *'an appearance*; *it is not real*. Vedantic philosophy, in which this is a fundamental dogma, has sought to clarify it by a number of analogies, one of the most attractive being the many-faceted crystal which, while showing hundreds of little pictures of what is in reality a single existent object, does not really multiply the object.'"

Also, he said, "'you may suddenly come to see, in a flash, the profound rightness of the basic conviction of Vedanta: . . . knowledge, feeling and choice are essentially eternal and unchangeable and numerically *one* in all men, nay in all sensitive beings.'" Similarly, "'the external world and consciousness are one and the same thing.'"[222]

I had seen a highly energized Oneness that responded to any event (information/movement) in our 3-D world. It was a different level—called transcendent by ancient wisdom teachings.

In the unified Consciousness every event, every bit of information was *instantaneously* processed—available *in potentia* for our 3-D use as insights and awarenesses: new information combinations nonlocally in the present. The "present," though eternal, was, in its self-organizing arrangement of information related to our world, yet as momentary as the tiniest division of time that exists. Or, wait—let's say it was available whenever the compass points aligned. However, they never disappeared *in potentia*. A paradox yet quite clear in transcendent Oneness, where duality did not exist. Or coexisted—blended—as if it did not.

34

SEPTEMBER 25, 2005

But there is one more event I will jump to: September 25, 2005—seven months after Hunter Thompson's suicide in February. He was often wheelchair-bound by then; his body had worn out. I thought that was why. Doug Brinkley quoted Hunter on suicide not long beforehand, when his options had narrowed down because of health: "Of course it's a fucking option of mine. Who the fuck do you think I am? Do you think I'm gonna go in to live with a goddam Nurse Ratched in the hospital and be put through some detox thing? Fuck that."[223]

September 25 was my birthday. I had begun *Keep This Quiet!*—in a very rough draft. Hard to write. But I always loved my letters from Hunter. I thought they added to his legacy. At this point I didn't even have publication rights, yet in a way I did. I'd dreamed about Hunter a couple of weeks before his death and woke feeling wonderful. I didn't know why but felt a closeness.

It seemed to me the dream had buffered me, for when soon afterwards, the TV set told me he'd died I heard in my inner ear the song line, "Please don't let me be misunderstood." Not that he was speaking but that the line nurtured me. For I had hoped to see him again. Nothing specific—just an opportunity waiting to happen. Impossible perhaps and inevitable at the same time.

So I started drafting *Keep This Quiet!* As mentioned, I had dreamed in 1991 I was "helping write The Hunter Thompson Story." It made sense now. Dreams often set up something, seed a thought. So I plunged in.

I now did guided meditations when I woke up, lying in bed, turning on light body music—in part because Snoepie, my dachshund, was seventeen. I had to take him out to pee in the middle of the night. It disrupted my sleep. Every night. I had made a deal with him that I wouldn't put him down, he'd have to figure it out—because I'd never imagined myself killing a living creature like a dog. It was a shock to think I'd probably have to.

However, I discovered that not getting straight up, I was never tired. The meditation adjusted my tiredness; I felt refreshed. Also, something else was going on. The meditations were delicious. As I lay there, with Snoepie (he loved the music), I felt wavelets of light travel through me, emitting an exquisitely sensual sensation. This happened as I was preparing daily for writing *Keep This Quiet!* I thought they were due to Hunter. (Hmmm. It felt like electricity baths.)

Exactly on my birthday I treated myself to a Native American shamanic ceremonial-chamber event with Kailash Kokopelli, who has performed on every continent; his website describes him as "a multi-instrumentalist, composer, songwriter and producer . . . playing a great variety of (wind) instruments ranging from Didgeridoo to (Native American) flutes, as well as reed instruments, percussive soundscapes, drums, crystal singing bowls, string instruments and vocals." Kailash, with his Inner World Music, is "recognized as a . . . pioneer sound therapist by medical practitioners and international doctors."

I gathered up my Tibetan conch, bought from the Hungarian shaman Joska Soos de Sovar, and my sacred Sanskrit conch and drove an hour to the Watersong Peace Chamber on Periwinkle Farm just outside Pittsboro.

There, an initiation occurred. Warm, compassionate, Kailash added my instruments to his with delight. He knew of Joska. In Dutch, Joska had written a book: *I Do Not Heal, I Restore Harmony.* Joska had spoken to us of "traveling without moving," as well as the fact that distance didn't exist (he meant it didn't have to).[*]

As Kailash led a group meditation, swept up in the

---

[*] For those wanting to know more about Joska, there is a good English partial translation of his 1985 Dutch autobiography—free at http://www.soul-guidance.com/houseofthesun/soosbio.htm.

indigenous-instrument sounds, I had this physical sensation—of the delicacy of sensuality; it was unforgettably intense. In *Love in Transition,* I had written what seemed like fantasy, describing how the cells can feel: that "a man in space was waiting to release into the universe its own memory"—of an unknown sensual capacity on the cellular level.

And now here I was, experiencing the sensation of the cells . . . light moving like wavy, flowing rivulets that exploded. More: this overwhelming sense awoke in me of the holiness of the mere trace of a touch—here, a subtle touch—on the skin, so holy it is, this body we live in; how the cells can potentially feel that subtle sacredness: the particles of light meeting light; the flowers, the trees, the music, the utter sensuality of the merest encounter.

Such a purity of sensuality, I'd never remotely felt before. I took it to be a human condition: one we don't know about, or rarely know: an extreme peak—or delicacy—of sensation. Something anyone has the potential to feel. Perhaps that was in the archetype of the feminine (and the masculine) at its most awakened. It fit that description of Magdalena as "very sensual and very pure"—an awareness almost too dangerous to release out to the public, as I'd written in *Love in Transition,* where it was only intuition. The body renewed itself with the sheer essence of life, the creativity at its heart, based on touch, on contact as the particle level crossed into expression, feeling, in matter, in my body.

Author Ziad Masri, in his Amazon best-selling *Reality Unveiled: The Hidden Keys of Existence That Will Transform Your Reality (and the World),* tells us—echoing Walker—that nothing is solid. He explains in language I did not know back in 2005: sitting in your chair, you're 100-millionth of a centimeter above it; you are not touching it but sensing the atomic repulsion between its atoms and yours.

At home in guided meditations before working on the HST materials, I continued to feel the exploding rivulets of light. Atomic repulsion? This independent movement inside me energized me to work on "The Hunter Thompson Story."

That experience went on for two or three years, like the bell of years before. Then was gone. During that time sometimes I closed my eyes and saw this indescribable, fast-moving geometric energy shape, there and gone so fast my brain barely had time to register— zero time to get descriptive words. But something in me gasped as my brain struggled to even register, *what just went past? It was like a chunk of rock or a meteor or star, black-bluish, lumpy, brilliant without rays, twinkling without traditional light. Fast like a cosmic bullet in another dimension my brain was out of sync with, but in sync long enough to let me see it and smile. Stay, don't go. Show me more. It didn't come often. I loved the fact that it might show up at any time. Here. Gone. Zoom. Swoosh. Hot damn. Kazaar.*

So what did this all mean about my relationship with Hunter? Why had I persisted in keeping him posted about my journeys as they diverged from his? Very late, in 2017, to check on myself before publication, I asked the akashic masters. Their answer rings true: they described two sisters in the Middle East, who were quite evolved and could talk freely with no one but each other. Imagine the danger if anyone had found out what they thought. And a nun and priest in Tibet, who, likewise, uncharacteristic to their orders, shared close communication. That helps explain the sense of wanting to discuss my situation with him, wanting him to come along on the journey. On the other hand, he had places to be. He was not available, this lifetime, to take the path I'd chosen, after a certain point. Yet, said Doug Brinkley, he kept the feeling of closeness. That never left, not till the day he died.

Recently, in 2014, I mused, waking in the middle of the night, about how we are light; born with codes into the universe.

And I thought: were those codes I released at Kailash's in 2005? I had felt they were an unknown aspect of the body's ability to feel—that is, in everyone. Something universal held back because, as with consciousness—parts of which had in the past been closely guarded—it would be so easy to abuse this great hidden faculty. I don't mean sheer ecstasy on the physical level but something in addition; deeper, going through every mystical pore to the place of Revelation.

I have not reached this type of bodily feeling again but can easily hold on to the memory.

Then I thought of Dhyanyogi-ji's dream instruction: "Come to where I am"; of the phrase "My Father and I are One," and of Al Miner's website note that "Father" here means "Mother-Father."

I thought: my assignment from Dhyanyogi-ji, then, must have been to come to *where he was*: "One with God." That, then, was where he was calling me? A big assignment.

Another assignment I had was "Measure me." I was left to muse over it, and ruminate over it, and finally absorb the answer to it. I was sure I would.

One day I read about the Grail codes in us, awakened in a group initiation led by a formidable spiritual teacher, Jonette Crowley, at Malta. And suddenly things started coming together yet again. It was from Malta a stranger joined me at Delphi when, by chance at twenty-four years old, I took my first trip to Europe and a side excursion from Athens to the land of Know Thyself.

At Delphi I met this British stranger *stationed at Malta.* In a brief time-off from his Royal Air Force post he hopped over to Mount Parnassus to climb rocks. Meeting him was numinous—including a particularly symbolic moment that night. As we sat on a restaurant balcony, our eyes surveying the pitch-black sky over the valley, inexplicable pairs of phosphorescent birds began to streak across the sky. He came from Malta. Streaks of light in pairs. I had long wondered what it was all about in the deep sense. It felt symbolic, but of what? A real-life vision, a symbolic action. An activated sky.

And now I got it: Malta, *pairs of streaks of light.* A code of love in a frequency in our cells. Streaking across the blackness.

The spiritual teacher above received a message in Malta that universalized the message she got further—through a spirit form of the Great Mother. It was that the Grail codes are in our DNA, facilitating "the merging of [our physical self with] our spiritual/light component."

> We are the Grail! What is happening now is the merging of our humanity with our divinity . . .
>
> Once the activation is given to us, it spreads throughout the human matrix, empowering each of us to become beings of light.[224]

I have so many people to thank. Who shared everything. It's all I am anymore, the *experiences that reshaped my cells—their readiness—including my dogs Snoep, Snoepie, Hans; including my friends and the dedicated editing of Virginia P. Williams; including the blastoff of Hunter, sending me into orbit with this series; including all the blastoffs shaping Life as we will know it this century and the next—taking each of us into new orbits of lucidity, awareness, self-knowledge, gumption, experimentation, freedom, sacredness, respect.*

In the beginning was the Word. But it was not somebody else's word. Now we can take our own word for it, and that is the challenge facing us each—to get to that place where our word is gold, transformed through

the fires of transition, the Fourth Amendment, the Rites of Home, inter-
nally, where no one can gain admittance except sacredly being admitted
through the door, all the while we are, each of us, part of All of us.

And the experience in 2001 where I saw how the Whole twirls into
ever-new forms BEHIND *a point—that point being anyone, and, at some*
times, definitely each one if they but ask and step up to the plate. For
Ciao. As Ciao.

So there, my contribution to the Ciao D Hunter. The great blastoff,
the loudspeaker transmission, the holodeck place of imagination, the fu-
ture as each craftsperson creates it, fueled by freedom, honesty, imagina-
tion, a knowing without and within. Fearlessness too, in a world where
fear might take over. Denying it further options; for fearlessness rules,
and all citizens opt for it, or some do—enough—to make it a viable Path
into the future. This, for our Earth.

If the unidentified Montparnasse beggar—I saw in a symbolic act
that triggered the beginning of my Love in Transition *series—initially*
had finished his meal but wanted to light up after lunch and had noth-
ing to put the light to, then as the Whole twirls and steps up behind this
scene, this time at the plate, on the plate—as food for the next century,
in the Sole for Breakfast tradition[*]*—let's sign on. Signon. A signature of*
love, one for the next century, when many signatures of Love are made,
and let's put this one there, inside the Chow tradition.

---

[*]   The "sole for breakfast" reference will be unfamiliar to many readers. Please see
the "Brief List of Important Personal References" at the end of this book; this motif
is a pun in the poetry translated by Mihai Ursachi, page 147; see more verses, pages
379–80; Also, read up on the Ciao puns on page 392.

CODA

To go far out

Roland: "Sure, I believe in the akasha chronicles.

"In my vision it is a place in our consciousness, it is a part of our mental body and mental capacity, but we can't reach it with the rational mind.

"It is like the library of the soul, an enormous amount of memories. You can go there by way of the soul.

"The more we know our soul, the more we can reach this immense information and use it for our purpose on earth."

Today

I had predicted—in 1985—a massive energy onslaught coming to Earth, with the guide feeding the thoughts into me then—an onslaught that required preparation.

By 1998 I was ruminating that it appeared to me that (after writing in my apartment), when I stepped outside onto the grounds, by staring up at the clouds, focusing, perhaps I was "bringing in," as it were, some visual form of the ideas I'd been working in.

Well, this idea wasn't far off. Many years later it clicked that in falling into a reverie, focusing on the clouds, looking for edges, etc., I was applying a process I would later learn for working in energy. The clouds were not only a canvas; they represented my energy field visible behind my shut lids in meditation. Eureka. What does that mean? Today I would call it projecting one space onto another.

Now I ask, was this tool a technique I remembered? This slow awareness is just as good a way as any of remembering "past lives." Or, better still, of recovering those lost skills. As the meaning slowly sinks in, I feel just like I stepped into a school of Pythagoras, telling myself alertness is called for.

ALL OF THIS MEANT THE END WAS TRULY THE BEGINNING.

Hanuman image in the sky

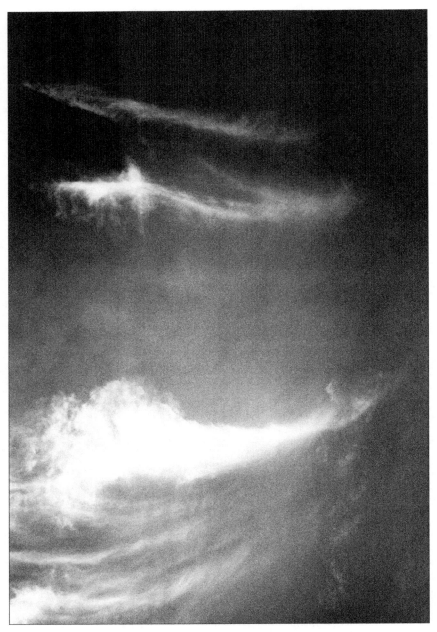

Conch under Flying Gold and White Duo

It was clear and I could have read about how the East knew these secrets.

THE BEGINNING of another level of CONSCIOUSNESS, in arriving at the END OF THE STORY—conscious and unconscious information brought into a unity for just one minute, from which new structure would inevitably result.

I sat down to finish the book with an alive sky outside. Masses of faces and folds, forming and moving.

The universe of change, Plato had called it.

In bed today, 2011, I was listening to the LuminEssence light body cofounder geophysicist Duane Packer channeling DaBen on CD, when suddenly I realized my mind had wandered. I found myself thinking: "Where is my guide? Too high to come down to this level my mind went to, in a human-frequency range." So I looked for the moving waves and pulses that I identified the guide by. I easily found that level. Then thought: "But how much distance between the two. My identity is of a nonmoving energy (physically speaking). That consciousness of identity is moving, because the energy is, the energy identifying with its movement, which is how it gets its consciousness."

So, I thought: "I'll just have to create a frame of reference of me that spans those two points. I'll just have to hold them both."

This made a huge perception shift, to think of me as, at all times, most basically, also in that pulsing-waves frequency and position— which saw differently and identified with itself differently than was possible in my human self, no matter how many times I fused with Universal Consciousness and got my ideas from there.

Then I thought of myself as a particle being. I had for a long time written as if I were but had not published the text. Then I realized: Okay, a particle too can't identify with me on this level. Bingo! Suddenly I blinked. I couldn't believe it. So I was part of the Earth DNA. No wonder I had certain experiences and thought as I thought. Wooooo.

That made me part of everyone. That made me universal. Wooooo. Hadn't I started out with this premise? Hadn't this been what the Universal Guide had taught me in the Zurich Initiation. Wooooo. Pause. But I can't stop. Reflect. Yes, but keep moving. Let that level—wooooo. That level doesn't wait around like this. It's made its point. It's moving. It's—

And so I knew who I was at last. At least for now. I knew this much. There was always more. If I looked into the mirror, I would see an old face, a once-beautiful face that had years of lifetime here on it. But if I at the same time reached up to that other frequency, that face lightened and I also didn't overidentify with it in its physical form. Yet it was representing all of me. It could now receive more. What an adventure.

BASICS: Things I've Learned

Keep This Quiet! Workbook Preview

Esoterics of the Earth in Exercises

Moving Patterns Around

How to Work with Patterns—demonstrated to me through myself. Not for widespread use. Here is how we did it (do it): a pattern was plopped over a situation in Zurich. That is, a piece of my earlier life was, I discovered, being used in the 1980s in Zurich, by spirit guides, as a pattern for me to walk into. It was not the original situation in which the pattern occurred. It was thought (by guides) too difficult to carry through the original pattern there. At least, some of those who were overseeing thought it too difficult. They thought it would fail. They thought I didn't have enough desire and certitude. They thought the energy wasn't there, that I couldn't rise to my full height and play it out in the location the pattern was lifted from.

Lifting patterns from one location to another was an ancient esoteric system of assisting the Earth (in the macro-sense) by using a micro-pattern that represented it (an analogy). And through changing the analogy changing the macroscopic scene. It was "action at a distance."

Secret Exercises

PULLING IT ALL TOGETHER:

Maintenance

Back in the U.S., there was no more PK. So that time was past. Second, no more cloud photography. How to bring the photography out? Third, I was shifting energy. I saw how I had been (we all do) pattern-shifting, using my own patterns. And I was a "distributor" to those who "stepped down" those understandings to levels closer to Earth, forms that would be met with a good reception here now. Okay. So I understood why I was a kind of invisible behind-the-scenes person. It was a relief to understand. But could I go beyond behind-the-scenes?

Before, I was apprenticing. But now my teachers were stepping back. I was listening to my own quotations from within. It was a new stage, of embodying. I hoped I could do it.

As time passed, I would feel a gradual shift. Clearly inside I wanted to find out things *from* myself. Not just "for," but *from*. As if some key had been turned, I was getting a key to myself, deep inside, answers, even memories, knowledge I just "knew" deep inside—that "knowing" becoming an "I." Or the location where I could connect with it. This was different. In fact, it would become as if an invisible force stepped in to repel me from getting my answers in any other way. From within, from myself, there was some deep tunnel there to the Light.

So I am wrapping up what I learned over nineteen years, readying for the next challenge, which may be—I thought it was—to bring the new consciousness to public form. What? As a pattern that in its Omega returns to the Alpha to set out again, but before that touch bases.

A Question for Mother Meera

I remember a question someone asked Mother Meera in a little book of Q & A: was she always conscious of where her energy was? She said no. In some instances, yes, but in other types of situations it was not necessary:

Q: Are you consciously aware of calls for your help or does your power work automatically?

MM: The grace works automatically when the aspiration is sincere. It is not necessary for me always to know. If I had twenty telephones in this room and they were all ringing, it would not be helpful. But I can know what I want and when I need.

Q: When you are asked a question, how does the answer come?

MM: I SEE it. Even as a child it was this way.[225]

Remember that in addition to your personal energy, you can also at any time tap into the vastness of cosmic energy.

All things, in their connectedness, amplify one another. I do not amplify everything. I do amplify some things. And with those, I connect.

So from that ending note, we have something to take off on. Far be it from me to think that this is any more than a drop in the bucket. But it is a point, a focused point, a swelling, an ambitious point that wants to voyage, to set off into experiences far beyond what it can understand. Pull back curtains. Dance into the days ahead.

Bringing it all together

Two levels, two aspects, not merging, assisting—

Well, aligning, assisting—

2010

The end and the beginning

I'm sitting in the bed, meditating to contact readers. Readers I can't see. Readers in the future. I was the writer. I didn't think about readers. I saw only the writing. My personality had a subpersonality that prevented me from looking for receptive readers. I, the writer, had the drive, but didn't turn the job of audience expectation over to the rest of me. I therefore had to work on opening up the channel to the audience. And my expectation of it.

But why does this image at the end—of the most recent nineteen-year cycle—look so much like 1985, the beginning of my Zurich Initiation?

Eerily, a connection gradually dawned on me. The reader may remember that, through a computerized numerology chart in Charlottesville in 1984, I'd been advised to get ready for a massive upheaval, which did indeed burst upon me in 1985/1986, with the Zurich Initiation.

The chart revealed I had big shifts in nineteen-year cycles. Well, checking backward with the full view of hindsight, I find that nineteen years *before that* cycle began is 1966, the year I met Hunter, having just met Milton Klonsky and Jan Mensaert in 1965. Eerily still, nineteen years *after* 1986 (the second year of the Zurich Initiation) lands smack in 2005, the year that in February Hunter died.

The Initiator had been unique in my life in his first appearance, in Zurich in September 1985, when I went into his consciousness and he imprinted me: never forget this picture. At that moment I saw *him standing before an empty stadium, looking up at the audiences of the future who would read his book.* What book(s)? By whom? I assumed by him. I was mightily impressed. His determination struck awe in me. I raised him in my mind to the highest pinnacles. But maybe, now, I ask, was he transmitting out more broadly?

And I dared wonder if he'd shown me a picture to use myself. Even, suppose somewhere—could it be possible?—somehow he was me. Suppose in a twist I looked at the whole thing in terms of past or future lives. I could take a cue from the child of seven I was who met, inside herself, a much more evolved being and resolved to catch up— i.e., live up to an unknown potential he expected "himself" (herself) to have; threw down the gauntlet that it should be so, musing internally thoughts that the child me heard.

This was where things stood when I realized, at sixty-nine, there was one more step to bringing out these books. I had to pay attention now to the audience, the audience that didn't exist. Not in linear time. And he had shown me how. Had materialized in my mind as a consciousness I'd been taken to, where he was. That was his hello. That, I would need as my secret weapon one day to carry forth.

So I figured there was a pattern of Alpha–Omega where the "end" came in with the beginning, infiltrating at the start. We saw no shape of the future. But in this line of thinking, it was there—creating events parallel to the "birth" event that seemed to have no connection. But they did. As it opened into the future, the future, the end point, was there as well.

So I surmised—played with the idea—that my dream of my mother hesitating at my birth, delaying a beat while an unknown male (who stopped her from pushing me immediately forth) went first . . . that this depicted symbolically the fully aware end consciousness. Stepping into me at birth, while I would then go through all the steps of Knowing nothing.

This presence, I thought much later, was the higher wisdom and consciousness of what I had to learn, the end point—where the circle closed.

So, finally in 1985 I reached that state, the Christ State, he was calling to readers from—that's how I'd interpreted it—those in the future who would read his work. Was the future now? Was it this?

Had he planned all along to get me to the moment when he stood inside me at seven, when he focused me on (or I fixed my sight on) at twenty-four a miming beggar in Paris outside a café: the desperate beggar symbolically missing matter to incarnate his consciousness into? Giving a "smoke signal."

And when he came as the Initiator (I was forty-five)—all those appearances. Was it enough? Had I learned enough? If not, people were in line to carry the ball the next segment. But could I, this time, do it myself? I sat in bed, calling the readers. Calling to them, believing in their receptiveness. It was up to me, after all, to have that perspective: *Believe, believe. This is what it takes from you now.*

But is it relevant that before deciding to write *Man and His Symbols*, Jung rejected the idea—not wanting to write for laypeople so late in his career—and then had a dream? Of himself communicating before a crowd—*that understood him.* Not scholars, doctors, psychiatrists but laypeople. This was unheard of. So he changed his mind. Did that decision, that dream, consult with—give a model for—the vision I saw when I shot up into the Initiator's consciousness at the very start of my "Confrontation with the Self"? Saw him standing before an empty stadium, preparing what he would say to the audiences of the future, crafting his words for that invisible crowd he was sure would come. At any rate, we have so many potentials to harvest, planted by so many people before us and alongside us. It's sometimes easy to forget that. But we are all plowing the way for all of us *now*.

As landscape, nature becomes a collection of objects and interactions, the product of inexorable laws operating upon fundamental elements of reality. But to see the world as inscape is to take each experience and each perception as unique and authentic. It is to realize that each person, rock and tree has infinite possibility and unbounded richness.

—F. David Peat

AUTHOR EXERCISES, KITCHEN EXERCISES, AND A FEW SUNDRY OTHERS

41

AUTHOR AND SUNDRY EXERCISES

The exercises and commentary below are associated with specific sections and chapters of the book. To do them, get into a centered state with a relaxed mind, perhaps some meditation music in the background.

Part One: "A Peek into My Apartment"

JUNG ON SYMBOLS

Jung was interested in a bizarre aspect of synchronicity: "How does it come that even inanimate objects are capable of behaving as if they were acquainted with my thoughts? This is . . . a thoroughly paranoid speculation which one had better not ventilate in public, but I cannot deny my fervent interest in this aspect of the problem."[226]

Elsewhere he said: "But symbols, I must point out, do not occur solely in dreams. They appear in all kinds of psychic manifestations. There are symbolic thoughts and feelings, symbolic acts and situations. It often seems that even inanimate objects co-operate with the unconscious in the arrangement of symbolic patterns." He cites the pendulum clock that stopped in the palace of Frederick the Great upon the death of the emperor. Even *time* marks the moment physically, by the hands of a clock suddenly still. The lost potential to strike itself reflecting the human loss of potential to move.

"Involuntary spontaneous manifestations" of symbols, as in dreams, he points out, can be "'collective representations,' emanating from primeval dreams and creative fantasies."[227]

EXERCISE

Can you think of an occasion when an object seemed to symbolically act out—echo, illustrate—an event or a thought? Take a few moments to reflect on any instances of this in your life. Any you know of. If nothing comes to mind, you can intend to watch for them. For instance, ask your unconscious to give you an illustration.

Try this tonight. Ask your dreams to show you how the world of inanimate objects might be intertwined with your world or ask it to show you an unknown part of you that has this awareness.

Part Two: "Interstices"

EXERCISE ON MOVING ENERGY AROUND

I was, for most of my life, shy about public speaking. Then suddenly in my room at an Athens conference in 1994, I felt I'd received the use of "the personality" of a friend. At the end of the conference, the audience members were invited to say a word. I found I could easily speak to the group.

Now, let's imagine how that might play out for you. Think of someone whose energy is quite different from yours. Imagine that person visiting you. If you can, recall an actual situation. Around that person—perhaps even in anticipating his or her arrival—do you suddenly switch gears? Do you feel your energy adjusting? Does it seem more in tune with the other person's, as if mixing portions of two styles?

If you don't typically have a lot of energy and that person does, do you have more? Do tasks you've put off seem easy *if that person has go-to-it energy*? Or what can you find that's changed temporarily? How can you make the most of it?

On the flip side, that person may likewise respond to you. Can you—energetically speaking—"lend" some of your forte and borrow some of that person's (an aspect, a flavor, where that person excels)—both of you benefiting, in synch, rebalancing with a different approach or outlook that temporarily just rubs off?

Part III: "Marlowe"

EXERCISE ON RECEIVING A TRANSMISSION

In the chapel in the Palace of Versailles I received a transmission. If you wish, you can do the same. Sit quietly in a spot with a history you are curious about. Get relaxed. If outdoors, feel nature: the trees, the leaves, the smells—pine, honeysuckle, cherry blossom—the wind. You are getting in touch with prana, chi, life force.

If inside, do whatever makes you relaxed, confident, spontaneously certain. Nothing you do is "wrong." Don't have expectations. Empty your mind. Let your curiosity be alert . . . your awareness. For fifteen minutes, sit following your breath . . . breathe in . . . breathe out . . . Ask to receive a *transmission* from this place. It could even be a sense of communion with the nature there.

Maybe you get nothing, just as happened to me in the Paris chapels. Another time, perhaps something will click. If you set the intention, you'll attract a communication of some sort because your own unconscious will be busy announcing and preparing for it.

RECEIVING A TRANSMISSION BY EMAIL

The following exercise can be stimulating if used sparingly. In a quiet state open an email from someone who often has interesting reflections. Intend to tune into any resonant ideas. Notice whether when opening it, you get a stream of lively thoughts jumping into your mind. Pay attention. Could you be tapping into spillover thoughts not written down in the email? Or thoughts on the topic from "out there" in space-time? Try it. Not always, but sometimes, this can be inspirational.

To go further, in conversation listen to what *isn't* said. As with body language, there is unspoken "frequency communication." Have no expectations. *No projections.* Think open-endedly. Just let the empty mind receive whatever is in tune with it, whatever message mirrors that emptiness and state.

When a person communicates with you, there is information like an aura surrounding the words. See if you can get in touch with it. Sometimes it is unconscious to the other person.

Part IV: "Bipod Metalism and a Cave"

ARNOLD MINDELL AND PROPRIOCEPTION (MOVEMENT–AND–POSITION SENSE),

OR HOW ONE LOCATION, ONE FORMAT, IS SOMETIMES SUPPLYING AN IMPRINT, A SHAPE, TO PUT A SIMILAR SITUATION INTO. THIS EXERCISE IS TO BE USED WITH CARE

In the chapter "Bipod Metalism and a Cave" many ideas from ancient traditions and from Carl Jung about the unconscious were speculated on.

Arnold Mindell, founder of process-oriented psychology, is a later-generation Jungian who taught at the Jung Institute Zurich while I was there. Mindell's work has centered around his depiction of the "dreaming process" of the unconscious. As an interviewer puts it, "Rather than a repository of archetypes, as Jung had suggested, the unconscious, or dreambody, according to Mindell, is a dynamic, flowing continuum of which archetypes are only 'snapshots.' Dreams, physical symptoms, relationships, accidents, altered states of consciousness—all are manifestations of the dreambody in action."[228]

When this unconscious process is blocked, it is likely to tell us so by presenting symptoms, "even chronic illnesses. . . . Mindell's approach is to amplify and follow them until they reveal their hidden messages."[229]

In a 1990 interview Mindell recounted the story of a woman with a negative inner voice. "I'll have her listen to the inner critic for a while, asking who it is, whether it's a man or a woman, her mother or her husband or her boss, etc. Then she might say, 'Oh,

my stomach hurts.' Now she's switched to the proprioceptive channel."[230] (The sensory receptor channel is "found chiefly in muscles,
tendons, joints, and the inner ear, that detects the motion or position of the body or limb by responding to stimuli arising within the
organism."[231])

How did the pain feel? While answering, she made a fist. Mindell
asked her to amplify it "by making a muscle in her bicep, tightening
her neck, and tensing her face." Abruptly, *as she amplified*, she identified the facial expression with her father, whom she said Mindell
resembled. It was easy to point out to her that she had *internalized*
feelings about her father into an "inner critic."[232]

EXERCISE ON AMPLIFICATION CHANNELS

Try this for yourself. Locate a physical discomfort. Notice what you
do as you describe it. Do you make a movement, shift position? Or
does a thought runs through your mind? Consider that your unconscious, your "dreambody," is trying to give you clues—by amplifica-
tion. Hold the gesture, the position. Detect, if you can, any association. Just as the woman tightened her fist, her biceps, her neck,
amplify your gesture or position. What comes to mind? Is it relevant?
Is it is a memory? A clue?

THE PROPRIOCEPTIVE CHANNEL: A ROCK

Mindell describes how a feeling can carry over. Say, you have a stomach ache. Your stomach feels heavy. At night you dream of a rock. "The proprioceptive experience of the weight in the stomach was coupled to the dream rock."

Suppose, to treat the stomach ache, you take a pill, you feel better. However, be aware that deeper still, "the gestalt or archetype behind [the symptom remains] . . . If the individual needs to be heavier or more like a stone, . . . this experience is going to try to reach consciousness in every way possible."

In reverse, for the same reason, "You can dream of a volcano and have a splitting headache the next day."[233]

VECTORS

Regarding vectors, if you want to remember a dream, don't change position when you wake; the information is accessible while you stay *exactly as you first began to recall it.*

EXERCISE ON VECTORS

See if the feel of an exact position that your feet are in, your arms are in, gives you information about a *different* situation or person that you suddenly realize associates to it. Explore it as a *vector*, that is, that *your position in space* at this moment is relative to a similar position/configuration. Walk a few steps, in the pattern-shape, as if "in someone else's shoes." Listen to your body as you do this. Try this exercise several times to get a result.

KITCHEN EPIPHANIES/
EXERCISES

Thoughts come to me in the kitchen. For instance, squeezing the last drop out of a lemon: *"Every particle of life wants to fulfill itself."*

EXPLANATION

No, I don't mean the lemon is thinking or the lemon drop feels its destiny, but that *without thought* there's a connection. The field the lemon drop sits in, as it were, has patterns that even the lemon is harmonized with. Also, fulfillment—being in the flow—is part of a universal pattern of giving and withholding. Patterns that balance.

And these micro-actions—micro-models—have an impetus we repeat, which subtly get into our consciousness. We squeeze the lemon to the last drop. Squeezing *to the last drop* is in our psyche, as if the idea jumped from the lemon into us—which it did as a symbol. But it is more.

It is a pattern we copy. We squeeze something else. And it is the pattern—to stay with this example—of squeezing the lemon, how we felt when we did. Which is quite different in another context, we think.

But no, the pattern may carry over. Micro-patterns affect us, scaled up. And it's as if—*as if*—the small scale has awareness in this line too as they too emit weak light, just like us; so it's not too big a stretch. This light is synchronizing, achieving coherence. I was right before knowing why. That even squeezing the lemon drop, I'm helping the universe achieve fulfillment—in the spirit of it, coherent with that sense.

As if the action is applying a universal law, to either squeeze to the last drop or squander—and the choice is right there in the smallest example. I know, lighten up. But the idea is persistent, at least in the kitchen, as if that environment is its own world, teaching me. Who would have thought?

MAKING CORRELATIONS: HANDS AND THE DISHWASHER

When I lived in Zurich, I often bought beautiful cut flowers—lilies, gerbera, daffodils—and arranged them in a hallway vase. I noticed that my intuition often intervened. It seemed to be directing my hands beyond making a pretty arrangement. Suddenly as I put a yellow Asiatic lily stem here, a red Gerbera there, the placements were connecting with something else. That is, my sensation function (here, hands) in Jung's personality types was communicating with my intuition. Let's amplify that.

In Raleigh in 2014, I load the dishwasher: a fork in one slot, a knife in another. Again I catch myself: the relative positions are not arbitrary. Imagine if this fork is a, that knife is x, and *that fork* z. Sensing what is going on, I realize I am making a symbolic pattern: a statement about the relationship of x to a to z. I myself have no idea whatsoever what a is or x or z is—what it stands for, correlates to—but if I pay attention I might find out. That is, in the case where the unconscious is making an association.

Imagine that it is digesting my opinion about a matter that symbolically "sets up" when my hands (the sensation function) talk to my intuition and listen to what it tells them these objects *momentarily* "stand for." Functionally, they are just kitchen flatware. Practically speaking, I am loading the dishwasher.

But there is a little matter the unconscious wants my input on. It can get it by subterfuge—i.e., simply by speaking *its* language. By asking my hands to "act out" the answer if, it says: *This means that. And this that. Now, in that framework what's the answer?* I've no idea I'm voting on my (mental) persuasions. But mental and physical positions can collaborate. Who knew?

My intuition is finding a way to communicate; in this case—to use Jung's personality typing—my "inferior sensation" has become "the transcendent function." That is, my/our most unconscious aspect—here, sensation function—can transcend its fairly unconscious state and bring information *out* of the unconscious.

SCIENCE: CORRELATION WAVE IN PSI TESTS

Fortunately, there is relevant science to bring in—from University of Illinois at Chicago neuroscientist Norman S. Don and his clairvoyant subject Olof Jonsson. In experimenting in long-distance ESP with Jonsson, Don et al discovered unexpectedly that psi might operate as a correlation wave.[234]

Don was the lead writer in a related paper that got a fair amount of attention, "Signal Processing Analysis of Forced-Choice ESP Data: Evidence for Psi as a Wave of Correlation."

In it, Don et al analyzed the subjects' *signal processing* when guessing high-imagery targets. For those whose cognitive style was visual, they found significant or marginally significant correlation waves (p< .037 and p < .063). But only by including misses *alongside* hits. That is, if they examined the individual's total test results—not distinguishing between hits and misses.[235]

As previously mentioned, Australian psychologist/Jungian Lance Storm speculated that the Self, not being concerned with hits and misses in a psi test, could be "correlating" the individual's answers to something entirely outside the test objectives. Thus, the correlation wave represented the Self's goals. If so, he speculated, results attained in hit/miss ESP scores reflected the *ego's* intent to follow instructions, while the Self had a mind of its own.[236]

EXERCISE ON CORRELATION

In a familiar place—say, the kitchen or workroom—when doing an activity involving your hands, try this. Not in each instance *but sometimes* you can sense the action has an unconscious correlation—a configuration your unconscious is paying attention to. Play with this possibility at odd moments. See if your unconscious begins to tell you about this tool. See if it eventually alerts you to it, as mine did in the kitchen at the dishwasher.

KITCHEN EPIPHANIES ON PARTICLES

I suddenly realized that—obviously—the particle experience pre-dates our own. (Of course, I knew this. But the thought arrested me numinously.) I was looking at a piece of salad. Feeling a sympathy—it was about to go down the drain—knowing that the lettuce is not feeling anything.

And suddenly I realized: *The perspective I'm tapping into . . . it's looking through time.* I'm here in 2012 in my own body, but also, looking at the lettuce in the sink about to be chopped up in the garbage disposal . . . looking at another time—another place that will vibrate with this memory by association. That the tiny piece of lettuce went down the sink drain to be chopped in the garbage disposal is embedded in our history, in our predictions, our expectations, our DNA.

Thinking this, I plucked the lettuce out of the sink, put it into the garbage bin without trauma, and more and more understandings came.

The particles have the experience before us, sitting inside decisions we make. As if this particle were a telescope or magnifying glass that I can look through time with.

Where is this going?

I detect it's about the fact that the particles are nowhere and everywhere, and I catch myself looking at a piece of lettuce in a sink facing two possibilities, one painful, one not—that is, painful to me—*if it were me,* and it's not. And somehow the particle carries all those possibilities and locations, that instant—the piece of lettuce does—as if it were throughout time or could carry this instant, this choice I make, throughout time into other, very different moments. *Can it?*

Can this compassionate instant with the lettuce, its fate decided by a choice of *cruelty or not*, move into more places? Even scenarios? When and why? This is 4:24 p.m. 4/23/2012, at the conclusion of a DaBen workshop (DaBen, a scientific and healing spirit entity, co-founder of LuminEssence light body studies).

Not that this means the particles feel anything, but as I look at the lettuce as if I'm a particle of that experience—from the perspective of the lettuce, supposing it had one—I experience *the universe experiencing cruelty, indifference, or some other emotional pattern*, some expression of a consciousness. I practice a quality in the moment I shift and take the lettuce out of the sink. At that moment, was it my universal self that brought this experience to me? And if so, what? 5/9/2012.

To be clearer, when I see a piece of lettuce—rescue it from the sink—it is not the lettuce itself I rescue. It is *the universe's patterns of feeling*. It is *anything* in such a position now or ever.

Anywhere, in any subject matter. It is the organization of life and how we respond. It's whether I even notice or not the possibility of pain. The lettuce is a stand-in, a substitute. The pain is not real, but the possibility of it in similar situations is. Naturally, I don't go around like this all the time.

I feel this, of course, from the particle me—or the transpersonal me. Or just the relationship between the particles spreading through the universe—passing through us—and us here doing things, feeling things.

EXERCISE

Imagine a positive feeling about a flower, an animal—kindness, peace . . . indulge in it. Imagine it is a quality the universe receives, an emotion that goes into its atmosphere—that somebody might pick it up, resonate with it. Somebody who will not even know your context in the slightest. But that you are planting finer replications, future experiences of this quality. That it's a contribution to just sit quietly and smell a rose. Who knew?

MORE—IN THE KITCHEN

Back at the kitchen the idea expanded: *The perspective I'm tapping into, re the particles: It's looking through time.*

Then almost flippantly, it popped into my head penetratingly: *The particles carry time in them.* As if: *Well, you asked.*

Hold on. What did that mean? The clue was as clear as in the deepest altered state, though I was, in full practicality, preparing dinner for myself.

ON PAST LIVES: 2014

As described, my unconscious was quick to turn little configurations—relative locations of objects—into models and hypothesize from one situation how I would, spontaneously, from my gut, react to another it correlated to it. As if one vector "stood in" for another.

Then in 2014, I had a reading. I do that rarely now. But sometimes it's good to see how my perspectives compare with someone else's. So I had an akashic records reading. And a lot of things the akashic masters said jived with my findings. One in particular resonated.

It sounded like a fairy tale. And it might be. Do we literally have past lives? Or do we continue on with lessons others bring forward to be finished? Is it "us" or "our consciousness" that survives?

Anyway, here is a story of a consciousness skill I seem to have inherited. The akashic masters said it was my focus in a past life. However it is explained, I instantly loved this woman. She was (I was) a nun in Tibet. Her small group had the lifework of bringing in patterns and releasing them into the world. Sounds idyllic to me. And based on my intuitive, unconscious knowledge described above, it sounds right on.

Recently, in old files, I found this forgotten rumination (by me): "To have the universe on one's eyelids must be a new tool—of 'shaping' space. Could one consciously 'bend' space—how? And not just into one shape."

When I was twenty-four, I smoked a joint for the first time, given to me by a New York City friend, who said, "Take this for your dreams." Instantly, as I puffed it, the universe jumped onto my eyelids if I shut them. I opened them—all clear. Shut them—the universe was there. But what if it wasn't, say, a "star map," but was a flashback to this tool. What if—yes—the vision was a clue to, a point of contact with, the consciousness tool of this nun.

AN "I AM" MEDITATION

At times, Norman Don told me, he went to a retreat where attendees did nothing but focus on "I am." The whole time. No thoughts, no cares. Just sit somewhere quiet and turn your mind inward, thinking: *I am.*

Try this yourself. Sit in a quiet space. Stay as long or short a time as you want initially—ten minutes will do—and watch your mind empty, your consciousness shift, your focus narrow to the single two words. Not "I am a teacher," "I am a father," "I am a human being." *I am.*

IN CLOSING

In the end there are at least 100 billion planets right in our Milky Way galaxy and 100 billion galaxies just in the observable universe. The vastness of our universe prompted Newton—who in his day knew of just seventeen celestial bodies—to think of himself as having been "only like a boy playing on the sea-shore, and diverting myself in now and then finding a smoother pebble or a prettier shell than ordinary, whilst the great ocean of truth lay all undiscovered before me." How much of this can any one of us know?

Yogis say, "I have nothing to prove."

Jung said, "In the psyche there is nothing that is just a dead relic.

Everything is alive, and our upper story consciousness is continually influenced by its living and active foundations. Like the building, it is sustained and supported by them."[239]

HOW AN ARCHETYPE FUELED TERRORISM

But more specifically, right now, as the times—the twenty-first century—caught up with my 1985–'86 initiation, the predictions, the analyses, which I was not ready for then, can't I bring them out now with emphasis? End on that note? I think so, especially as in continuing Jung's work, with Jung's blessing, Erlo van Waveren's dive into the unconscious produced some of the same apparently top secret material that mine did. Not that it had to be top secret at all, just that almost no one seemed to be looking in that direction.

Pages earlier, I wrote about "the threat of the growth of extremist groups, that would misconstrue the Archetype of Home, of the End of the World, interpreting it literally." And consequently, line up for the great apocalyptic death drive against us. It would be a mistake. A tiny misreading. Almost on the level of a typo, that, crossing dimensions, grew, inflated. Why did not someone shout, "Hold it! Wait! This archetype is not literal. Stop the presses. Alert the symbolic mind that it is being literalized, this time with dire consequences"?

When the ego got the incorrect game plan, bloodshed would be the result. Couldn't I emphasize here the wrong read-out that was occurring?

Especially as the Zurich Initiator not only warned of this, he further was worried at the prospect that one such group might gain a bomb of some sort; he was working against that prospect, given the probabilities of the future thirty years ago! A full thirty years in which we had the chance to steer away from this but were blindsided by not taking seriously the thoughts in the air.

We wanted to stamp them out of people's heads through the internet. But had a more active internet right in the atmosphere itself, through which the thoughts traveled. In earlier pages of *Keep This Quiet!* IV, I rather timidly addressed the situation, doing due

diligence but not charged up as I feel now. I wrote: "These warnings in 1985–'86 have seemed prescient to me with the more recent development of Al-Qaeda, ISIL, and other terrorists." I spoke
of this in terms of "the ego's misunderstanding of the Archetype of
Home—an archetype constellated in the psyche as the planet went to
a higher level of consciousness. In Jungian terms, . . . it was activated
in the collective unconscious." The double-sword danger came, "said
the Initiator, if this archetype was taken literally . . . Another name
for this drive, he said, was the 'Archetype of the End of the World,'
meaning a *nonliteral* end of 'the old Earth consciousness.'"

It's as if a gap in dimension translation, a flaw in our consciousness,
is to blame. Consciousness was expanding, becoming more transparent
to us. We needed mass consciousness to hold this understanding of how
thoughts interconnected in the atmosphere and that our invention of the
internet mirrored this basic system, not the other way around.

LOOKING FOR TERRORISTS IN THE WRONG PLACE

Who would ever guess that the correct place to look for terrorists
might be in the "mental body"? That's what I learned in the mid-
1980s in an initiation I've tried to report about—notably, in *Keep
This Quiet!* III and to a lesser degree in *Keep This Quiet!* IV. Predicted
because of the probabilities in the air, based in the stirrings of archetypes. And stirrings of archetypes based in the logical, dynamic
organization of the point in time we had reached. The shift from the
Piscean consciousness to the Aquarian, some would say. Leaving that
aside, others would point to and join in with the increasing global-
ization—ease of travel, of surfing the net. But there was something
else. As technology relentlessly brought us closer, these facts and beliefs became thoughts in our minds, and they mingled even before
we were aware that we were sharing mental space. But I was made
starkly aware of the predictions in the 1980s, because of my Zurich
Initiation. This meant that *somewhere, consciousness knew*. Foresight,
that was looking beyond our visible, rational reality.

However, we stopped the analysis in too short a projected time-line. Not so, more aware, deeper consciousness. Not that everyone here even wants a more expanded consciousness, but right now it could come in extremely handy in a practical way. Who would guess that archetypes, misconstrued, were at the root of some of the terrorist activity? It is easy to see if the premise is accepted that activity in the unconscious can sweep the globe. A focus there can become a mass eruption. In this case, to eradicate extremist ideology, apocalyptically driven, we could just look at the archetype in motion behind it. The Archetype of the End of the World. But it meant the end of the world as we knew it. A new consciousness—incipiently inside us—was roaring in, slaying patterns that had held sway. That was what Carl Jung called the Aquarian consciousness. We could simply title it the twenty-first-century-and-beyond consciousness. The unconscious had a dramatic role. Ideas—for better or worse—could spread faster than wildfire in it. We just didn't give it that credit.

I did. I did because I had written about it—with the spirit of Milton Klonsky, in a much more evolved form, a cosmic form (so that he was an entirely different spirit, at my side, prodding me, at the typewriter). What I wrote was in part this—in 1985 or 1986—wrote it not by myself but with these whisperings in my ear. Earlier in *Keep This Quiet!* IV, I discussed the fact that Mihai Ursachi translated the opening (see page 147 for the Romanian) of *The Christ State*:

Extra, extra, read all about it—
The End of the World
Everywhere, alarms were going off,
People waking up
Waiting for this signal
The end of the world
Waiting to bring it about
The end of the world

Jumping some stanzas:

> People waking up
> Inner alarms going off
> Rung from the astral plane
> A man on the astral plane clanging the dinner bell
> Saying there was food for the masses
> That man was to come to the gathering
> Meet here to dine
> That the food long in preparation was ready
> That there was sole for breakfast

To cut it short: "The breakfast of the New Age was being pre-pared"—it was "sole for breakfast." The outwardly chaotic scene, I wrote—with his energy and words stirring into my ear—was mirroring

> something seen from across a window
> a window into man's soul
> and in that soul the end of the world is a blessing
> An age is being carried out.
> People waking up
> inner alarms ringing
> ringing in
> the New Age

And:

> Man was getting the story secondhand.
> Living a version that was secondhand
> but a revision had been sent
> the manuscript as it really was . . .

> Not secondhand
> But firsthand

There is much much more, all poetry, recounting the positive outlook for this new century. I will cut it off here, though, and find a way to step out of the book, as the author, and let its pages go into other hands.

I went to sleep, asking for help in getting this ending right, and what came? I woke and fiddled with the Gonzo Fest photo from 2014 outside Carmichael's Bookstore. Okay. That prediction of my book in a window came true.

But as I enlarged the image to "view pixels" for the first time, I peered closer. Because I'd just seen it: tiny clapping hands. Wow. Somewhere in my energy field—or whatever explanation you want to give—there they are. Materialized cheers, that I have to squint and peer with all my being to take in. A cue to rejoice. I felt a wave of excitement as I cropped and inserted the bookstore photos. Another experiential finding, another addition to my Big Picture. A thrill each time I glanced down at the printout. Something mysterious lurks out there. There are still mysteries waiting for us to tap into. That makes my heart burst with youthful energy. Well, then let's see what the next chapter brings. I thank you so much, dear readers, for going along with me, and I cheer and clap for you and your dreams as well. Together we are connected in this spiritual quest of Being/for Wholeness. Together we create momentum and space for each other. Blessings. And now *arrivederci*.

For in truth great love is born of great knowledge of the thing
loved.
—Leonardo da Vinci

Appendix

Part Two: "The 1990s"

The "Wave of Correlation"

Spirituality Perspective

By Jef Crab, founder of E.A.S.T. (Energetic Awareness, Sensitivity & Transformation) Institute

After contemplating this chapter, I am very much inclined to subscribe to your propositions. I highlighted the text:

> My hands ran through the Tai Chi form while my mind, in the group, emptied into a high state of awareness. . . .
>
> This meant that I could—we can—in an altered state, use a physical exercise to edit (map out) a manuscript—find an energy geography. It showed the interchangeability of space-rime and space-time, energy and matter, even one activity and something it could be made to correspond to. (end quote)

as an essential condition for the "wave of correlation."

As a matter of fact, some shamanistic techniques, especially healing at a distance, will use this wave, and even more the correlations . . .

Finding the "energy-similarity" between two (or more) totally separate and most of the time different objects/persons/situations requires a deeper state of awareness . . . (You seemingly experienced this state in Leuven.)

Other realities are entered through certain passages consisting of landscape/objects/energies/sounds, etc. An apprentice will need "power tools" or "techniques" to get in the right state of mind. For an accomplished shaman time-space is just a kind of wormhole thing combined with spacewarp. . . . Neither distance, time, nor matter are fixed realities. Distance is here and time does not exist.

Concluding, also in my personal view, there is no difference between (let's say) the shape of our brain/mind, the universe and all the situations with all their persons and objects, during our life. What we live is what we are in micro-cosmos and macro-cosmos.

The Self projects itself continuously on the screen of our awareness. That makes things happen (or not) . . . Nice chapter, nice work. Enjoyed reading it.

Appendix

"Event Balls"

The unification of time and space "implies that subatomic particles are dynamic patterns, that they are events rather than objects . . . In Buddhism you discover exactly the same thing."

—Fritjof Capra

The more cells you bring together, the more detailed the information. See, it's characteristic of the hologram that if you illuminate a part of the hologram you will get the information about the whole picture but it will be *less detailed.* (italics added)

—David Bohm

This idea of a Greek-like, Olympus-like relay of deaths traced back to my dream of a car accident in 1981. In it, a man spoke to a group. I vaguely grasped a project was involved and in his view the momentum would be furthered by what he was about to do. Next, he solitarily sat inside the car, no longer human—elongated like a figure by El Greco, focused to such an extent it was eerie. He apparently was no longer in control of the decision. It was a superhuman effort. Then he disappeared.

The empty car reappeared, parked outside a Greek temple; two male figures descended the steps. One put his hand through the car window; a "spotlight" was shown on a few drops of blood on the glove compartment. From this, I understood there was human pain, wordless sacrifice. These dream scenes, not long before Milton Klonsky died, gave me the first clue a project was under way. So when Lama Sing told me about a soul grouping spreading its consciousness across dimensions, the Christ consciousness, I asked if they were pursuing a project. He said yes. In the intense questioning I was in, I connected the dots.

Depth psychologist Carl Jung had stipulated in *Man and His Symbols* that there is an *adumbratio,* or *anticipatory shadow,* preceding death—present in such expressions as dreams.

Though Milton's death by cancer had been, I thought, *symbolically* portrayed in this example of the "wave of announcements" leading up to it—among a slew of dreams and other foreshadowings—it *literally* mapped out Willy's death in a car accident, inside Milton's energy ten years later.

I will not go into here all the uncanny clues and synchronicities and forecasts that made this the first inkling of the existence of event balls. But—connected to the Little Dot I took to be my soul I saw, in a vision, speeding through the universe as a compressed ball on a dead-serious mission—it's a little platform to start ruminations from.

Bohm: "Time itself is an order and manifestation, you see. We are going to say that it is possible to have an implicate order with regard to time as well as to space, to say that in any given period of time the whole may be enfolded . . . *the moment is atemporal, the connection of moments is not in time* but in the implicate order." (italics added)[240]

This rudimentarily opens the discussion of how in nonlinear time a whole ball of the future—of *potential* entangled together—like a superposition that had one string pulled, one collapse of the wave function, might be lofted into the air; some related events to take place, some perhaps not. But the entanglement meant that from the moment x occurred, other events entangled with it (or people) were in the air as well, undated, unmanifested, but now more probable. Or—how did I know—perhaps definitely scheduled? But not yet determined as to when? More like related by "if." If this, then there goes that.

In a dream flash before my mother's sudden death, I had seen: DEATH SET FOR 1983. I had not thought that was in the event ball. Possibly yes, possibly no. But Willy Van Luyten's death, ten years after Milton's, was so surrounded in kundalini episodes, warnings, attempts apparently to stop it, that I detected it literalizing the 1981 dream (see *Keep This Quiet!* III, Chapter 27). And if a dream ten years before could make an event ten years later probable, describing the outlines of it, then it was a little less incredulous that while Willy was dying I was dreaming, as it were, all unknowingly, the death of Hunter. Dreaming of packing up, going to the U.S., and helping write "The Hunter Thompson Story." A story predicated, it would turn out, upon Hunter's death.

So it became more and more uncanny. It seemed to add up to entanglement, an event ball, probabilities, the dancing Shiva particles of our non-3-D world. Event balls would be a "form" of time. Of "multidimensional gravity"?

How much of the universe can you pinch between your thumb and finger? Maybe a lot more than you think. Far reaches of the cosmos may lie less than a millimeter away. Whole other universes may be within your grasp. Even if you cannot see these distant places and other worlds, you may be in communication with them through that most familiar of forces, gravity.

In just two years this seemingly preposterous proposal has become one of the hottest theories of physics.[241]

Afterword

In fact, it has been calculated that if you took the entire population of the Earth, all seven billion of us, and removed all the empty space from all of our combined atoms, the entire human race would fit into a *single sugar cube*. If that doesn't boggle your mind, then I don't know what will—so much for a solid world.

—Ziad Masri

Looking back now—in 2017—far from Tienen, how can I believe such tales as I've written?

I sit here as rather an observer of my own observation. I have no doubt whatever I reported accurately. At the very same time, rather contradictorily, I marvel at it all. Yes, Nabokov, it reads to me like a novel now, but I did not make anything up. I have to keep pinching myself and telling myself that. These experiences, these events, happened. Ladies and gentlemen, guys, everybody out there. This is our world. Even though 95 percent of it is invisible to us, it is—based on all the hints and clues given us—amazing.

Acknowledgments

A heart full of appreciation to the following people: to Adam Sorkin for permission to reprint his translations of Mihai Ursachi's poetry and to the late Mihai Ursachi for translating poetry by me. To Virginia Parrott Williams for finding hours to do her incomparable developmental editing. To Brad Weber, Joy Haynie Ayscue, Mary Paul Thomas, Frank Despriet, Suzanne Brown, and Martin Flynn for priceless feedback. To Jyoti for page-by page textual confirmations. Many thanks for discussions on Taoist philosophy with E.A.S.T. Institute founder, Jef Crab. Also, to Didi-Ionel Cenuşer, my SUP publisher in Romania, for unfailing belief in me. To Ishwari (Ellen Balis) and Jayshree (Jan Handel) of Dhyanyoga Centers for fact-checking about Dhyanyogi-ji. To Rebecca Helgesen and the Akashic masters for input and confirmations, as to Diana Henderson for inspiration and kindness. To Doug Brinkley, Literary Executor of the Hunter Thompson Estate, for reprint permission and support. And to Hunter himself. To Ron Whitehead for friendship and the honor of presenting at the 2014 Gonzo Fest; to Nick Storm for filming the event and sending me the beautifully professional DVD. To Nick Garing for putting me into the impressive 2017 Gonzo Fest panel. Also, to Jinn Bug, for, with Ron, arranging my unforgettable Brown Hotel dinner with Hunter's son, Juan Thompson. To the late Rhea A. White for inviting me into her EHE publications. To Norman S. Don, for his research, cf., "Condition Three" (on Olof Jonsson). To E. H. Walker for our few conversations. To Alice Osborn for beautiful final edits, as on *KTQ Too!* and III. Lastly, to Gaelyn Larrick of www.wakingworld.com for the cover design; Lumena Atherton for tweaks for the new edition; and Darlene Swanson of Van-garde Imagery for the interior design.

Photos: *Asiatic Lion, Gir Forest* by Nikunj Vasoya: Wikipedia ("Gir

Forest Wildlife Sanctuary"); *Facade of the Chota Hathi Gumpha, or Small Elephant Cave, Udayagiri* by William Henry Cornish, c. 1892: British Library Online Gallery, http://www.bl.uk/onlinegallery/onlineex/apac/photocoll/f/019pho000001003u00394000.html.

Cover Images: *Dhyanyogi-ji*: reprinted with permission of Dhyanyoga Centers and assistance from Jayshree; *Mary Magdalene*: icon given me in Romania, scanned by J. W. Photo Labs, who did many other scans as well; *Eagle nebula*: NASA; *Yin-yang*: © "making faces," http://www.123rf.com/profile_makingfaces (Shutterstock).

Brief List of Important Personal References

Keep This Quiet! I–IV

From My Biography

Forgotten piano recital piece at seven: a Bach keyboard composition arranged for beginning piano at which I got stage fright. But I stayed on the stool and played from the beginning over and over up to different passages, till finally remembering the whole baroque piece, I played it start to finish, trills and all. I loved the trills.

Another "I" at seven: a "I" inside me who suddenly "woke" with the thought, the frozen awareness, that he couldn't fathom the paradox of his memory of himself yet having a puny record so far in this lifetime (my seven years). Reflecting on the Zurich workshop of May 1992, it was as if that kind of thing happened in reverse.

Vision at twenty-four (my first out-of-body experience): of a Little Dot of myself, my soul, traveling—with intense concentration. A determined dot whose sense of mission impacted me so I left my body without further thought and went with her. This happened to occur at the time I was losing my virginity.

***Signon* (rare, as in steak):** one of many puns (sign on, sig[arette] no) associated with the beggar below.

Unidentified Montparnasse beggar at twenty-four (at Le Dôme café-restaurant in Paris): I saw him as he made a wavy sign with his head across the window, elaborately mouthing a request for a cigarette (in a symbolic act that triggered the beginning of my *Love in Transition* series).

FROM DREAMS

Bipod Metalism, 1981: a jabberwocky term in my dream of visiting Jung's "museum"; there his assistant suggested this area of study to me.

Number 4 (the quaternity, "the timeless four"): for Jung, meant wholeness, individuation, the Self. There is much discussion of the symbolism (or archetype) of four in *Keep This Quiet!* III. "Four," as I use it, is part of the motif of Meta4. It's also significant in a Dream of My Life in which I received an award of Number 4. Four also is the heart chakra. And *four* in French means oven (as in alchemy).

"Chou de [pronounced 'Ciao D'] Hunter": a dream phrase from March 1981. I painted and repainted it in red ink on my palm every time it washed away—recalling the intensity of Hunter Thompson's letters to me in red ink, not to mention his convertible, the Red Shark.

FROM A.R.E. ASTROLOGY

Mars-Neptune: a Mars-Neptune conjunction at a rare intensity of 24.6 in my astrological chart—as pointed out by Edgar Cayce's A.R. E. in preparing the chart in 1984. The opposites of Mars-Neptune (male–female / fiery aspiration–mystical intuition) were a helpful lens to see my life through.

FROM THE ZURICH INITIATION

Sole (soul) for breakfast: a pun by the Zurich Initiator (in *Love in Transition* III, 14): "the food long in preparation was ready / that there was sole for breakfast / make from one fish food for everyone / for the New Age breakfast was ready / and the breakfast of the New Age / was the sole of man / The breakfast of the New Age was being prepared. / Now everything fell into place." Mihai Ursachi's translation is on page 147.

Notes

1. Bair, *Jung*, 329.
2. Atomic Heritage Foundation, http://www.atomicheritage.org/history/who-built-atomic-bomb; Jung, *Earth Has a Soul*, 21, 11.
3. This letter is in the Parapsychology Laboratory Records, Correspondence Series, in the Rubenstein Rare Book and Manuscript Library at Duke University. I have a copy of it.
4. Thompson, *Kingdom of Fear*, 28.
5. Sabbadini, *Synchronicity: Multiple Perspectives*, 79.
6. Jung, foreword, http://www.iging.com/intro/foreword.htm.
7. Roth, *Return of the World Soul* I: 165.
8. Tyson, "The Star in You," http://www.pbs.org/wgbh/nova/space/star-in-you.html.
9. Jung, *Man and His Symbols*, 57.
10. Gilder, *The Microcosm: The Quantum Revolution in Economics and Technology*.
11. Backström, "Interview with Edgar Mitchell," http://cabinetmagazine.org/issues/5/esp.php.
12. Jung, *Memories, Dreams, Reflections*, 225.
13. Harrell, *Keep This Quiet!* III.
14. Jung, *Letters* II: 343–344. Quoted by Donati in *Synchronicity: Multiple Perspectives*, 48.
15. Brinkley, *Rolling Stone* 970, http://www.rollingstone.com/culture/features/contentment-was-not-enough-20050324#ixzz3kydHZtKD.
16. Thompson, *Generation of Swine*, 44.
17. Slackman, "Outlaw Journalist Is Dead at 67," http://www.nytimes.com/2005/02/22/books/22thompson.html?pagewanted=2&_r=1.
18. Hodgson and Guest, "Late, Great Godfather of Gonzo," http://www.independent.co.uk/news/media/my-crazy-hazy-days-with-the-late-great-godfather-of-gonzo-412652.html.

19. "What are the Signs and Symptoms of a Kundalini Awakening?" https://www.goldenlighthealingnyc.com/index.cfm?id=56164.

20. Thompson, Juan, "My Father the Outlaw," http://totallygonzo. proboards.com/thread/19/father-outlaw-juan-thompson.

21. Park, Russell, and Jyoti, "Christina Grof," http://centerforsacred studies.org/remembering-teachers-christina-grof/.

22. "Jyoti's Background," Mother's Grace (website), http://www.mothersgrace.org/profile/background.html.

23. Wilson, foreword, *LifePrints*, x.

24. "Right-Brain Hemisphere," *Psychology Encyclopedia*, http:// psychology.jrank.org/pages/545/Right-Brain-Hemisphere. html#ixzz3MTKrqdfb.

25. Jyoti, *An Angel Called My Name*, xxxix.

26. "International Institute of Biophysics: Dr. Fritz-Albert Popp," http://www.biontology.com/international-institute-of-biophysics/.

27. Bischof, "Biophotons: The Light in Our Cells," http://www.bibliotecapleyades.net/ciencia/ ciencia_fuerzasuniverso06.htm

28. Bischof, *Biophoten* book description, http://www.marcobischof. com/en/arbeitsgebiete/biophotonen.html.

29. Levarek, "Prof. Fritz-Albert Popp," http://biontologyarizona.com/ dr-fritz-albert-popp/.

30. Ibid.

31. McTaggart, *The Field*, 40.

32. Levarek, "Prof. Fritz-Albert Popp," http://biontologyarizona.com/ dr-fritz-albert-popp/.

33. Joines and Kruth. "Current Research," http://www.rhine.org/ what-we-do/current-research/235-a-study-of-human-biofields-by-bill-joines-ph-d.html. The Rhine Research Center added clarifying words to the website quote of this and the following note.

34. Ibid.

35. Warren-Hicks, *Indy Week*, http://www.indyweek.com/indy-week/durhams-rhine-research-center-one-of-the-countrys-last-parapsychological-institutes-seeks-to-quantify-the-ethereal/ Content?oid=4163344.

36. Keutzer, "Kundalini FAQ," http://www.eecs.berkeley.edu/~keutzer/kundalini/kundalini-faq.html#1c.

37. Ibid., #1b.

38. Jyoti, *An Angel Called My Name*, xxiii–xxiv.

39. Ibid., 110.

40. Dhyanyogi-ji, *This House Is on Fire*, 81.

41. Ibid.

42. Jung, *Memories, Dreams, Reflections*, 215.

43. Bair, *Jung*, 294; Jung, *Memories, Dreams, Reflections*, 207.

44. Jung, *Memories, Dreams, Reflections*, 215–16.

45. Jung, *The Essential Jung*, 120.

46. Ibid., 120–21.

47. Jung, *Seven Sermons to the Dead*, http://gnosis.org/library/7Sermons.htm.

48. Jung, *Memories, Dreams, Reflections*, 217.

49. Jung, *Liber Novus*, vii.

50. Campbell, "Dr. Hector Kuri-Cano Lectures and Notes 1989–1994."

51. "Dhyanyogi Madhusudandas," Wikipedia.

52. Perry, "The Face of Jesus," http://www.nhne.com/articles/safaceofjesus.html.

53. "Thompson," "Fear and Loathing in Elko," 24.

54. Othitis, "Fear and Loathing in Elko," http://www.gonzo.org/books/rsm/rsm.asp?ID=a.

55. Thompson, "Elko," 24–25.

56. McTaggart, *The Field*, 147ff.

57. Peat described the dinners of Einstein and Jung at Jung's home in several places. I drew the information for this passage specifically from Peat, "Divine Contenders," 15.

58. "The Soul and Death" is reprinted in *Jung on Death and Immortality*. The quotation here is found on pages 19–20.

59. Don, McDonough, and Warren, "Signal Processing," 357, 379.

60. Storm, "Synchronicity and Psi," in *Synchronicity: Multiple Perspectives*, 286–87.

61. Keen, "Cross Correspondences," http://www.montaguekeen.com/page46.html.

62. Ibid.

63. Jyoti, *An Angel Called My Name*, 140.

64. "Biography of Rupert Sheldrake," http://www.sheldrake.org/about-rupert-sheldrake/biography.

65. Adams, "Rupert Sheldrake," http://www.theguardian.com/science/2012/feb/05/rupert-sheldrake-interview-science-delusion. See also Sheldrake, *Morphic Resonance: The Nature of Formative Causation.*

66. Sheldrake, "Morphic Resonance," http://www.sheldrake.org/research/morphic-resonance/introduction.

67. Roth, *Return of the World Soul* II: 159.

68. Johnsen, *Yoga Journal,* July/August 1988, 52.

69. Davis, Review of *The March to the Stars,* http://www.raintaxi.com/vinea-press/

70. Biography of Mihai Ursachi, http://www.archipelago.org/vol5-3/contributors.htm.

71. Ursachi, *Poetry Bay* (Summer 2003), http://poetrybay.com/summer2003/mihaiursachi.

72. Love, "Thompson from the other end of the Mojo Wire," http://connection.ebscohost.com/c/articles/16945768/technical-guide-editing-gonzo-hunter-s-thompson-from-other-end-mojo-wire. Robert Love was an adjunct professor at the Columbia University Graduate School of Journalism and an editor-at-large at *Playboy* and other titles, and is currently the editor-in-chief at *AARP* magazine.

73. Frawley, http://www.davidicke.com/forum/showthread.php?t=145836.

74. "Bapuji Writes," in *Shakti* (newsletter), XXVI: no. 4 (July 2009), 6.

75. Shri Dhyanyogi Madhusudandas, *Shakti: An Introduction* (glossary), 145.

76. Das, "The Hindu View of Time," http://hinduism.about.com/od/basics/a/time.htm.

77. Das, "The Four Yugas or Epochs," http://hinduism.about.com/od/basics/a/fouryugas.htm.

78. Laszlo, *The Self-Actualizing Cosmos*, 36–37.

79. Ibid., 32.

80. Shri Anandi Ma, in Dhyanyogi-ji, *Shakti: An Introduction*, 10.

81. Dhyanyogi-ji, *This House Is on Fire*, 12.

82. Ibid., 36.

83. "Asiatic Lion," Wikipedia.

84. Dhyanyogi-ji, *This House Is on Fire*, 36.

85. Shri Anandi Ma, in Dhyanyogi-ji, *Shakti: An Introduction*, 14–15.

86. Dhyanyogi-ji, *This House Is on Fire*, 36–37.

87. Shri Anandi-Ma, in Dhyanyogi-ji, *Shakti: An Introduction*, 11.

88. Ibid., 10.

89. Dileepji, in Dhyanyogi-ji, *This House Is on Fire*, iii.

90. Ibid., v.

91. Dhyanyogi-ji, *This House Is on Fire*, 153.

92. Ibid., 83.

93. Ibid., 111.

94. Calder, *The Meditation Handbook*, http://alchemylab.com/meditation_handbook.htm.

95. Laszlo, *The Self-Actualizing Cosmos*, 45.

96. Lazslo, "Toward a Physical Foundation for Psi Phenomena." This highly recommended address is now online, http://www.goertzel.org/dynapsyc/1996/ervin.html.

97. Laszlo, "Be Supercoherent," http://www.huffingtonpost.com/ervin-laszlo/supercoherence_b_1839520.html.

98. Dhyanyogi-ji, *Shakti: An Introduction*, 74

99. Dhyanyogi-ji, *Brahmanada*, 4.

100. Jones, "David Bohm and the Holographic Universe," https://futurism.com/david-bohm-and-the-holographic-universe/.

101. "Pilot Wave" and "De Broglie–Bohm Theory," Wikipedia.

102. Turner, "Deliberate Accident in Art," http://www.tate.org.uk/context-comment/articles/deliberate-accident-art.

103. "Prominent Swedish-Born Psychic Jonsson Dies at 79," *Las Vegas Sun* (May 21, 1998), http://www.lasvegassun.com/news/1998/may/21/prominent-swedish-born-psychic-jonsson-dies-at-79/.

104. "Ayahuasca Fast Facts," http://reset.me/ayahuasca-fast-facts/. This site has since been revamped.

105. Mizrach, "Santo Daime," http://www2.fiu.edu/~mizrachs/daime. htm.

106. "Versailles," http://www.castles.org/castles/Europe/Western_ Europe/France/france6.htm.

107. Hochman, "Molière," *McGraw Hill Encyclopedia of World Drama* I: 399.

108. "Hall of Mirrors," Wikipedia.

109. "Marie Antoinette Reviled," http://www.fsmitha.com/h3/h33-fr3.htm.

110. Castle, "Contagious Folly," in Chandler et al, eds. *Questions of Evidence*, 11–42, Excerpt: "The Ghosts of Versailles," http://www. museumofhoaxes.com/versailles.html.

111. Narrative of Marie-Thérèse de France, from *The Ruin of a Princess*, 210.

112. Jung, *Memories, Dreams, Reflections*, 314–15.

113. Ibid., 315.

114. Ibid., 316.

115. Ibid., 317.

116. Ibid.

117. Don, "Condition Three" (unpublished book), 64.

118. Ibid., 82.

119. Ibid., 61.

120. Yogananda, *God Talks with Arjuna: The Bhagavad Gita*, 372. Passage reprinted at http://www.yogananda.com.au/pyr/pyr_ kundalini1.html.

121. Yanush, "Paramahansa Yogananda Best Quotes," http://www. yogananda.com.au/gurus/yogananda_quotes36consciousness.html.

122. Peat, "Divine Contenders," 22.

123. Roth, *Return of the World Soul* I: 100.

124. Ibid., 102.

125. "The Emerald Tablet of Hermes," *Internet Sacred Texts Archive*, http://www.sacred-texts.com/alc/emerald.htm.

126. Miller, *137: Jung, Pauli, and the Pursuit of a Scientific Obsession*, 221.

127. "Hexagram," Wikipedia.

128. Peat, *Pathways of Chance*, 90.

129. Roth, "Remo F. Roth, C.G. Jung, Marie-Louise von Franz and Wolfgang Pauli," https://www.facebook.com/permalink.php?story_fbid=468655896566217&id=300564096708732.

130. Roth, *Return of the World Soul* I: 104–105.

131. Roth, *Return of the World Soul* II: 53.

132. Ibid., 89, 99–100.

133. Ibid., 21.

134. Roth, "Remo F. Roth, C.G. Jung, Marie-Louise von Franz and Wolfgang Pauli," https://www.facebook.com/permalink.php?story_fbid=468655896566217&id=300564096708732.

135. Konstin, "Balance Yin-Yang Energy: Ki," http://www.superlife.ws/group/reikiforsuperlife/forum/topics/balance-yin-yang-energy-qi.

136. Peat, "Divine Contenders," 23.

137. Roth, *Return of the World Soul* II: 98–99.

138. Moss, http://www.beliefnet.com/columnists/dreamgates/2014/07/the-pauli-effect-on-the-pauli-effect.html.

139. Goswami, *The Physicists' View of Nature* II: 68.

140. Roth, *Return of the World Soul* II: 98.

141. Lindorff, *Two Great Minds*, 83; Roth, *Return of the World Soul* I: 104–105.

142. Harrell, *Space Encounters* III, 474.

143. Jung, *Memories, Dreams, Reflections*, 317.

144. Yatri, 229.

145. Ibid.

146. Ibid., 232. "Showing Marlowe the Cave" comes from *Love in Transition* IV: 347.

147. Yatri, 233.

148. Press Release, "Princeton's PEAR Laboratory to Close," http://www.princeton.edu/~pear/press-statement.html.

149. Rhine and Rhine, "The Psychokinetic Effect," 20–43.

150. Fourmilab Switzerland, "Introduction to Probability and Statistics," https://www.fourmilab.ch/rpkp/experiments/statistics.html.

151. "Experimental Research," Princeton Engineering Anomalies Research: Scientific Study of Consciousness-Related Physical Phenomena (website), http://www.princeton.edu/~pear/

experiments.html; "Implications and Applications,"
http://www.princeton.edu/~pear/implications.html.

152. Dhyanyogi-ji, *Brahmanada*, 77.

153. Ibid., 75.

154. "Statistical Hypothesis Testing," Dartmouth,
http://www.dartmouth.edu/~matc/X10/Show.htm.

155. Radin, *The Conscious Universe*, 155.

156. Ibid., 157.

157. Ibid.

158. "Understanding—Thou Art That," Divine Life Society,
http://sivanandaonline.org/public_html/?cmd=displayrightsection
&section_id=1597&parent=1338&format=html.

159. Gribbin, *Q Is for Quantum: An Encyclopedia of Particle Physics*, 436.

160. Bierman, "Consciousness Induced Restoration of Time-Symmetry,"
http://deanradin.com/evidence/Bierman2010CIRTS.pdf.

161. Sarfatti, http://stardrive.org/stardrive/index.php/all-blog-articles/
myblog-ftd/dick-biermans-experiments-on-presponse-evidence-
for-violation-of-quantum-mechanics-in-living-matter.html.

162. "Is This REALLY Proof That Man Can See into the Future?"
http://www.dailymail.co.uk/sciencetech/article-452833/Is-
REALLY-proof-man-future.html#ixzz3r1wO75xf.

163. Ibid.

164. White, "The More We Are," http://www.ehe.org/display/ehe-
pagea229.html?ID=70.

165. White, "*Love in Transition*," review, http://www.ehe.org/display/
ehe-bookreviews39ca.html?formtype=d1&revid=81.

166. Harrell, *EHE News*, 9–10.

167. Ibid., 10–11.

168. White, *EHE News*, 11.

169. Goswami, *The Visionary Window*, 48.

170. "Wave Function," Wikipedia.

171. "Mind and the Wave Function Collapse: John Hagelin in
Conversation with Henry Stapp," https://www.youtube.com/
watch?v=hSv0NLSCEYo.

172. *Nanotechnology* glossary, http://whatis.techtarget.com/definition/superposition.

173. Goswami, *The Visionary Window*, 15.

174. Lindorff, *Two Great Minds*, 185.

175. Shri Anandi Ma, in Dhyanyogi-ji, *Shakti: An Introduction*, 10.

176. Walker, *Noetic Journal* I: 100–107, 1998; the exact phrase is emphasized there. The concept is found repeatedly in the book: see Walker, *The Physics of Consciousness*, 182.

177. Author's Note.

178. "Who Was Evan Harris Walker?" http://archived.parapsych.org/members/e_h_walker.html.

179. "Quantum Theory Demonstrated," Weizmann Institute of Science, http://www.sciencedaily.com/releases/1998/02/980227055013.htm.

180. Dhyanyogi-ji, *This House Is on Fire*, 98.

181. Walker, *The Physics of Consciousness*, 142–143.

182. Ibid., 217.

183. Ibid., 194.

184. Nimtz and Haibel, *Zero Time Space: How Quantum Tunneling Broke the Light Speed Barrier*, 3.

185. "Quantum Tunneling," *Science Daily*, https://www.sciencedaily.com/terms/quantum_tunnelling.htm. This article excerpts from Wikipedia.

186. Becker, "Is Information Fundamental?" http://www.pbs.org/wgbh/nova/blogs/physics/2014/04/is-information-fundamental/.

187. Walker, *The Physics of Consciousness*, 181.

188. Ibid., 151.

189. Ibid., 181.

190. Ibid., 151.

191. Ibid., 152.

192. Ibid., 182.

193. Rosenblum, and Kuttner, *Quantum Enigma*, 72.

194. "Einstein-Podolsky-Rosen," http://www.informationphilosopher.com/solutions/experiments/EPR/

195. Goswami, *The Visionary Window*, 36.

196. Stapp, http://www-physics.lbl.gov/~stapp/jcs.txt.

197. Wiseman, http://www.tandfonline.com/doi/abs/10.1080/00107510600581011#.VSU-12fTDiE.

198. Pais, Reviews of Modern Physics 51, 863-914 (1979): 907.

199. Bell, Physics 1: 195–200 (1964). Quoted on http://www.nature.com/news/physics-bell-s-theorem-still-reverberates-1.15435#/ref-link-1.

200. Mermin, "Is the moon really there when nobody looks?" http://www.theory.caltech.edu/classes/ph125a/istmt.pdf.

201. Ibid., 93.

202. "Mind and the Wave Function Collapse: John Hagelin in Conversation with Henry Stapp," https://www.youtube.com/watch?v=hSv0NLSCEYo.

203. Stapp, "Minds and Values in the Quantum Universe," in Davies and Gregersen, ed., *Information and The Nature of Reality*.

204. Atwood, "Buddhism and the Observer Effect," http://jayarava.blogspot.com/2014/07/buddhism-and-observer-effect-in-quantum.html.

205. Miller, "Amit Goswami's Theory," http://www.bibliotecapleyades.net/ciencia/ciencia_psycho08.htm.

206. Walker, *The Physics of Consciousness*, 95–96.

207. Bell, Physics 1: 195–200 (1964). Quoted on http://www.nature.com/news/physics-bell-s-theorem-still-reverberates-1.15435#/ref-link-1.

208. Walker, *The Physics of Consciousness*, 330.

209. John Stewart Bell quote in "Quantum Mechanics for Cosmologists," 611.

210. Zyga, "Quantum Mysticism," http://phys.org/news163670588.html#jCp.

211. Walker, *The Physics of Consciousness*, 150.

212. Ibid., 153.

213. Ibid., 154.

214. Ibid., 163.

215. Rosenblum and Kuttner, *Quantum Enigma*, 238.

216. Goswami, *The Visionary Window*, 15.

217. Walker, *The Physics of Consciousness*, 163.
218. Ibid., 172.
219. Ibid., 214.
220. Planck, as quoted in *The Observer* (January 25, 1931), http://www.spiritscienceandmetaphysics.com/proof-that-consciousness-creates-reality/#sthash.ntD9zwx8.dpuf.
221. Marin, "Mysticism in Quantum Mechanics," 807–22, http://www.academia.edu/260503/_Mysticism_in_quantum_mechanics_the_forgotten_controversy_
222. Harrison, "The Development of Quantum Mechanics," http://www.upscale.utoronto.ca/PVB/Harrison/DevelQM/DevelQM.html.
223. Seymour and Wenner, *Gonzo*, 414.
224. Crowley, http://www.soulbodyfusion.com/storyofashtatara.htm.
225. Mother Meera, *Answers*, 23.
226. Jung, *Letters*, I–II, 343–44. Quoted by Donati, in *Synchronicity: Multiple Perspectives*, 48.
227. Ibid., 41, 42.
228. Bodian, "Interview with Arnold Mindell," http://www.sonic.net/~billkirn/mindell_interview.html.
229. Ibid.
230. Ibid.
231. Free Dictionary online.
232. Bodian, "Interview with Arnold Mindell," http://www.sonic.net/~billkirn/mindell_interview.html.
233. Mindell, *City Shadows*, 22.
234. Don, McDonough, and Warren, "Signal Processing," 358.
235. Ibid, 374.
236. Storm, "Synchronicity and Psi," in *Synchronicity: Multiple Perspectives*, 287.
237. Max Planck Institute, "Einstein's Geometric Gravity," http://www.einstein-online.info/elementary/generalRT/GeomGravity.
238. "Theory of Relativity," http://www.allaboutscience.org/theory-of-relativity.htm.
239. Jung, *The Earth Has a Soul*, 68–69.
240. "The Enfolding-Unfolding Universe."

241. Paul Preuss, "New Theory Proposes Strong Gravity and a Universe at Your Fingertips," http://www2.lbl.gov/Science-Articles/Archive/multi-d-universe.html.

Works Cited

Articles and Book Chapters

Bapuji. "Bapuji Writes." *Shakti* XXVI, no. 4 (July 2009), 6.

Bell, J. S. "On the Einstein Podolsky Rosen Paradox." *Physics* 1 (1964), 195–200.

————. "Quantum Mechanics for Cosmologists." In *Quantum Gravity 2: A Second Oxford Symposium*, edited by C. J. Isham, R. Penrose, and D. W. Sciama. Oxford: Oxford University Press, 1981.

Castle, Terry. "Contagious Folly: *An Adventure* and Its Skeptics." In *Questions of Evidence: Proof, Practice, and Persuasion across the Disciplines*, edited by Harry Harootunian, James Chandler, and Arnold Davidson, 11–42. Chicago: University of Chicago Press, 1994. Excerpt: "The Ghosts of Versailles." http://www.museumofhoaxes.com/versailles.html.

Corrie, Damon. "A Personal Encounter with Einstein's Theory of Relativity and the Fourth Dimension." http://lastrealindians.com/a-person-al-encounter-with-einsteins-theory-of-relativity-and-the-fourth-dimension-of-unseen-reality-by-damon-corrie/.

Donati, Marialuisa. "Beyond Synchronicity: The Worldview of Carl Gustav Jung and Wolfgang Pauli." In *Synchronicity: Multiple Perspectives*, edited by Lance Storm, 42–63.

Harrell, Margaret A. "The Gift of the Natural Mind: A Consciousness." *Exceptional Human Experience* (2004).

————. "The Will to Initiate and Evolve." *EHE News*, vol. 8, no. 1 (March 2010), 8–13.

Johnsen, Linda. "Women Saints of India." *Yoga Journal* (July/August 1988), 52–55, 109.

Jung, C. G., "The Soul and Death." In *Jung on Death and Immortality*, edited by Jenny Yates, 3–10. Princeton: Princeton University Press, 1999.

Pais, Abraham. "Einstein and the quantum theory." *Reviews of Modern Physics* 51 (1979), 863–914.

Peat, F. David. "Divine Contenders: Wolfgang Pauli and the Symmetry of the World." In *Synchronicity: Multiple Perspectives*, edited by Lance Storm, 15–24.

Sabbadini, Shantena Augusto, "Synchronicity, Science and the *I Ching*." In *Synchronicity: Multiple Perspectives*, edited by Lance Storm, 79–83.

Stapp, Henry. "Minds and Values in the Quantum Universe." In *Information and the Nature of Reality*, edited by Paul Davies and Niels Henrik Gregersen.

Storm, Lance. "Synchronicity and Psi." In *Synchronicity: Multiple Perspectives*, edited by Lance Storm, 273–92.

Thompson, Hunter S. "Fear and Loathing in Elko," *Rolling Stone* 622 (January 23, 1992), 22–28.

Walker, E. H. *Noetic Journal* I (1998), 100–107.

Wilson, Frank E. MD. Foreword. In Richard Unger. *LifePrints: Deciphering Your Life Purpose*.

BOOKS

Bair, Deirdre. *Jung: A Biography*. Boston: Little, Brown and Co., 2003.

Davies, Paul, and Niels Henrik Gregersen, ed. *Information and the Nature of Reality*. Cambridge, England, and New York City: Cambridge University Press, 2014.

Dhyanyogi-ji. *Brahmanada: Sound, Mantra and Power*. Antioch, CA: Dhyanyoga Centers, 1979.

————. *Shakti: An Introduction to Kundalini Maha Yoga*, rev. 2nd ed. Antioch, CA: Dhyanyoga Centers, 2000.

————. *This House Is on Fire: Loot All You Can—The Life of Shri Dhyanyogi As Told by Anandi Ma.*

Don, Norman S. "Condition Three." Unpublished book manuscript (168 pages).

Goswami, Amit. *The Physicists' View of Nature* II. Springer (2001 edition/ February 2002).

————. *The Visionary Window: A Quantum Physicist's Guide to Enlightenment.* Wheaton, IL: Quest Books, 2000.

Gribbin, John. *Q Is for Quantum: An Encyclopedia of Particle Physics.* New York: Simon & Schuster, 1999.

Harrell, Margaret A. *Keep This Quiet!* III: *Initiations.* Raleigh, NC and Sibiu, RO: Saeculum University Press, 2014.

————. *Love in Transition* I, II: *Voyage of Ulysses—Letters to Penelope.* Hermann Press: Sibiu, RO, 1996.

————. *Love in Transition* III: *The Christ State.* Hermann Press: Sibiu, RO, 1996.

————. *Love in Transition* IV: *The Bedtime Tales of Jesus, a History of the Unconscious Mind.* Sibiu, RO: Hermann Press, 1998.

————. *Space Encounters* I, II: *Chunking Down the 21st Century.* Sibiu, RO: Saeculum University Press, 2002.

————. *Space Encounters* III: *Inserting Consciousness into Collisions.* Sibiu, RO: Saeculum University Press, 2003.

Jung, C. G. *The Earth Has a Soul: C. G. Jung on Nature, Technology & Modern Life*, edited by Meredith Sabini. Berkeley: North Atlantic Books, 2002.

————. *The Essential Jung*, edited by Anthony Storr. Princeton: Princeton University Press, 1983.

————. *Jung on Death and Immortality*, edited by Jenny Yates. Princeton: Princeton University Press, 1999.

————. *Letters* II: *1951–61*, edited by Gerhard Adler. Translated by Jeffrey Hulen. Princeton: Princeton University Press, 1976.

————. *Memories, Dreams, Reflections*, edited by Aniela Jaffé. Translated by Richard and Clara Winston. London: Fontana Press, 1993.

————. *The Red Book: Liber Novus, edited by* Sonu Shamdasani. New York: W. W. Norton & Co., 2009.

————, et al. *Man and His Symbols*. London: Picador, 1978. First published 1964 by Aldus Books Ltd.

Jyoti (Jeneane Prevatt). *An Angel Called My Name*. Prague, the Czech Republic: DharmaGaia Publishing, 1998.

Klonsky. Milton. *Speaking Pictures: A Gallery of Pictorial Poetry from the Sixteenth Century to the Present*. New York: Harmony Books, 1975.

Laszlo, Ervin. *The Self-Actualizing Cosmos: The Akasha Revolution in Science and Human Consciousness*. Rochester, VT: Inner Traditions, 2014

Lindorff, David. *Pauli and Jung: The Meeting of Two Great Minds*. Wheaton, IL: Quest Books, 2004.

McTaggart, Lynne. *The Field: The Quest for the Secret Force of the Universe*. New York: Harper, 2008.

Miller, Arthur I. *137: Jung, Pauli, and the Pursuit of a Scientific Obsession*. New York: W. W. Norton & Co., 2010.

Mindell, Arnold. *City Shadows: Psychological Interventions in Psychiatry*. Zurich: Lao Tse Press, Ltd., 2009.

Mother Meera. *Answers*. Ithaca, NY: Meeramma Publications, 1991.

Nimtz, Günter, and Asrid Haibel. *Zero Time Space: How Quantum Tunneling Broke the Light Speed Barrier*. Wiley-VCH (Germany)/New York: John Wiley and Sons, 2008.

Pais, Abraham. *Inward Bound: Of Matter and Forces in the Physical World*. New York: Oxford University Press, 1986.

Peat, F. David. *Pathways of Chance*. Pari, Italy: Pari Publishing, 2005.

Radin, Dean. *The Conscious Universe: The Scientific Truth of Psychic Phenomena*. Reprint. San Francisco: HarperOne, 2009.

Roth, Remo. *Return of the World Soul: Wolfgang Pauli, C. G. Jung, and the Challenge of the Psychophysical Reality* I: *The Battle of the Giants*. Pari, Italy: Pari Publishing, 2011.

———. *Return of the World Soul: Wolfgang Pauli, C. G. Jung, and the Challenge of the Psychophysical Reality* II: *A Psychophysical Theory*. Pari, Italy: Pari Publishing. 2012.

Sheldrake, Rupert. *Morphic Resonance: The Nature of Formative Causation*, 4th U.S. ed. (rev.). Rochester, VT: Park Street Press, 2009. First published 1981 as *A New Science of Life*.

Rosenblum, Bruce, and Fred Kuttner. *Quantum Enigma: Physics Encounters Consciousness*. New York: Oxford University Press, 2008.

Seymour, Corey, and Jann S. Wenner. *Gonzo: The Life of Hunter S. Thompson*. Boston: Little, Brown, and Co. 2007.

Storm, Lance, ed. *Synchronicity: Multiple Perspectives on Meaningful Coincidence*. Pari, Italy: Pari Publishing, 2008.

Thompson, Hunter S. *Kingdom of Fear: Loathsome Days of a Star-Crossed Child in the Final Days of the American Century*. New York: Simon and Schuster, 2003.

Unger, Richard. *LifePrints: Deciphering Your Life Purpose from Your Fingerprints*. Berkeley: Crossing Press, 2007.

Walker, Evan Harris. *The Physics of Consciousness: The Quantum Mind and the Meaning of Life*. Cambridge, MA: Perseus Publishing, 2000.

Yatri, *Unknown Man: The Mysterious Birth of a New Species*. Reprint. New York: Simon & Schuster, 1988.

URLs & E-mail

Any URLs that are not here are identified fully in the Notes.

Adams, Tim. "Rupert Sheldrake: the 'Heretic" at Odds with Scientific Dogma." *The Guardian* (Feb. 4, 2012). http://www.theguardian.com/science/2012/feb/05/rupert-sheldrake-interview-science-delusion.

Atwood, Jayara. "Buddhism and the Observer Effect in Quantum Mechanics." *Jayarava's Raves* (blog). http://jayarava.blogspot.com/2014/07/buddhism-and-observer-effect-in-quantum.html.

Backström, Fia. "Private Lunar ESP: An Interview with Edgar Mitchell." *Evil Winter* 5 (2001–2002). http://cabinetmagazine.org/issues/5/esp.php.

Becker, Kate. "Is Information Fundamental?" /http://www.pbs.org/wgbh/nova/blogs/physics/2014/04/is-information-fundamental/.

Bell, J. S. Physics 1, 195–200 (1964). Quoted in Wiseman, Howard. "Physics: Bell's Theorem Still Reverberates." http://www.nature.com/news/physics-bell-s-theorem-still-reverberates-1.15435#/ref-link-1.

Bierman, Dick J. Bio. Open Sciences (website). http://www.opensciences.org/people/dick-bierman.

———. "The Consciousness Chronicles: Time and Consciousness." https://www.youtube.com/watch?v=biPJJD4DFlU.

———. "Consciousness Induced Restoration of Time-Symmetry (CIRTs): A Psychophysical Theoretical Perspective." Reprinted from *The Journal of Parapsychology* 74: 273–99. http://deanradin.com/evidence/Bierman2010CIRTS.pdf.

Bischof, Marco. "Biophotons: The Light in Our Cells." http://www.bibliotecapleyades.net/ciencia/ciencia_fuerzasuniverso06.htm.

———. Book description of *Biophotonen* (*Biophotons*). http://www.marco-bischof.com/en/arbeitsgebiete/biophotonen.html.

Bodian, Stephen. "Field of Dreams: An Interview with Arnold Mindell." First published in *Yoga Journal* (March–April 1990). Reprint. http://www.sonic.net/~billkirn/mindell_interview.html.

Bradford, Michael. "Brahma–Randhra: The Evolving Center in the Brain." http://thedaobums.com/topic/4943-secret-of-the-big-accumulator/.

Brinkley, Doug. "Hunter S. Thompson: Contentment Was Not Enough." *Rolling Stone* 970. http://www.rollingstone.com/culture/features/contentment-was-not-enough-20050324#ixzz3kydHZtKD.

Campbell, Jean. Email. "Dr. Hector Kuri-Cano Lectures and Notes 1989–1994.

Calder, Christopher. *The Meditation Handbook.* http://alchemylab.com/meditation_handbook.htm.

Crowley, Jonette. "Soul Body Fusion: The Goddess and the Grail Codes." http://www.soulbodyfusion.com/storyofashtatara.htm.

Davis, Robert Murray. Review of *The March to the Stars* by Mihai Ursachi. Translated by Adam Sorkin with the author. Vinea Press, 2006. http://www.raintaxi.com/vinea-press/.

Das, Subhamoy. "The Concept of Time: The Hindu View of Time." http://hinduism.about.com/od/basics/a/time.htm.

———. "The Four Yugas or Epochs," http://hinduism.about.com/od/basics/a/fouryugas.htm.

Don, Norman S., Bruce E. McDonough, and Charles A. Warren. "Signal Processing of Forced Choice ESP Data: Evidence for PSI as a Wave of Correlation." *The Journal of Parapsychology*, vol. 59 (December 1995), 357–80.

Dyer, Kim. "Castles of the World: Versailles." http://www.castles.org/castles/Europe/Western_Europe/France/france6.htm.

Frawley, David. Foreword. In Shri Dharma Pravartaka Acharya. *The Vedic Way of Knowing God.* http://www.davidicke.com/forum/showthread.php?t=145836.

Gilder, George. *The Microcosm: The Quantum Revolution in Economics and Technology*. New York: Simon & Schuster, 1990.

Harrison, David M. "The Development of Quantum Mechanics." March 30, 2004. http://www.upscale.utoronto.ca/PVB/Harrison/DevelQM/DevelQM.html.

Hodgson, Martin, and Katy Guest, "My Crazy, Hazy Days with the Late, Great Godfather of Gonzo." *The Independent* (August 20, 2006). http://www.independent.co.uk/news/media/my-crazy-hazy-days-with-the-late-great-godfather-of-gonzo-412652.html.

Joines, William, and John G. Kruth. "Current Research at the Rhine Research Center." http://www.rhine.org/what-we-do/current-research/235-a-study-of-human-biofields-by-bill-joines-ph-d.html.

Jones, Marina. "David Bohm and the Holographic Universe." https://futurism.com/david-bohm-and-the-holographic-universe/.

Kruth, John. "The Nature of Psi: The First Sight Model and Theory of Psi." https://tunsasays.wordpress.com/author/drpsi/.

Jung, C. G. Foreword. In *The I Ching, or Book of Changes*. Translated by Richard Wilhelm. http://www.iging.com/intro/foreword.htm.

———. *The Seven Sermons to the Dead*. Translated by H. G. Baynes. The Gnostic Society Library. http://gnosis.org/library/7Sermons.htm.

Jyoti and Russell Park. "Remembering Our Teachers: Christina Grof." http://centerforsacredstudies.org/remembering-teachers-christina-grof/.

Keen, Montague. The Montague and Veronica Keen Foundation. "Cross Correspondences: A Brief Introduction." http://www.montaguekeen.com/page46.html.

Keutzer, Kurt. "Kundalini FAQ." http://www.eecs.berkeley.edu/~keutzer/kundalini/kundalini-faq.html#1b.

———. Ibid. #1c.

Laszlo, Ervin. "Be Supercoherent: Tune into Your Consciousness." *HuffPost* (September 26, 2012). http://www.huffingtonpost.com/ervin-laszlo/supercoherence_b_1839520.html.

Levarek, Sandra. "Prof. Fritz-Albert Popp." http://biontologyarizona.com/dr-fritz-albert-popp/.

Love, Robert. "A Technical Guide for Editing Gonzo: Hunter S. Thompson from the other end of the Mojo Wire." *Columbia Journalism Review*, vol. 44, issue 1 (May/June 2005), 61. http://connection.ebscohost.com/c/articles/16945768/technical-guide-editing-gonzo-hunter-s-thompson-from-other-end-mojo-wire.

Marin, John Miguel. "Mysticism in Quantum Mechanics: The Forgotten Controversy." *European Journal of Physics* 30 (2009): 807–22. Reprint uploaded by Marin. http://www.academia.edu/260503/_Mysticism_in_quantum_mechanics_the_forgotten_controversy_.

Mermin, N. David. "Is the Moon Really There When Nobody Looks?" *Physics Today* (April 1985), 38–47. http://www.theory.caltech.edu/classes/ph125a/istmt.pdf.

Miller, Iona. "The Self-Aware Universe: A Synopsis of Amit Goswami's Theory of Physics and Psychic Phenomena." http://www.bibliotecapleyades.net/ciencia/ciencia_psycho08.htm.

Mizrach, Stephen. "Santo Daime." http://www2.fiu.edu/~mizrachs/daime.htm.

Othitis, Christine. "Fear and Loathing in Elko." The Great Thompson Hunt (website). http://www.gonzo.org/books/rsm/rsm.asp?ID=a.

Paramahansa Yogananda. *God Talks with Arjuna: The Bhagavad Gita*. Extract reprinted at http://www.yogananda.com.au/pyr/pyr_kundalini1.html.

Peat, F. David. "Active Information." http://www.fdavidpeat.com/ideas/activeinfo.htm.

Perry, Robert. "The Face of Jesus." http://www.nhne.com/articles/safaceofjesus.html.

Planck, Max. As quoted in *The Observer* (January 25, 1931). http://www.spiritscienceandmetaphysics.com/proof-that-consciousness-creates-reality/#sthash.ntD9zwx8.dpuf.

Roth, Remo. "Remo F. Roth, C.G. Jung, Marie-Louise von Franz and Wolfgang Pauli" (September 8, 2013). https://www.facebook.com/permalink.php?story_fbid=468655896566217&id=300564096708732.

Sangha, Ananda. "Yogananda on Kriya Yoga." http://www.ananda.org/meditation/meditation-support/articles/yogananda-on-kriya-yoga/.

Sarfatti, Jack. "Dick Bierman's Experiments on Preresponse Evidence for Violation of Quantum Mechanics in Living Matter." *Stardrive* (Jack Sarfatti's blog). http://stardrive.org/stardrive/index.php/all-blog-articles/myblog-ftd/dick-biermans-experiments-on-presponse-evidence-for-violation-of-quantum-mechanics-in-living-matter.html.

Sheldrake, Rupert. "Morphic Resonance and Morphic Fields: An Introduction." http://www.sheldrake.org/research/morphic-resonance/introduction.

Slackman, Michael. "Hunter S. Thompson, Outlaw Journalist, Is Dead at 67." *New York Times* (Feb. 22, 2005). http://www.nytimes.com/2005/02/22/books/22thompson.html?pagewanted=2&_r=1.

Sorkin, Adam. "Contributors: Mihai Ursachi." *Archipelago*: 100th Anniversary Edition, vol. 10, no. 3 & 4 (2007). http://www.archipelago.org/vol5-3/contributors.htm.

Stapp, Henry P. "Attention, Intention, and Will in Quantum Physics." http://www-physics.lbl.gov/~stapp/jcs.txt.

Stapp, Henry P., and John Hagelin, "Mind and the Wave Function Collapse: John Hagelin in Conversation with Henry Stapp," https://www.youtube.com/watch?v=hSv0NLSCEYo.

Thompson, Juan F. "My Father the Outlaw," http://totallygonzo.proboards.com/thread/19/father-outlaw-juan-thompson.

Turner, Christopher. "The Deliberate Accident in Art: Blots." Tate. http://www.tate.org.uk/context-comment/articles/deliberate-accident-art.

Tyson, Peter. "The Star in You." http://www.pbs.org/wgbh/nova/space/star-in-you.html.

Ursachi, Mihai. *Poetry Bay* (Summer 2003). http://poetrybay.com/summer2003/mihaiursachi.html.

Warren-Hicks, Colin. "Durham's Rhine Research Center, one of the country's last parapsychological institutes, seeks to quantify the ethereal." *Indy Week* (May 14, 2014). http://www.indyweek.com/indyweek/durhams-rhine-research-center-one-of-the-countrys-last-parapsychological-institutes-seeks-to-quantify-the-ethereal/Content?oid=4163344.

Weizmann Institute of Science. "Quantum Theory Demonstrated: Observation Affects Reality." *ScienceDaily* (February 27, 1998). http://www.sciencedaily.com/releases/1998/02/980227055013.htm.

White, Rhea A. "Exceptional Human Experience and the More We Are." http://www.ehe.org/display/ehe-pagea229.html?ID=70.

———. *"Love in Transition: The Bedtime Tales of Jesus."* Book review. http://www.ehe.org/display/ehe-bookreviews39ca.html?formtype=d1&revid=81.

Wiseman, H. M. "From Einstein's Theorem to Bell's Theorem." *Contemporary Physics*, vol. 47, issue 2 (2006), 79–88. http://www.tandfonline.com/doi/abs/10.1080/00107510600581011#.VSU-12fTDiE.

Zyga, Lisa. "Quantum Mysticism: Gone But Not Forgotten." http://phys.org/news163670588.html#jCp.

Websites without Author's Name

"Akashic Records—The Book of Life." Adapted from: *Edgar Cayce on the Akashic Records* by Kevin J. Todeschi. Edgar Cayce's A.R.E (website). http://www.edgarcayce.org/are/spiritualGrowth.aspx?id=2078.

"Einstein's Geometric Gravity." Einstein Online (website), copyrighted by the Max Planck Institute for Gravitational Physics, Potsdam, Germany. http://www.einstein-online.info/elementary/generalRT/GeomGravity.

"Façade of the Chota Hathi Gumpha or Small Elephant Cave, Udayagiri." British Library Online Gallery. http://www.bl.uk/onlinegallery/onlineex/apac/photocoll/f/019pho000001003u00394000.html.

"Marie Antoinette Reviled (1789 Continued)." Macrohistory: World Timeline (website). http://www.fsmitha.com/h3/h33-fr3.htm.

"Who Was Evan Harris Walker? (1936–2006)." Parapsychological Association (website). http://archived.parapsych.org/members/e_h_walker.html.

Index

Author's Bio

Margaret A. Harrell is a three-time fellow of MacDowell Colony who recently authored the memoir series: *Keep This Quiet! My Relationship with Hunter S. Thompson, Milton Klonsky, and Jan Mensaert*; *Keep THIS Quiet Too! More Adventures with Hunter S. Thompson, Milton Klonsky, Jan Mensaert*; and *Keep This Quiet! Initiations.* A free-lance editor, she was Hunter Thompson's copy editor at Random House for *Hell's Angels.* She teaches light body meditation courses in the DaBen and Orin school of LuminEssence, which explore the dynamics and untapped potential of ourselves in various forms and translations of our energy. She is also a cloud photographer, who has been listed in the Marquis Who's Who in American Art since 2008. Her work has been exhibited in Italy, Romania, Canada, and the U.S.; a selection is housed in the het Toreke museum in Belgium. Academically, she graduated from Duke University (honors and distinction in history) and Columbia University (contemporary English and American literature). She has studied at the C. G. Jung Institute Zurich and been trained in numerous types of energy work. After living abroad in North Africa and Europe for lengthy periods, she now lives in Raleigh, North Carolina.

Books in the *Keep This Quiet!* Series

Keep This Quiet!

*My Relationship with Hunter S. Thompson,
Milton Klonsky, and Jan Mensaert*

Keep THIS Quiet Too!

*More Adventures with Hunter S. Thompson,
Milton Klonsky, Jan Mensaert*

Keep This Quiet! III:

Initiations

Keep This Quiet! IV:

Ancient Secrets Revealed

Connect with Margaret Harrell

I really appreciate that you read my book. If you would like to connect with me on social media, you can find me at the places below:

On Facebook: https://www.facebook.com/margaret.a.harrell.3

On Linked In: https://www.linkedin.com/in/margaretharrell

On Goodreads: https://www.goodreads.com/author/dashboard

On my website: http://margaretharrell.com/

Before You Go

If you liked this book, please consider reviewing it on Amazon, B & N, and/or Good Reads. And if you would like to subscribe to my blog for updates and announcements of future books, just click this link to be on my mailing list: http://margaretharrell.com/news/

Printed in Great Britain
by Amazon

39885864R10248